EXODUS

Allan Harman draws of a lifetime of teaching and preaching the Old Testament in this commentary. With careful attention to the Hebrew text of Exodus, he brings out nuances that otherwise might be missed, and shows the connections with other parts of Scripture to underscore the foundational character of this book for the faith of the people of God.

John A. Davies
Principal Emeritus
Christ College, Sydney

EXODUS

God's kingdom of priests

Allan M. Harman

Scripture quotations are from *The Holy Bible, English Standard Version*, copyright © 2001 by Crossway Bibles, a division of Good News Publishers. Used by permission. All rights reserved.

Scripture quotations marked (NIV) are taken from *The Holy Bible, New International Version®*. NIV®. Copyright©1973, 1978, 1984 by International Bible Society. Used by permission of Zondervan. All rights reserved.

Scripture quotations marked (NASB) are taken from the *New American Standard Bible®*, Copyright © 1960, 1962, 1963, 1968, 1971, 1972, 1973, 1975, 1977, 1995 by The Lockman Foundation. Used by Permission. (www.Lockman.org)

Scripture quotations marked (NKJV) are taken from the *New King James Version*. Copyright © 1982 by Thomas Nelson, Inc. Used by permission. All rights reserved.

Allan Harman has had a life-time interest in exposition of the biblical text. He is Research Professor at the Presbyterian Theological College in Melbourne, Australia. He has lectured and preached in many countries and served as the senior editor of the Reformed Theological Review, Australia's oldest theological journal until he retired at the end of 2013.

Copyright © 2017 Allan M. Harman

ISBN 978-1-5271-0025-1

10 9 8 7 6 5 4 3 2 1

Printed in 2017
by
Christian Focus Publications Ltd.,
Geanies House, Fearn, Ross-shire,
IV20 1TW, Scotland, U.K.

www.christianfocus.com

Cover design by Daniel van Straaten

Printed and bound by
Bell & Bain, Glasgow

All rights reserved. No part of this publication may be reproduced, stored in a retrieval system, or transmitted, in any form, by any means, electronic, mechanical, photocopying, recording or otherwise without the prior permission of the publisher or a licence permitting restricted copying. In the U.K. such licences are issued by the Copyright Licensing Agency, Saffron House, 6–10 Kirby Street, London, EC1 8TS www.cla.co.uk.

Contents

Abbreviations 9
Glossary 13
Notes on Hebrew 15
A Note on Terminology 19
Foreword 23
Suggestions for Further Reading 25

Introduction 27
  1 The Place and Significance of Exodus in the
     Old Testament 27
  2 The Authorship of Exodus 28
  3 The Theology of Exodus 32
  4 The Date of Exodus 36
  5 Outline of the Book of Exodus 38

Part I Redemption from Egypt 1:1–15:21 45
      1 Oppression in Egypt 1:1-22 47
      2 The Provision of a Deliverer 2:1–4:31 57
      3 Increased Oppression 5:1-21 87
      4 Promised Deliverance 5:22–7:5 93
      5 Redemptive Judgment 7:6–12:51 105
      6 Exit from Egypt 13:1–15:21 147

Part II The Journey to Mount Sinai 15:22–18:27 167
      7 The Waters of Marah and Elim 15:22-27 169
      8 The Grumbling Community 16:1-36 173
      9 Water from the Rock 17:1-7 181
     10 The Amalekites Defeated 17:8-16 185
     11 Provision of Judicial Help 18:1-27 189

Part III	The Covenant at Sinai 19:1–24:18	197
	Introduction	199
12	At Mount Sinai 19:1-24	203
13	The Ten Words 19:25–20:17	211
14	The Theophany 20:18-21	223
15	Worship Regulations 20:22-26	227
16	The Laws 21:1–23:33	231
17	Ratification of the Covenant 24:1-18	259

Part IV	Instructions Regarding the Tent of Meeting 25:1–31:18	267
	Introduction	269
18	Contributions for the Sanctuary 25:1-9	275
19	The Ark of the Covenant 25:10-22	279
20	The Table 25:23-30	283
21	The Lampstand 25:31-40	285
22	The Dwelling Place/The Tent 26:1-37	287
23	The Altar of Burnt Offering 27:1-8	293
24	The Courtyard 27:9-19	295
25	Oil for the Lampstand 27:20-21	299
26	The Priests' Garments and Their Consecration 28:1-29:46	301
27	The Altar of Incense 30:1-10	317
28	The Census Tax 30:11-16	319
29	The Bronze Basin 30:17-21	321
30	Anointing Oil 30:22-33	323
31	Incense 30:34-37	325
32	Bezalel and Oholiab 31:1-11	327
33	The Sabbath 31:12-17	329
34	Concluding Summary 31:18	331

Part V	Rebellion and Restoration 32:1–34:35	333
	Introduction	335
35	The Golden Bull 32:1-6	337
36	The Lord's Verdict 32:7-10	341
37	Moses' Intercession 32:11-14	343
38	The Broken Covenant and Its Curse 32:15-29	345
39	Vicarious Atonement 32:30-35	351
40	The Call to Move from Sinai 33:1-6	355
41	The Temporary Meeting Place 33:7-11	357
42	Moses and the Glory of the Lord 33:12-23	359
43	Preparation for New Revelation of God's Glory 34:1-4	363
44	God's Glory Revealed 34:5-9	367
45	The Renewal of the Covenant 34:10-28	371
46	Moses' Radiant Face 34:29-35	377

Part VI	Building the Tent of Meeting 35:1–40:38	381
	Introduction	383
47	The Call to Build 35:1-29	385
48	Bezalel and Oholiab 35:30–36:7	389
49	The Progress of the Work 36:8–39:31	391
50	Moses' Inspection of the Tent 39:32-43	397
51	Setting up the Tent 40:1-33	399
52	The Lord's Glory 40:34-38	403

Subject Index	405
Scripture Index	415

Diagrams

The Proposed Route of the Exodus 171
Proposed Entrance to Tent of Meeting 296
Diagram of Tent of Meeting 382

Abbreviations

ABD	*Anchor Bible Dictionary* (New York: Doubleday, 1992).
ANET	*Ancient Near Eastern Texts relating to the Old Testament*, 3rd ed. with supplement, ed. J. B. Pritchard (Princeton: Princeton University Press, 1969).
ASV	*American Standard Version*
AV	*Authorised (King James) Version*
BDB	Brown, Driver and Briggs, eds., *A Hebrew and English Lexicon of the Old Testament* (Oxford: Clarendon Press, 1975 reprint).
Bib	*Biblica*
BS	*Bibliotheca Sacra*
c.	Latin, around, about
CHAL	*A Concise Hebrew and Aramaic Lexicon of the Old Testament* (Grand Rapids: Eerdmans, 1988).
DCH	*Dictionary of Classical Hebrew*, ed. David J. A. Clines, 7 vols. (Sheffield: Sheffield Academic Press, 1993–2011).
DIHG~S	J. C. L. Gibson, *Davidson's Introductory Hebrew Grammar-Syntax*, 4th ed. (Edinburgh: T. & T. Clark, 1994).
DOTT	*Documents from Old Testament Times*
EBC	*Expositor's Bible Commentary*, revised ed. 2003.
ESV	*English Standard Version*
EQ	*Evangelical Quarterly*

ET	*Expository Times*
fem.	Feminine
GKC	*Gesenius' Hebrew Grammar*, 2nd ed., Gesenius, Kautsch, Cowley, eds (Oxford: Clarendon Press, 1966).
HALOT	*The Hebrew and Aramaic Lexicon of the Old Testament* (Leiden: Brill, 2000).
Heb.	Hebrew
IBD	*The Illustrated Bible Dictionary* (Leicester: InterVarsity Press, 1986).
IBHS	*An Introduction to Biblical Hebrew Syntax*, Bruce K. Waltke and M. O'Connor (Winona Lake: Eisenbrauns, 1990).
IDB	*Interpreter's Dictionary of the Bible*, 4 vols. (Nashville: Abingdon Press, 1962).
ISBE	*International Standard Bible Encyclopaedia*, 4 vols. (Grand Rapids: Eerdmans, 1979).
JBL	*Journal of Biblical Literature*
JETS	*Journal of the Evangelical Theological Society*
JSNT	*Journal for the Study of the New Testament*
JSOT	*Journal for the Study of the Old Testament*
JSS	*Journal of Semitic Languages*
JTS	*Journal of Theological Studies*
JTVI	*Journal of the Transactions of the Victoria Institute*
lit.	literally
LXX	The Septuagint, the oldest and most important Greek translation of the Old Testament, made in Egypt about 250 B.C.
mg.	margin
ms(s).	manuscript(s)
MT	Massoretic text, the Hebrew text of the Old Testament that became recognised as authoritative after the fall of Jerusalem in A.D. 70.

NASB	*New American Standard Bible:* Updated Edition. Anaheim, CA: Foundation Publications, 1997.
NEB	*New English Bible.* New York: Oxford University Press, 1976.
NICOT	*New International Commentary on the Old Testament*
NIDOTTE	*New International Dictionary of Old Testament Theology and Exegesis,* ed. Willem A. VanGemeren, 5 vols. (Grand Rapids: Zondervan, 1997).
NIV	*New International Version.* Colorado Springs: International Bible Society, 1984.
NKJV	*New King James Version.* Nashville: Thomas Nelson, 1982.
NLT	*New Living Translation.* Wheaton: Tyndale House, 1996.
NRSV	*New Revised Standard Version.* Grand Rapids: Zondervan, 1989.
part.	participle
pass.	passive
REB	*Revised English Bible.* Oxford: Oxford University Press, 1989.
RSV	*Revised Standard Version.* The Bible Societies, 1952.
RTR	*Reformed Theological Review*
RV	*Revised Version*
TB	*Tyndale Bulletin*
TDOT	*Theological Dictionary of the Old Testament,* 15 vols. (Grand Rapids: Eerdmans, 1974-2006).
TWOT	*Theological Wordbook of the Old Testament,* 2 vols. (Chicago: Moody Press, 1980).
VT	*Vetus Testamentum*
WTJ	Westminster Theological Journal
x	The number of occurrences of a word in a particular verse or section is marked by this multiplication sign, e.g., 2x.

Glossary

Dead Sea Scrolls
: About 800 scrolls containing all or part of Old Testament books discovered at or near Qumran, on the north-western side of the Dead Sea.

fixed pair
: The term 'fixed pair' refers to words that regularly occur in parallel expressions in Hebrew, e.g., head/skull, earth/dust, mouth/lip.

ellipsis (or, gapping)
: This occurs when a normal element of a sentence is missing and has to be understood from the context.

hapax legomenon
: A word occurring only once (pl. *hapax legomena*).

homonym
: A word having the same sound as another, but with a different meaning and origin. In the text, these Hebrew words are marked by the addition of a Roman numeral as listed in the *Dictionary of Classical Hebrew*, e.g., *rav* II.

inclusio
: A literary device by which a repeated theme both introduces and concludes a passage, so marking it as a separate section.

Massoretes
: Groups of Jewish scholars (A.D. 600–1000) who produced the final form of the OT text, adding the vocalisation, accents, and various notations.

Qumran
: See above, 'Dead Sea Scrolls'.

targum
: An Aramaic translation or paraphrase of some part of the Old Testament. They were oral at first but were later written. The earliest examples (found at Qumran) are from the second century B.C.

theophany
: A visible appearance of God.

Vulgate
: The Latin version of the Bible produced by Jerome in the period A.D. 380–405, which became the official Bible of the Roman Catholic Church at the Council of Trent in 1546.

Notes on Hebrew

Verbal Themes

Qal	Qal
Ni.	Nifʻal
Pi.	Piʻel
Pu.	Puʻal
Hi.	Hifʻal
Ho.	Hofʻal
Hitp.	Hitpaʻel
Hitpo.	Hitpolel
Hitpalp.	Hitpalpel

Grammatical Expressions

cognate accusative — The use of a noun as the object of a verb which comes from the same root, e.g., 'They dreaded [with] dread' (Ps. 14:5).

coh. — cohortative: indirect imperative forms in the 1st person singular and plural, e.g., 'Let me (us) send'.

constr. — construct: a noun, usually in a shortened form, placed before another noun and with a close semantic relation to it, covering all the nuances of the English *of*.

enclitic *mem* — A final *mem* added to words in poetry. This is a rare survival of an archaic form that has no obvious function.

fem.	Feminine
imper.	Imperative
imperfect	A verbal conjugation in Hebrew that identifies a situation as fluid or in motion.
inf.	Infinitive
inf. absol.	Infinitive absolute: a verbal form normally placed before another form of the verb in order to emphasise it.
interrogative marker	The use of h^a prefixed to a sentence to change it into a question.
jussive	3rd person forms of the indirect imperative, e.g., 'Let him (them) send'.
m.	masculine
object marker	The particle *'et* (untranslated) used to mark the direct definite object of a verb.
pass.	passive
part.	participle
perfect	A verbal conjugation in Hebrew that identifies a situation as static or at rest.
pers.	person
pl.	plural
s.	singular
vav consecutive	The use of the conjunction *vav* ('and) and a verbal form to indicate a simple action that has arisen out of something that has gone before.

Transliteration of Consonants

alef	ʼ
bet	b/v
gimel	g
dalet	d
he	h
vav	v
zayin	z
chet	ch (as in German *ich*, or Scottish *loch*)
tet	t
yod	y
kaf	k
lamed	l
mem	m
nun	n
samek	s
ayin	ʻ
peh	p/f
tsadeh	ts
qof	q
resh	r
sin	s
shin	sh
taw	t

Note:

1. Long vowels are marked with a circumflex, e.g., â, ê, î, ô, û.

2. Hebrew words are normally accented on the final syllable. However, there is a group of nouns in which the stress is placed on the first of a pair of vowels, resulting in next-to-last syllable stress. This is marked by the use of an acute, e.g., *régel* (foot). The acute is also used with a small number of other nouns that do not have the stress on the final syllable, e.g., *shâmáyim* (heavens).

A Note on Terminology

At various points in the book of Exodus, terms are used that require translation into English. How this is done is important, as it can affect our understanding of the message of the book. Significant theological points can be missed if our English terminology does not reflect the use of particular Hebrew words and phrases. On five points in this commentary I deviate from common practice (consult the appropriate exegetical comments for fuller information and justification).

1. The Plagues (Exod. 7-11)
In the biblical text the combined judgments on the Egyptians are never called 'the plagues', but 'signs and wonders'. Hence, in the commentary they are simply called 'signs'.

2. The Ten Commandments (Exod. 20:1-17)
The Hebrew text never contains the expression 'the Ten Commandments'. Rather, it designates them 'the Ten Words', of which *Decalogue* (via Latin) is a precise translation. They are referred to in the commentary as 'the Ten Words', or individually as 'the First Word', 'the Second Word', etc.

3. The Book of the Covenant (Exod. 24:7)
The use of 'book' is an anachronism, as books only developed from the use of codices in the early Christian centuries. The writing material was probably leather or papyrus, and 'scroll' or document' are suitable English translations.

4. The Mercy-Seat (Exod. 25:17)
The lid or cover of the ark is often translated as 'mercy-seat', but no suggestion is ever made in the biblical text that the ark was God's seat or throne. As the Hebrew word for this lid is

from the same root as the verb 'to make atonement', it is far better to refer to it as the 'place of atonement'.

5. *The Golden Bull* (Exod. 32:1-35)

There is no suggestion in the text that the idol made at Sinai was diminutive. The word used for it can designate a mature bull, and this would fit in with the Israelites knowledge of bull worship in Egypt. The term used in the commentary is 'golden bull'.

6. *The Tabernacle* (Exod. 25-31)

God's meeting place with Israel is called 'a tabernacle' in practically all English versions. However, the word 'tabernacle' is Latin for a tent, and using it obscures the fact that God chose to live symbolically in a tent like his people. This gracious condescension of God is better marked by using the expression 'Tent of Meeting', and then the direct connection with John 1:14 becomes apparent: 'The Word became flesh and made his dwelling (*eskênôsen*, lit. 'lived in a tent') among us. We have seen his glory, the glory of the One and Only, who came from the Father, full of grace and truth'.

*In memory of my parents
Joseph and Jessie Harman*

Foreword

This volume is the fifth commentary I have written for either the Focus or the Mentor series of Christian Focus Publications. I take the opportunity to thank all the staff for their ready assistance, and for the privilege it has been to cooperate in publications that seek to explain the text of Holy Scripture for today's readers. The task of writing commentaries will never cease until the Lord Jesus returns, as new information surfaces and new interpretations must be assessed. As with my other commentaries, I have not entered into debate with other writers, but have tried to present what I think is the meaning of the Hebrew text of Exodus. Footnotes are there for the sake of students and pastors in particular, who may seek further information on specific points, especially those relating to Hebrew.

As with my other commentaries, my wife Mairi and I have worked through the text of Exodus together in our evening devotions, and in so doing we have learned much. I thank Mairi for all she has done to further my writing, and her continued participation in all aspects of my ministry.

ALLAN M. HARMAN
Wallington, Victoria

Suggestions for Further Reading

Commentaries

John Currid, *Exodus*, Vols. 1 and 2 (EP Study Commentary: Darlington: Evangelical Press, vol. 1, 2000; vol. 2, 2001).

W. H. Gispen, *Exodus* (Bible Student's Commentary; Grand Rapids: Zondervan, 1982).

Victor Hamilton, *Exodus: An Exegetical Commentary* (Grand Rapids: Baker Academic, 2011).

Walter C. Kaiser Jr, 'Exodus', *The Expositor's Bible Commentary*, 2nd ed. (Grand Rapids; Zondervan, 2008), pp. 287-497.

John L. Mackay, *Exodus* (Fearn: Christian Focus Publications, 2001).

Douglas Stuart, *Exodus* (The New American Commentary: Nashville: B. & H. Publishing Group, 2006).

Other Studies

John A. Davies, *A Royal Priesthood: Literary and Intertextual Perspectives on an Image of Israel in Exodus 19:6* (London: T. & T. Clark International, 2004).

Meredith Kline, *The Structure of Biblical Authority* (Grand Rapids: Eerdmans, 1972).

Jeffrey J. Niehaus, *God at Sinai: Covenant and Theophany in the Bible and Ancient Near East* (Grand Rapids: Zondervan, 1995).

J. A. Motyer, *The Message of Exodus: The Days of Our Pilgrimage* (Nottingham: Inter-Varsity, 2005).

Geerhardus Vos, *Biblical Theology: Old and New Testaments* (Edinburgh: Banner of Truth Trust, 1974), pp. 100-82.

Introduction

1. The Place and Significance of Exodus in the Old Testament

The Book of Exodus is the first of four books that deal with the period of Moses. Between Genesis and Exodus there is a long time gap without any biblical record of the events in the intervening period. The opening chapter of Exodus highlights the change in circumstances for Abraham's descendants. Whereas the total number of Israelites in Egypt was seventy after Jacob arrived there (Gen. 46:26-27), by the time the account opens in Exodus they had been 'fruitful and multiplied greatly' (Exod. 1:7). There was also a change in relations with the Egyptians, for their favourable attitude towards the Israelites, depicted in the closing chapters of Genesis, is replaced by hostility, demonstrated first by oppressive treatment, and then by steps to kill all infant boys.

Exodus is concerned with two forms of servitude. The first is the harsh slavery imposed on the Israelites in Egypt and from which they sought deliverance by their God (Exod. 2:23-25). The other servitude is the submission of Israel to God as a result of His gracious deliverance of them from their bondage, and the choice of them to be His treasured possession (Exod. 19:4-6). From Exodus 20 to the end of the book the focus is on God's demands on His people, expressed in concise form in the Ten Words (Exod. 20:1-17), and then in greater detail in what follows through to the establishment of the Tent of Meeting and the visible symbol of God's glory in the cloud over it (Exod. 40:34-35).

The Exodus events are repeatedly referred to in the book of Deuteronomy (a covenantal renewal document; see, e.g, Deut. 7:8ff., 18-19; 8:14; 9:7-21; 26:5-8). The same applies in the historical books (see, e.g., 1 Sam. 2:27-28; 8:8; 2 Sam. 7:6, 23; 1 Kings 8:9, 21, 51; 2 Kings 17:7; Neh. 9:9-15; Dan. 9:15), the Psalms (77:7-20; 78:12-16, 42-53; 105:23-37),[1] and the prophets (Jer. 2:6; 16:14; Amos 2:10; 3:1; Micah 6:4).

Clearly the redemptive activity of God in relation to His enslaved people in Egypt forms the sub-structure of the message of the remainder of the Old Testament. In accordance with His covenantal promises God fulfilled His word, and redeemed a people for Himself, not because they were larger or more powerful than other nations but simply because He sovereignly set His love on them (Deut. 7:7-8).

2. The Authorship of Exodus

No ascription of authorship appears in the book of Exodus, nor does it in any of the other books of the Pentateuch. The same applies to most of the Old Testament literature. However, in Exodus there are several references to Moses writing documents, containing both historical and legal material. The first reference to writing in the Pentateuch occurs when God commands Moses to write on a scroll (*sêfer*) a memorial (*zikkârôn*) about the defeat of the Amalekites (Exod. 17:14). That the Israelites were acquainted with writing should not cause any surprise, as they were not just desert nomads. Men like Moses, Bezalel, Oholiab and others were doubtless knowledgeable about Egyptian scribal practice.[2] Later references in Numbers and Deuteronomy indicate that Moses recorded the itinerary of the Israelites from the time they left Egypt (Num. 33:2-49), the song the LORD gave to him and Joshua as a testimony against the people (Deut. 31:19-22), and also the names of the leaders of the tribes on their staffs (Num. 17:1-2).

More significantly, Moses' writing activities, according to the Book of Exodus, were connected with the Decalogue and related legislation. After recording them on the scroll of the

---

1. On the Psalms in particular, see my discussion, 'The Exodus and the Sinai Covenant in the Book of Psalms', *Festschrift in Honor of Dr. Prof. In Whan Kim* (Seoul: Chongshin University, 2011), pp. 128-68.

2. The article by Alan Millard, 'Writing', *Dictionary of the Old Testament: Pentateuch*, edd. T. Desmond Alexander and David W. Baker (Downers Grove: InterVarsity Press, 2003), pp. 904-11, contains much information on writing in the period covered by the Pentateuch.

covenant, he read them to the people (24:4, 7). Following the rebellion of the people under Aaron's leadership, the covenant was renewed and Moses was instructed by the LORD (34:27) to write down 'the words', that is, the covenantal requirements he has just been given (34:10-26). The most comprehensive description of Moses' writing of the law is in Deuteronomy 31:24, where it is stated that he 'finished writing in a book the words of this law from beginning to end'.

These references reveal that Moses was involved in scribal activity, but they do not prove that he wrote the whole of the book of Exodus. As with other parts of the Pentateuch (especially portions like the early chapters of Genesis), divine revelation as well as oral and written accounts were blended by inspiration into the books as they have come down in the Hebrew manuscripts. Moses had the background of education in Egypt (cf. Acts 7:22: 'Moses was educated in all the wisdom of the Egyptians and was powerful in speech and action'), as well as many years in the Sinai desert when living among the Midianites. It is significant that a major part of the Pentateuch is situated in the Sinai Peninsula (Exod. 16 to Num. 20). From the book of Joshua onwards the Old Testament has many references to 'the law of Moses', or to 'the book of Moses'. For example, at the covenant renewal ceremony at Ebal, Joshua built 'an altar of uncut stones, on which no iron tool had been used'. This was done 'according to what is written in the Book of the Law of Moses' (Josh. 8:31), alluding to Exodus 20:24-25. The Book of the Law is probably to be equated with the scroll of the covenant (Exod. 24:7; see the commentary on this verse).

The books of the Bible were accorded canonical status, not because of any human decision-making process, but because of divine inspiration.[3] As inspired and inscripturated revelation, individual books had objective authority that was acknowledged by the believing church, and functioned as canon before the various books were brought together as a completed and closed unit. Canonicity is something inherent in the books because of their inspiration, and they speak

---

3. This position is set out in the Westminster Confession of Faith, chapter 1, sections II-IV.

for themselves as God's written revelation. For believers in biblical times, and for us today, there is also the internal witness of the Holy Spirit, convincing of the antecedent divinity and authority of the Scriptures.[4]

While we do not know precisely how the whole of the Pentateuch came together, certainly it appears that the beginning of the process of canonisation was with parts of what ultimately became the book of Exodus. Canon and covenant are closely connected, and the formal inscripturisation of God's revelation with His covenantal people, the nation of Israel, in the form of the covenantal scroll (Exod. 24:7) probably marked the first stage.[5] This means that Moses was at the forefront of documenting the divine revelation.

The response of the people at Mount Sinai to Moses' reading of the covenantal document (Exod. 24:7) is paralleled in later incidents in the Old Testament. These include the reading of the law by Hilkiah (2 Kings 22-23; 2 Chron. 34), and the reading of the law by Ezra (Neh. 8:1-9, 14-17; 10:28-39; 13:1-3). In the case of the references in Nehemiah, it is significant that though the one in 8:1 is to 'the book of the law of Moses' (*sêfer torat mosheh*), the designation is abbreviated in 13:1 to 'the book of Moses' (*sêfer mosheh*). This is ambiguous in more than one way. First, it is unclear if 'book' refers only to a section of the Pentateuch (such as Exodus or Deuteronomy), or whether it refers to all parts of it. Probably, the latter is correct. Secondly, it is unclear whether the reference to Moses implies authorship, or whether it is simply a reference to the covenantal mediator through whom the law was given. This ambiguity carries over into the New Testament references as well. Moses was deeply involved personally with all the material in the book of Exodus except for 1:1–2:10, the information in which section must have been passed on by oral or written tradition.

---

4. For discussion on the witness of the Spirit, see John Murray, 'The Attestation of Scripture', in *The Infallible Word*, 3rd revised edition, edd. N. B. Stonehouse and Paul Woolley (Nutley, NJ: Presbyterian & Reformed Publishing Company, 1967), pp. 1-54.

5. Meredith Kline discussed this conjunction in his articles, 'Canon and Covenant', in the *WTJ* 32, 1 (1969), pp. 49-67; vol. 32, 2 (1970), pp. 179-200; vol. 33, 1 (1970), pp. 45-72. These articles are incorporated in his book *The Structure of Biblical Authority* (Grand Rapids: Eerdmans, 1972).

Clearly by the time of Ezra and Nehemiah the Pentateuch was being called either 'the law of Moses' or 'the law of the LORD', and several times the phrase 'the book of Moses' occurs (Ezra 6:18; Neh. 13:1; 2 Chron. 25:4). The first of these passages is important as it is dealing with the reinstatement of the priests and Levites. The relevant laws are not in only one book of the Pentateuch, but in several (cf. Exod. 29:1-46; Lev. 8:1-36; Num. 3:5-9; 8:5-22). It is not surprising that the New Testament is replete with references to 'the law of Moses' or 'the book of Moses'. One of the quotations from Exodus falls into this second category, for Jesus quoted Exodus 3:6: 'I am the God of Abraham, the God of Isaac, and the God of Jacob'. In doing so, He said to the Sadducees who were in discussion with Him: 'Now about the dead rising—have you not read *in the book of Moses*, in the account of the bush, how God said to him …?' (Mark 12:26). The New Testament epistles also have many quotations from the Pentateuch, including from Exodus, and often the term 'Moses' is used as denoting 'the books of Moses'.[6]

This discussion points to the prominent place of Moses in the writing of the Pentateuch, while noting that the Scripture does not claim that every single part of it was from his pen.[7] As far as Exodus is concerned, much of it comprises revelation given by God to Moses for transmission to the Israelites. The terms like 'the law of Moses' and 'the book of Moses' are not claims that he was the original source of the law, or that he was the author of the book.[8] Rather, they indicate respectively that he was the covenantal mediator through whom the law was given, and the central figure in the exodus and the subsequent events. While the *fact* of inspiration is clear, much less is known about the *process* of inspiration, except that all Scripture is breathed out by God (2 Tim. 3:16), and that 'men spoke from God as they were carried along by the Holy Spirit'

---

6. A good listing of passages in the New Testament quoting from Exodus is given by C. John Collins, in *Understanding Scripture: An Overview of the Bible's Origin, Reliability and Meaning* (Wheaton: Crossway, 2012), pp. 191-92.

7. Some helpful comments are given by O. T. Allis on 'What does "Moses wrote the Pentateuch" Mean?' in *The Five Books of Moses* (Philadelphia: Presbyterian & Reformed Publishing Co., 1943), pp. 12-14.

8. Daniel I. Block has many relevant things to say about Moses and Deuteronomy that have relevance for the discussion relating to Exodus. See his article 'Recovering the Voice of Moses: The Genesis of Deuteronomy', *JETS* 44, 3 (2001), pp. 385-408.

(2 Pet. 1:21). What we do know, however, is that in both the Old and New Testaments there is definite acknowledgement that Exodus forms part of the canon, for our Lord and His apostles endorsed the canon of the Old Testament. The law of Moses, the prophets, and the Psalms formed the inspired source of instruction for the church's proclamation of the prophecies concerning the mission and message of Jesus (Luke 24:44). Exodus, however it reached canonical finality, stands as a covenantal document that is foundational for all that follows in the biblical message of salvation.

3. The Theology of Exodus

Many studies have been published that highlight the theology of Exodus,[9] so that a full discussion is unnecessary. But certain matters need emphasis, and so particular aspects are taken up here. The first is that Exodus cannot be understood without reference to the book of Genesis that precedes it, nor to the following books that complete the Pentateuch: Leviticus, Numbers, and Deuteronomy. The opening chapters of Exodus make the connection with Genesis very clearly (cf. Exod. 1:1-5 with Gen. 46:8-27, and Exod. 2:23-25 with Gen. 15:17-19; 17:7; 17:19; 26:24; 35:11-12). Genesis 1–11 is foundational for the rest of the Bible, while from Chapter 12 onwards the concept of covenantal blessings become predominant. Exodus sets out the basic requirements of the covenant with the nation that God adopted as His people, while Leviticus expands on many of the detailed requirements for priests and people. Numbers, among other things, relates how the promise of land starts to become so prominent as the people begin their move to the territory the Lord had sworn to give them. Deuteronomy is not a second law (cf. the LXX of 17:18, *to deuteronomion touto*, 'this repetition of the law'), but it is a reiteration of the covenant of Sinai (see Deut. 5:1-3).

---

9. See among others Geerhardus Vos, *Biblical Theology: Old and New Testament* (Edinburgh: Banner of Truth Trust, 1974), pp. 100-82; Eugene Merrill, in *A Biblical Theology of the Old Testament*, ed. Roy B. Zuck (Chicago: Moody Press, 1991), pp. 30-56; J. Gordon McConville, 'Exodus', *NIDOTTE*, 4, pp. 601-05; Paul House, *Old Testament Theology* (Downers Grove: InterVarsity Press, 1999), pp. 87-125; Douglas Stuart, *Exodus* (The New American Commentary: Nashville: B. & H. Publishing Group, 2006), pp. 34-49.

Introduction

There are two comments by Geerhardus Vos that are pertinent here. He remarked: 'The exodus from Egypt *is* the Old Testament redemption. This is not an anachronistic, allegorising manner of speaking. It is based on the inner coherence of Old Testament and New Testament religion itself.'[10] God's rescue of His enslaved people in Egypt is the redemption *par excellence* of the Old Testament, though some expressions for 'redemption' (especially when the Hebrew verb *gâ'al* used), do not include the specification of any ransom price. No suggestion occurs in the biblical text that there was some actual payment made to Egypt as part of the redemptive process.[11] God's redemptive activity in Egypt was promised to the patriarchs, reaffirmed in Exodus 2:23-25, and in Exodus 6:6-8 not only described as being freedom for His people but linked intimately with the central feature of the covenant. God promised to take His redeemed as His own people and to be their God. Covenant and redemption are tied together in Exodus and in the Old Testament as a whole.

The second comment by Vos is that the outstanding principles of the exodus-deliverance were 'made regulative of all future salvation and bind things past and things to come indissolubly together'.[12] For the rest of Scripture the exodus provides the pattern of God's redemptive activity. The nature of the redemption and its vocabulary become the standard for the redemptive return of Israel from exile, and pre-eminently for Christ's deliverance of His people from the thraldom of bondage to Satan.[13] Using the Old Testament 'exodus' as the exemplar, the New Testament deals with the state of sin out of which we must be redeemed, the price that was paid by the Lord Jesus in offering Himself as a sacrifice, and the new

---

10. Geerhardus Vos, *Biblical Theology*, p. 109.

11. As B. F. Westcott put it: 'It cannot be said that God paid to the Egyptian oppressor any price for the redemption of His people. On the other hand the idea of the exertion of a mighty force, the idea that "redemption" costs much, is everywhere present': *The Epistle to the Hebrews*, 3rd ed. (London: Macmillan & Co., 1903), p. 298.

12. Geerhardus Vos, *Biblical Theology*, p. 110.

13. For discussion on how the New Testament appropriates the language of redemption from the exodus period in the Old Testament, see B. B. Warfield, 'The New Testament Terminology of "Redemption"', *Biblical Foundations* (London: Tyndale Press, 1958), pp. 199-245, and L. L. Morris, *The Apostolic Preaching of the Cross* (London: Tyndale Press, 1955), pp. 9-59.

relationship that follows as a consequence of redemption.[14] What happened at the time of the release of the Israelites from slavery in Egypt was intended to prepare for, and to teach concerning, the same principles coming to higher expression in the freedom from the bondage of sin through Christ.

One of the most central features of the theology of the book of Exodus is the theme of God's presence with His people. The divine promise was, 'I will be with you [2 m.s.]. And this shall be the sign to you that it is I who have sent me to you: When you have brought this people out of Egypt, you [2 m. pl.] will worship God on this mountain' (3:12). God proceeded to reveal His nature, using the Hebrew verb 'to be' (*hâyâh*), denoting that He was the living and life-giving God. One good suggestion has been that the words of God, 'I am who I am' (3:14), can be taken to mean 'I am, I the God who appears in action'.[15] The name derived from this verb, *yhwh* (rendered in our versions by 'the LORD'), was used in making the declaration by God: 'And I [the LORD] have promised to bring you [2 m. pl.] up out of your misery in Egypt' (3:17). This name became the salvation and covenantal name of God, occurring over 6,800 times in the Old Testament. The intention was that His people would have an on-going relationship with Him, so that He would be with them, and that He would continue to make Himself known to them ('you will know that I am the LORD', 6:7; 10:2; 16:12; 31:13). The reality of the Lord's abiding presence with them was going to be displayed in the Tent of Meeting, and His glory seen in the cloud that was over it. His presence was not only manifested at Mount Sinai, but He symbolically went with the people on their pilgrimage to Canaan (40:34-38). Like the tents of the Israelites, God's tent, the Tent of Meeting, was able to be disassembled, and it led the people on each stage of the journey to Canaan.

Another significant aspect of the teaching of the book of Exodus is the relation between the Sabbath and the sanctuary.

---

14. For tracing the biblical pattern of release from slavery, see the excellent popular treatment by John H. White, *Slavery to Servanthood: Tracing the exodus throughout Scripture* (Philadelphia: Great Commission Publications, 1987), and for the New Testament the short treatment by R. E. Nixon, *The Exodus in the New Testament* (London: Tyndale Press, 1963).

15. This is the view of Professor B. Holwerda, *Dictaten, I, Historia Revelationis Veteris Testamenti*, Aflevering II (Kampen, 1954).

This comes out in the positioning of the instructions regarding the Sabbath in the narrative sections dealing with the Tent of Meeting. At the conclusion of the instructions for building the sanctuary, the Sabbath ordinance was enjoined as a sign between the Lord and His people (Exod. 31:17). However, in the account of actually building the sanctuary, the Sabbath ordinance, somewhat abbreviated, comes first, before any of the other details (Exod. 35:1-3). The Sabbath instruction thus forms the link between the command and the fulfilment passages relating to the Tent of Meeting. That this is not just an accidental placement of these commands is made plain later, as twice the identical instruction is given: 'Observe my Sabbaths and have reverence for my sanctuary. I am the LORD' (Lev. 19:30; 26:2). The Sabbath was a sign of the covenant (31:13). That is to say, observance of it was a visible weekly acknowledgement of commitment to the Lord. It was also the day for the major worship activities of Israel, so that the Sabbath and the Tent of Meeting were inextricably joined together. Both were of divine appointment, not dictated by human desire.

A final aspect concerning the theology of this book concerns the way in which that theology was communicated. The people of Israel had both spoken and written revelation. That is to say, Moses had to communicate orally God's words to the people, and later there was written revelation (17:14; 24:4; 32:15-16; 34:27-28). However, in addition to oral and written theology, there was visual theology embodied in the sacrificial system, and especially in the whole symbolism of the Tent of Meeting. That Tent was in effect a continuation of the Sinai experience, for there were distinct zones in operation. The most holy zone was where Moses met God on the top of the mountain. The next, a lower zone, was an area into which only Moses and the elders could enter. Finally, the people as a whole could assemble at the base of the mountain, and an altar was built there (24:4). The Tent of Meeting replicated that threefold pattern: the Most Holy Place, the Holy Place, and the courtyard where the people could sacrifice on the altar.[16]

---

16. W. J. Dumbrell, *Covenant and Creation: An Old Testament Covenant Theology*, revised and enlarged edition (Milton Keynes: Paternoster, 2013) develops this position on pp. 136-37.

Experiences in connection with the ritual worship in Israel were genuine, but the various elements were intended to point forward to the real sacrifice of the Lamb of God. The writer to the Hebrews teaches that Jesus is the eternal High Priest, and that He is 'a minister in the holy places, in the true tent that the Lord set up, not man' (Heb. 8:2 ESV). Furthermore, he says, Jesus entered into the holy places 'through the greater and more perfect tent (not made with hands, that is, not of this creation)' (Heb. 9:11 ESV). The question arises, though, as to how the people of Israel could have understood this. They had the picture language, but they needed spoken instruction as well. Otherwise, they would have been in the same position as we would be in regarding baptism and the Lord's Supper if we did not have spoken words of explanation accompanying their observance. There must have been priestly spoken ministry, so that word and sacrament were conjoined. Unfortunately, we have few passages in the Old Testament to guide us, though the experience of Hannah and Eli was doubtless not an isolated case (1 Sam. 1:9-18). Many must have received 'true instruction' from the mouth of priests (Mal. 2:6). Visual theology needed supplementation by the spoken word. Prophetic proclamation and priestly ministry most probably combined to teach and instruct the people, leading them from the visible symbols in the Sabbath and the sacrificial system to consider 'the sufferings of Christ and the glories that would follow' (1 Pet. 1:11).

4. The Date of the Exodus

Probably no other issue of biblical chronology has been discussed as frequently as this one. It has become the perennial controversy relating to the Book of Exodus. Little change has taken place in the discussions over the last fifty years, as can be seen by consulting a representative selection of evangelical writers.[17] The matter is complex, since it involves many

---

17. The following discussions show how stable has been the debate: Leon T. Wood, 'The Date of the Exodus', in *New Perspectives on the Old Testament*, ed. J. Barton Payne (Waco: Word, 1970), pp. 66-87; Bruce K. Waltke, 'Date of the Conquest', *WTJ* 52 (1990), pp. 181-200; Herbert Wolf, *An Introduction to the Old Testament Pentateuch* (Chicago: Moody Press, 1991), pp. 141-48; J. H. Walton, 'Exodus, Date of', *Dictionary of the Old Testament: Pentateuch*, edd. T. Desmond Alexander and David W. Baker (Downers Grove: InterVarsity Press,

aspects, biblical and extra-biblical. Only one biblical passage (1 Kings 6:1) expressly gives a chronological note that allows a calculation of the date of the exodus. The extra-biblical evidence relates to issues such as the place names mentioned in Exodus 1, the Pharaoh of the exodus, the evidence for the Israelite occupation of Canaan, and the identification and dating of relevant archaeological remains.

The reference in 1 Kings 6:1 provides the length of time, 480 years, between the exodus and the commencement of the temple construction by Solomon. The date of the latter is fairly certain (966 B.C.), and thus the exodus is understood to have happened around 1446 B.C. That date seems to be supported by the reference in Judges 11:26 to the period of 300 years before Jephthah's time that Israel controlled Transjordania.[18] This early date for the exodus conflicts with the view of many scholars that the extra-biblical evidence points to a late date around 1250 B.C. The view that the 480 years is a round figure for twelve generations of forty years each was popularised by John Bright.[19] This would give a period of about 300 years between the exodus and the building of the temple, and would place the exodus in mid-thirteenth century B.C. Some evangelical scholars have supported this position,[20] though the majority still favour the early date.[21] Nothing in the context in 1 Kings 6 suggests that the number of years is to be taken in any way other than the normal. The

---

2003), pp. 258-72; William H. Shea, 'The Date of the Exodus', *Giving the Sense: Understanding and Using Old Testament Historical Texts*, edd. David M. Howard and Michael A. Grisanti (Leicester: Apollos, 2003), pp. 236-55.

18. This figure is not as definite as that in 1 Kings 6 since it is uncertain in some cases in Judges whether judgeships overlapped. But even making that allowance, the length of time given does not support a late date for the Exodus.

19. John Bright, *The History of Israel*, 4th ed. (Louisville: Westminster/John Knox Press, 2000), p. 123.

20. Support has been given by Kenneth Kitchen, *Ancient Orient and Old Testament* (London: Tyndale Press, 1966), pp. 72-75; *ABD* 2, pp. 702-03; *On the Reliability of the Old Testament* (Grand Rapids: Eerdmans, 2006), pp. 307-12; and R. K. Harrison, *Introduction to the Old Testament* (London: Tyndale Press, 1970), p. 317.

21. For representative presentations, see J. J. Bimson, *Redating the Exodus and Conquest*, 2nd ed. JSOT Supp 5 (Sheffield: Almond, 1981); G. L. Archer, *A Survey of Old Testament Introduction*, rev. ed. (Chicago: Moody Press, 1979), pp. 223-34; E. H. Merrill, *A Kingdom of Priests*, 2nd ed. (Grand Rapids: Baker Book House, 2008), pp. 66-78.

supposition of forty years for a generation is artificial, and it appears to be an attempt to make the chronological reference in 1 Kings 6:1 fit extra-biblical evidence.[22] According to the list of the priestly line from Sinai to the time of Solomon given in 1 Chronicles 6:33-37, there were eighteen generations in between, not twelve.

The external data from Egypt and Palestine is inconclusive. This is simply part of the nature of archaeological investigation, which can never be complete and which is open to a variety of interpretations. The differing conclusions advanced by archaeologists about the extra-biblical evidence relating to the date of the exodus demonstrates this amply. Accepting the statement in 1 Kings 6:1 in a straightforward arithmetical sense points to the early date as correct. To go against this biblical statement requires adoption of a procedure in which extra-biblical considerations take precedence over intra-biblical evidence. The reverse procedure must always be adopted.

5. Outline of the Book of Exodus

No indication is given within the book itself as to how its structure is to be portrayed. It is different from Genesis which has the recurring formula, 'these are the generations' (*tôlᵉdot*), that serve as divisional markers. Various schemes can be proposed for Exodus, but redemption from Egypt, the journey to Sinai, the covenant made there, the rebellion of the people and the renewal of the covenant, and the detailed instructions and description of the Tent of Meeting must all feature prominently. Hence, the contents of the book have been set out in this commentary in a six-fold pattern:

---

22. Cf. the comment of Kenneth Kitchen, *Ancient Orient and the Old Testament*, p. 73: 'But what shall be make of the 480 and plus 553-plus-x years, as compared with the roughly 300 years' interval required by our primary evidence?' The reference to 553 years is to the total years for all the individual figures from Exodus to 1 Kings plus some unknown figures. Michael W. Chavalas and Murray R. Adamthwaite, in discussing the way in which archaeology throws light on the Old Testament, conclude that 'one suspects that the conventional explanation of the 480 years, that it represents twelve generations of the biblical "forty years" (in reality twenty-five), owes more to consideration of harmony with Egyptian history than to the demands of exegesis of the text.' *The Face of Old Testament Studies: A Survey of Contemporary Approaches*, David W. Baker and Bill T. Arnold edd. (Grand Rapids: Baker Books, 1999), p. 85.

Introduction

Part I Redemption from Egypt 1:1–15:21

1. Oppression in Egypt 1:1-22
   1. The Increase in Population 1:1-7
   2. The First Attack on the Israelites 1:8-14
   3. The Second Attack on the Israelites 1:15-21
   4. The Third Attack on the Israelites 1:22
2. The Provision of a Deliverer 2:1 –4:31
   1. Moses' Birth 2:1-10
   2. Moses the Refugee 2:11-25
   3. Moses' Call 3:1–4:17
      i) The Choice of Moses 3:1-10
      ii) Moses' Response and His Objections 3:11–4:17
   4. Moses' Return to Egypt 4:18-31
3. Increased Oppression 5:1-21
   1. Additional Burdens 5:1-14
   2. Rebuff by the Israelites 5:15-21
4. Promised Deliverance 5:22–7:5
   1. God's Revelation of His Name 5:22–6:12
   2. Moses' and Aaron's Family Line 6:13-27
   3. A Promise of Signs and Wonders 6:28–7:5
5. Redemptive Judgment 7:6–12:51
   1. The First Sign: Confirmation of Moses and Aaron 7:6-13
   2. The Second Sign: Water Turned to Blood 7:14-24
   3. The Third Sign: Frogs 7:25–8:15
   4. The Fourth Sign: Gnats 8:16-19
   5. The Fifth Sign: Flies 8:20-32
   6. The Sixth Sign: On Cattle 9:1-7
   7. The Seventh Sign: Boils 9:8-12
   8. The Eighth Sign: Hail 9:13-35

9. The Ninth Sign: Locusts 10:1-20
10. The Tenth Sign: Darkness 10:21-29
11. The Eleventh Sign: 11:1–12:51
    i) Judgment Announced 11:1-10
    ii) Preparations for the Passover 12:1-13
    iii) Preparations for the Unleavened Bread 12:14-20
    iv) The Passover Celebration 12:21-28
    v) Judgment on the Egyptians 12:29-32
    vi) The Exodus 12:33-42
    vii) The Passover Regulations 12:43-51

6. Exit from Egypt 13:1–15:21
    1. Consecration of the Firstborn 13:1-16
    2. Crossing the Red Sea 13:17-22
    3. At the Red Sea 14:1-14
    4. Through the Red Sea 14:15-31
    5. The Song of the Sea 15:1-18
        i) The Saving Power of the LORD 15:1-3
        ii) Victory over Egypt 15:4-10
        iii) Confrontation with the Living LORD 15:11-16
        iv) Worship on the Mount 15:17-18
    6. A Summary of Events at the Red Sea 15:19-21

Part II The Journey to Mount Sinai 15:22–18:27

7. The Waters of Marah 15:22-27
8. The Grumbling Community 16:1-36
9. Water from the Rock 17:1-7
10. The Amalekites Defeated 17:8-16
11. Provision of Judicial Help 18:1-27
    a) *The Meeting with Jethro 18:1-12*
    b) *Jethro's Advice 18:13-23*
    c) *The Appointment of Judicial Assistants 18:24-27*

Part III The Covenant at Sinai 19:1–24:18

12. At Mount Sinai 19:1-24

1. The Chosen People 19:1-6
2. Consecration of the People 19:7-15
3. Meeting with God 19:16-24
13. The Ten Words 19:25–20:17
    1. The First Word 20:1-3
    2. The Second Word 20:4-6
    3. The Third Word 20:7
    4. The Fourth Word 20:8-11
    5. The Fifth Word 20:12
    6. The Sixth Word 20:13
    7. The Seventh Word 20:14
    8. The Eighth Word 20:15
    9. The Ninth Word 20:16
    10. The Tenth Word 20:17
14. The Theophany 20:18-21
15. Worship Regulations 20:22-26
16. The Laws 21:1–23:33
    1. Slavery 21:1-11
    2. Homicide 21:12-17
    3. Bodily Injuries 21:18-32
    4. Property Matters 21:33–22:15
    5. Social Responsibilities 22:16-31
    6. Relationships with Others 23:1-9
    7. The Sabbatical Principle 23:10-13
    8. The Three Annual Festivals 23:14-19
    9. Promises and Warnings 23:20-33
17. Ratification of the Covenant 24:1-18
    1. The Formal Covenant Ceremony 24:1-11
    2. The Revelation of God's Glory 24:12-18

Part IV Instructions Regarding the Tent of Meeting 25:1–31:18

18. Contributions for the Sanctuary 25:1-9

19. The Ark of the Covenant 25:10-22
    1. The Nature and Use of the Ark 25:10-16
    2. The Lid of the Ark 25:17
    3. The Cherubim 25:18-20
    4. Atonement and Revelation 25:21-22
20. The Table 25:23-30
21. The Lampstand 25:31-40
22. The Dwelling Place/The Tent 26:1-37
    1. The Linen Curtains 26:1-6
    2. The Goats'-Hair Curtains and the Two Additional Coverings 26:7-14
    3. The Frames and Crossbars 26:15-29
    4. Confirmation of the Building Plan 26:30
    5. The Veil 26:31-35
    6. The Curtain at the Entrance of the Holy Place 26:36-37
23. The Altar of Burnt Offering 27:1-8
24. The Courtyard 27:9-19
25. Oil for the Lampstand 27:20-21
26. The Priests' Garments and Their Consecration 28:1–29:46
    a. The High Priestly Garments 28:1-5
    b. The Ephod 28:6-14
    c. The Breastpiece 28:15-30
    d. Other High Priestly Garments 28:31-39
    e. Dress of the Ordinary Priests 28:40-43
    f. Installation of the Priests 29:1-46
        i. Preparation of the Priests 29:1-6
        ii. The Priestly Anointing 29:7-9
        iii. The Removal of Defilement 29:10-28
    g. The sin-offering 29:10-14
    h. Offering of the First Ram 29:15-18

i. The Offering of the Second Ram 29:19-25
   j. The Future Priests 29:26-30
      i. The Covenant Meal 29:31-34
      ii. Details of the Priestly Installation 29:35-37
      iii. The Regular Offerings 29:38-43
      iv. Concluding Summary 29:44-46

27. The Altar of Incense 30:1-10
28. The Census Tax 30:11-16
29. The Bronze Basin 30:17-21
30. Anointing Oil 30:22-33
31. Incense 30:34-37
32. Bezalel and Oholiab 31:1-11
33. The Sabbath 31:12-17
34. Concluding Summary 31:18

Part V Rebellion and Restoration 32:1–34:35

35. The Golden Bull 32:1-6
36. The Lord's Verdict 32:7-10
37. Moses' Intercession 32:11-14
38. The Broken Covenant and Its Curse 32:15-29
39. Vicarious Atonement 32:30-34
40. The Call to Move from Sinai 33:1-6
41. The Temporary Meeting Place 33:7-11
42. Moses and the Glory of the Lord 33:12-23
43. Preparation for New Revelation of God's Glory 34:1-4
44. God's Glory Revealed 34:5-9
45. The Renewal of the Covenant 34:10-28
46. Moses' Radiant Face 34:29-35

Part VI Building the Tent of Meeting 35:1–40:38

- **47.** The Call to Build 35:1-29
    1. The Sabbath Regulations 35:1-3 (cf. 31:12-17)
    2. Materials for the Tent of Meeting 35:4-29 (cf. 25:1-9)
    3. The Liberality of the Israelite Community 35:20-29 (cf. 31:1-11)
- **48.** Bezalel and Oholiab 35:30–36:7
- **49.** The Progress of the Work 36:8–39:31
    1. The Dwelling Place 36:8-38
    2. The Ark 37:1-9
    3. The Table 37:10-16
    4. The Lampstand 37:17-24
    5. The Altar of Incense 37:25-29
    6. The Altar of Burnt Offering 38:1-7
    7. The Bronze Basin 38:8
    8. The Courtyard 38:9-20
    9. The Costly Materials Used 38:21-31
    10. The Priestly Garments 39:1-31
- **50.** Moses' Inspection of the Tent 39:32-43
- **51.** Setting up the Tent 40:1-33
- **52.** The LORD's Glory 40:34-38

PART I
Redemption from Egypt
(1:1–15:21)

1

Oppression in Egypt
(1:1-22)

1. Increase in Population (1:1-7)

This book begins without any explanation of why the children of Israel found themselves in adverse circumstances in Egypt. Consulting the closing chapters of the previous book, Genesis, helps to explain the presence of the Israelite community in Egypt, but we need to go back earlier to see it in its true perspective. When God made a covenant with His servant Abraham He assured him that his descendants would sojourn in a land that was not theirs, and there they would be afflicted for 400 years. God told Abraham that after divine judgment his descendants would come back to the land of Canaan (Gen. 15:12-16). The scene is now set in the opening chapters of Exodus for the afflicted people of Israel to be brought out with a mighty hand and a stretched out arm from their slavery in Egypt. The major theme of Exodus is redemption.

1 The Book of Exodus commences with the words, 'And these are the names of the sons of Israel' (Heb. *v^e'êlleh sh^{e}mot*), and from this the Jews derived its title, 'and these are the names of.' 'These names' are said to be those 'of the sons of Israel who went to Egypt with Jacob'. This commencement immediately makes a connection with Genesis 46:8 where the exact words have already occurred. This is important as it shows that Genesis and Exodus have a close relationship, in that the latter is a continuation of the narrative begun in the former. Many later historical books in the Old Testament also manifest this same consciousness of being part of an interconnected record of Israel's history.

The NIV does not translate the opening word 'and' (Heb. v^e), nor does it note that the verb 'came' occurs twice in this verse. The NASB has: 'Now these are the names of the sons of Israel who came to Egypt with Jacob; they came each one with his household' (cf. the similar rendering in the NKJV). The stress is placed on the fact that all these sons (with the exception of Joseph who was already there) came down to Egypt with Jacob, and also that they came with their families. It was a migration of the whole clan. 'Sons of Israel' here refers literally to the children of Jacob, while elsewhere in this book the expression means the whole nation.

2-4 The names of those who came down to Egypt are given in a distinctive way:

> Reuben, Simeon, Levi *and* Judah
> Issachar, Zebulon *and* Benjamin
> Dan *and* Naphtali, Gad *and* Asher

This threefold division gives the first four sons of Leah, followed by the last two sons of Leah, and separated by 'and', Benjamin, the second son of Rachel. Finally, the sons of the handmaid Bilhah are given, and then the sons of the handmaid Zilpah, in each case the two names of each pair linked by 'and'. This order is different from that given in Genesis 46:8-17, and it is hard to be sure of the reason for the change. The listing comes near to giving the sons by age.[1]

5 The tally of those coming down from Canaan to Egypt is given as seventy, which agrees with Genesis 46:27 and Deuteronomy 10:22, but disagrees with the assertion of Stephen the martyr that there were seventy-five who arrived in Egypt (Acts 7:14). The figure of seventy-five is taken from the LXX of Genesis 46:27 and Exodus 1:5. This total was achieved by omitting Jacob and Joseph but including *nine*

---

1. As suggested by W. H. Gispen, *Exodus* (Bible Student's Commentary; Grand Rapids: Zondervan, 1982), p. 30.

sons and grandsons of Joseph.² There may also be significance in using seventy in order to indicate completeness, i.e., the whole family of Jacob came down into Egypt. If Er and Onan had not died earlier in Canaan (Gen. 38:7-10) this would have been the ideal and complete number of descendants.³

This genealogy and the number 'seventy' are making an important theological point. That number stands in marked contrast to the information in the following verse that Israel so multiplied in Egypt that 'the land was filled with them' (v. 6). God fulfilled His promise to Abraham to give him innumerable descendants, and the number 'seventy' simply highlights how abundantly Israel proliferated under divine blessing.

6-7 Joseph was the means through whom his family came down into Egypt, but he and his brothers all died there. That generation did not see the redemption from slavery that God was going to accomplish in his time, nor did they see the massive increase in the Jewish population. The words in verse 7 emphasise this increase by repetition of the idea. The NIV rendering – 'were fruitful and multiplied greatly and became exceedingly fruitful' – disguises the fact that in Hebrew there are four verbs used, all of which point back to the creation narrative. Other translations, such as the NRSV, preserve the use of four verbs: 'But the Israelites were fruitful and prolific; they multiplied and grew exceedingly strong.' The first three verbs point back to the creation mandate that God gave. God's command to man was to be fruitful and to become numerous (Gen. 1:28), while the seas were to swarm with living creatures (Gen. 1:20). This juxtaposition of the

---

2. A Heb. fragment from Qumran (4QExᵃ) also gives the number as seventy-five. For further discussions on the calculation of the numbers, see Victor Hamilton, *The Book of Genesis Chapters 18-50* (NICOT: Grand Rapids: Eerdmans, 1995), pp. 596-99, and F. F. Bruce, *The Acts of the Apostles: Greek Text with Introduction and Commentary*, 3rd ed. (Grand Rapids: Eerdmans, 1990), pp. 195-96. The LXX does not provide a full list of Joseph's family, but it does name Manasseh and his son Galaad, Ephraim and his sons Sutulaam and Taam, and Sutulaam's son Edom. While the general principles of the enumeration are fairly clear, various possibilities exist for establishing some of the persons involved.

3. For this interpretation, see both Ronald Youngblood, *The Book of Genesis: An Introductory Commentary*, 2nd ed. (Grand Rapids: Baker, 1991), p. 269) and John Currid, *Genesis Volume 2: Genesis 25:19–50:26* (Darlington: Evangelical Press, 2003), p. 341.

statement of verse 7 with the creation vocabulary draws attention to a significant point. Israel was fulfilling the mandate God had given, and when it came to assessing how great it had become, a repeated noun helps to highlight this fact (*bim'od m^e'od*), 'with exceeding greatness.'

Study Questions

1) What other biblical books start with a genealogy? Why are these genealogies so important?

2) What significance do you see in the use of both names, Israel and Jacob, in verse 1?

3) How did the wrong action of Joseph's brothers in selling him turn out to be part of God's plan?

4) What is the significance of the fact that the growth in the Israelite population in Egypt is expressed in terms of God's original mandate given at creation (Gen. 1:28)?

2 The First Attack on the Israelites (1:8-14)

The account of the Israelite occupancy of Lower Egypt is carried forward until the time of a new Pharaoh. The scene being painted is of an oppressed people, out of favour with the ruling powers in the land, and unable to rescue themselves from their plight. What was needed, and later chapters describe it, was an intervention of God on behalf of His special people (Exod. 19:4-6; Deut. 7:6-8). He was going to carry them out as on eagles' wings (Exod. 19:4).

8 This verse notes that in course of time another Pharaoh came to the throne, who was ignorant of Joseph's story. Both verbs in the sentence (NIV, 'know', 'came to power') have been explained in different ways. 'Came to power' represents the Hebrew verb 'to rise up' (*qûm*). It could simply be noting that a new king arrived on the scene, or it could be linking this new ruler with the Hyksos invasion of Egypt around 1730 B.C. If the latter is the meaning, then it is indicating the Hyksos ruler who arose *against* Egypt at that time (for the use of the verb in this sense, see Deut. 19:11; 28:7; Judg. 20:5; 2 Sam. 18:31; 2 Kings 16:7). The verb 'know' (Heb. *yâda'*) is also ambiguous. In addition to the meaning 'know', it can convey the idea of 'know about', 'have knowledge of.'[4] It may even denote something stronger still, namely, that this new ruler did not acknowledge the worth of Joseph's work or the legacy that he left to succeeding generations.[5] Which ruler this was depends upon the date of the Exodus (see discussion in the Introduction). If the early date is accepted, then it could have been a Hyksos ruler, or the Pharaoh, Amosis I, or on the late date it could have been Rameses II.

9 This Pharaoh saw the reality of the situation in the delta region of the Nile. The number of Israelites was so great that they posed a security threat to Egypt. To his own people he proclaimed the fact that another people (Heb. 'people of Israel', NIV 'the Israelites') was, in that region at least, greater in number and more numerous than the Egyptians.

10 He called for wise counsel to deal with the situation. If further increase took place among the Israelites, then there could be a serious military situation in the event of war. Any enemy could try and ally the Israelites with their own forces, and so become an extremely potent army against Egypt. The end result, too, could be that the servitude of Israel to the Egyptians could be finished, as they would take the opportunity to escape and go up from the land. Pharaoh's reference to going up from the land comes much earlier than the LORD's first reference to the exodus of His people from Egypt (Exod. 3:7-10).

11 Pharaoh's plan to keep the Israelites in control was, first of all, to appoint officials over them as they provided forced labour for the Egyptians. These officials (Heb. *sârê missîm*; NIV 'slave masters') were 'to oppress them', that is, to inflict on them hard labour so that not only were they slaves but they were also subjected to brutal treatment as they gave compulsory service to the Egyptians. The Hebrew word used for 'forced labour' (*sêvel*) is used later in the Old Testament of the program of state labour under the rule of Solomon (1 Kings 11:28). In particular, this labour program

---

4. *DCH*, IV, p. 99.

5. This is the view taken by Victor Hamilton, *Exodus: An Exegetical Commentary* (Grand Rapids: Baker Academic, 2011), pp. 7-8.

was directed towards the building of store cities, called here Pithom and Rameses. These cities cannot now be identified. They were intended as 'store cities' (Heb. *'ârê misk^{e}nôt*). Most probably, these were fortified cities with supplies stored there for military purposes. The building of these cities was part of the protective measures being undertaken to safeguard Egypt's interests. In later history, Solomon had similar cities built (1 Kings 9:19), as did the Judean kings, Jehoshaphat (2 Chron. 17:12), and Hezekiah (2 Chron. 32:28). Play on words may well be present, as *misk^{e}nôt* at the beginning of Exodus is echoed at the end of the book with the account of the setting up of God's *mishkan*, 'the tent of meeting'. This verse is also important because the picture of harsh slavery in Egypt is being drawn, before God's plan of redemption from slavery and bondage is announced.

12-13 The Egyptian plan misfired, for the harder the Israelites were oppressed the more they increased in number. In an echo of God's promise to Jacob, 'Your descendants will be like the dust of the earth, and you will spread out (lit. 'burst forth'; Heb. *pârats*) to the west and to the east, to the north and to the south' (Gen. 28:14), the narrative records that Israel 'spread out' (Heb. *pârats* imperf.). So great was the increase of Israel that the Egyptians were in dread of them. Their fear resulted in a decision to work them even harder, and with physical compulsion. Perhaps 'with brutality' is not too strong a term to describe their treatment of these slaves. According to Leviticus 25:43, 46, 53, ruthless behaviour like this was outlawed in Israel.

14 The subject of the opening verb in this verse (Heb. *vay^{e}mâr^{e}rû*) is not given, but in the context it appears best to take it as being 'the Egyptians'. They made bitter the lives of the Israelites by imposing such hard labour on them, both with bricks and mortar and also out in the fields. Building and farm work were the means used both to gain good outcomes for Egypt and at the same time to oppress the Israelites. The identical idiom is used at the end of the verse as occurred at the end of the previous one, so emphasising the harsh nature of their life. 'They ruthlessly made them work as slaves' (ESV). The fact that the Hebrew verb for work (*'âvad*) is also the root of the word for a slave (*'éved*) adds to the poignancy of the account. Later the repeated refrain is going to be that Israel was rescued by God's power from 'the house of slavery' (Heb. *bêt ʿᵃvâdîm*, Exod. 13:3, 14; 20:2; Deut. 5:6).

3. The Second Attack on the Israelites (1:15-21)

The second way that the Pharaoh chose in attempting to limit the power of the Israelites was by having all male babies killed. This would have the effect of reducing the fighters belonging to exiled Israel, and limiting the danger that they brought to Egyptian power. If successful this would limit the number of males able to procreate and ensure the continuity of the Jewish population.

15 Instructions are given to 'the Hebrew midwives'. This expression is ambiguous as it could mean either that the midwives were of Hebrew ethnicity or that they were the midwives who were serving the Hebrew women. Since the two named, Shiphrah and Puah, bore Semitic names, the first option is probably right. The meaning of the term, 'Hebrew', is debated. It is unlikely that it is connected with the Habiru, a term descriptive of a group of people mentioned in Near Eastern documents for over 1000 years. The Habiru were most probably intruders into the Fertile Crescent from the north, and were opponents of Israel.[6] The biblical text links them with Eber, the name of one of Shem's sons (Gen. 10:21; 11:14, 16). There is no suggestion here in Exodus that the two named midwives were the only ones, which makes it very possible that they acted in some supervisory role.

16 The instruction given to the midwives was that when the Hebrew women were on 'the stones' and gave birth to a child, if it was a son then it was to be killed, but if a daughter it was to be preserved alive. 'The stones' represents a Hebrew dual form (*'ovnâyim*). The word must describe some form of birthing-stool that was in use, for the only other use of the dual is in Jeremiah 18:3 where it refers to the potter's wheel. The connection between these two occurrences is unclear. The Hebrew text says that if the child was a 'son' it was to be killed, while 'a daughter' was to be kept alive. While some

---

6. For this interpretation of the term 'Habiru', see Meredith G. Kline, 'The Ha-Bi-ru – Kin or Foe of Israel', *WTJ* 19 (1956-57), pp. 19-24, 170-84; 20 (1957-58), pp. 46-70.

versions have followed the AV in translating the Hebrew literally ('son', 'daughter'; see NASB, NKJV, ESV), others have changed to 'boy' and 'girl' (REB, NRSV). This change removes the terms from the realm of family relationships, and the more abstract terms do not have the same emotional force. The Israelites were being told that it was *their* sons and daughters that were in view.[7] That increases the abhorrence of what was planned.

17 Pharaoh had not reckoned with the fact that he was dealing with women whose loyalty was to another master. They 'feared God', that is, their relationship with Him was one of devotion and obedience, a combination found elsewhere where this fear is mentioned (see Pss. 19:9-11; 34:8-14).[8] Not concerned with Pharaoh's anger, they refused to conform to the order, and let all the sons and daughters live. Divine authority must always take precedence over human instructions (cf. Acts 5:29).

18-19 Pharaoh proceeded to interrogate the midwives for the reason why they failed to obey his order. He disdainfully called their actions 'this thing'. In reply, they claimed that a difference existed between the Egyptian women and their Hebrew counterparts. The Hebrew women were more 'lively' than the Egyptians and gave birth quickly. No evidence exists to confirm this assessment. It could be that it was the case, or that God made it so as part of His redemptive activities on behalf of Israel. While what the midwives said may not have been untrue, yet it was only a partially true response. The Bible does not hide the faults of God's people, but sets them out without normally making any comment on them.

20-21 The language of these verses suggests that the midwives were definitely from the Israelite community. God's attitude to the midwives was one of kindness (lit. 'God was good to the midwives'). The verb used (*yâtav*) often comes in the setting of the covenant, as demonstrated by Jacob's words when he was preparing to meet his brother Esau (Gen. 32:9-10;

---

7. This point is brought out well by J. A. Motyer, *The Message of Exodus* (Nottingham: Inter-Varsity Press, 2005), p. 28.

8. For discussion on the wider usage of the expression 'the fear of the Lord', see H. Blocher, 'The Fear of the Lord as the "Principle" of Wisdom', *TB* 28 (1977), pp. 3-28.

note the cluster of covenantal terms, the divine name *yhwh*, and the words 'loving kindness', 'faithfulness', 'truth', and 'servant'). The usage of this verb helps in understanding the reference here. God's favour was on His covenantal servants, the faithful midwives, and blessings flowed also to all the Israelite community. The language describing this increase echoes that of verse 7, which emphasises how ineffective was Pharaoh's first plan of selective genocide. In spite of his evil designs the increase of the people of Israel continued as before. The midwives were rewarded for their commitment to their covenantal LORD (v. 21, 'they feared God') by a gift of families from His hand. The Hebrew text denotes the gift as being 'houses' (*bāttîm*), but 'house' can often denote a household or a family (see Gen. 18:19; 35:2; 46:27; Exod. 12:3; 2 Sam. 7:11-16).

Study Questions

1) Do you think there was any indication that the Israelites were a warlike people and therefore would be a danger to the Egyptians?

2) What indications are there in this passage of how serious was the attempt by the Egyptians to make life very difficult for the Israelites?

3) What is the connection between fearing God and receiving blessing from Him?

4) Was the partial answer of the midwives to Pharaoh's question morally acceptable?

4. The Third Attack on the Israelites (1:22)
22 The first plan of genocide having failed, Pharaoh had another step to take. He gave the instruction that every boy that was born had to be thrown into the Nile, while every girl was to be kept alive. To make it quite plain that this applied only to Israel, the Samaritan Pentateuch, the LXX, and the Targums all have 'born to the Hebrews'. This action is parallelled in the New Testament by Herod's decree that all the boys aged two years and under were to be killed

(Matt. 2:16-18). In both cases the statements are reserved, the decision being indicated but no detailed description given of the way in which it was carried out.

2

The Provision of a Deliverer
(2:1–4:31)

1 Moses' Birth (2:1-10)

The narrative now focuses on one particular family, who managed to circumvent Pharaoh's scheme and save their son. The account in Exodus of Moses' birth, life, and ministry has as its complement two New Testament passages. These are the speech of Stephen, in which he spoke of some parts of Moses' life (Acts 7:20-44), and the section in Hebrews 11 dealing with him (Heb. 11:23-29). In several respects these commentaries add important details to the Exodus account (e.g., Moses thought that by killing the Egyptian his people would understand that God was going to use him to rescue them, Acts 7:25). These are illustrations of the way in which later revelation helps in understanding earlier passages. The Egyptian provenance of the account is marked by the use of several Egyptian words in the text, such as 'papyrus basket' and 'reeds'.

1 Attention now focuses on one particular child born at that time, Moses. A man and woman, both from the family of the Levites, married. The parents are not named, and while it is often noted that they were Amram and Jochebed, mention of them in Exodus 6:20 need not necessarily to be taken to mean that they were Moses' immediate parents. They could be mentioned as Moses' ancestors (see the note in the NIV Study Bible on Exod. 6:20). The name Jochebed is important because it contains a shortened form of the divine name *yhwh* (Jo-), together with a noun meaning 'glory', and so seems to mean 'The LORD is glory'. This is noteworthy and has relevance for understanding Exodus 6:2-3, for it means that the name 'the LORD' (*yhwh*) was indeed known and used before the time of Moses.

2 The couple already had at least two children, as the wife had given birth to Aaron and Miriam (see 2:4 and 7:7). She conceived again and gave birth to a son. She saw that he was 'good' (Heb. *tov*), which in the context means 'healthy', 'well', though it could signify special (see comment on v. 3). There was danger that he was going to die, so she took steps to hide him, which worked for the first three months of his life. However, by that time it would have been clear that another avenue of deception would have to be found if he was to be saved. Both Acts 7:20 and Hebrews 11:23 mention the period of three months.

3 The substitute plan involved making a reed basket (Heb. *têvat gome'*), coated with bitumen and pitch. The word for the basket (*têvâh*) is only used of Noah's ark in Genesis 6–8 and in Exodus 2 of the receptacle in which Moses was placed. It was probably a small replica of the type of boats used on the Nile for carrying passengers and cargo. The mother placed Moses in the basket, and set it among the reeds on the edge of the river. The Hebrew word for 'reeds' (*sûf*) occurs in the name 'Sea of Reeds' (*yâm sûf*, Exod. 10:19), traditionally translated as 'the Red Sea'. The English versions have followed the LXX in that rendering, which was a borrowing of an expression (*erythra thalassa*) from the classical Greek writers such as Herodotus. Hebrews 11:23 points out that the action of Moses' parents was motivated by two factors: they saw he was 'no ordinary child' (cf. the use of 'good' in v. 2) and their faith was in God as the deliverer. The first of these explanations agrees also with the words of Stephen recorded in Acts 7:20, that Moses was 'beautiful to God' (*asteios tô theô*).[1] The saving

---

1. This may be an elative expression, 'exceedingly beautiful', possibly a reflection of the similar idiom in Hebrew in which divine names could be used to express superlatives. See the articles by D. Winton Thomas, 'A Consideration of Some Unusual Ways of Expressing the Superlative in Hebrew', *VT* 3 (1954), pp. 209-24; 'Some Further Remarks on Unusual Ways of Expressing the Superlative in Hebrew,' *VT* 18 (1968), pp. 120-24.

of Moses was a foreshadowing of the salvation of Israel as a whole.

4-5 Moses' sister, Miriam, stationed herself (so the Heb. verb *yâtsav*, Hitp., implies) at a distance to observe what the outcome was going to be of her mother's actions. She wanted to know what was going to happen to her young brother, so that she could report back to her parents. From her vantage point she saw Pharaoh's daughter come down to the river 'to bathe'. This seems an unusual action, for surely facilities for bathing existed in the royal palace. It may be that there was thought to be some magical significance through bathing in the Nile, and it was for that purpose Pharaoh's daughter came. While at the riverbank she saw the papyrus basket and sent one of her women servants to get it.

6 Immediately on opening the basket, she saw Moses. The Hebrew text says: 'she saw him, the child!' i.e., the one already spoken about in the previous verses. He was crying, and she recognised that this was one of the babies of the Israelites, and had compassion on him. She clearly would have known the decree commanding death to infant Hebrew babies, but she chose to disregard it and save this child. Her words at the end of verse 6 could either be a statement, 'This one is from the children of the Hebrews,' or else a question without an interrogative marker, 'Is this one of the Hebrews' children?'

7-8 While Miriam earlier had been at a distance (see v. 4), she had come much closer so that she was able to ask if Pharaoh's daughter wanted a nursemaid for the baby boy she had just discovered. In response to a favourable answer, Miriam went to find her mother. Miriam is referred to here by the Hebrew word *'almâh*, the same word that is used in Isaiah 7:14 in the prophecy concerning the virgin birth.

9 Miriam called her mother, to whom Pharaoh's daughter entrusted the baby, promising due payment for her work in caring for him. This action was highly significant, for it meant that Moses was brought up in his own home, and his parents had the opportunity to teach him about Israel's God.

10 The narrative records the next major event in Moses' life, though no mention is made of his age. When he was grown up he was adopted by Pharaoh's daughter as her son. The Hebrew text uses a verb (*gâdal*) that is used quite frequently to denote the maturing process, and it is sometimes accompanied by the verb 'to be weaned' (*gâmal*; see Gen. 21:8). Here that accompanying verb is not used, and hence no specific age can be attributed to Moses. His mother relinquished her son to be brought up and educated in the royal palace of Egypt. He was then in a position of great privilege, wealth and education. In his speech Stephen the martyr referred to the fact that 'Moses was educated in all the wisdom of the Egyptians and was powerful in speech and actions' (Acts 7: 22). Pharaoh's daughter gave him the name Moses, and the added explanation she gave was: 'For from the water I drew him out.' The name (Moses, '[one] who draws out [of the water]') may well have connections with both Egyptian and Hebrew languages, but as in other Old Testament cases, the accompanying explanation should not be taken as an exact translation of the name in question (cf. Ichabod, 1 Sam. 4:21-22; Ebenezer, 1 Sam. 7:12).

Study Questions

1) What comparisons can you draw between the rescue of Moses in the ark on the Nile with the salvation of Noah and his family?

2) How do you think that Moses' parents knew he was not 'an ordinary child' (Heb. 11:23)?

3) Why should a daughter of Pharaoh have felt sorry for a Hebrew baby?

4) In what ways did the time in Pharaoh's palace prepare Moses for his later work?

2 Moses the Refugee (2:11-25)

This section of the narrative deals with the period after Moses had come to maturity, and Acts 7:23 puts his age at forty when the incident related in verses 11-15 took place. He was by then well-educated, enjoying 'the pleasures of sin', and the recipient of great wealth (Heb. 11:25-26). However, an incident took place that was crucial for him in more ways than one. He had to identify with the people of God, and he had also to learn that he himself could not redeem Israel.

11 The NIV translation of the opening of this verse is very idiomatic: 'One day, after Moses was grown up' (cf. the NASB: 'Now it came about in those days, when Moses had grown up'). This marks a transition from the early life of Moses to a stage in which he identifies with fixed purpose with his people. In his early upbringing by his parents, he must have been told about their origins, and so he went out to his people in order to see their situation. He had made up his mind to visit his relatives (Acts 7:23). No fixed point can be given to his decision to refuse to be called a son of Pharaoh's daughter (Heb. 11:24). What he saw was the harsh slavery being endured by them, the Hebrew text using a word for their forced labour (*s^{e}valôt*) that has been used already in 1:11. In particular, he saw a fellow Israelite being abused by an Egyptian overseer.

12 Looking around, 'here and there' (Heb. *koh vâkoh*), he could not see anyone watching and he took the law into his own hands and struck the Egyptian. What was being meted out to his fellows (being struck) he now metes out as punishment and struck the Egyptian, killing him (the same verb *nâkâh*, Hi.). He disposed of the body by burying it in the sand. At this stage of his life, Moses thought that by his own power and actions God was going to rescue His people from their slavery, but they did not share his mistaken belief (Acts 7:25).

13-14 The next day Moses went out and saw two Hebrews fighting each other. He asked the reason why one man was striking the other, but the answer must have surprised him greatly. Having looked around before he hit the Egyptian the previous day, he thought his action was unseen, but now he is disabused of this idea. The man asks him if he had been appointed as a judge with power over life and death. He wondered if Moses was going to kill him in the same way he killed the overseer the previous day. This question forced Moses to realise that his murder of the Egyptian had not gone undetected. It was indeed 'known' to both Israelites and Egyptians.

15 The news was carried even to Pharaoh, who then wanted to take Moses' life. There could be no defence for Moses' actions, and he realised that he had to get out of the country quickly, and so went to 'the land of Midian'. Knowledge of the Midianites is virtually restricted to what is recorded about them in the Bible. Midian was one of the sons of Keturah, Abraham's third wife (Gen. 25:2; 1 Chron. 1:32). In the story of Joseph the Midianites are traders (Gen. 37:28), while here in Exodus they are pastoralists (Exod. 2:17). Their territory seems to have been without precise boundaries, but was probably on the eastern side of the Sinai Peninsula. Knowledge of the desert was going to be very important for Moses, as he would lead the children of Israel there for forty years. No indication is given as to how long Moses had been living in Midian before the incident at the well took place. The text simply says that he was living there (Acts 7:29 calls him a *paroikos*, an alien or foreigner), and on a particular day sat down at a well, that was often the gathering point in the Near East. A well is the setting in several stories concerning the patriarchs (see Gen. 24; 29).

16-19 To that well came Jethro's daughters, though the father is not named until later. He is referred to as the priest of Midian. It is possible that in Midian, as in Salem (Gen. 14:18-20), the chief official was a priest/king. His daughters had come to draw water, and filled the troughs to satisfy the needs of the flocks. After the arduous task was finished, they were deprived of it by ruthless shepherds who drove 'them' away. 'Them', however, is masculine in the Hebrew text, which suggests that the daughters were superintending the work of male servants engaged in the task. Moses intervened in the situation and became the rescuer, and watered the flocks (again with a m. pl. suffix, 'their flocks').[2] The daughters returned home, and when their 'father' Reuel asked why they had come back so early, they told him what had happened. The name Reuel appears to mean either 'friend of God' or 'shepherd of God'. In later narratives he is called Jethro (Exod. 3:1; 18:1), which suggests that the two names refer to the same person. As early as the first century A.D., the Jewish historian Josephus suggested that Reuel was his personal name while Jethro was his official designation.

---

2. This is the first time in the Old Testament that the verb 'to save' (*yâsha'*, Hi.) occurs. What Moses did was a foreshadowing of the far greater work of God in saving His people (Exod. 14:30). The verb does not become frequent until the book of Judges, other synonymous verbs being used instead (cf. the use of *nâtsal*, Hi., 'to deliver' in v. 19).

Many examples occur in the Old Testament where dual names were used (cf. Pul/Tiglath Pilezer, 2 Kings 15:19, 29; Eliakim/Jehoiakim, 2 Kings 23:34-36). Outward appearance suggested to the women that Moses was an Egyptian, and so they reported to their father. Both his speech and dress would have distinguished him from the desert dwellers of Midian. The action of Moses is described using the verb 'to deliver', a verb used repeatedly from Exodus onwards of God's action in delivering His people from bondage and slavery. He did indeed draw water (the Heb. *dâloh dâlâh*, inf. absol. + pf. suggests some emphasis is needed in translation) for their flocks. Reuel inquired about the location of the man, and rather than leave him, he wanted his daughters to invite him to eat with them (lit. 'that he may eat bread').

21-22 Moses was agreeable to staying with Reuel and his family, and Zipporah (meaning 'bird' in Heb.) was given to him as his wife. She bore him a son whom Moses named Gershom. The explanation that Moses gave for this name was that he had become an alien in a foreign land. There may well have been a double play on words in this use. The verb *gârash* means 'to drive out' (cf. its use already in v. 17, and its later use in reference to Pharaoh in 6:1), and the form 'he drove them out' would have been *gᵉrâshâm*. However, if divided differently, it could be made up of the Hebrew words *gêr*, 'stranger', 'alien', and *sham*, 'there'. Moses had been driven out and forced to become an alien in Midian.

23-24 The opening words suggest a long time elapsed before the death of the Pharaoh (Heb. 'those many days'). Meanwhile, no change had taken place in the condition of the Israelites, and they 'groaned' under their burdens. This is the only time in Exodus that this verb (*'ânach*) occurs, though its use alongside terms such as 'to cry out' (*zâ'aq*), 'a cry for help' (*shav'â*), and 'a groan' (*nâ'âqâh*) points to the deep sense of misery out of which the Israelites were appealing to God for deliverance. They were not only aliens in Egypt, but were subjected to harsh slavery. God's response is highlighted by the use of four verbs: 'God heard ... remembered ... looked upon ... was concerned.' He was attentive to their combined cries, and remembered His covenant with Abraham, with Isaac, and with Jacob. In a context like this, 'remember' means to act in faithfulness to His word of promise (cf. 'God remembered Noah', Gen. 8:1). While the commencement of this book assumes knowledge of God's covenant with the patriarchs (for Abraham, see Gen. 15:17-19; 17:7; for Isaac, Gen. 17:19; 26:24; for Jacob, Gen. 35:11-12), the covenantal relationship between God and His people as a key to the whole narrative is made explicit. This is the first of thirteen occasions in Exodus in which the word 'covenant' (b^erit) appears. A covenant is a bond between God and man, given by a sovereign God as an expression of His grace. In this formal way He expressed the relationship that existed between them. The central core of the covenant was that God promised, 'I will be your God, and you shall be my people.'

25 The outcome for Israel was that God showed compassion on His afflicted people. The prophet Isaiah was later to reflect on this, saying of the people of Israel, that 'in all their distress he too was distressed, and the angel of his presence saved them' (Isa. 63:9). The NIV translation, 'and was concerned about them,' is an attempt to render in modern English the Hebrew text that simply says, 'and God knew' (*vayyêda'*). In this case the Hebrew verb 'to know' (*yâda'*) is used in the sense of 'knowing intimately' (cf. its use of God's knowledge of Moses, Exod. 33:17; Deut. 34:10; or His knowledge of the psalmist's sitting and rising, Ps. 139:2). God looked with compassion on His people, identified with them in their tribulation, and set in process the divine plan for their rescue.

Study Questions

1) Moses' action in killing the Egyptian was to protect his people. What attitude should we take towards this murder?

2) Can you suggest reasons why Moses made his way to live among the Midianites?

3) Quite a few events in the Bible take place at wells. Can you recall some of these and their significance?

4) The language detailing God's response to the cry of the Israelites in their slavery (2:23-25) is given in terms that

normally apply to humans ('heard', 'remembered', 'was concerned'). How does this language help us to understand God's actions?

3 Moses' Call (3:1–4:17)

i) The Choice of Moses (3:1-10)
The text now moves on to note how God chose Moses as the leader of Israel, and, from a human point of view, as their deliverer. God 'made known his ways to Moses' (Ps. 103:7), sovereignly revealing to him His purposes for the redemption of Israel and the settlement of the people in the land of Canaan. The nature of that revelation, as supernatural, comes out in this passage, as God uses something quite contrary to normal experience, a bush burning but not being consumed, to arrest Moses' attention and from it to speak to him. This marks the end of the patriarchal period, and the commencement of a new era in the history of redemption.[3]

1 For a period of time Moses was tending the flocks of his father-in-law, Jethro, who has already been introduced into the narrative in 2:16 (see comment there). The fact that he was a priest is noted three times (2:16; 3:1; 18:1). Moses led or drove the flock 'to the far side of the desert' (*'achar hammidbâr*), seemingly an indication of a considerable distance away from the normal grazing area. This may have been over 100 miles in distance (160 km) and the journey would have taken considerable time. He came to Horeb that is called the mountain of God. 'Horeb' means 'the dry place', and in parts of the Old Testament, especially in Deuteronomy, it is used rather than 'Sinai'. The expression 'the mountain of God' does not indicate that there was only one mountain on which God revealed Himself. Various mountains were places of revelation (cf. Moriah, Gen. 22:2; Perazim, 2 Sam. 5:20; Carmel, 1 Kings 18:20-39) but Horeb/Sinai was particularly known as 'the mountain of God' because of its connection with covenant-making and also because of God's self-revelation of Himself there.

---

3. In addition to commentaries on this passage, the important article by E. J. Young, 'The Call of Moses,' *WTJ* 29 (1966-67), pp. 117-35, 30 (1967-68), pp. 1-23, contains many significant insights.

2 What Moses saw was the angel of the LORD 'in flames of fire from within the bush'.[4] The angel of the LORD, who is called elsewhere 'the angel of God' (Judg. 13:6, 9), appeared first in the patriarchal narratives (see Gen. 16:7-13; 22:15-18). He claimed on the one hand to be God's messenger, declaring His word, while on the other hand claiming to exercise the prerogatives of God Himself. That Moses was looking at a revelation of God is made plain in verse 4 where the angel is called 'God' (*'elohîm*). Here the angel of the LORD appears in the bush (*s^eneh*), and then in verse 4 God calls to Moses from the bush. The word for bush only occurs in this chapter and in Deuteronomy 33:16, where the promise is made concerning the tribe of Joseph that it would have the blessing of the presence of the God of the covenant, who had revealed Himself in the burning bush to Moses. No identification can be made of the bush with any specific species. The emphasis is not on the particular type of desert shrub but on the revelation that takes place by sight and hearing. No rationalistic explanation can satisfactorily explain the phenomenon of the burning bush. It was a means chosen by God to demonstrate His sovereignty and His holiness, and also to produce in Moses a proper sense of reverence towards God as he is commissioned to go back to Egypt on his mission of redemption. Fire is often used in the Bible in connection with the holiness of God (cf. Exod. 19:18; 24:17; Lev. 9:24).[5] The fact that the bush was burning, yet not consumed by the flames, is only one of a number of miraculous happenings in the Mosaic era. A similar cluster of miracles occurred in the ministry of Jesus, in a period when the old covenant gave way to the new.

3 As Moses contemplated the appearance of God in the burning bush, he decided to turn aside and see what the vision was or meant. He was looking at something quite outside of normal experience, because the bush was burning yet not burnt up. The Hebrew word 'to burn' (*bâ'ar*) is used in two senses in

---

4. The Hebrew text has *b^elabbat 'êsh* ('in the flame of fire'), where *labbat* ('flame of') must be a contracted form for *lahevet 'êsh* (see *DCH*, IV, p. 520).

5. Some commentators make the burning bush a symbol of the afflicted people of God, and this is certainly the origin of the use of the burning bush by Presbyterian churches, with the Latin motto: *Nec tamen consumebatur* ('Nevertheless not consumed'). While it is a biblical truth that the church will survive all persecutions, for the Lord will not cast off His inheritance (Ps. 94:14), yet the burning bush is a revelation of God, not of the church.

this passage. In verse 2 it means 'burn', while here in verse 3 it means 'burn utterly', 'be consumed'. Not surprisingly, Moses wondered at the meaning of this 'strange sight'.

4 Anthropomorphic language is used to describe God's reaction to Moses' actions and words. The language is striking because it says: 'When the LORD (*yhwh*) saw ... God (*ʾelohîm*) called to him.' Though the matter of the name of God has not yet arisen, the name particularly associated with God's revelation and redemption at the time of the exodus is used here in the narrative. It seems clear that the name was already known and used, even though its significance was not fully understood (see the comments on 6:2-5). In addition, *ʾelohîm* is used, equating 'the angel of the LORD' with God Himself. The words spoken are a call from God: 'Moses, Moses,' probably intending the repetition to indicate urgency (cf. 1 Sam. 3:10). The response of Moses is that of Isaiah much later (Isa. 6:8): 'Here I am' (*hinnênî*). The call is answered by immediate readiness on Moses' part. When God speaks in power, those called respond with willingness to His command, as demonstrated in the calling of the disciples by Jesus in the Gospel accounts.

5 The instruction immediately follows to Moses not to come any closer and to remove his sandals, for the place where he was standing was holy ground. This same instruction to remove the sandals was given later to Joshua by the commander of the LORD's army (Jos. 5:15). In both passages the idea was not that the ground was intrinsically holy, but made so because of God's immediate presence there. Boundaries were set lest Moses, lacking in humble reverence, approached too near to the God of glory. A sovereign God sets the manner in which sinners draw near to Him.

6 God again identified Himself to Moses as 'the God of your father, the God of Abraham, the God of Isaac, and the God of Jacob' (see 2:24). The singular, 'your father,' may seem strange at first sight, and although it is not as common as the plural, 'your fathers,' it does occur elsewhere (see Gen. 26:24; 31:5, 42, 53; 46:1, 3; 49:25; 50:17; Exod. 15:2; 18:4). It points to Abraham as the one to whom the promises were originally given, and those promises were repeated to Isaac and Jacob.[6] The successive

---

6. The Samaritan Pentateuch had 'fathers' here, and it may be from that source,

covenants were not altogether new covenants, but rather reaffirmations of the basic one given to Abraham.[7] Jesus in verse 6a quoted the words here in relation to His teaching on marriage at the final resurrection (Matt. 22:23-33//Mark 12:18-27). His use of the passage seems to reflect on the fact that the wives of the three patriarchs all had difficulty in conceiving. It was only by God's power and faithfulness that children were born, and so He remains the one who can give life from the dead.[8] Moses' reaction was to hide his face, for he feared to look on God. As in a later incident, he saw something of the form of God, but realised that he could not look with impunity on it (see Exod. 24:9-10). With one exception (Isa. 50:6), this is the only place in the Old Testament in which a person hides (using the verb *sâtar*) his face from God.

7 The divine declaration continued, with a wonderful expression of God's tender care for His afflicted people in Egypt. He had indeed seen (Heb. *râ'oh râ'îtî*) their affliction, heard their cries, and understood their suffering. The prophet Isaiah, in his ministry to Judah, referred to the exodus experience of redemption, saying that he was going to tell of all the many good things that the LORD had done for the house of Israel, in love and mercy redeeming them (Isa. 63:7-9). The use of the word 'my people' (*'ammî*) is significant. God was no longer dealing with just a family, but a group who had become a nation. Out of all nations they were His 'treasured possession' (Exod. 19:5), chosen not because they were more numerous than other nations, but simply because the LORD loved them (Deut. 7:7-8). For the first time the expression 'slave drivers' (*nôgêsîm*) occurs, but it seems similar in meaning to the 'slave masters' (*sârê missîm*) of Exodus 1:11. Oppressive labour was resulting in cries of distress to God.

8 God's saving work was not just something for the future, but He reassured Moses that He had already come down (*vâ'êrêd*) to rescue the people (*lᵉhatstsîlô*, lit. 'to deliver

---

or from of a Greek version, that Stephen quoted the words, 'I am the God of your fathers', in his speech (see Acts 7:32).

7. It is significant that the Heb. word for 'covenant' (*bᵉrît*) never occurs in a plural form in the OT, reinforcing the essential unity of the various covenantal formulations.

8. Cf. the discussion by J. G. Jantzen, 'Resurrection and Hermeneutics: On Exodus 3:6 and Mark 12:26', *JSNT* 23 (1985), pp. 43-58.

him', i.e., the nation). While He had appeared to others earlier in patriarchal history, He had come down and appeared in the burning bush. The redemptive mission was twofold. On the one hand, it involved release from the slavery in Egypt, while on the other hand it involved bringing Israel up out of Egypt to the land that God had, by solemn oath, sworn to give them. The verb 'bring up' (*ʿâlâh*, Hi.) became one of the standard terms used to describe either the LORD's or Moses' actions in leading the people out of Egypt (for the LORD, see Exod. 33:15; Lev. 11:45; Num. 21:5; Deut. 20:1; Josh. 24:17; for Moses, see Exod. 17:3; 32:1, 7, 23; 33:1). The land to which Israel would be brought is described as 'a good and spacious land, a land flowing with milk and honey.' These expressions also became standard ones in relation to the nature of Canaan, especially in the Book of Deuteronomy (for 'the good land', see Deut. 1:25, 35; 3:25; 4:21, 22; 6:18; 8:7, 10; 9:6; 11:17; for 'the land flowing with milk and honey', see 6:3; 11:9; 26:9, 15; 27:3; 31:20). The use of the reference to 'milk and honey' parallels a similar expression in Ugaritic (another Semitic language). On a tablet found on the Mediterranean coast to the north of Israel Baal is said to send fertility and abundance in the form of fat/oil and honey:

> 13 The heavens rain fat/oil
> 14 the wadis flow with honey.[9]

These expressions were a way of denoting the bounty that was to be available to them. The land that the Israelites were to inherit was 'the home of the Canaanites, Hittites, Amorites, Perizzites, Hivites and Jebusites'. This list of the inhabitants of Canaan is one of several that occur in the Old Testament. The fullest list in Genesis 15:18-21 names ten Gentile nations, while others give varying numbers (see Gen. 10:15-17; Deut. 7:1; Josh. 3:10; 11:3; 24:11). No explanation is given why the variation occurs from passage to passage, but there is a parallel with the description of the land promised to Israel. The boundaries are stated in different ways (cf. Gen. 15:18-21; 28:13-14; Exod. 23:31; Josh. 1:2-5), probably indicating that the promised land was a concept, not a piece of territory to be

---

9. This appears in the Ugaritic document KTTU 1.6.

marked out with arithmetical precision. Sometimes the full ten nations are enumerated; at other times an abbreviated list is given. It was enough to know that these were the representative nations who would have to be disinherited before Israel could occupy the land.[10]

9-10 Twice in these verses the expression 'and now' (*vᵉ'attâh*) appears. It forms a marker to indicate a change in the dialogue; the first occurrence links in with the preceding account, while the second one at the start of verse 10 indicates the consequence. The NIV captures the meaning well with the translation, 'And now ... so now.' The LORD's word reiterates what had already been declared in verse 7 regarding the cry of the Israelites reaching Him. He had heard them and also seen how the Egyptians were maltreating them. The word for 'oppression' (*lachats*) here is used almost exclusively of the oppressive treatment meted out to the Israelites by the Egyptians. The Israelites had always to remember their experience in Egypt and hence they were commanded not to oppress foreigners (Exod. 22:21; 23:9). The second 'and now' introduces the action required to remedy the situation. Moses was instructed that he was being sent to Pharaoh to bring God's people out of Egypt.[11] Again Israel is identified as God's people ('*ammî*, 'my people'), though with the qualifying phrase, 'the sons of Israel' (*bᵉnê yisrâ'êl*).

Study Questions

1) Quite frequently in the Old Testament it is said that God appeared to one of His servants. What other passages can you locate, and do they also involve some dramatic visual appearance?

2) How did taking off his sandals show Moses' response to God's holiness?

---

10. For discussion on the individual national names, see Walter C. Kaiser Jr, 'Exodus', in *The Expositor's Bible Commentary*, 2nd ed. (Grand Rapids; Zondervan, 2008), pp. 367; and for fuller discussion, *Peoples of the Old Testament World*, edd. Alfred J. Hoerth, *et al* (Grand Rapids: Baker Book House, 1994), pp. 127-250.

11. The LXX and the Vulgate both have 'and *you* will bring out', but the *Hif'il* inf. absol. (*lᵉhôtsê'*) is acceptable without any need to emend the text.

3) At this stage in Moses' life and ministry, how important was the reassertion by God of the fact that He was the God of the covenant made with Abraham, Isaac, and Jacob?

4) Moses' commission from God was daunting, but what elements in God's word to him would give hope and encouragement?

ii) Moses' Response and His Objections (3:11–4:17)

11 Moses' immediate response was to question his own ability to effect the deliverance of the people from their bondage. This is the first of several occasions on which Moses showed reluctance to fulfil the role God had in mind for him (for later ones, see 4:1, 10, 13). Earlier Moses was confident of his own ability to redress at least some of the grievances of his people (see commentary on 2:12). Now he was apprehensive of what lay ahead, knowing, of course, the anger of Pharaoh towards him (2:15).

12 The answer came in two parts. The first was that God gave reassurance regarding His presence. The form, 'I will be with you' (*'ehyeh 'immāk*) is the same in Hebrew as the promise that God gave Jacob (Gen. 26:3). This is the first occurrence in these early chapters of Exodus of the Hebrew verb 'to be' (*hāyāh*) that is going to be crucial in the passages dealing with God's self-revelation of Himself (see especially, 3:13-15; 6:2-8). The special name for God (*yhwh*, 'the LORD'), used in verse 15, is thought to come from this verb, though some satisfactory explanation has to be given of a change of the middle consonant from *yod* to *vav*.[12] As events proceeded, Moses was to understand that God's presence would constantly sustain him. The second part of the response was a declaration concerning a sign. The word for 'sign' (*'ôt*) can mean either an immediate demonstration to show the truthfulness of a message, or one given later to confirm what has been said or done. Here the sign is clearly of the latter variety. The proof of God's presence with His people in their escape from slavery would be worship 'on this mountain', i.e. on Horeb/Sinai. This was why Moses was so insistent to Pharaoh that the Israelites must be allowed to worship *yhwh* in the desert

---

12. See also the discussion on the divine name on pp. 95-96.

(5:1). The fulfilment of the promise of a sign came about when Israel entered into a formal covenantal relationship with the LORD after the exodus from Egypt (recorded in Exod. 19 onwards).

13 Moses sought further information to assist him in his mission. His concern was, that in going to his own people, 'the sons of Israel', and making a declaration that he had been sent by 'the God of our fathers', they would ask about God, 'What is his name?' The form of the suggested question is not, 'Who (*mî*) is he?', but 'What (*mâh*) is his name?' It is significant that the Israelites would immediately identify the God who had sent Moses as the covenantal God of Israel. But if he used the name *yhwh*, would they recognise of whom Moses was speaking? The evidence points to the fact that this name, the so-called *tetragrammaton* (the four-lettered word), was already in use before the time of Moses. It is used in narrative, but also in shortened form in the name of Moses' mother/grandmother, Jochebed. What the Israelites needed to know was the significance of this name. Hence, 'What is his name?' is to be viewed as a request for understanding the name *yhwh*. On occasions of new revelation by God of Himself in the Pentateuch, a new name was given (see Gen. 16:13 and 17:1). So here too at this crucial stage in the history of Israel, a name is given added significance as it is tied in intimately with God's redemptive purposes for Israel. Moses wanted words from God that would satisfy the people.

14 God's reply was in enigmatic form: 'I will be what I will be' (*'ehyeh ᵃsher 'ehyeh*). Various possibilities exist as to the translation and significance of this name. The verbal form *'ehyeh* could be translated as a past tense in English, 'I was', or as a present, 'I am', but as it has already been used as a future in verse 12, it is best to retain the form 'I will be'. This is not the name of God but rather it was a statement concerning His nature. Moses was told that he must inform the Israelites that he has been sent by 'I will be' (*'ehyeh*).[13] This is a reference back to verse 10, which contains the commission given to Moses. He was to go to Pharaoh and then bring the Israelites out of Egypt.

---

13. The LXX has *ho ōn*, 'he who is', that conveys the idea of God being the living one, but no Heb. ms. supports this.

15 The narrative continues the instructions that God gave to Moses. He was told to go and say to the Israelites that the God of their fathers, the God of Abraham, Isaac, and Jacob, had sent him. The repeated reference to the God of the patriarchs is important, as it highlights the fact that God, the redeemer, was well-known to the people, and, while not mentioning the covenant with Abraham, yet implies that He is the God of the promises. In addition, Moses was instructed to tell the people that God's name (it is implied it is *yhwh*) was a perpetual one (*lᵉʿolâm*), a name to last for generation to generation (*lᵉdor dor*). In perpetuity, this distinctive name for God was going to express His character.

16-17 These verses contain the instructions regarding Moses' delivery of God's message to the Israelites. It was to be mediated through the assembled elders. Very significantly the message was from the LORD (*yhwh*). Whatever ambiguity might appear in the preceding verses over God's name (especially verses 13-14), from this point onwards 'the LORD' is the predominant self-designation of God, and also the most frequent title used of Him. The pronunciation is uncertain, as the Jews regarded the name as being so sacred that they substituted instead the word *ʾᵃdonay* (Lord) whenever they came across *yhwh* in the Hebrew text. From early transliteration it appears that the first syllable was *yâh*, and, if so, the verbal form may be a causative, 'he who causes [or, gives] life.' As no definition is given of 'LORD', contextual usage must determine its meaning. It is clearly a covenantal name, and appears repeatedly in contexts denoting the LORD as the gracious redeemer of His people (see the later discussion of 6:1-5).[14]

The mode of God's revelation to Moses is described in the same way as used of Abraham (Gen. 17:1, 'appeared', Heb. *nirʾâh*). In the case of Moses the revelation was in the burning bush (3:2). The message made reference to God's cognisance of what had happened to Israel in Egypt. The Hebrew text does not say that God had seen the affliction but that He had

---

14. There is an helpful discussion by R. Laird Harris, 'The Pronunciation of the Tetragram', in John H. Skilton, ed., *The Law and the Prophets: Old Testament Studies in Honor of Oswald T. Allis* (Nutley, N.J.: Presbyterian and Reformed Publishing Co., 1974), pp. 215-24.

indeed visited the people (*pâqod pâqadtî*). The verb *pâqad* has a variety of meanings in the Old Testament; sometimes, as here, it refers to God's gracious presence with His people.¹⁵ All the ill-treatment meted out to Israel is summed up in one word in Hebrew, 'what has been done' (*heʿâsûy*).

The message was one of promised deliverance from Egypt and the transfer of Israel to Canaan. Biblical Hebrew has no word for 'promise', but simply uses the verb 'to say' (here, 'and I said', *vâ'omar*).¹⁶ The deliverance is described as causing them to go up to Canaan (Heb. *ʿâlâh*, Hi.), one of the ways in which the deliverance from Egypt is recorded in the Old Testament (other terms include 'redeem', and 'bring out'). The description of the destination of Israel when delivered from slavery in Egypt is set out in terms similar to, but not identical with, what Abraham had earlier been told (see Gen. 15:18-19). The point was clearly to show that the land of Canaan was not empty territory but occupied by various ethnic groups who would defend their territorial rights. Occupation of the land was going to be by divine intervention.

18 The assurance was given that the elders would listen to Moses and that there would be a joint delegation to Pharaoh. The group¹⁷ were to inform him that 'the LORD, the God of the Hebrews' had met with them. The Hebrew verb 'met' (*niqrâh*) is very similar to the verb 'called' (*niqrâ'*), having only the final consonant different. In spite of variations in both Hebrew manuscripts and versions, the meaning 'meeting with' makes good sense and should be retained. The result of this meeting with God was the demand to Pharaoh that the Israelites should be allowed to go three days' journey into the desert and there to sacrifice to one called 'the LORD our God'. The mention of 'three days' raises questions regarding the ethics of this request. Were the Israelites to tell a lie in order to secure their release? The best explanation appears to be that of Augustine (A.D. 354-430) who suggested that the requests to Pharaoh were graded, getting more and more difficult for

---

15. For the varied meanings of *pâqad*, see *TWOT*, II, pp. 731-32.

16. The LXX changed it to 3 pers. m. s., 'and he said'.

17. Two Heb. mss., the LXX, and the Vulgate make the verb 2 pers. m. s., 'you (s.) are to say', instead of the MT, 'you (pl.) are to say'. The ms. evidence is not strong enough to compel an alteration.

him to grant. There was no intention to deceive. The full truth was not disclosed because he had no right at this stage to the information.[18] No mention is made previously in Genesis or Exodus of the people of Israel sacrificing in Egypt, but now provision is made for sacrifice after some separation occurs from Egypt.

19-20 The LORD's pre-knowledge was disclosed in relation to Pharaoh's reaction to the request. The king of Egypt was not going to 'give [permission]' for any movement of the Israelites away from his immediate control. A release would only take place if there were an intervention with 'a strong hand' (*b^{e}yâd ch^{a}zâqâh*). This description of God's omnipotence was to become part of a standardised expression for His deliverance of Israel from slavery in Egypt (see Deut. 4:34; 9:26; 'with a strong hand and an outstretched arm', 6:21; 7:19).[19]

The solution for Israel lay with the LORD who promised to 'send' His hand so that Pharaoh will 'send away' the children of Israel. This is a play on two verbal forms of the same Hebrew verb (*shâlach*: 'send', Qal; 'send away', Pi.). What was going to convince Pharaoh was the exhibition of God's wonders (*niflâ'ot*). This word is very significant as it is from a root that is used of acts that only God could perform. Deliverance from Egypt was going to need divine intervention. Whatever was to take place as a consequence of this assurance, it would be the direct action of God ('*I* will perform'). Ultimately the position would be reached that Pharaoh would send the Israelites away.[20]

21-22 Exit of Israel from Egypt was not to mean that the people lacked material possessions. God pledged to so alter the feelings of the Egyptians towards them that they would not leave 'emptily', that is, with empty hands. Shepherds and their families were to come into possession of gold, silver, and

---

18. This argument is developed by Walter C. Kaiser, Jr., 'A Three-Day Journey to Offer Sacrifices to the Lord', *Hard Sayings of the Old Testament* (Downers Grove: InterVarsity, 1988), pp. 63-64.

19. The expression in the MT is: 'The king of Egypt will not let you go and not with a strong hand.' A number of Hebrew mss. have *halô' b^{e}yâd chazâqâh*, 'will it not be with a strong hand?' The LXX has *ean mê*, 'If not …?' that seems to be an interpretation of the MT.

20. The verbal form here (*shâlach*, Pi.) is used of divorce in the Old Testament. Hence, it carries here the implication of a definitive dismissal of Israel from Egypt.

clothing. Whereas Jacob's family had come down relatively poor to Egypt, it was God's intention that they would go out much richer. Hence He promised to so touch the hearts of the Egyptians ('to give this people grace in the eyes of the Egyptians') that they would willingly enrich Israel.[21] While the text here only directs women to ask from their neighbours, the account at the time of the exodus makes it plain that men and women were involved by description of it in plural terms: 'The Israelites (3 m. pl.) did as Moses instructed .... [The Egyptians] gave them what they asked for, so they plundered the Egyptians' (Exod. 12:35-36).

Study Questions

1) Why should Moses have been so reluctant to go and speak with Pharaoh, and how does his explanation here fit in with his later hesitation as well (see 4:1, 10)?

2) Can we explain why God should give Himself a name that could be interpreted in more than one way?

3) Do you think we can trace a connection between the use of 'I am' here with the 'I am' sayings of Jesus as recorded in the Gospels?

4) The land that God swore to give His people was 'a land flowing with milk and honey'. Seeing the similarities, climatewise, between Egypt and Canaan, what was the significance of this specific promise?

4:1 Moses raised another objection regarding his mission, for he was concerned that his own people would not believe him, or pay attention to his message. He was correct in that lack of faith was to be shown to be characteristic of Israel. Unbelief would mark the history of God's people (cf. Ps. 78:22, 32). He was also worried lest his own folk denied that he had received divine revelation.

---

21. Many Heb. mss. enlarge the text to make the requesting apply to both men and women: 'A man shall ask from his neighbour and a woman from her neighbour.' This looks like a clarification of the MT to include both genders, and also to substitute the words rêa' and râ'ot for the rarer word for neighbour, miskenet. The MT is the harder reading and should be retained.

The Provision of a Deliverer 2:1–4:31

2-3 God's response was to perform two miracles in order to convince him, and all Israel, that the LORD had indeed appeared to, and spoken with, him. The first was through the command to throw his staff on to the ground, where it became a snake. Moses ran in fear from it.

4 The next instruction to Moses was to reach out and take the snake by the tail, and when he did so it became again a staff in his hand. It reverted to its normal form. God's power was able to change its character and then change it back to its original status.

5 The purpose of this miracle was related to Moses' question in verse 1. It had been performed 'in order that' (*lᵉma'an*) Israel might believe that the God of the patriarchs had indeed appeared to Moses. The miracle was intended to confirm the message that Moses was to deliver. As elsewhere in the Bible, God's miracles were not only designed to display aspects of His character, but given in order to propel people to a specific course of action, or to point forward to later revelation of God's omnipotence. Once again God is identified as 'the LORD', the God of Abraham, Isaac, and Jacob. The God who was directing Moses and the people was none other than the God who had entered into binding commitments first to Abraham (Gen. 12, 15, 17) and then renewed with Isaac (Gen. 26:24) and Jacob (28:13-15).

6-7 An additional miracle was given in case the first one did not have the desired effect of bringing Israel to genuine faith. Moses was instructed to put his hand inside his cloak (lit. 'in his bosom'), and when he did so it was 'leprous, like snow' (*mᵉtsora'at kashshéleg*). The Hebrew word used here for 'leprosy' (Pu. fem. part. of *tsâra'*) is not restricted to what is strictly leprosy (Hansen's Disease) but it can denote a variety of skin diseases.[22] On obeying a further instruction, Moses' hand was restored like the rest of his skin. Again, God's omnipotence was displayed in this sign.

8-9 Further provision was made in case of persistent unbelief on the part of Israel. The incidents relating to the staff and to Moses' hand were the first and second 'signs'.

---

22. For further information on the use of this word, see G. J. Wenham, *The Book of Leviticus* (NICOT: Grand Rapids: Eerdmans, 1979), pp. 194-214.

Whereas in 3:20, God promised to perform miraculous deeds (*niflâ'ot*), now the word for a sign (*'ot*) is used. A sign could either be intended, as here, as a stimulus to immediate action, or else, something to confirm later that what had happened was divinely planned. If these signs had not convinced Israel, then a further one would be added. If Moses took some water from the Nile and spilled it on the ground, it would become blood. Later, changing water into blood occurred in the second major sign (Exod. 7:14-17).

10 A third objection was raised by Moses, on this occasion citing his lack of eloquence as the reason why he should not be the spokesman of God. He acknowledged God's relationship to him as that of sovereign to a servant, but claimed that he was never a fluent speaker, despite being called to his present mission. 'Slow of speech and tongue' is a fine descriptive phrase for lack of eloquence. Similarly, lack of fitness to speak on God's behalf was cited by both Isaiah (Isa. 6:5-7) and Jeremiah (Jer. 1:4-8), while the apostle Paul's opponents derided his speaking ability (2 Cor. 10:10). Paul himself disclaimed being eloquent (1 Cor. 2:1), and denied speaking with 'wise and persuasive words' (1 Cor. 2:4).

11-12 The answer that God gave rested on His sovereign creative power that determines a man's speech, or hearing, or sight. There was no need for any response from Moses to the questions, 'Who gave .... ?'; 'Who gives ....?'; 'Who makes....?' The LORD Himself claimed the prerogative of bestowing such abilities, and He emphatically drew attention to His own self-existence: 'Is it not I, the LORD?' Furthermore, He reassured His servant that He would graciously provide for his task by both offering assistance and giving the necessary words to speak.

13 A supplementary question from Moses showed that he was still reticent to accept the role. In spite of promised grace (see the previous verse) he requested that someone else be sent by the LORD on this mission to Pharaoh. In effect, he asked for a substitute to do it.

14 For the first time in the account of Moses' life, it is recorded that God was angry with him (for later incidents, see the references in Deut. 1:37; 4:21; 9:18). The alternative that God proposed was that Moses' brother Aaron should be his 'prophet' (as he is later called, 7:1). The reference to him as 'the Levite' (*hallêvî*) should not be overlooked. As became clear later, Aaron was given the privilege of heading the order of priests, not Moses. The three reasons advanced here were that Aaron was a good speaker, he was already on his way to meet Moses (the same verb 'meet', *qârâh*, as used in 3:18), and that Aaron was going to be joyful in spirit when the meeting took place. The implication was that Aaron would be a ready spokesman in Moses' place.

15 The process was established whereby what Moses wished to say would be communicated to Aaron. This passage is very helpful in understanding the later role of the prophets who were not the originators of their messages but rather served as covenantal enforcement mediators.[23] What was promised was divine assistance to both Moses and Aaron. The MT makes this plain by saying that the teaching would be of the two of them ('will teach you (pl.) what to do'). The form of words here, 'And *I* will be with your mouth and with his mouth' (*v^e'ânokî 'ehyeh 'im pika v^e'im pîhû*) appears to be an allusion back to 3:12 with its assurance of continuing divine presence and aid.

16 Aaron's role was to be the communicator of God's word to the people. The way in which this is expressed is significant both for the situation in Egypt and for the wider implications for God's revelation of Himself. What was to happen in Aaron's ministry was analogous with the way in which God was to reveal Himself to Moses. In effect, Moses would be God to his brother ('as if you were God [*^elohîm*] to him'). This provision ended Moses' reluctance to speak to Pharaoh and it concluded his questioning of God's directive to go in His name.

17 Proclamation of God's word to Pharaoh was to be accompanied with signs. The same staff that Moses had thrown down on the ground at God's direction was to be used again. The NIV rendering, 'perform miraculous signs', while periphrastic, does convey the significance of the Hebrew expression 'the signs' (*'et hâ'otot*).

---

23. The term 'covenant enforcement mediators' comes from Douglas Stuart in his discussion on the prophets in G. D. Fee and Douglas Stuart, *How to Read the Bible for All Its Worth: A Guide to Understanding the Bible*, 4th ed. (Grand Rapids: Zondervan, 2014), p. 190.

Study Questions

1) Many signs and wonders were performed in Egypt. Why was God's message spoken through Moses and Aaron not sufficient?

2) Was Moses' claim that he was 'slow of speech and slow of tongue' a genuine claim, or an attempt to avoid confrontation with Pharaoh?

3) God's pleasure was not always shown to His servants. Can you think of other later examples when Moses' experienced God's disfavour?

4 Moses' Return to Egypt (4:18-31)

God's intention for Moses had been stated in 3:10. His mission was to go to Pharaoh so that he could lead God's people out of Egypt. The preceding section has clarified the roles of Moses and Aaron, and now the narrative follows Moses' return there in order to fulfil his divinely appointed mission.

18 On return from Horeb, presumably with the flock (see 3:1), Moses went with a request to his father-in-law. He did not explain fully his reasons, but rather expressed a wish to see if any of his people were still alive (*ha'ôdâm chayyîm*). The way it was stated in Hebrew is the same as that used by Joseph to ask about the condition of his father Jacob (*ha'ôd 'âvî chây*, Gen. 45:3). His request did not distort the truth, for time had now gone past and he genuinely wanted to know how his people were getting on. The decision was made prior to the knowledge that no longer was he a wanted fugitive in Egypt. Jethro's response was to encourage him to go with his blessing. The Hebrew expression is to go in, or with, peace (*l^eshâlôm*).

19 Moses was told by the LORD to return to Egypt because the manhunt for him over the death of the Egyptian (2:15) had subsided, and it was evidently safe to go back. While the Hebrew text simply says that the LORD 'said' to Moses, the NIV is right in translating this as a pluperfect, 'had said'.[24] In the account of Moses' arrival in Midian, no reference is made to his explaining the reason why he fled from Egypt. The text

---

24. See the citation of this example of the pluperfect in *IBHS*, 33.2.3, p. 552.

does not provide any information about how much Jethro's family knew of the situation in Egypt.

20 Moses made the necessary preparations for travel to Egypt. While the birth of his first son, Gershom, has been noted already (2:21-22), no mention has been made of the birth of his second son, Eliezer (cf. 18:4). Presumably, both sons were taken back to Egypt, and this explains the use of the plural 'sons'. With a donkey for transport, Moses set off for Egypt with his wife and sons.[25] Along with their other possessions, Moses had 'the staff of God' in his hand. In a significant way it was going to be demonstrated that the staff did not just belong to Moses. It was the instrument through which God was going to display His superiority over Pharaoh and over the Egyptian gods.

21 Before setting out on his journey God told Moses some further facts about his mission. In particular, he had to perform in Pharaoh's presence all 'the wonders' ($mof^e t\hat{\imath}m$) that he had been empowered to do. The word 'wonder' ($m\hat{o}f\hat{e}t$) occurs 36 times in the Old Testament, almost half of them (17) being in reference to the miraculous events recorded in Exodus. These wonderful deeds have already been called 'the wonders' ($nifl\hat{a}'ot$, 3:20), and 'signs' ($'otot$, 4:8, 9, 17), while later they will be called 'judgments' ($sh^ef\hat{a}t\hat{\imath}m$, 7:4). These terms, which are practically synonymous, all refer to the extraordinary, divinely initiated actions that were intended to show to the Egyptians that the LORD was truly God. God's actions extended further still. He would act judicially against Pharaoh, an obstinate sinner, by further hardening his heart. This passage, and the use of it by the apostle Paul in Romans 9:14-18, raises many issues related to divine action and human response.[26] Both are in view here, as they are in Peter's

---

25. The Heb. text has 'the donkey' ($hach^amor$). This could be a case where in English the indefinite article is required, which is the choice that the NIV translators made, 'a donkey'. For this usage, see *DIHG~S*, §30 (e), p. 27. On the other hand, the definite article could function as a possessive pronoun, 'his donkey', as proposed by James Barr, 'Determination and the Definite Article in Biblical Hebrew', *JSS* 34 (1989), pp. 307-35.

26. See, in particular, the discussions on Romans 9 in William Hendriksen, *Exposition of Paul's Epistle to the Romans* (Grand Rapids: Baker Book House, 1980), pp. 320-26; John Murray, *The Epistle to the Romans, Vol. II, Chapters 9 to 16* (Grand Rapids: Eerdmans, 1965), pp. 24-30. For other discussions on the

speech on the day of Pentecost (Acts 2:22-23). In reference to Jesus' death, Peter related it to the sovereign purpose of God ('This man was handed over to you by God's set purpose and foreknowledge'), but yet he held those involved in the crucifixion responsible for their actions ('And you, with the help of wicked men, put him to death by nailing him to the cross'). The heart of Pharaoh, a rebellious sinner, was further hardened in order to show God's power and that His name might be proclaimed in all the earth (Exod. 9:16).

22 The LORD's message for Pharaoh attributed a very specific status to Israel, namely, that of being the LORD's son, His first-born. The relationship between God and Israel was that of father/son (see Deut. 32:6; Jer. 3:4; 31:9), and this fact explains the LORD's complaints against His people for acting in a 'foolish and unwise' manner' (Deut. 32:6), or of being 'a perverse generation, children who are unfaithful' (Deut. 32:20; see also Isa. 1:4). However, added to this concept was the designation 'first-born', the only time this expression is used of Israel in the Old Testament. The first-born of a family in Israel occupied a position of privilege (the law regarding the first-born is set out in Deut. 21:15-17). Here, Israel having been chosen by God, and as the first fruits among the nations (Jer. 2:3), is to be publicly acknowledged as having that status.

23 The contrast between Israel and Egypt is clear. Pharaoh is to be told that God's son, the first-born, has to be sent away to worship Him (see the earlier reference in 3:18 to a three-day journey into the desert). On the other hand, Egypt's first-born son is going to undergo the judgment of death because of Pharaoh's refusal to accede to God's demand. This is the first of five occurrences of the combination of the verbs 'refuse' (*mâ'an*, Pi.) and the verb to 'send' (*shâlach*, Pi.) in the narrative in Exodus detailing Pharaoh's obstinate refusal to allow Israel to go and worship the LORD (Exod. 4:23; 7:14; 8:2; 9:2; 10:4). The repetition of this idea highlights the consequences of Pharaoh's heart being hardened.

---

issue, see Walter Kaiser Jr., 'The Lord Hardened Pharaoh's Heart', *Hard Sayings of the Old Testament*, pp. 66-68; Victor Hamilton, 'An Excursus on Heart Hardening', *Exodus*, pp. 170-74, and especially John Frame, *The Doctrine of God* (Phillipsburg: Presbyterian & Reformed, 2002), pp. 64-69.

24 Verses 24-26 comprise a unit that has produced much discussion, and probably no single section of Exodus is more difficult to explain. Among the questions that have arisen are the subject of the meeting with God (Moses or Gershom), the person circumcised (Gershom, or his younger brother, Eliezer), and the one at whose feet the foreskin was thrown (Moses, Gershom, or Eliezer).[27] The overall understanding of the passage has also produced very different interpretations. Here one particular view will be given, with footnote references to other discussions. Some of the main points can be summarised:

1. The incident occurs as Moses is returning to Egypt from Midian in order to take up the leadership of Israel, both in regard to negotiations with Pharaoh for the release of the people and the subsequent events at the time of the exodus. In the context, the pointers are to Moses as the person with whom the LORD met and whom He threatened with death.

2. At that time, one of Moses' sons had not been circumcised as set out in the Abrahamic covenant (Gen. 17:10-14). The essential link between circumcision and the covenant was evident, and this was repeated by Stephen when in his speech to the Sanhedrin he reminded them that God 'gave Abraham the covenant of circumcision' (Acts 7:8).

3. The failure to perform the rite of circumcision, like the absence of circumcision, was punishable by death. This means that the threat was that the token cutting of the flesh in circumcision would become total in the cutting off by death.

4. Moses could not become the leader of Israel if he himself or his sons did not bear the sign of the covenant in their bodies. It would have been completely incongruous for him to assume this leadership role if he was not faithful

---

27. For a listing of nine problems presented by these verses, see Victor Hamilton, *Exodus*, pp. 81-83. Hamilton's general approach is the same as I have adopted. A contrary opinion, that the object of God's attack was Gershom, is set out by John Currid, *Exodus, Vol. 1 chapters 1-18* (EP Study Commentary: Darlington: Evangelical Press, 2000), pp. 115-17.

to the demands of the covenant. Hence, the LORD met with him on the way to Egypt and tried to kill him.

While on the way back to Egypt, at a lodging place, Moses came face to face with God. The verb used here for 'meet' (*pâgash*) seems to have been practically synonymous with the other more common verb for 'meet' (*qârâh*), as is shown by the use of both verbs in verse 27 ('Go into the wilderness to meet [*qârâ*] Moses …. So he went and met [*pâgash*] him …. [ESV]').[28] While a 'lodging place' could denote some form of inn, more likely it simply speaks of a campsite or some form of temporary hut. The location was 'in the desert' (v. 27), an expression that refers to an uninhabited area. There God met him and 'tried' to kill him. Rather than suggesting in a translation that God attempted to kill him but was not able to accomplish this, it is wise to follow the NIV and accept that it was an action on the point of taking place. The penalty for covenantal disobedience was death. No indication is given of how the judgment was to be carried out. It could have been by some fateful illness. The LXX says that 'the angel of the Lord met him', which may have been an attempt to weaken the force of the MT expression, and possibly also to link it with the appearance of God to Jacob at the brook (Gen. 32:22-32). Previously, Pharaoh had tried to kill Moses (Exod. 2:15). Now it is the LORD who did so.[29]

25 Moses' wife, Zipporah, intervened in the situation, and with a flint knife (*tsor*) cut off her son's foreskin. The use of flint as a cutting tool for the administration of circumcision is also mentioned in Joshua 5:2-3. No explanation is given of why a flint knife in place of a metal one was used. The 'son' was most likely the younger one, Eliezer (Exod. 18:4). Probably the scenario was like this. Gershom the elder son had been circumcised, but, because of Zipporah's opposition, the second son, Eliezer, had not. Now, without any prompting but realising the danger of the situation, Zipporah proceeds to perform the circumcision. The cut foreskin she throws at Moses' 'feet', which is probably

---

28. Inexplicably the NIV translation omits that verb, 'and he went'.

29. The expressions are slightly different in the two passages, but the meaning is the same. Exod. 2:15 has, 'And he sought to kill Moses', while Exod. 4:24 has, 'And he sought to put him to death'. No difference between the two expressions can be discerned.

a euphemism for the genital area.[30] Her action was probably more than just 'touching' (*vattaggaʿ*). Rather, the way in which she showed her displeasure at having to perform this ritual was by 'throwing'. She also made a statement explaining the situation. To Moses she said: 'Surely you are a bridegroom of blood to me.' By this act of blood-shedding she averted divine judgment, and in doing so acquired her husband again. For a second time, Moses is saved by a woman (cf. 2:1-10).

26 The consequence of the action was that 'he let him alone'. Though the subject of the verb is not stated, the NIV rendering 'the LORD' is probably right. It seems as if the act of circumcision cancelled the attack on Moses, so that, if it was an induced illness, he recovered. The second sentence in this verse picks up Zipporah's statement referring to a 'bridegroom of blood'. Whatever else this phrase meant, it certainly reinforced the concept that circumcision was a vital matter for the people of the covenant. Specifically, the text says that this statement was so 'because of the circumcision' (*lammûlot*). The circumcision of Eliezer was essential if Moses was to lead his people out of their slavery. While this passage does not mention what happened to Zipporah and the sons, it is most probable that they returned to live with Jethro in Midian (cf. 18:1-14).

27 The text now brings Moses and Aaron together as they jointly take up the role that God intended for them (see vv. 14-16). By specific divine instruction, Aaron went into the 'desert' to meet Moses. They met at 'the mountain of God'.[31] Aaron had to leave Egypt, presumably secretly, in order to come into personal contact with his brother again. The narrative here presupposes instruction had been given to Aaron, and also more precise directions as to where he was to find his brother. They met and greeted another with a kiss (cf. the same action when Jacob and Esau met up with one another, Gen. 33:4).

28 Moses then related to his brother 'all the words' that had been part of his commission, and also 'all the signs' concerning which he had received instruction (for comment on 'signs,

---

30. Victor Hamilton, *Exodus*, lists the passages that have been appealed to for this understanding of 'feet', p. 81. Cf. also the entries in *NIDOTTE*, 3, p. 1048, and *DCH*, VII, p. 411.

31. For further detail on Horeb/Sinai as the 'mountain of God', see the comment on 3:1.

see on 3:12 and 4:8-9). The MT is terse here, highlighting the 'words' and 'signs' that were going to be so central in the work ahead in Egypt. English translation needs some additional words: 'sent him [to say]', 'commanded him [to do].' Spoken words were going to be reinforced by miraculous signs.

29-31 It was necessary for Moses and Aaron to let the elders of Israel know of God's intentions for His people. Hence they gathered together the elders (referred to already in 3:18), and communicated to them all that Moses had been told. Aaron now assumed the role of acting as Moses' 'prophet' (see vv. 14-17), and he performed miracles (v. 30). Earlier Moses had been concerned that the people would not believe him (v. 1), but now the signs had convinced them of the truth of his message and so they believed. The response of the people even went further. Hearing about how God had visited them and taken notice of their affliction, 'they bowed down and worshipped.' The two verbs in this expression are always used in conjunction with one another ('bowed down', *qâdad*; 'worshipped', *shâchâh*, Hitp.). They occur at important occasions in Old Testament history and especially mark out the devout worship of the Lord and obeisance to Him (cf. Gen. 24:26; Exod. 12:27; 2 Chron. 29:30). Even though the people were later to sin against the Lord, at this stage they accepted the message from Him and responded with adoration.

Study Questions

1) Moses' relationship with his father-in-law seems to have been good. How is this confirmed by the later incident in chapter 18?

2) In 4:2 Moses is said to have a rod in his hand, while in verse 20 it is called 'the rod of God'. Why should this language now be used concerning it?

3) In verse 22 the language of adoption is used for the first time of the Israelites. How important did this become both for Israel and for Christians, as the New Testament teaches?

4) The relationship between Moses and Aaron was important, but yet it was not always a congenial one. Why should the brothers have had some strident disagreements?

3

Increased Oppression
(5:1-21)

1 Additional Burdens (5:1-14)

The opening chapters of Exodus have set the scene for confrontation with Pharaoh. The location and condition of Israel have been described, along with the call of Moses and Aaron. Now the account details their first meeting with Pharaoh. He responds by an intensification of their hardship in relation to their brick-making activities.

1 No further information is given of the preparations for an audience with Pharaoh. All that is mentioned is the fact that Moses and Aaron went to Pharaoh with God's message, just as God had told Moses earlier (3:18-20). The message that they brought begins in a manner that afterwards became one of the hallmarks of prophetic speech: 'Thus says the Lord' (*koh 'âmar yhwh*). Pharaoh is told that 'the God of Israel' (a phrase synonymous with 'the God of Hebrews', 3:18, and used again in v. 3) instructs him to let His people go in order to keep a feast to their God in the desert. Such a feast involved the offering of sacrifices, an indication that sacrificial worship was part of the religious experience of Israel prior to the Mosaic law.

2 Pharaoh's response was predictable, as God had already indicated to Moses (3:19). He questioned as to who this Lord was who sent such commands to him, and why he should obey Him (Heb. 'listen to his voice') and release the children of Israel. This rhetorical question is typical of a group of such questions introduced by 'Who?' (*mî*) that express insult.[1] Blatant refusal was linked with denial of any knowledge of the LORD. This may have been Pharaoh's way of indicating the new name for God made no difference to him.

3 The message to Pharaoh continued with the announcement that God had met with Israel. The same expression 'met with' (Heb. *niqrâ' 'âlênû*) has already occurred in 3:18.[2] Moses and Aaron request permission to journey for three days into the wilderness to offer sacrifices to the LORD. What is additional here, as compared with the statement in 3:18, is the threat that is expressed. The sacrificial worship in the wilderness was proposed 'lest he fall upon us with pestilence or with the sword' (RSV, ESV). What was suggested was that failure to comply on Israel's part would result in divine judgment, either by fatal disease or by the sword.[3]

4 The response is an accusation by Pharaoh that Moses and Aaron are 'taking the people away from their labour'. The verb translated 'take away' (*pâra'*) is usually used in reference to letting hair fall loose, though it does occur in Exodus 32:25 (twice) in reference to the children of Israel running wild while Moses was on the mount. The same sort of meaning could apply here. In Pharaoh's eyes Moses and Aaron had lost control of their people and consequently their work is suffering. The command to get back to work was probably not just directed to the two leaders but to all the people.

5 The threat that Israel posed for Egypt is reflected in Pharaoh's further comment. He raised the question of the comparative size of Israel in relation to the Egyptians, a matter that caused the attempts to reduce the number by the

---

1. For further comment on this practice, see *IBHS*, p. 322. This discussion is based on George W. Coats, 'Self-Abasement and Insult Formulas,' *JBL* 89 (1970), pp. 14-26.

2. *BDB*, p. 897, lists the meaning here as 'meet unexpectedly', but there is no indication in the usage of this verb elsewhere that supports this. Though the consonantal text has this verb as *qârâ'*, this is just a by-form for *qârâh*, as is shown by the fact that the following preposition is *'al*, not the expected *'el* or *lᵉ* if the verb was *qârâ'*.

3. Hebrew uses the article with the words 'pestilence' and 'sword' contrary to English usage. It is the practice in Hebrew to use the generic article of things that are well known. See *DIHG-S*, pp. 28-9, *Rem.* 1.

expedients related in chapters 1–2. The Israelites are referred to as 'the people of the land' (*'am hâ'ârets*). While in the Old Testament this may have later taken on a more technical meaning, here it seems to be a general description of the Israelites as not professional classes but agricultural workers and slaves.[4] The aspect of the number is stressed by the word order: 'Behold many now are the people of the land ….' Of the modern versions the NRSV comes closest: 'Now they are more numerous than the people of the land ….' The size of Israel was a continuing problem for the Egyptians. Moses and Aaron were held responsible by Pharaoh, for he accused them of stopping the people working. The same Hebrew word for 'labour' is used in verses 4 and 5 ('their burdens', *siv^elotâm*), and this should be reflected in English translations.

6-7 Immediately Pharaoh put his intentions into effect, giving the slave drivers and foremen over the Israelites instructions that no more straw was to be provided for the brick-makers.[5] The word for slave drivers (*hannog^eshîm*) has already been introduced at 3:7, while 'foremen' (*shot^erîm*) is quite widely used in the Old Testament of officials or leaders. While it could be that the straw improved the bricks, most probably it made the process of mixing the clay easier, and so facilitated the task. From that time onward, the responsibility lay with the people. They had to gather the straw for themselves.[6]

8 No diminution of the number of bricks was to take place as a result of this direction to the slave masters. They were still to be laden with the identical quota. Pharaoh claimed that laziness was the real reason why they were crying out and wanting to go and worship the LORD in the desert. What he

---

4. For further discussion, see E. W. Nicholson, 'The Meaning of the Expression *'Am Ha'ares* in the Old Testament, *JSS* 10 (1965), pp. 59-66.

5. It is hard to be certain whether the Heb. text has the verb *yâsaf*, 'to add', or *'âsaf*, 'to gather'. If the former, then the presence of the consonant *'alef* is just a scribal variation. If it is the latter, then the vocalisation of the word has to be altered. Cf. the note by John I. Durham, *Exodus* (Word Biblical Commentary: Waco: Word Books, 1987), p. 62. Whichever verb is selected, the basic meaning of the verse does not alter.

6. Hebrew has no reflexive pronouns, but instead uses a variety of ways to express reflexive idea. Here a preposition and suffix (*lâhem*) is employed, as in v. 11 (*lâkem*).

did not reckon with was that Israel was not only approaching him in their distress (*tso'ᵃqîm*, 'crying out'), but that they cried (*vayyiz'âqû*) to the LORD.⁷ That cry had reached His attention (see 2:23-24).

9 The reference to making the work harder seems to be connected with the loss of the provision of straw, rather than some additional burden. The slaves had to continue working at their task, and the overseers were not to pay any attention to their words, for they were reckoned as being lies.

10-11 The slave drivers and the foremen carried out Pharaoh's command, declaring to the people his decree: 'I will not give you any more straw'.⁸ The animosity towards the Israelites was not at a subordinate level. It came from the Pharaoh himself. The leaders were told that everyone had to go and get straw for himself, wherever it could be found.⁹ No compensation was given for this additional labour, for there was no reduction in their workload. The picture the narrative paints is of the increasing harshness of the slavery endured in Egypt.

12-13 No nearby source of straw was available, and so the people had to scavenge throughout the land for what they needed. The taskmasters had to hurry them along. The verb used ('*ûts*, Qal part. pl. m.) has the meaning of being too narrow, or to urge on, and though no object is expressed it is clear from the context that it is 'the people' mentioned in the previous verse. The words of the slave drivers that follow are somewhat unusual in the Hebrew text: 'Complete your works a day's thing in its day, just as the straw was.' The expression 'a day's thing in its day' does occur elsewhere in the Old Testament (Exod. 5:19; 16:4; Lev. 23:37; 1 Kings 8:59; 2 Kings 25:30). The modern English versions pick up the meaning well: 'the work required of you each day'(NIV); 'your

---

7. No great difference in meaning can be discerned between the verbs *tsâ'âq* and *zâ'aq*.

8. The Heb. is '*ênennî notên lâkem téven*. The use of the partic. 'giving' (*notên*) carries the idea of continuous action, while the neg. particle 'is not' ('*ên*) has added to it the 1 pers. s. pronominal suffix, marking out the subject. For this usage, see *DIHG~S*, p. 136, §113, (d), and *IBHS*, p. 661, 39.3.3.

9. Lit. 'from where you find [it]'. Adverbs such as 'there' or 'thither' are often omitted when 'where' ('*ᵃsher*) is used in a compound expression. *DIHG~S*, p. 10, §10, Rem. 2.

daily task each day' (ESV). The point was that just as when the straw was provided, so now they had to complete the set daily allocation.

14 It was not only the ordinary people who were called upon to suffer, but the Israelite foremen were beaten because of their perceived failure to achieve the normal quota.[10] Almost all English translations read 'were beaten *and were asked*'. This clause does not represent any words in the MT, but it is necessary in the context. The Hebrew word for 'quota' is *choq*, which normally refers to a divine decree. However, it has wider meanings than that, and can quite appropriately, as here, refer to an instruction issued by a human ruler.[11]

2 Rebuff by the Israelites (5:15-21)

15-16 The Israelite foremen went directly to Pharaoh, perhaps without knowing what had already transpired between Moses and Aaron and him. They cried out to him (the same verb as used in v. 8), seeking some redress in their situation. Their complaint was that they were being beaten, when really the sin had to be laid at the feet of Egyptians, Pharaoh's 'own people' (*'ammekâ*).

17-18 The response by Pharaoh was as they should have expected. He hadn't changed his opinion of the Israelites, only making his accusation of laziness more emphatic. The NIV translation captures the meaning well: 'Lazy, that's what you are—lazy!' In doing so, it retains the order of the words in Hebrew. Pharaoh also repeated his claim that the request to go and worship the LORD in the desert was only motivated by their laziness. The Israelites had to get back to their work, and without provision of straw had to produce the same daily quota of bricks. A different word is used for quota (*tóken*) than used in verse 8 (*matconet*), though both words come from the same Hebrew root (*t-k-n*).

19-21 Pharaoh's reply brought home to the foremen that the situation was not going to be resolved quickly, and especially the fact that no change was going to be made to

---

10. Victor Hamilton, *Exodus*, p. 91, suggests that the verb *nâkâh* be translated by 'scold' or 'berate' here. However, all the other occasions when it is used in the Old Testament suggest physical force was involved.

11. The variety of meanings can be found in *DCH*, III, pp. 299-302.

the quota. Coming out from their audience with Pharaoh, the foremen met Moses and Aaron who were waiting for them. The verb 'to meet' (*pâga'*) is a strong one, and probably an English verb like 'confront' is more suitable here than simply 'meet'. This is confirmed by the words of the foremen that follow. They accused Moses and Aaron of making the people odious in Pharaoh's eyes, and desired that the LORD would intervene as the judge. They were ungrateful, forgetting the words and miracles of the LORD. Their fear was that the Egyptians would have an excuse to take extreme measures against them, even extermination by the sword.

Study Questions

1) Why do unbelievers like Pharaoh not want to listen to God's word?

2) Was Pharaoh's opposition to Israel leaving to worship because of the danger their numbers posed, or simply because of the lack of production of bricks that this would involve?

3) The Israelites were in harsh service. Why then did they later long to return to Egypt (see 16:3)?

4

Promised Deliverance
(5:22–7:5)

1. God's Revelation of His Name (5:22–6:12)

This section is critical for the whole book of Exodus. It commences with Moses' complaint to the Lord that He had not rescued His people. God's response integrates instruction regarding His covenantal name, the Lord (*yhwh*), with reassurances regarding His future saving work on behalf of His people. In verses 6-8 the themes of divine initiative in redemption and the on-going relationship that God was confirming with Israel are brought together. When He delivered them from their bondage, then they would indeed know that He was the Lord their God, who was going to bring them to the land He had promised to the patriarchs. But the people were hard of heart and wouldn't listen to Moses.

Several significant features of this section can be summarised before fuller explanation is given.

(1) Moses responded to the complaints of the Israelite foremen by himself first complaining to God. His questions are really accusations (5:22). Then he claimed that God had not acted decisively to redeem His people.

(2) God gave two answers.

(a) First, He gave the reassurance that in the future the omnipotent God would cause Pharaoh to let the people go (6:1).

(b) Secondly, He also identified Himself by using the formula, 'I am the Lord' (v. 2). The use of this phrase is highly significant, and it recurs in verses 6, and finally its third use rounds out the whole episode (v. 8). The promises given to the patriarchs regarding a land for the people were reasserted (vv. 4-5).

(c) God indicated by repeated assertions that He was the saviour/redeemer: '*I will bring you out* …'; '*I will free you from being slaves* …'; '*I will bring you to the land* …' Sovereignty in salvation belongs to Him alone.

(d) He pointed forward to Israel becoming His people, with whom He will sustain a lasting relationship: 'I will take you as my own people, and I will be your God' (v. 7). This phrase was to be the enduring summary of the covenantal relationship in both Old and New Testaments.

(e) The final word is again the formula relating to the self-identification of God: 'I am the Lord'. The God who appeared to Moses in the burning bush (3:1-22) was the Lord, the God of the covenant, and the gracious redeemer of His people.

22 Moses turned to the Lord in prayer. The idiom here (Heb. *shûv 'el*) does not indicate any harshness in Moses' action but rather coming into God's presence, albeit with puzzlement. He could not grasp from the flow of events how God's purposes were going to be worked out in the life of the Israelites. Rather than rescue there had come trouble. This seemed on the face of it a contradiction of what God had already told him (3:10). So Moses queried whether what had happened was the reason why he was sent. The presence of two 'Why?' questions is unusual in Old Testament narrative, and this points to Moses' problem as he wrestles with this turn of events.

23 The claim that Moses made was that from the outset of negotiations with Pharaoh, only trouble had come upon the Israelites. Further, he pointed to the fact that God had not delivered His people *'at all'* (AV, and followed by most English versions including NASB, RSV, NIV, and NRSV). This expression is an attempt to bring out the force of the Hebrew (*hatstsêl lo'-hitstsaltâ*).[1] The accusation is that, seemingly contrary to God's express declarations (cf. 3:8, 10, 17), no rescue had *really* taken place.

6:1 The LORD's answers did not specifically respond to Moses' questions, but rather reassert that deliverance of His people is indeed His intention. The questions do not elicit a rebuke but a promise. The word 'now' (Heb. *'attâh*), with which the first answer commences, accentuates the truth that the timing of the rescue was God's prerogative. Moreover, the deliverance was not going to be in secret but worked out before their eyes. Twice in this verse the power behind the deliverance is said to be by 'a mighty hand' (*b^{e}yâd ch^{a}zâqâh*). While the NIV inserts '*my* mighty hand' on both occasions, other translators were clearly reticent to do so (cf. AV, RSV, NASB, ESV, NRSV). Because there has already been a reference to God's mighty hand (3:19), the first occurrence here would seem to be similarly a reference to His mighty hand. The second occurrence is not so clear, as later on the same root **(*ch-z-q*)** in a verbal form is used of the pressure put on the Israelites to hurry and leave Egypt (12:33). Whatever the translation and interpretation here may be, the point is clear that the LORD was going to act upon Pharaoh so that Israel could go free ('what I will do to Pharaoh').

2 This verse opens with the statement: 'God spoke to Moses and said to him'. Many translators have felt that some additional word is needed, and so the NIV and NRSV add 'God *also* said', while the NASB inserts 'further'. The declaration follows, 'I am the LORD', linking this passage with the explanation about His name that God gave to Moses at the burning bush (3:13-17). This formula, from the time of Moses onward, often appears as though it was God's signature attached to a proclamation. Here it introduces the name itself

---

1. For the use of the inf. absol., see *DIHG~S*, pp.122-26, especially §101.

(v. 3), is used to indicate God's purpose for Israel (vv. 6-8), and then terminates the speech with finality (v. 8).

3 The declaration that followed concerned the transition in regard to God's name. Whereas previously in the patriarchal times, God made Himself known as El Shaddai, now He used a name that He had not employed previously. This statement has been widely discussed, and it is the basis by which many critical scholars distinguish various strands in the Pentateuch, dependent on whether they use the name *ᵉlohîm* or *yhwh*. But the contrast here is not between these two names, but between *yhwh* and *'êl shadday* (God Almighty). The problem is how to reconcile this statement with the fact that the name *yhwh* (the Lord) does appear many times in Genesis, and even the name of Moses' mother/grandmother, Jochebed, contains an abbreviated form of it (*jo-*).

Several different explanations have been given to explain Exodus 6:3. One main line of argumentation is to focus on the use of the preposition 'by' (Heb. *bᵉ*) and the significance of the verb 'know' (Heb. *yâda'*). On this explanation, God had revealed Himself by the name *yhwh*, but the Israelites did not know the significance of the name until the time of Moses. The vocable was known but not its true meaning.[2] On the other hand, it has been claimed that there is a question here without the normal interrogative marker: 'Did I not make myself known to them?'[3] While this argument is possible, yet the former viewpoint seems preferable. The patriarchs knew the name, but did not understand the full import of it. It was only when the exodus event was imminent that the people came to realise the true significance of the name *yhwh*.[4] Moreover, giving a new name at this juncture would have created suspicion. Moses had to confirm for his people that he was acting for the God of the patriarchs, not some unknown God.

4 The relation between God and His people was governed by a formal covenant. This was made initially with Abraham

---

2. See the argument set out by J. A. Motyer, *The Revelation of the Divine Name* (London: Theological Students Fellowship, 1959).

3. For this argument, see W. J. Martin, *Stylistic Criteria and the Analysis of the Pentateuch* (London: Tyndale Press, 1955), pp. 16-20.

4. See, in particular, the recent discussion by Jared Hood, 'I Appeared as El Shaddai: Intertextual Interplay in Exodus 6:3', *WTJ* 76, 1 (2014), pp. 167-88.

but re-affirmed to Isaac and Jacob. Central to that covenant was the promise concerning occupation of the land of Canaan (cf. Gen. 15:18-21; 17:8; 28:13). It was a land about which they already knew a great deal, for they had already lived there. Their occupancy of it was uncertain, as they were only sojourners there, residents without ownership rights. Now they were reminded that possession of the land was certain, as God was giving it to them as a gift. In the book of Deuteronomy the promise of land receives more detailed treatment, especially in chapter 26:1-11.

5 The cries of the Israelites had not gone unnoticed. God had heard the pleas of His enslaved people and remembered His covenant. This expression, to 'remember' on God's part, is an anthropomorphism. To say that He remembers His covenant is to assert that He faithfully fulfils its promised provisions.

6 In this and the following verses (vv. 6-11), Moses is commanded by God in reference to the Israelites. He has to go again to them with a divine message. First, God identifies Himself as the LORD. Then He sets out His chosen ministry to Israel. The repeated 'I' emphasises the role God has in salvation. It appears in this passage seven times. The second sentence in verse 6 contains three words relating to redemption that form part of a cluster of terms associated with the exodus. First of all, it uses the verb 'to bring out' (*yâtsâ'*, Hi.) to describe the release from slavery and going out into the wilderness. Secondly, the verb 'to deliver' (*nâtsal*, Hi.) has already been used twice in the preceding narrative (3:8; 5:23) when reference is made to God's act of releasing Israel from slavery. Thirdly, the verb 'to redeem' (*gâ'al*) is introduced to convey the idea of purchase of the people by the LORD. The best-known use of this verb is in the book of Ruth in regard to Boaz' redemption of Ruth (Ruth 4:1-12). The harshness of life in Egypt for the Israelites is emphasised by stressing the heavy yoke that they carried, and the fact that they really were slaves. Deliverance for them was going to be redemption from the objective realm of sin and evil.

7 God's promise to Israel also involved the relationship between Himself and the people. At Sinai the nation was to be given its constitutional charter, with its life regulated by its sovereign. He would adopt Israel as His children, while from the reciprocal point of view He would be their God. This basic statement of God's relationship with Israel will be elaborated later (see commentary on 19:3-6). The events surrounding Israel's exodus from Egypt were intended to be proof that the LORD really was God, unlike the gods who were worshipped by the Egyptians.

8 The focus turns in this verse to the gift of Canaan. Whereas verse 6 used the verb 'bring out' (*yâtsâ'*, Hi.) to speak of deliverance from Egypt, now the verb 'bring' (*bô'*, Hi.) is employed to speak of entry into the land promised to Abraham, Isaac, and Jacob. The promise was made by an oath-taking ceremony that involved an uplifted hand (cf. Num. 14:30: Ezek. 20:5).[5] This land was to be God's gift to His people so that it would be their 'possession'. The word used here for 'possession' (*môrâshâh*, from the root *y-r-sh*) only occurs nine times in the Old Testament, seven of which are in Ezekiel. The verb, though, occurs over 230 times, especially in reference to Israel's taking possession of Canaan.[6] The message to the Israelites of God's intentions for them concludes with another use of the self-identificatory formula, 'I am the LORD'.

9 Moses declared to the Israelites just what the LORD had told him (Heb. *vay^edabbêr mosheh kên*), carrying out his role as covenantal mediator between God and His people. He was, however, rebuffed by the people who refused to listen to him. Two reasons are given why this happened. The first is because of their 'discouragement' (*qôtser rûach*). The word *qôtser* comes from a root meaning 'to cut short' (*q-ts-r*) and it is a *hapax legomenon*. It was rendered as 'faint-hearted' (*oligopsuchia*) by the LXX, and this seems to fit well with the context and also the meaning of *qôtser rûach* ('short of spirit'). The second and related reason was because of their 'hard labour' (*mê^{ʿa}vodâh qâshâh*). Bondage, plus hard labour, accentuated now by the absence of the provision of straw, brought about deep depression. A dispirited people was in no mood to accept what Moses told them.

---

5. It was not only in oath-taking that a hand was uplifted, since the expression is also used of rebellion (2 Sam. 20:2) and giving a blessing (Lev. 9:22; Ps. 134:2).

6. I have discussed the concept of the land for Israel in *Deuteronomy: The Commands of a Covenant God* (Fearn: Christian Focus Publications, 2007 reprint), pp. 15-24.

10-11 The people were not the only ones to receive a message from the Lord. Moses had to go to Pharaoh and deliver to him a second message just like the one he had first received (5:1). The command to him was to release the Israelites and let them depart from Egypt.

12 Moses' response to the instruction was to express again doubts about his mission to Pharaoh. The reaction of his own people suggested a negative answer from Pharaoh. Why would he listen to someone who spoke with 'faltering lips'? (lit. 'uncircumcised lips'). This phrase is significant for it marks the development of the idea of circumcision to embrace the idea of what is unfit or undedicated to the Lord. Similarly, Jeremiah applies the word 'uncircumcised' to hearing, saying 'uncircumcised ears' (Jer. 6:10). Moses' attitude to his own speaking ability had not altered from his earlier defensive statements (3:11; 4:1; 4:10). The answer to his question comes in 7:1-5, interrupted by an insertion regarding genealogies.

Study Questions

1) Moses clearly at this stage could not understand what God's purposes were for His people. How does this help us as Christians as we view events affecting us and the church today?

2) In the commentary two different explanations are offered of verses 2-3. Which do you personally think fits best the context here?

3) God knows everything, and therefore does not need to 'remember'. Can you think of other biblical passages that use language like this to remind us of His faithfulness?

4) In verses 6-7 some very important terms are used of God's actions on behalf of His people ('bring out', 'rescue', 'redeem', 'take'). Can you explain how these terms still apply under the Gospel?

2 Moses' and Aaron's Family Line (6:13-27)

The narrative is broken at this point by the insertion of a limited genealogy. It is limited in that it is of Reuben and

Simeon, the two oldest sons of Jacob, that are cited as preliminary to the record of the tribe of Levi. Clearly the focus is on the descent of Moses and Aaron, as leaders in the Israelite community. It will be shown that the brothers were fitted for their role because of their descent from Levi, and, after giving the genealogy, reference is made to the fact that it was the very same Aaron and Moses mentioned in it that were the spokesmen for God. Some general comments about the genealogies are as follows:

1. The information follows the listing in Genesis 46, giving the basic information about Reuben, the firstborn, and Simeon, the second born.
2. Levi follows as the third son, but much additional information is given of his family.
3. Whereas the genealogy in Genesis 46 only lists Levi and three sons (i.e., first and second generations), here the genealogy of Levi is traced down to the fifth generation.
4. The genealogy reads as if it was an extract from some other document, and various other genealogies have to be compared with this one (e.g., Numbers 3 and 26).
5. There are surprising features in it, e.g. the number of women included – Jochebed, Elisheba, and an unnamed daughter of Putiel[7] – the concentration on Aaron rather than Moses, and the marriage of Aaron to a woman from Judah (see comment on v. 23).[8]
6. The choice of Moses rather than his older brother Aaron points to God's sovereignty in action. The first-born is passed over as the leader in favour of his younger brother, demonstrating God's purpose for the Israelites.

13 Note is taken of the charge given to Moses and Aaron that had reference both to their own people, the Israelites, and to

---

7. The LXX and the Samaritan Pentateuch also insert the name of Miriam in v. 20 to make it accord with Numbers 26:59, but the Hebrew mss. do not support this insertion.

8. For a very informative discussion of the genealogy, see Victor Hamilton, *Exodus*, pp. 108-10.

Pharaoh (the wording in the RSV or ESV is preferable to that of the NIV). Both were involved, as the message concerned the exodus of Israel from Egypt. God's purpose is constantly to the forefront in this record of slavery in a foreign land.

14-15 The list commences with the statement: 'These are heads of their fathers' houses' (ESV). This is the way that the Old Testament refers to a patriarchal house, which was made up of many clans (*mishpᵉchot*, vv. 14, 15, 17, 19, 24, 25). Then follows the names of Reuben and Simeon, together with their sons' names.

16-25 At this point the focus shifts to Levi and his family and remains with them. Levi's age is given, together with the names of his sons, Gershom, Kohath, and Merari. While the names of Gershom's and Merari's sons are given, the concentration is on listing the descendants of Levi by his son Kohath, down to Phinehas in the fifth generation (v. 25). Amram in turn married Jochebed, who bore Aaron and Moses. The name Jochebed is significant, as it carries the abbreviated form of the covenantal name *yô-*, showing that the name *yhwh* was in use prior to the events related in the book of Exodus. This means that Amram married his father's aunt, a marriage of relatives that was prohibited under the later biblical law (Lev. 18:12). Another significant marriage is that of Aaron, who married Elisheba, son of Amminadab (v. 23). Rather than marrying a woman from the family of Levi, Aaron married a woman from Judah (see 1 Chron. 2:10). This fact is significant in relation to the ancestry of Jesus, for the biblical genealogies show the names of Elisheba's father, Amminadab, and her brother, Nahshon, as links in the line from Judah, via David, to Christ (Ruth 4:18-22; 1 Chron. 2:10-11; Matt. 1:4; Luke 3:32-33). Here the priestly and the kingly are blended, foreshadowing the same combination in the person and work of the Lord Jesus.

26-27 The final verses in the section resume the narrative, drawing attention to the facts already stated earlier in verse 13 regarding Moses and Aaron, though with the reversal of the order of their names between verse 26 and verse 27. To the instruction regarding bringing the Israelites out of Egypt is added that they were to exit 'according to their divisions' (*'al tsivᵉ'otâm*). The word for division or battalion (*tsâvâ'*) is a term used in the Pentateuch several times to denote Israel as the people wandered in the desert (see Exod. 7:4; 12:41; Num. 10:14, 18, 22, 25). Later its most frequent usage (c. 200 times) is in the phrase 'the LORD of hosts'. The point here is that the Israelites were not going to depart from Egypt as mere slaves but as warriors in battle array, ready to initiate occupancy of Canaan. The final verse, verse 27, confirms the identity of those designated to represent the Israelites before Pharaoh. No change had been made in regard to God's spokesmen; they were still the same Moses and Aaron. The switch in the order of the names points now to the fact that not birthright but God's sovereign choice determined who was the leading figure.

3 A Promise of Signs and Wonders (6:28–7:7)

Another episode is related here of a renewed commission for Moses. He was reluctant to take up the task, but proved obedient to the LORD's directions when told again that Aaron would be his 'prophet'.

6:28-29 The NIV abbreviates the beginning of verse 28. It is better to follow the NRSV and the ESV: 'On the day when the LORD spoke to Moses, in the land of Egypt . . . .' The narrative brings the reader up to the time when Moses again professed lack of the necessary gifts for this ministry. God had identified Himself as 'the LORD' (see comment on 3:13-15), and He now indicated that the whole content of His revelation to Moses was to be communicated to Pharaoh – 'everything I am telling you'.

30 Again, Moses returned to his own lack of oratorical gifts, citing once more his claim that he had 'faltering lips' (lit. 'uncircumcised lips', *ʿral sᵉfâtáyim*: see 6:12). His assertion was that if he were to go, then Pharaoh would refuse to listen to him.

7:1 How graciously God dealt with his servant Moses! He informed him that he was to be like God to Pharaoh, while his brother Aaron occupied the office of prophet (see comments on 4:14-17). This pattern is most important for the way in which the prophets operated in the Old Testament times. Their ministry was structured on that of Moses and Aaron. Divine revelation was communicated to chosen servants, who in turn communicated it to their audiences.

2 Moses was given no choice in regard to his message. It was to be everything that the LORD commanded. There is no discernible difference between the expressions 'everything I command you' (*kol-ʾªsher ʾªtsavvekâ*) and 'everything I tell you' (6:29; *kol-ʾªsher ʾªnî dovêr ʾêlekâ*). Revelation had to be transmitted in its entirety. Once more the central theme of the message is reiterated. Pharaoh had to be brought to the realisation that he had to let the Israelites leave Egypt.

3-4 Once more Moses is told that God would sovereignly harden Pharaoh's heart, something already stated back in 4:21. There is a change here in that a different verb is used to denote 'hardening' (*qâshâh* instead of *châzaq*, Pi.). No discernible difference in meaning occurs between these two verbs, or the other verb for 'hardening' that is also used in Exodus 4-14 (*kâvêd*). From the outset, Pharaoh's heart was set against the Israelites, but God's actions towards him were judicial in order to demonstrate that the exodus was solely dependent upon divine power. The same duality was apparent in the death of Christ, for though it was part of God's 'set purpose and foreknowledge', yet those who crucified Him were guilty of putting Him to death (Acts 2:23; 4:27-28). Mere multiplication of 'signs and wonders' (for 'sign', see 3:20 and 4:8) was not going to change Pharaoh's heart; he would refuse to listen to Moses and Aaron. All the plagues were to be called 'signs', while 'judgments' (*mishpâtîm*) point to them as judicial acts. The actual exodus would take place because of 'mighty acts of judgment' that God would execute when He laid His hand on Egypt. These were clearly events synonymous with 'miraculous signs and wonders'. God's concern was for *His* people, the Israelites, whom He now designates as His 'divisions' (see comment on 6:26). The message was that the Israelites would leave Egypt as an organised body, going out in military formation.

5 It was not just the Israelites who were to be convinced by the redemption from Egypt by God's 'outstretched arm' and 'mighty acts of judgment' (6:6-7), but also the Egyptians. Recognition of the redeeming God as 'the LORD' was to be the outcome of the judgment on Egypt and the bringing of the Israelites out from there. This statement needs to be set over against Pharaoh's assertion that he did not know the

Lord (5:2). The subsequent events of the exodus were aimed at convincing the taskmasters in Egypt that their gods were mere vanities without any claim to reality, whereas the God of their slaves was living and powerful.

6 This verse draws the narrative back to 6:13, so that, following the parenthesis of 6:14–7:5, attention falls once more on Moses and Aaron as chosen servants and messengers. What had been commanded of them, that they did. The MT is even more definite and emphatic than the NIV translation suggests: 'Moses and Aaron did just as the Lord commanded them'. Better is the ESV: 'Moses and Aaron did so; they did just as the Lord commanded them'. Their actions were demonstrations of complete obedience to God's directions.

7 The respective ages of Moses and Aaron are listed. Moses, the second born, was eighty years of age, while Aaron was eighty-three years old. No mention is made in Exodus of any danger to the children at the time of Aaron's birth, so presumably the decree was issued shortly before the birth of Moses (see 1:22).

5

Redemptive Judgment
(7:8–12:51)

From 7:8 to 12:30 the narrative deals with the visitations of God's judgment on Egypt by means of the eleven signs, and then the miraculous deliverance of the Israelites from their slavery by way of the dry Red Sea. Several important factors about the signs have to be borne in mind:

1. Though the signs are often referred to as 'plagues', and while the biblical text refers to individual signs as 'plagues' (9:3, 14, 15; 11:1), yet collectively they are either called 'signs' (7:3; 8:23; 10:1) or 'wonders' (4:21; 7:3; 11:9, 10). Also, eleven signs were performed, as the incident with Moses' staff (7:6-13) has to be included.

2. The signs were part of the events that set the pattern of redemption for all the rest of the Scriptures. The language of the New Testament, in describing the redemption purchased by Christ, echoes in many places the language of the book of Exodus (cf. Acts 2:22). Many of the details of the exodus have typological significance.

3. The signs were judgments of God on Pharaoh and his people. They were directed against the people, the things that they depended upon for life and existence, and even against their gods (12:12). The events in

connection with the signs constituted a polemic against the Egyptian gods.

4. No indication is given of the time frame of these events. There is no suggestion in the text that they occurred in close chronological proximity to one another.

5. Many have suggested that the signs were just natural disasters, even if they happened in a heightened form. While this position has been widely adopted, yet it faces numerous objections.[1] Nothing in the text suggests mere natural phenomena were utilised by God to being judgment on Egypt. Attempts to find natural explanations for the eleven signs fail to explain the earlier miracles performed before the elders by Moses (4:2-5; 4:8-9). The narrative in Exodus points to divine intervention in connection with the signs.[2]

6. Leaving aside the first demonstration of supernatural power (7:6-13), the following nine are arranged in threes. In the first three, warning is given to Pharaoh in the morning (7:15; 8:20; 9:13). While in the first and second of each three, the plague is announced beforehand, in the third it is not. At the third sign the Egyptian magicians acknowledge the finger of God in the event (8:19), in the sixth they were unable to stand before Moses (9:11), and in the final one, the ninth,

---

1. Perhaps the most quoted source for this viewpoint is the presentation by Gerta Hort, 'The Plagues of Egypt', *ZAW* 69 (1957), pp. 84-103; 70 (1958), pp. 48-59. Her position, except in relation to what is usually called the tenth plague, is held by K. A. Kitchen, *On the Reliability of the Old Testament* (Grand Rapids: Eerdmans, 2006), pp. 249-54. For discussion of the plagues in general, and specifically a criticism of this approach, see J. D. Currid, *Ancient Egypt and the Old Testament* (Grand Rapids: Baker Books, 1997), pp. 104-20. Brevard Childs, *The Book of Exodus: A Critical Theological Commentary* (OT Library: London: SCM Press, 1974), p.168, comments on Hort's thesis: '... this genre of apologetic literature suffers from the strange anomaly of defending biblical "supernaturalism" on the grounds of rationalistic arguments.'

2. T. D. Alexander, *From Paradise to Promised Land,* p. 161, rightly notes that the 'text consistently emphasises the divine provenance of these events. This is indicated, for example, by the references to Moses and Aaron stretching out their hands or a staff in order to bring about the different signs or wonders. Although some of these may be associated with natural phenomena, their occurrence is clearly attributed to divine intervention'.

Pharaoh declares that he will not see Moses' face again (10:28).

7. There is also progression in intensity among the plagues. No distinction is made in the first two plagues between any of the inhabitants in Egypt. But in the next seven, it is only the Egyptians who are exposed to the consequences of the plagues. Moreover, the punishment inherent in the individual plagues became more severe. The first three touched aspects of human comfort, the second three impinged on the maintenance of life, and the third group brought death.

8. The signs must also be viewed in their connection with creation. Exodus 1–15 has strong affinity with the account of creation in Genesis 1–2 and also other parts of Genesis 1–11. The early verses of Exodus make the connection explicit by alluding to the creation mandate (cf. Exod. 1:7 with Gen. 1:28). When the judgment of the signs occurs, creation goes into reverse. There is uncreation, or decreation. The work of creation in six days as related in Genesis 1 was attacked and chaos ensued. By the ninth sign, darkness again marks out the created world.[3]

1 The First Sign: Confirmation of Moses and Aaron (7:8-13)
Before the other varied signs came, another incident with Moses' staff took place (for the previous one, see 4:1-5). While verses 9 and 10 seem to imply that it was Aaron's staff, yet verses 10-18 make it clear that it was Moses' staff that was involved, since reference is made back to the fact that it had been changed into a snake (7:15). The context suggests it forms the first of eleven sequential demonstrations of God's wonders.

8-9 Implicit in the text is a command to Moses and Aaron to return to Pharaoh. When he would issue a challenge to them by demanding a miracle, a portent (Heb. *môfēt*, cf. v. 3), Moses would follow the LORD's direction and got Aaron to

---

3. See the discussion by John D. Currid, *Ancient Egypt and the Old Testament*, pp. 113-17.

throw his staff down on the ground so that it could become a snake.

10-13 Following the divine directions, both men went into the presence of Pharaoh, where the predicted incident took place. The staff indeed became a snake. The word used here for 'snake' is not the usual one, *nâchâsh* (cf. its use in 4:3), but *tannîn*. While *tannin* is often translated as 'great sea creature' (Gen. 1:21; Ps. 148:7), here it is used as a synonym for *nâchâsh*. On seeing what happened, Pharaoh called for his 'wise men and sorcerers' (*lach^{a}kâmîm v^{e}lam^{e}kashsh^{e}fîm*). The first of these terms is a general word for 'wise men', while the second, which occurs in this form only five times in the Old Testament, denotes those who practised sorcery. It was a practice forbidden in Israel (Deut. 18:10). They are also called 'Egyptian magicians' (*chartummê mitsráyim*). They did the same things according to their 'mysterious lore' (*lah^{a}tîm*), a term coming from a root that indicates 'wrapping up' or 'covering completely'. Each of the Egyptians threw his staff on the ground, and they became snakes. Then Aaron's staff 'swallowed' these snakes. No explanation is given in the text as to how the magicians achieved their duplication of the miracle, whether by some illusory trick, or whether it was a genuine transformation of the sticks by satanic power. Similarly, the reference to the swallowing of the snakes by the one that came from Moses' stick carries no further elaboration. Rather than Pharaoh having his heart changed, he hardened his heart further, refusing to listen to Moses and Aaron even as the LORD had said. Even miracles do not by themselves change hearts set against God (cf. Ps. 78:12-17; John 10:25).

Study Questions

1) Lists of names are a feature of the Bible. What purpose does this list (6:14-27) serve at this point in the book of Exodus?

2) Prophecy was to become an important function in Israel (see Deut. 18:9-22). How did the relationship between Moses and Aaron help set the pattern for later prophets?

3) Was Pharaoh's heart naturally hard, or did God act sovereignly to change it?

4) How could the Egyptian wise men and sorcerers imitate what happened here as related in verses 8-11, and also later?

2 The Second Sign: Water Turned to Blood (7:14-24)

The scene has now been set for the narrative to describe the further ten signs that God sent on Egypt. Redemptive judgment would occur, wherein the same acts of God that brought deliverance to His people were expressions of divine punishment. This principle came to its highest expression in the death of Christ on the cross.

14-15 Directions were given by the LORD to Moses concerning his next meeting with Pharaoh. Lest he take an optimistic approach to this meeting, he was reminded of the hardness of Pharaoh's heart, and his unwillingness to accede to the demands relating to the Israelites. Moses had to go out to the Nile the next morning and wait on the river bank for Pharaoh to approach. No indication is given as to the reasons why he went there. It could have been for bathing, or for some worship activities that involved the river Nile. Moses and Aaron were there as representatives of the living God.

16 The message to be conveyed to Pharaoh was an announcement from 'the LORD, the God of the Hebrews'. Once more the command taken to Pharaoh was, 'Let my people go'. No action, other than release of the Israelites from bondage, would satisfy. It was not that Pharaoh had not received this message previously. The problem was with himself, for up to that very time he had neither listened nor obeyed.

17-18 Earlier Pharaoh had claimed he did not know the LORD (5:2). The time had now come for the display of 'miraculous signs and wonders' (7:3-5) so that the Egyptians would have no excuse. Knowledge of the LORD would come through their own experience of His power. They, and many of the things in which they trusted and worshipped, would become subject to divine judgment. The announcement is made in a dramatic way: 'Behold, I am about to smite with the staff that is in my hand over the waters that are in the Nile, and they shall be turned to blood.' This construction, commencing with the particle 'behold' (Heb. *hinnêh*), often marks out a dramatic development. In narrative it is often accompanied, as here, by a participle that can indicate something is on the point of happening.[4] The effect of the water turning to blood would result in the death of the fish, the smell from the river becoming foul, and the water being unfit for drinking. This important resource for the Egyptians would be unavailable.

19 The instruction to Aaron, via Moses, was to stretch his staff over all the water supplies of Egypt, not just the river Nile but also over canals, ponds, and pools of water. No explanation of a naturalistic kind can explain the word 'blood' (*dâm*) here. It can be used metaphorically (see, e.g., Joel's reference to the moon turning to blood, Joel 2:31), but there is no hint here that this sort of explanation can account for the change to the water. The transformation of water to blood was to take place even in storage vessels, whether wooden or stone (the Heb. text says 'in trees and in stones', but the context implies vessels made of these products).

20-21 Moses and Aaron explicitly followed the LORD's instructions. They had Pharaoh and his officials as their audience as the water was changed to blood. The three consequences of this, already stated (v. 18), came to pass – dead fish, a bad smell, and inability to drink any of the water. God's judgment through this smiting was the presence of blood everywhere in the land.

22-24 Again, the Egyptian magicians attempted to replicate the miracle by their 'sacred arts'.[5] In some unstated way they were able to approximate to the miracle that Moses and Aaron had performed. Pharaoh realised that this was God's judicial action, as the miracles caused him to harden further his heart against the LORD. Pharaoh returned to his palace and the verdict passed on him was: 'and he did not take even this

---

4. The Heb. participle can be used in all three time settings – past, present and future. The context must determine the tense used in English translation. The final clause, 'and they shall be turned into blood' (*vᵉnehpᵉkû lᵉdâm*) is a good example of a vav consec. perf. that continues on the tense from the preceding participle. On this point, see *DIHG-S*, p. 94, §76 (c).

5. Here the spelling is different from that in 7:11 where *lahᵃtêhem* occurs. The spelling here lacks the *hê*, *lâtêhem*.

to heart.' This idiomatic phrase simply means 'to consider'.[6] Even these events made no difference to Pharaoh's thinking. His people were reduced to digging holes to try and get drinking water, as the water from the Nile was not potable. Presumably, the water of the Nile was altered to cause the fish to die, while subsurface water was unaffected. New wells were needed to provide a water supply.

3 The Third Sign: Frogs (7:25–8:15[7])

The next sign, involving frogs, came a week later than the previous one. Notification was given to Pharaoh before it happened, and again his magicians were able to replicate the events.

7:25–8:2 Seven days after the Nile was struck, the LORD instructed Moses to go to Pharaoh with the same message as previously (cf. 5:1; 7:16). The threat was that if he refused, then the whole of Egypt would be plagued with frogs. The phrasing concerning this new judgment highlighted the impending event. The participle of the verb 'to strike with' [plague, or death] is used (*nogêf*). Two nouns from this same root are used later in the narrative (*maggêfot*, 9:14; *négef*, 12:13).[8] The Hebrew word for 'frogs' (*ts^{e}pard$^{e\,\prime}$îm*) occurs thirteen times in the Old Testament, all of them appear here in Exodus, except for two psalms that refer to this event (Pss. 78:45; 105:30). The word itself may be onomatopoeic, 'the croakers'.[9] It is possible that this plague was an attack on the concept of the frog-headed god of the Egyptians.

3-4 Nowhere in the country was to be exempt from the plague of frogs. Even Pharaoh's palace would be invaded, including his bedroom and bed. The houses of everyone, high

---

6. The phrase 'to take to heart' (*shît libbô*) occurs ten times in the Old Testament, and does not seem to differ in meaning from the parallel expression 'to set to heart', *sîm libbô*.

7. There is a difference in the chapter divisions at this point. The MT and the LXX include vss. 1-15 as part of chapter 7.

8. Two other words are also used in the narratives in Exodus for 'plague', *néga'* in 11:1, and *déver* in 9:3, 15. While most English versions use 'plague' for all these Hebrew words, the NASB makes an effort to differentiate among them: *nogêf*, 'smite'; *maggêfot*, 'plague'; *négef*, 'plague'; *néga'*, 'plague'; *déver*, 'pestilence'.

9. See Alan Cole, *Exodus: An Introduction and Commentary* (Tyndale series: London: Tyndale Press, 1973), p. 91.

and low, would experience the frogs, and the kitchens where food was prepared would also be affected.

5-7 As with the previous sign, stretching out by Aaron of the staff would symbolise God's power. The streams, canals and ponds (all mentioned already in 7:19) would produce abundant numbers of frogs so that the land would be covered with them. When Aaron did this, it happened as the LORD had said. For the second time, the Egyptian magicians imitated a divine action, and were able to claim that they had brought up frogs from the Nile. There was no reversal of the judgment, rather an intensification of it.

8 Pharaoh's response was a request for prayer to the LORD. While he didn't confess that he now knew that the God of the Israelites was really God, yet he acknowledged the source of the sign. He made a promise that if the frogs were removed, then he would accede to the request for sacrificial worship in the desert.

9 The opening clause of Moses' answer to Pharaoh is hard to translate, though the general meaning is clear from the context. The verb (*pâ'ar*, Hitp.) is more often used of vaunting one's glory (cf. Isa. 44:23; 60:21; 61:3). The implication here is that Moses conceded that Pharaoh was worthy of more honour than himself. A variety of translations can indicate that: 'prove yourself glorious before me = please determine for me' (CHAL); 'I leave to you the honour' (NIV); 'be pleased to command me' (ESV); 'kindly tell me' (NRSV).[10] The request was for Pharaoh to designate a time when Moses would pray for him, his officials, and people that their homes would be free of the frogs. The one exception that was made was that the request did not extend to the river Nile. Only there they would remain.[11] The verb (*'âtar*) used in this passage and elsewhere (see 8:28-30 [Heb. 8:24]; 9:28; 10:17-18) in the narrative concerning the signs God brought to pass is not the normal one (*shâ'al*). This verb here may have had the connotation of offering sacrifices as one prayed.

---

10. *DCH*, VI, p. 646, suggests that there may have been a *pâ'ar* III meaning 'choose', but no other passage can be cited to support this suggestion.

11. 'Only' represents the Heb. adverb *raq* that has an 'immediate restrictive sense' when it stands initially in a clause following a positive clause, as here. *IBHS*, p. 669, §39.3.5.

10-11 Pharaoh tried to put off the timing of the prayer, perhaps indicating that he thought that the sign would come to an end of its own accord. His request for a cessation of the sign was going to be heard, and that too would again be a demonstration of the LORD's power. It was a revelation of God that should have led to the acknowledgement of His existence and omnipotence.

12-15 The Hebrew text implies that as soon as Moses and Aaron left Pharaoh, they cried out to the LORD *(vayyêtsê' mosheh v^e'ah^{a}ron ... vayyits'aq mosheh ...)*. The verb 'cry out' *(tsâ'aq;* Heb. 8:8)[12] is interesting because if often implies crying out in a distressful situation (cf. Gen. 27:34; Exod. 17:4), and it has already appeared earlier in this book concerning the Israelites' cry to God for deliverance from Egypt (2:23) and the related noun, *tse'âqâh*, in 3:7, 9. The divine response was to kill all the frogs in the houses, the enclosures,[13] and the fields. But the outcome was different from what Pharaoh would have expected. The frogs did not disappear but were simply piled up in heaps,[14] and the whole land stank because of them. In spite of these circumstances, Pharaoh thought that there was going to be some alleviation of the conditions in the land. The MT says that he saw *r^{e}vâchâh*, 'respite', or 'relief', a word that only occurs here and in Lamentations 3:56 in the Old Testament. He may well have been under the impression that there would at least be some lessening of the problems for Egypt, but the outcome was that he hardened his heart, refusing to listen to Moses and Aaron.

4 The Fourth Sign: Gnats (8:16-19)

The fourth sign in the series was an infestation of gnats or lice. Two things were different about this sign. First, no pre-warning was given to Pharaoh, and secondly, his magicians

---

12. The Hebrew verbs *tsâ'aq* and *zâ'aq* appear to be variants of the same root, as it is not unusual to find such variation in Hebrew in verbs with similar initial consonants. The difference between the two verbs, and their derived nouns *ts^e'âqâh* and *z^e'âqâh*, is simply orthographic.

13. The word for 'enclosures' (*ch^{a}tsêrot*) can be used for enclosures containing houses, and hence it may be just another way of describing villages.

14. The MT has *ch^{o}mârim ch^{o}mârim*, 'heaps, heaps.' This is a Hebrew way of denoting emphasis. See *IBHS*, p. 119, §7.4.1.

were unable to reproduce this miracle. They went further than merely acknowledging their inability to do similarly, by attributing the sign to 'the finger of God'.

16-17 Whereas the previous sign related to water, this one was concerned with insects in the dust. Moses carried out God's instructions, and, in turn, Aaron stretched out his hand with the staff. When the staff hit the dust of the earth, lice came on humans and animals alike. The Hebrew word for 'lice' (*kên*) is rare, but some small insect, with dust as its habitat, is clearly in view. The last sentence of verse 17 re-emphasises how widespread was the infestation – 'all the dust throughout the land of Egypt'.

18-19a The magicians made the attempt to do the same as Moses and Aaron had done, but failed: lit. 'And the magicians by their secret arts tried to bring forth the gnats, and they were not able'. This marked a new phase in the series of events. The magicians made the admission; 'This is the finger of God'. It is hard to be sure how much this meant. Was it a real admission that the God of the Israelites was indeed the source of the miracles? The context suggests that it was (see also 9:11).

19b The outcome was exactly as was the case with the previous signs. Rather than Pharaoh being brought to repentance, he hardened his heart still further. This refusal to listen and obey was just as the Lord had earlier declared.

Study Questions

1) Why was the use of the rod so significant in these signs, and not just a command in God's name?

2) Was the fact that Pharaoh's servants witnessed these signs intended to put even more pressure on him to change his mind and let the people go?

3) Do you think the reaction of the magicians (8:19) was a realisation that the God of the Israelites was really the living God, or was it simply an attempt to persuade their ruler to act on Moses' request? A true confession, or just a convenient comment in the situation?

5 The Fifth Sign: Flies (8:20-32)

The next sign was introduced in the same way as the previous ones, 'And the LORD said to Moses' (8:20). A divine word formed the basis for what transpired. More interaction took place between Moses and Pharaoh than with the previous signs, and a sharp differentiation was made between the Israelites and the Egyptians. The principle stated here (vv. 22-23) came to fuller expression at the time of the Passover and the exodus itself (12:12-13; 14:29-30).

20-21 Another rendezvous at the riverbank was planned (see the previous reference in 7:15), and the same command of the LORD was transmitted to Pharaoh: 'Send my people away so that they may worship me'. The threat that followed had play on words in it, involving the verb 'to send'. If Pharaoh didn't send (*mᵉshallêach*, Pi. part. m.s.) the people away, the LORD would send (*mashlîach*, Hi. part. m.s.) a swarm of flies to cover the ground and to penetrate into all the Egyptian houses. The word for 'a swarm of flies' (*'ârov*) only occurs here in Exodus 8, and in the two psalms that speak of the signs in Egypt (see Pss. 78:45; 105:31). Exact identification of the insect is impossible, and as the noun *'ârov* is derived from a verb (*'ârav*) meaning 'to mingle' or 'intermix', the probability is that an assorted infestation of small insects is intended.

22-23 These verses set out a very important principle that operated in relation to the exodus of the Israelites from Egypt. It was a demonstration of God's sovereignty in grace in the redemption of His people through His judgment on the Egyptians. The declaration of God to Moses was: 'I will set apart the land of Goshen in which my people live'. The verb for 'set apart' (*pâlâh*, Hi.) should not be confused with the verb 'to redeem' (*pâlâ'*). It means 'to set apart', 'to make a distinction'.[15] It occurs three times in the narrative concerning the signs (8:22 [Heb. 8:18]; 9:4; 11:7). The Israelites were exempt from this judgment due solely to God's sovereign determination, and in itself the invasion of the insects was to show that the LORD was really God. The idea was emphasised by its repetition in a slightly different form: 'I will put a

---

15. See *DCH*, VI, p. 689; *NIDOTTE*, 3, p. 620.

deliverance between your people and my people' (NIV margin). The word for 'deliverance' is really 'redemption' (*pᵉdût*), and it is rare, occurring only here and in Psalms 111:9 and 130:7. Though emendation has often been suggested, it is best to retain the MT as the word fits the context well. How God was going to show differentiation between Israel and Egypt would ultimately revolve around redemption.[16] Pharaoh and his people did not have long to wait for this distinction to be made, for intimation was given that it would occur the very next day.

24 God carried out His word, and a heavy infestation of the insects took place. The narrative then indicates that the land was 'ruined' (*shâchat*, Pi.). The usage of this verb shows that it often connotes a devastation caused by God's judgment. Thus it appears in relation to the destruction of Sodom and Gomorrah (Gen. 13:10; 19:13, 29), while later it occurs in relation to both Babylon (Jer. 51:11) and Tyre (Ezek. 26:4).

25-27 The effect of the sign was that Pharaoh relented to the extent that he would let the Israelites sacrifice in Egypt, not in the desert, as was their request. He does go some way, however, to acknowledging their God – 'Sacrifice to *your* God.' Nothing but the release of the Israelites from their slavery would suffice. In reply, Moses indicated that the offering of sacrifices by his people could lead to an outbreak of violence against them. His reference to stoning is not to it as a means of execution, for Egypt did not practise stoning in that way, but to communal violence instigated by an intense dislike of their sacrificial customs. This seems to be the meaning of 'detestable in their eyes', not that it was detestable in God's sight. Moses insisted that God demanded a three-day journey into the desert rather than sacrifices in the locations where they lived.

28 A short trip into the desert for sacrificial activities was acceptable to Pharaoh, and he even names the Israelites' God as '*the* LORD *your God*'. He spoke imperiously to Moses and Aaron, shown both by the form of his statement, '*I* [*'ânokî*] am sending you', and also by the instruction that continued the

---

16. Walter Kaiser Jr, 'Exodus', *EBC*, p. 409, has a good note on *pᵉdût*, along with bibliographical information.

prohibition that they were not to go far. The more unusual negative prohibition form (*'al* + jussive) is replaced by the form denoting either a strong prohibition, or one of more permanent nature (*lo'* + imperf.). This is the form that divine commands normally take in the Old Testament. Here Pharaoh is depicted almost as exercising divine control. Finally, he requested prayer on his behalf, so that the current sign would be removed.

29 Moses promised an immediate response to Pharaoh's request, with the assurance that by the next day the flies would disappear. Appended to this was a warning. Pharaoh had already acted deceitfully, and Moses was trying to ensure this did not happen again. Action, not prevarication, was demanded.

30-32 The promise to Pharaoh was kept, and Moses' prayer was answered. All the people, from Pharaoh downward, were relieved of this plague. Not one fly remained. However, Pharaoh's heart was not touched; instead he hardened it still further.

6 The Sixth Sign: On Cattle (9:1-7)

Another sign was directed against the livestock in Egypt – cattle, horses, donkeys, herds [of cattle] and flocks [of sheep and/or goats]. These were the animals that provided the population with many things needed for day-to-day living, including milk, meat, clothing, and transportation. Bulls in particular were worshipped as part of a fertility cult, while female gods were depicted as cows. Once again, one of the 'signs' had a sharp polemical edge to it. It was directed against animals necessary for life, but also against the false gods of Egypt. This 'sign' also differs from the earlier ones in that there is greater emphasis on specification of time, on the distinction made between the Israelites and the Egyptians, and on death of the animals.

1 It is made plain that Moses was not the originator of the messages being relayed to Pharaoh. It is the Lord who sent him to Pharaoh and who gave him the words to speak. The message did not change, for it was identical with previous ones (see 7:16; 8:1; 8:20). It remained: 'Let my people go, so that they may worship me'.

2-4 The Lord's word to Moses assumed the situation that Pharaoh would continue to hang on to the Israelites. The Hebrew text speaks of his still seizing them (*vᵉ'ôdᵉkâ machᵃzîq bâm*). The warning to Pharaoh was clear. Refusal to allow the Israelites to go would result in the hand of the Lord being expressed against them in the form of 'a very heavy pestilence' (*déver kâvêd me'od*). Any kind of pestilence that produced death can be encompassed by the word *déver*. It could be by sword, or famine, or, as here, by fatal illness. All the domesticated animals were to be affected ('all the livestock in the field'). The principle of making a distinction between the Egyptians and the Israelites was to be carried out in a very telling way, for the animals belonging to the Israelites were to be exempted from the infliction of the judgment.

5-6 The Lord even set the time when the pestilence would occur. The word used for this (*mô'êd*) is often used in the Old Testament for a determined time or place.[17] It happened in accordance with His warning to Pharaoh. The difference, sovereignly determined between the two groups in Egypt, was manifest in the death of the Egyptians' livestock, whereas not one died belonging to the Israelites ('not one dead', *lo'-mêt 'echâd*; cf. 8:31 [Heb. 8:27], 'not one left', *lo' nish'ar 'echâd*). Redemptive judgment was on display again.

7 The MT simply says at the beginning of this verse that 'Pharaoh sent ....' There is no need to expand like the NIV, 'Pharaoh sent *men to investigate*', as the simple and accurate translation, 'Pharaoh sent', is quite sufficient. He needed to satisfy himself that the warning had become a reality. His investigation confirmed the fact that the disease had affected not one of the Israelites' animals. Despite another miracle, he hardened his heart again, and did not release them.

7 The Seventh Sign: Boils (9:8-12)

The next sign from the Lord affected not only the animals but also the Egyptians themselves. Even the magicians had no answer to this miracle, and could not even stand their ground in Moses' presence because of the boils.

---

17. The word appears frequently in the expression 'the tent of meeting' (*'ôhel mô'êd*), i.e., the place where the Lord appointed a meeting with his people. See *TWOT*, 1, pp. 388-89.

8 The instruction was for a fistful of dust from the furnace to be tossed into the air before Pharaoh. The word for 'dust' (*pîach*) only occurs in this passage in the Old Testament, while the word for 'furnace' (*kivshân*) only appears in two other passages in the Old Testament (Gen. 19:28; Exod. 19:18). It would appear that 'furnace' comes from a Hebrew verb meaning 'to subdue' (*kâvas*), though the connection between verb and noun is unclear.[18] What is probably more significant is that the reference to 'furnace' may be to the ovens that the Israelites used to fire the bricks that they were compelled to make. From the instrument of slavery came a sign of God's judgment. The command to Moses was to 'scatter' (*zâraq*) the soot. This word is normally used of ritual occasions such as sprinkling blood on the people and the altar (Exod. 24:6-8; 29:20; Lev. 1:5). Here it is used of the dramatised judgment that was to be inflicted because of the Egyptians' refusal to let the Israelites go.

9 When tossed in the air, the soot was to change to fine dust that would cause 'festering boils' on both the Egyptians and their animals. The word for 'festering boils' (*ªva'ebu'ot*) only appears in verses 9-10, and seems to refer to some skin disease, whether a form of leprosy or skin anthrax. This affliction may be the background for the reference in Deuteronomy 28:27, in which Israel was warned by Moses that one of the covenantal curses would be affliction 'with the boils of Egypt and with tumours, festering sores and itch'. In that case, the message was that the exodus and its accompanying events would be reversed, and Israel would suffer many of the diseases that had been inflicted on the Egyptians.

10-11 Both Moses and Aaron took soot as directed and appeared before Pharaoh. Open and public demonstration of God's power was part of the revelatory aspect of the signs and wonders. Moses threw the soot into the air (lit. 'heavenwards'), and men and animals were affected with the threatened festering sores. The Egyptian magicians, who have not been mentioned since the incident with the gnats (8:19), were themselves included in the judgment, and could not even maintain their position in Moses' presence.

---

18. For a note on this word, see Victor Hamilton, *Exodus*, p. 144.

Occult practices could not sustain them in the face of divine power.

12 Pharaoh's obstinacy, maintained in the face of this further demonstration of God's power, caused him to harden his heart and refuse to listen to Moses and Aaron. In God's sovereignty he worked on Pharaoh and further strengthened his rebelliousness; Pharaoh's own antagonism was now being confirmed by God's action (cf. Rom. 9:18).

Study Questions

1) God promised to put a distinction between His people and the Egyptians (8:23; 9:4). How was this carried out both in these signs and also in the exodus itself?

2) Constantly God was saying to Pharaoh, 'Let *my* people go'. What could convince the Israelites that this was indeed the real relationship between them and their God?

3) Does the wording of 8:26 suggest that in Egypt the Israelites weren't sacrificing correctly to God, but had adapted their worship to that of the Egyptians?

4) Why should Pharaoh have normally been told when the next sign was to occur? Would surprise not have been an even more effective way of changing his attitude?

8 The Eighth Sign: Hail (9:13-35)

As the signs continue, the narrative concerning each one is longer than the earlier ones, and no more mention is made of the Egyptian magicians. In this one, humans were subjected to a hailstorm, along with all the country. The very things that sustained life (crops and animals) were directly attacked by this sign. Once more the distinction between the Israelites and the Egyptians was maintained, and Goshen, where the Israelites lived, was off-limits for the hail.

13-15 On this occasion Moses was told to rise early and take up his position in Pharaoh's presence. The NIV translates this verse as: 'Then the LORD said to Moses, "Get up early in the morning, confront Pharaoh"....'

'Confront' is too strong, as the verb here (*hityatstsêv*) just conveys the idea of taking up a position in a place, or appearing before someone. The message of the God of the Hebrews remained the same: 'Send my people away so that they may serve me'. The accompanying threat was made in the same way as previously (see 8:20-21). If Pharaoh didn't act obediently in sending the people away, then God reserved the right to send His hand against Pharaoh and his people with full destructive force. He would send His plagues (*maggêfotay*) to the heart of Pharaoh. This is the only time this word for 'plague' appears here in Exodus. It comes from the verb 'to smite' (*nâgaf*), that has already occurred in 8:2 (Heb. 7:22), and that appears again later in the account of the first Passover celebration (12:23, 27).

16-17 As part of God's plan for His people, He raised up Pharaoh in order to demonstrate through him His power. Proclamation of God's name was to be made to the world. Something much more than just the words 'God' or 'LORD' is intended. God's character was to be evident in the events leading up to the exodus, as well as the exodus event itself. 'Name' in a passage such as this represents the nature or attributes of God.[19] Moses recognised the continuing hostility of Pharaoh. The verb used of Pharaoh's attitude (*sâlal*, Hitp.) was one often applied to building a roadbed higher than the surrounding terrain (cf. our English word, 'highway', for a similar development). This could mean that Pharaoh was setting up barriers against messages of the LORD being brought to him, or else it could be a metaphorical use implying that he was exalting himself.[20] The former meaning gives good sense. Pharaoh was placing himself as a barrier in the way of the Israelites serving their God according to His demands.

18-19 The next announcement was in the form already used earlier of divine intimation of coming events ('behold I am causing it to rain an exceedingly heavy hailstorm'; on the form, see the comment on 7:17). The use of the participle in Hebrew (*mamtîr*, 'causing to rain') conveys both the certainty of the predicted event and also its immanency, and this accords with the indication of time – 'at this time tomorrow.'

---

19. On this point, there is a helpful discussion by A. P. Ross in *NIDOTTE*, 5, pp. 147-51. Ross says that the name of the Lord (*yhwh*) really stands for His nature (p. 148).

20. *CHAL*, p. 257, opts for the meaning 'behave haughtily, insolently'.

On no previous occasion since the foundation of the state of Egypt, had such hail occurred. The warning was that if people and animals did not take shelter, then the hail would kill them.

20-21 A sharp contrast is drawn in these verses between two groups in Egyptian society. On one hand, there were those who 'feared the word of the Lord'; on the other hand, those who 'ignored the word of the Lord'. Fearing God in this context is not the same as living a life governed 'by 'the fear of the Lord', as described in Psalms or Proverbs (see, e.g., Ps. 111:10; Prov. 1:7). Some realised the danger they were in, and reacted accordingly. With haste, they brought their slaves and cattle inside, while those who had not taken to heart the warning (*lo'-sâm libbô*) left both out in the fields.

22-26 Again Moses performed the task allotted to him. He used his staff in the same way as Aaron had done with some of the previous signs (8:6; 8:17), and thunder, hail and lightning came as the Lord had predicted. On other occasions in the Old Testament, thunder and lightning are presented as part of a theophany (Exod. 20:18; Deut. 5:23-25; 1 Sam. 12:18). The creator was in control of all the elements, and displayed His power in utilising them for His own purposes. They were His instruments of judgment, so that everything outside – men, animals, crops, and trees – were all struck down. From the foundation of the nation of Egypt no previous occurrence like this was ever known to have happened. Once more the Goshen region, home to the Israelites, was spared for the moment. Sovereign grace was shown to the undeserving. The Israelites were no better than the Egyptians, but God's choice in love spared them (Deut. 7:7-8).

27-28 The storm elicited from Pharaoh a grudging admission: 'This time I have sinned.' For a third time he promised submission, acknowledging that the Lord was in the right, while he and his people were in the wrong. From the sequel the reader knows that a confession of being guilty did not change his heart and behaviour. The loss of servants, livestock and crops had brought him to this point. He and his people had had enough rain and hail, so he asked for prayer to the Lord. As on previous occasions, he promised that if this divine action ceased, he would let the Israelites go, and in addition there was no need for Moses and Aaron to continue their audience with him.

29-30 No indication is given of the location of Pharaoh's residence. It was simply in 'the city', indicating that he had a palace there.[21] It could have been any one of a number of cities. Moses commits himself to spreading out his hands to the LORD (*'efros 'et-kappî el yhwh*). This is one way in which prayerful action is described in the Old Testament (for other instances, see 1 Kings 8:22, 38-39; Ezra 9:5; Ps. 44:20). The word for 'hands' is strictly the palms of the hands, which may show that hands were facing upward when prayer was made, indicating the one praying was seeking to receive blessing from God. The purpose of the prayer on this occasion was to ensure that the rain and hail ceased, and to bring about a true realisation that the earth belonged to the LORD. The wording here (Heb. *layhwh hâ'ârets*) is exactly the same as the opening verse of Psalm 24, a declaration that Israel's LORD was the creator to whom the whole world belonged. Pharaoh was dealing not only with Israel's God, but the one who had the entire world in His hands. Even though some of the people were earlier said to fear God (v. 20), Moses knew that there was no genuine repentance on the part of Pharaoh or his officials. In saying this he anticipated the actions of Pharaoh that were to follow.

31-32 These verses form a parenthesis that explains what happened to specific crops when the hail fell. The flax and the barley were destroyed, but the wheat and the rye were not. 'Flax' (*pishtâh*) was a well-known crop in Egypt from about 4000 B.C. After soaking, it went through a long drying process before it could be used to manufacture linen (cf. the account of Rahab hiding the Hebrew spies under the flax on the roof, Josh. 2:6). 'Barley' (*sᵉ'orâh*) and 'wheat' (*chittâh*) were the two main crops in Egypt, as they were later for the people in Israel. The other grain that was not destroyed, *kussémet*, is variously translated in the English versions. RSV, NASB, NIV, NRSV all opt for 'spelt', but the AV 'rie' [rye] may well have

---

21. The Heb. text has *kᵉtsê'tî 'et hâ'îr*, 'having gone out from the city'. This is an example of an accusative (marked by the use of object marker, *'et*) indicating the place from which a person departs. Another example occurs in v. 33. For the grammar, see *IBHS*, p. 169-70, §10.2.2b.

been closer to the mark. The word only occurs three times in the Old Testament (here and in Isa. 28:25, and Ezek. 4:9). The Gezer calendar, dated from about 900 B.C., helps by setting out the agricultural year in Israel, and three lines are very apposite to these verses in Exodus. They are:

> the month of hoeing the flax
> the month of reaping barley
> the month of reaping [wheat] and measuring.[22]

The beginning of the year was the flax harvest, which means that the barley crop was gathered in May, while the wheat was a month later in June. Here the point was that the hail destroyed the early crops, but not the two that were late in ripening.[23] While the early crops were destroyed, yet there would be food for the Egyptians from the later ones.

33 No explanation is given of why Moses had to leave Pharaoh's presence before he prayed.[24] It could be because the impact of the hail was far greater out in the fields rather than in a township location.[25] Moses did as he had already indicated to Pharaoh, and the narrative describes his mode of praying as in verse 29 ('he spread out his hands to the LORD'). The result was that the thunder and hail came to an end, as also the rain that was pouring down on the country. This is the first indication that rain (*mâtâr*) was an associated happening, though the verb for 'rain' (*mâtar*) was used in verse 23 ('So the LORD *rained* hail').

34-35 The cessation of this particular sign caused another change for Pharaoh. Again his rebelliousness asserted itself, and he sinned once more (for Pharaoh's previous admission of sin, see v. 27). More was needed than a miracle of this nature to change his attitude and influence his actions. Ultimately

---

22. For the full text, see J. C. L. Gibson, *Textbook of Syrian Semitic Inscriptions, Vol. I, Hebrew and Moabite Inscriptions* (Oxford: Clarendon Press, 1971), pp. 1-4.

23. The Heb. word describing the wheat and rye is *'âfîl*, 'late [ripening]'. This is its only occurrence in biblical Hebrew.

24. The Heb. text employs a double preposition to denote Moses' departure from Pharaoh; lit. "Moses went out *from with* (*mê'im*) Pharaoh'. Such a doubled preposition is fairly common in Heb.

25. This is suggested by John L. Mackay, *Exodus* (Fearn: Christian Focus Publications, 2001), p. 178.

it would be a work of God's Spirit that would bring him to the point of permitting the exodus to occur (see 12:31-32). The sin of Pharaoh and his officials was that they hardened their hearts. Sin often provokes reactions like this. With steely resolve Pharaoh refused to countenance any departure of the Israelites, and in so doing fulfilled the word of the LORD delivered through Moses (cf. 4:21; 7:4, 13).

9 The Ninth Sign: Locusts (10:1-20)

1-2 Another stage in the prolonged process of exiting Egypt was reached when the LORD issued a new instruction to Moses. The hearts of Pharaoh and his officials had been hardened by the LORD (the verb used is the causative of *kâvêd*, Hi.) for three stated reasons. The first was that He could manifest His power by His manner of dealing with the Egyptians[26] and by the miraculous signs.[27] The second was that succeeding generations would be able to communicate the knowledge of these events to children and grandchildren. Transmission of the LORD's deeds was an important responsibility of adults in the Israelite community (see the principle exhibited in Exod. 12:24-28; Deut. 6:20-25; and Ps. 78:1-8). The third reason was that the Israelites might know indeed that it was the LORD who had performed all these actions. The miracles were a form of revelation intended to show God's presence and power.

3 As on previous occasions, Moses and Aaron went on a joint delegation to Pharaoh. The announcement they made, 'Thus says the LORD, the God of the Hebrews ...', was again in the form of a solemn declaration, such as the prophets often made in later periods of Israel's history. The message commenced with a query about how long Pharaoh was going to refuse to let the Hebrews go. The LORD's demand was reiterated in the same format as on several previous occasions (7:16; 8:1, 20; 9:1, 13).

4-6 Failure to comply would bring swarming locusts by the next day. The word used here for 'locusts' (*'arbeh*) is,

---

26. The Heb. verb is *'âlal*, Hitpo. When used with persons, this verb has the idea of dealing harshly or abusively with them. See *DCH*, VI, p. 426.

27. The verb used is *shît*, that here has the meaning of 'perform' (*DCH*, VIII, p. 343, §16(2)e). In some of its semantic range it cannot be distinguished from *sîm*. Cf. its use in v. 2 with an identical meaning.

strictly speaking, the adult locust, though it is often used as a generic term. The threatened consequences of refusal would be an influx of locusts that would cover the ground, eat all plants and trees, and fill the houses of everyone, both officials and ordinary people. Such invasions of locusts are well attested from ancient times, and still occur. What was even more pointed about the threat is that the damage was going to be far greater than had ever been known. Going back even to the establishment of Egypt, this sign was unmatched in all its past history.

7-8 At that point Pharaoh's officials intruded into the discussion. They questioned concerning the length of time that Pharaoh would allow Moses to be a snare (*moqêsh*) to the Egyptians, that is, a hindrance to them. In referring to Moses, they speak of him simply as 'this [man]' (*zeh*). There is nothing derogatory in this expression, as this demonstrative pronoun simply picks up the implied references to Moses. They were prepared to deal with the problem of the Israelites in the way that Moses and Aaron wanted. Rather than see their country destroyed,[28] they wanted Pharaoh to grant the request and so send the people away. Moses and Aaron were brought back to Pharaoh (*shûv*, Ho.), implying that he had sent for them to return to him. He expressed willingness to let the people go so that they could serve 'the LORD your God'. Like other rulers in the Old Testament, he acknowledged who the God of the Israelites was, without himself being committed in faith to the same God (cf. the case of Cyrus, 2 Chron. 36:23; Ezra 1:2). All he wanted to know was exactly who was going. The expression used here in the Hebrew text (*mî vâmî*, lit. 'who and who') is a way of emphasising the question as to 'just who' (NIV) was going.

9 Moses' reply indicated that it was not to be only an exclusive group but rather a very mixed assembly of both sexes and ages who would go out to worship the LORD. He noted that it was to be a feast (*chag*) to the LORD that they celebrated. The word 'feast' indicated a religious festival or holiday. Its

---

28. The verb used to describe the condition of Egypt is '*âvad*, 'to perish, be destroyed'. One of its most frequent uses is to describe divine judgment against nations. Having just mentioned 'the LORD their God', the implication is that Pharaoh's servants recognised the hand of God in the events that were taking place.

most frequent use in the Old Testament is for the pilgrimage feasts of Passover, the Weeks, and the Tabernacles (cf. the related Arabic word *hajj*, to denote pilgrimage to Mecca).

10-11 Pharaoh's response was a sarcastic declaration. Yes, the Israelites, young and old, could go with the help of their God, the LORD (*yhwh*), but look out, for trouble was round the corner. The NIV text and margin capture well two differing interpretations of the final part of the verse. The renderings are either, 'Clearly you are bent on evil', or, 'be careful, trouble is in store for you'. Of these, the second one is preferable. As they were later to experience, the forces available to Pharaoh were very considerable (see 14:5-9). Permission to go and worship in the desert was not to be understood as freeing them from Pharaoh's power. A partial response to Moses' and Aaron's request was permission for the worship to be exclusively for males (NIV, 'Have only the men go'). That was clearly unsatisfactory, as it would leave the women and children still in bondage. Once Pharaoh had given his declaration, Moses and Aaron were dismissed from Pharaoh's presence. They didn't just leave, but were summarily expelled from his presence (lit. *vayᵉgâresh 'otâm mê'êt pᵉnê'y par'oh*, 'he drove them out from Pharaoh's presence').

12-15 The LORD's instruction followed the pattern of the previous signs. Moses was to stretch out his hand, and the locusts would come up and eat all that was growing in Egypt and what was left from the destruction by the hail. The effect of Moses' action in this case was for an east wind to blow all that day and all that night, bringing with it locusts to every part of the land. They covered the ground making it appear dark, and devoured all the crops in the fields, and all the fruit on the trees. This is the only occasion on which the verb 'to be dark' (*châshak*) occurs in Old Testament prose. Normally it is in poetic contexts, often denoting judgment and curse. Nothing that was green was left throughout Egypt, and this occurrence had no precedents, nor would there be any repetition of it in the future (v. 14).

16-17 Having sent Moses and Aaron away a little while previously, Pharaoh was forced to recall them. This he did speedily (lit. 'he hastened to call Moses and Aaron'), as he recognised that this sign was another demonstration of the

LORD's power. His confession of sin was the same as earlier (see 9:27), though now he added that he had sinned against Moses and Aaron as well. Presumably this meant that he realised that he was guilty in not recognising them as truly being the LORD's servants. What he wanted was forgiveness and the removal of his sin. 'Only', he asked, 'take this death away from me' (v. 17).[29]

18-19 Moses left Pharaoh's presence and went and prayed.[30] The outcome was that the LORD changed the wind direction. A strong sea breeze (*ruach yâm châzâq*) developed from the west, and carried the locusts towards the Red Sea. This is the first time that the Hebrew expression, *yâm sûf*, occurs. The expression simply means 'sea of rushes',[31] and it is used of the body of water that the Israelites crossed when they came out of Egypt (probably the Bitter Lakes or Lake Timsah, Exod. 14:21-22), but also of the Gulf of Suez (Num. 33:10-11) and of the Gulf of Aqaba (1 Kings 9:26). Here the record says that the locusts were carried *towards* the *yâm sûf*, which may well mean that not all of them were carried *into* the sea. The removal of them was so complete that not one was left anywhere in Egypt. Once more the LORD not only controlled nature by the use of the wind, but He exercised His sovereign power over Pharaoh. The wording regarding the LORD hardening his heart is identical with that in 9:12.

10 The Tenth Sign: Darkness (10:21-29)

Another dramatic sign brought darkness over all Egypt. Like the earlier signs of gnats (8:16-19) and boils (9:8-12), this one was unannounced, and was without any reference to Moses and Aaron appearing before Pharaoh.

21-23 Moses was instructed to stretch out his hand heavenwards, so that deep darkness would come over the land. This was to be so thick, that one could feel it. The verb

---

29. The NIV disregards the Heb. word *raq*, 'only'. Other versions attempt to translate it: cf. NKJV, 'Entreat the LORD your God, that He may take away from me this death *only*'; NRSV, 'Pray to the LORD your God that *at the least* he remove this deadly thing from me'.

30. The MT has simply: 'And he went out' (*vayyêtsê*). Some of the early versions (LXX, Syriac, Vulgate) insert 'Moses' as the subject, which is undoubtedly right.

31. This is the preferred translation of the phrase (see, *DCH*, VI, p. 134).

for 'feel' (*mâshash*, Hi.) is rare. If the translation 'feel darkness' is correct, then it is use of graphic imagery in attempting to say how dense the darkness was. The other alternative is taking the verb to refer to the resulting need to grope to find one's way in the dark (cf. this usage in Deut. 28:29; Job 5:14; 12:25), which also gives a satisfactory meaning. When Moses stretched out his hand, 'deep darkness' came over the land for three days. The expression 'deep darkness' is an attempt to translate the combination in Hebrew of two words for darkness (*chóshek* and *'afêlâh*). So serious was this darkness that not another person could be seen (lit. 'a man did not see his brother'), and it prevented people from going out-of-doors. Once more the principle of divine election was demonstrated, in that this sign was not applied to where the Israelites were living in Goshen. They, as God's people, did not have to walk in darkness but had God's light.

24 The statement in the previous verse that the darkness lasted three days, and no one could leave their place, has to be understood in a general and not in an absolute way. Pharaoh sent for Moses to come during that period, and probably Aaron with him.[32] Pharaoh relented, up to a point. He was willing that the Israelites should go out into the desert to worship, even taking their children with them.[33] However, flocks and herds had to stay behind. He rightly reasoned that if the whole Hebrew community, with their animals, went out, this would not be merely a worship time but a full exodus from Egypt.

25-26 The intent of Moses' reply is obscured by some of the English translations. Rather than render the opening words by, 'You must allow us to have sacrifices and burnt offerings' (NIV), what is needed is a more literal translation, 'You must also give into our hand sacrifices and burnt offerings' (NASB mg.). The point is that Moses was indicating that Pharaoh himself (the word 'you' is emphatic, *'attâh*) must provide some of the content of the sacrifices. He had to give it into

---

32. Two Heb. manuscripts, the LXX, and the Vulgate add that Aaron was also summoned before Pharaoh.

33. The NIV has, 'Even your women and children may go with you', but the Heb. text does not include the word 'women'. Presumably the NIV translators reasoned that the children would not be able to do this unless the mothers were with them.

Moses' hand (*gam-'attâh tittên beyâdênû*), an idiomatic way in Hebrew of saying to hand something over into the possession of someone else.[34] The offerings were going to be sacrifices (*z^evâkîm*) that were partially eaten by the worshippers, and burnt-offerings (*'olôt*) that were entirely consumed by fire. It was also necessary for the cattle and small animals (the word *tso'n* denotes sheep and/or goats) to be taken, as some of them would also be needed. The further explanation was that until they were out in the desert they would not know what other sacrificial animals they would need.

27-29 Once more the text indicates that the sovereign hand of God was in the whole affair and on this further occasion he hardened Pharaoh's heart (the same language is used as 9:12 and 10:20). He remained obstinate, refusing to send the people away. Moses was summarily dismissed from his presence, with the warning that he had to take care lest he come back before him again. A return to Pharaoh's court and presence would result in death. The reference to '*the day* you see my face' is simply a Hebrew way of saying 'when ...' The expression 'just as you say' (*kên dibbartâ*) in Moses' response to this stipulation is only found in two other passages in the Old Testament (Num. 27:7; 36:5). It denotes that Moses thought that Pharaoh had spoken what was right (*kên* is thus to be taken as an adjective here; cf. *DCH*, IV, p. 434).

Study Questions

1) These three signs are related in much greater detail than the earlier ones. Can you suggest any reason for this?

2) Does 9:20 imply that some of the Egyptians were by now convinced that the Israelites' God was indeed the living God and the one judging their ruler and their country?

3) Pharaoh was willing to confess he had sinned against the Lord (10:16). What was missing in this confession?

4) Sacrifice of animals was going to be a major part of Israelite religion as set out in the covenant at Sinai. Had

---

34. A good note on this can be found in Victor Hamilton, *Exodus*, p. 161.

it been significant up to this point in their history, or was it a new element?

11. The Eleventh Sign: The Death of the Firstborn (11:1–12:30)
The final sign related in chapters 11 and 12 was the most serious of God's judgments, for it involved all the Egyptian families and touched them deeply by taking the lives of all their firstborn, whether human or animal (12:29). It also involved the institution of the Passover celebration, the regulations for which are set out in Exodus 12:1-30, 43-51, and Deuteronomy 16:1-8.

i) Judgment Announced (11:1-10)
1 Further directions were given to Moses relating to the final smiting of the Egyptians (the Heb. text says '*ôd néga' 'echâd*, 'still one blow'). This was to be inflicted on Pharaoh and the whole land. The use of the Hebrew word *nega'* points to divinely inflicted punishment, and this is the only time it occurs in the narrative here in Exodus. The assurance was given that on this occasion the result would be release of the Israelites, with Pharaoh driving them out completely (the same verb, *gârash*, Pi., is used as in 6:1).[35]

2-3 Reference had already been made to the fact that the Israelites would not leave Egypt empty-handed (see comment on 3:21-22). Moses was to instruct both men and women to ask for vessels of silver and gold. These actions go back to a promise made to Abraham, that his people would leave the land of servitude 'with great possessions' (Gen. 15:14). This should not be understood to mean that the Israelites deceived the Egyptians, borrowing things they knew would never be returned. Rather, God caused the Egyptians to pity them (Ps. 106:46), so that the general populace of Egypt was quite willing to admit that their slaves had been ill-treated and that the God of Israel had been directly involved in the miraculous

---

35. There are difficulties in this verse especially around the word often rendered 'completely' (*kâlâh*). It is normally taken to be the verb *kâlâh*, or an adverb from it, though some have suggested it is the noun, 'a bride'. This latter suggestion does not seem to fit the context, and therefore the common rendering 'completely' is more feasible. For explanations, see Victor Hamilton, *Exodus*, p. 166, and Walter Kaiser Jr., 'Exodus', p. 370.

events that had occurred.³⁶ By God's own action, the attitude of the Egyptians was altered so that they were sympathetic to the Israelites. The attitude towards Moses himself was also a factor, God giving him favour in the eyes of the officials and the people.³⁷ The account of the actual asking for articles is given in 12:35-36.

4-6 No indication is given here of the person to whom Moses was speaking, but it is clear from the plural verbal form in verse 7 (*têdeʻûn*, 2 pl. m., 'that you (pl.) may know') and from verse 8 (*kol ʻavâdekâ*, 'all your officials') that it was to Pharaoh. The final judgment was not to be a further distortion in regard to nature (the Nile, insects, hail, locusts, etc.) but a direct attack upon the children and animals of the Egyptians. Every firstborn son, and all the firstborn among the cattle, were to die. The time when it would happen is said to be the middle of the night, without any explanation why this time was chosen. No exception was to be made among the Egyptians. It did not matter what social standing anyone had. From the ruler, the Pharaoh, to the humblest female slave working at her millstone, the same divine visitation would take place, causing such an outcry as had never occurred, nor would occur in the future. It is significant that the word for 'wailing' or 'outcry' (*tseʻâqâh*) is used of the response to this judgment. It occurred earlier of Israel's cry to God (3:7, 9). Now it is the Egyptians who cry in their distress, but there will be no relief for them.

7 God's sovereignty, and also His compassion for the enslaved Israelites, would be manifested in an appointed distinction between them and their captors. The same language is used here as in 8:23 and 9:4 (all these passages use the verb, *pâlâh*, Hi., 'to make a distinction'). What is notable here is the reference to the absence of barking dogs in the Israelite communities.³⁸ Presumably the idea is that with no

---

36. For a discussion of the moral issues in these happenings, see Walter Kaiser Jr., *Hard Sayings of the Old Testament*, pp. 69-71.

37. The idiom here, *vayittên yhwh ʼet chên hâʻâm beʻênê mitsrâyim*, 'and God gave the people favour in the eyes of the Egyptians', is very similar to what is said about Noah. Of him it is said, *venoach mâtsâʼ chên beʻênê yhwh*, 'and Noah found favour in the eyes of the Lord' (Gen. 6:8).

38. The MT has *yecherats kélev leshono*, 'a dog will not sharpen his tongue'.

crying out of people in this community, no dog would be disturbed and begin to bark.

8 It is clear now that Moses was addressing Pharaoh throughout this speech, as he speaks to him directly regarding the changed attitude of his officials. What was going to happen was spelt out to him, for his officials would reach the point where they would go looking for Moses in order to tell him to get out of the country, along with all his followers.[39] After doing obeisance before Moses, the officials will tell him to get out of the land along with his followers.[40] Following that, Moses gave the assurance that he would leave. At that point of the interview, the relationship between Moses and Pharaoh was so strained that Moses went out in anger. This can be understood as an expression of God's anger, or of Moses' anger at the stubborn sinfulness of the Egyptians.[41]

9-10 These verses form a summary statement of what had happened.[42] Moses was warned by the LORD as to the outcome of his mission, and the necessity of wonders to convince Pharaoh to release the Israelites (see 3:19-20, and for the words for 'wonders', the comments on 4:21). Moses and Aaron had performed[43] all these before Pharaoh, but his heart was so hardened by the LORD that he still refused to permit any exodus of the Israelites from his land.

ii) Preparations for the Passover (12:1-13)

The significance of this final sign is heightened by the instructions regarding the institution of the Passover celebration that are given in 12:1–13:16.[44] The first Passover

---

39. The MT has 'will come *down* (*yârad*) to me'. The use of 'come down' may reflect the position that Pharaoh's palace was elevated, or that Goshen was low-lying in comparison to other parts of Egypt.

40. 'Followers' is the translation of most English versions of the Heb. *b^eraglekâ*, 'at your feet'. *DCH*, VII, p. 412, cites this passage, along with others, for the meaning, 'at one's foot, i.e. following one'.

41. For the first interpretation, see J. L. Mackay, *Exodus*, p. 199, and for the second, Walter Kaiser Jr., 'Exodus', p. 424.

42. The NIV rightly translates the first verb in v. 9 as a pluperfect, *vayyo'mer yhwh*, 'And the LORD had said'. For the grammatical point, see *IBHS*, pp. 552-53, §33.2.3.

43. Again the pluperfect is needed, not the simple perfect as in the NIV.

44. I have discussed the Passover in *NIDOTTE*, 4, pp. 1043-46.

differed from all later ones, in that it was kept *in anticipation* of God's deliverance of His people from bondage in Egypt. Many of the detailed instructions parallel those concerning the sacrificial offerings, but it is also expressly stated that it was 'a Passover sacrifice to the LORD' (*zevach-hû'layhwh*, 12:27). Several things were unique about the first celebration. For example, as there were no Aaronic priests at that time, 'all the elders of Israel' had to select the animals and kill them (12:21). Also, the first Passover was eaten hurriedly as if departure from Egypt was to take place immediately (12:11), and it was observed at 'twilight' whereas later celebrations were in daylight (12:6).[45] All later celebrations were kept *in remembrance* of that deliverance. The various elements of the feast, such as the unleavened bread and the bitter herbs, were connected with Israel's slavery in Egypt. The ritual of the Passover also served to function as a teaching ministry, for there was a recital of the redemptive history, with attention drawn to God's sparing the households of the Israelites when He struck down the first-born of the Egyptians. This section of Exodus contains the fullest explanation of the Passover celebration, though later revelation supplements it (see, Exod. 34:25; Lev. 23:5-8; Num. 9:1-14; 28:16-25; Deut. 16:1-8; Josh. 5:10-11; 2 Chronicles 30:1-27; 2 Kings 23:21-23 compared with 2 Chron. 35:1-19; Ezek. 45:21-24; Ezra 6:19-22).[46]

It is difficult to determine accurately how frequently and precisely in accordance with the law it was observed owing to the paucity of references to it in the Old Testament text. Immediately Israel entered into Canaan, they kept the Passover (Josh. 5:10-11), while it appears from 2 Chronicles 8:13 that Solomon kept it throughout his reign (cf. 1 Kings 9:25, though the Passover is not specifically named).[47] During the reforms instituted by Hezekiah and Josiah, the Passover

---

45. The term 'twilight' translates the Hebrew *bên hâ'arbâyim*, 'between the evenings'. Presumably this meant between sunset and darkness, and hence 'twilight' seems a suitable translation.

46. For a discussion of all these passages, see T. D. Alexander, 'The Passover', in Roger T. Beckwith and Martin J. Selman, edd., *Sacrifice in the Bible* (Grand Rapids: Baker Book House, 1995), pp. 6-18.

47. This depends on linking the Feast of Unleavened Bread with the Passover. See the later discussion on Exod. 12:17-20.

celebration was central and also of unparalleled extravagance (cf. 2 Kings 18:6 with 2 Chron. 30:1-27, and 2 Kings 23:21-23 with 2 Chron. 35:1). After the exile, the religious festivals were again kept, seemingly with normality (Ezra 6:19-22).

1-4 These verses commence the section that gives the fullest directions relating to the Passover. It was to be a seven-day festival starting on the 14th day of the month Abib. Four days previously the head of each household had to take a young lamb or kid (the Heb. word *seh* can refer either to a lamb or kid; *DCH*, VIII, pp. 116-18). A calculation had to be made as to how much each person would eat before a particular animal was chosen. A small family could share the animal with nearby neighbours, thereby demonstrating the communal nature of this festival.

5-7 The provisions regarding the type of animal selected parallel those relating to other sacrifices, especially the specification that the chosen victim had to be without blemish (cf. Exod. 29:1; Lev. 1:3, 10; 3:1, 6-7; 9:3). The English phrase 'without blemish' represents the Hebrew adjective *tâmîm* that comes from a root meaning 'to be complete'. Its use placed a limit on the animal that could be chosen, as only a perfect or unblemished one was acceptable to God (Lev. 22:21-22). After the exile, among the sinful practices in Israel was the offering of blemished, diseased or crippled animals (Mal. 1:6-14). This provision of unblemished animals was part of Old Testament typology that directed attention to the nature of Jesus' offering of Himself 'without blemish or defect' (1 Pet. 1:19). It is expressly said that the animal could be from among the sheep or goats, and it was to be kept for four days before it was slaughtered. Probably this period of four days was to give time to ensure that no blemish was found on any animal. After being killed, some blood of the animals was used for ritual purposes on the houses where the Passover meal was taken. It was sprinkled on the top and sides of the doorframes. When previously God differentiated between the Israelites and the Egyptians (8:22-23; 9:5-7, 26), no special ritual was involved. Now, the difference is made by the marking of the Israelite homes with sacrificial blood, which was responsible for the safety of their firstborn. Substitutionary atonement was God's provision for them.

8-10 Another aspect of the Passover was that the sacrifice was itself eaten by the people. In this regard, the Passover resembled the peace or fellowship offerings, in which, after the prescribed parts of the animal were burned on the altar,[48] the rest was eaten by the offerer, family members, and friends. The Passover animal was roasted whole by fire. The word here for 'roasted' (*tsâlî*) is exceedingly rare, occurring only here and in Isaiah 44:16. The animal could neither be eaten raw, nor boiled in water. No indication is given why 'bitter herbs' (*mâror*) were included, or the reason of the link between them and 'flatbread' (*mâtstsôt*). 'Bitter herbs' such as chicory and endive were found in Egypt, and probably denoted the suffering the people had endured there. The use of flat bread is normally explained by the need for haste that precluded long preparation time for making bread with yeast. However, the lamb was prepared four days before the Passover, thus giving plenty of time for bread-making. Hence, no sure answer can be given why the bread had to be without yeast. The Passover was a feast for believing Israel, and due care had to be taken lest any of the feast be eaten by animals, or by those who were not entitled to share in it (v. 10).

11 The contents of the Passover feast having been given, the manner of partaking of it is set out. The cloak had to be tied up so that it did not impede walking or running (Heb. 'your loins girded'). The sandals had to be on their feet and the staff had to be already in their hand, both indicating that departure was imminent. No leisurely eating could take place but rather eating 'in haste' (*chipâzon*, only here, Deut. 16:3 and Isa. 52:12).

12-13 'Pass through' (*'âvar*) and 'pass over' (*pâsach*) are the dominant verbs in these verses. God announced to Moses and Aaron that He was going to 'pass through' the land, but 'pass over' the Israelites. He would strike all the firstborn, human and cattle, in Egypt, while no destroying blow (*négef l^emashchît*) would touch any on whose door-frames blood had been sprinkled. That blood was to be the indicator exempting people from judgment. The etymology of the verb

---

48. The parts burned were the fat around the intestines, the kidneys, the liver and the sheep's tail (Lev. 3:3-4). For a good summary of the requirements for the peace offerings, see the discussion by G. L. Carr in *TWOT*, 2, pp. 931-32.

'pass over' is debated,[49] though in the context it describes the way whereby God gifted salvation to the Israelites. God's passing through the land involved passing over them and their families. Salvation was God's provision. 'The destroyer' (so-called in v. 23, *hâmmashchît*) was none other than God Himself, and the judgment reached as far as the Egyptian gods (v. 12). The impotence of these gods has already been demonstrated in connection with the earlier signs, but now in this case the announcement of judgment is accompanied by another declaration, 'I am the LORD (*yhwh*)', that recalls the triple occurrence of this assertion in 6:6-8. Judgment and salvation are both His prerogatives.

iii) Preparations for the Unleavened Bread (12:14-20)
14 It is declared that 'this day' was to be a reminder (*zikkârôn*) for generations to come. The expression 'this day' probably incorporates all the events associated with the exodus, as the various things that happened were all intertwined. It was to be a festival to the LORD.[50] The description of it as a lasting ordinance (*chukkat 'ôlâm*) reinforces the importance of the Passover for succeeding generations. Until replaced by the Lord's Supper it was an annual remembrance of God's redeeming activity on behalf of His enslaved people (cf. 1 Cor. 5:7, 'For Christ, our Passover lamb, has been sacrificed').

15-16 The Passover festival was not just a short ceremony on one evening. Rather, it was a weeklong celebration during which *mâtstsôt* were exclusively the permitted bread (see comment on v. 8). At the start of the Passover week, all yeast had to be removed from the houses, with the penalty for disobedience on this matter stated as being cut off from Israel. Some suggest that this meant only exclusion from Israel, but other passages point to it being a reference to capital punishment (see Lev. 17:10; 20:3, 5, 6). Whichever

---

49. *DCH*, VI, p. 723, for example, lists four different verbs with the same consonants: *pâsach* I, 'to pass over'; *pâsach* II, 'to limp'; *pâsach* III, 'to protect'; *pâsach* IV 'to push, run into'. Certainly I and III are not contradictory, for protection was provided through the sprinkled blood. See also the discussion by Victor Hamilton, *Exodus*, pp. 184-86.

50. The MT says, 'And you shall celebrate it (the day) a festival to the Lord'. This involves the use of a cognate accusative (*chaggotem chag*), a construction fairly common in Hebrew but not in English.

the penalty, the point was made of how seriously the people had to take the Lord's directions for the Passover. A solemn assembly marked the Passover celebration on the first and also the closing day of the week. The word for solemn assembly (*miqrâ'*) denotes a called gathering of the people.⁵¹ No work was permissible on these two specific days, except for necessary preparation of food. This meant that these two 'sabbath' days were not to be kept so strictly as the ordinary Sabbath.

17 The Feast of Unleavened Bread was going to be an annual reminder of God's redemption of His people from their slavery. In exiting Egypt, Israel was not a rabble but an organised body in military-like divisions (see commentary on 6:26 and 7:4). The phrase 'this very day' (*be'étsem hayyôm hazzeh*) has, like 'this day' in verse 14, to be understood as a reference to the whole period, for the exodus had not yet occurred. Twice in this verse the NIV has the verb 'celebrate', but here it is not the verb used in verse 14 (*châgag*), but rather the verb 'to keep' (*shâmar*). The use of this latter verb is important as it is used of paying careful attention especially to things like covenantal obligations (Gen. 18:19; Exod. 20:6). The expression is unusual in that it simply says 'Keep the unleavened bread', whereas 'feast of unleavened bread' would be expected.⁵² The phrase 'a lasting ordinance for generations to come' is an exact repetition of the same phrase in verse 14.

18-20 These verses reinforce the description of yeast-free houses that was introduced in verses 8 and 15, and add some new further particulars, while not repeating some of those already given (e.g., the selection of the lamb on the tenth day of the month). The time of commencement for the celebration is stated very explicitly: 'In the first month ... from the evening of the fourteenth day until the evening of the twenty-first day' (v. 18). That week had to be a period when no yeast

---

51. It is derived from the verb *qârâ'*, 'to call', and later in the OT it came to designate reading of the Scriptures or even the Scripture itself (Neh. 8:8).

52. The Samaritan Pentateuch and the LXX both have a reading that is the result of changing one letter in the word for unleavened bread (*hammitsvâh* instead of *matstsôt*), yielding a translation 'keep the commandment'. Since no Hebrew manuscript has this reading, it should not be accepted.

was in the houses. Two different words for yeast are used in this chapter. In verse 15 *châmêts* occurs, while in verse 19 *se'or* appears. Possibly *châmêts* refers to something that has been leavened, such as bread, while *se'or* is the leavening agent.[53] The verb from which *châmêts* comes appears in this same verse to describe anything leavened with yeast (*machmétset*, Hi. part. fem. sing. of *châmats*). An important addition here is the reference to the penalty of being cut off from Israel being imposed on anyone transgressing this regulation, whether an alien (*gêr*) or native inhabitant (*'ezrach hâ'ârets*). This is significant as it shows that non-Israelites, i.e., Gentiles, could participate in this festival, and they must also have been included in the mixed group of people who left Egypt (see v. 38). Later, when Solomon dedicated the temple he asked that God would hear the prayer of the foreigner (the *gêr*) who came to pray at the temple (1 Kings 8:41-43). The final verse in the section reiterates the requirement that no one was to eat any leavened bread at this time, no matter where they lived (lit. 'in all your residences').

iv) The Passover Celebration (12:21-28)
21 The stage had been reached when Moses had to implement the instructions that he had already been given. He proceeded to gather the people and to pass on God's requirements: 'Go at once and select the animals for your families ....' (NIV) The initial clause in the NIV appears to accept a possible emendation of the Hebrew text (*mish^ekû ûq^echû lâkem tso'n*), 'draw out and take you a lamb' (AV). The problem is the first verb (*mâshak*)[54] that appears normally to mean 'to drag', 'to pull [off, along, away]'. Significantly, this verb appears here in parallel with the verb 'to take' (*lâqach*), and probably should be translated as 'pull out [from the flock]'. This gives good sense without having to resort to emending it to the verb 'to hasten' (*mâhar*).[55] The instruction, then, is to 'draw and take from the flock for yourselves animals'. The earlier instructions had made provision for joint sacrifices if the

---

53. This is the view taken by John Hartley in *NIDOTTE*, 2, p. 181.
54. Not to be confused with the verb *mâshach*, to 'anoint'.
55. This is the way that DCH, V, p. 523, takes this verb.

numbers were too small in any household (v. 4). Now they had to select out, take, and kill the Passover lamb.[56]

22-23 The additional instructions specify how the blood was to be applied to the door-frames of the houses. Hyssop, after being dipped into the blood in a bowl, was to be used to mark the door-frames of their houses. The word 'hyssop' (*'êzôv*) is used ten times in the Old Testament, normally in connection with sacrificial acts.[57] Using the hyssop, the blood of the sacrifice was to be applied to the top and sides of the door frames. When that had been done, no one was to venture outside lest they be smitten by the angel of death (see 12:12). The danger was that they would be confronted by the destroying angel, who was not permitted to enter the houses to inflict judgment there (v. 23).

24-25 These stipulations were for Israel as she left Egypt and entered the land of Canaan, the land that God promised by oath to Abraham (Gen. 15:18-21; 17:8). That they related not just to the immediate time is made plain by the words 'a lasting ordinance to you and your descendants' (*l^echoq l^ekâ ûlevânekâ 'ad 'ôlâm*). Until the anti-type appeared (Christ's sacrifice), the type (the Passover) would persist. The people had to take care that they kept this divinely instituted act of worship.

26-28 The didactic aspect of the Passover was an important element, for it was a teaching tool, especially for the children. In future, children, when present at the Passover, would ask questions about its significance. They would say: 'What is this worship to you?' That is, 'for you, what is the meaning of this ritual?' The reply to be given was important, since it designated this ritual as a sacrifice:[58] 'It is the Passover

---

56. The same Heb. word, pésach, can designate either the individual lamb or the Passover festival (2 Kings 23:21).

57. The botanical identification of hyssop is uncertain. It may be *origanum maru* or *majorana syriaca*.

58. This is important, because in the discussions following the Reformation, in the face of Roman Catholic assertion of the Passover-Mass relationship, some of the Reformers got out of the dilemma by asserting that the Passover was not a sacrifice, and thereby the argument was invalid. However, the Scriptures make it plain that the Passover was indeed a sacrifice. They should simply have said the Passover pointed forward to Christ, and when He died on the Cross there was no longer any need for a further sacrifice.

sacrifice to the LORD'. The commemorative aspect was affirmed strongly. By this festival Israel had to recall how God passed over the houses of the Israelites, when He was striking down the Egyptians (see the comments on v. 13 in relation to the verb 'pass over'). Some interval of time has to be proposed between the instructions of Moses and Aaron to the elders of the people and the response of the people noted at the end of verse 27. The word from Moses and Aaron brought forth a worshipful attitude from the people. The combined expression, 'the people bowed ... worshipped', is a fixed one, with the verb 'bowed' (*qâdad*) always appearing with the verb 'worshipped' (*shâchâh*, Hitp.). The response of the people was devout and reverent (see the commentary on the earlier occurrence of this expression, 4:31). The concluding verse in this section (v. 28) is important, for it notes how the children of Israel did precisely what had been commanded them. As in the case of other sacrifices, precise instructions had to be followed as the Passover had a typological significance. The NIV is rather free in its rendering of this verse. A more literal translation brings out the meaning well: 'Then the children of Israel went away and did so; just as the LORD had commanded Moses and Aaron, so they did' (NKJV). Strict compliance was given to the instructions regarding the Passover.

Study Questions

1) In view of the experience of the Egyptians with the various judgments, how do we explain their favourable attitude to the Israelites?

2) Why was the Passover such a communal event for Israel?

3) The regulations for the Passover were very detailed. Was this partly to provoke questions in the minds of the Israelites concerning its significance?

4) The Passover was to be not just a celebration but also a teaching medium, especially for the children? Does this have any application for our celebration of the Lord's Supper?

v) Judgment on the Egyptians (12:29-32)
29-30 In the middle of the night the final sign was given. The LORD struck down all the first-born, this judgment touching all who did not have the blood sprinkled on the door-frame. From the highest in the land ('Pharaoh ... who sat upon the throne') down to the lowest ('the prisoner who was in the dungeon'), every home was affected. Realising something of what was happening, Pharaoh and his servants all got up and began wailing. Their grief was so very real to them. The wailing was but an outward expression of deep inward sorrow, not necessarily in repentance towards God, but because 'there was not a house without someone dead' (v. 30).

31-32 Sometime during that night Pharaoh sent for Moses and Aaron. His abrupt instruction was: 'Up! Go out from my people, you and Israel's sons; go, worship the LORD as you spoke'. 'Up' (*qûmû*, imper. 2 m. pl.) is frequently used, as here, with the meaning 'make a move, start, set out',[59] and also in combination with other imperatives (as in Gen. 19:14; 21:18, 27:19, 43; 44:4). Pharaoh had finally relented, and was prepared to see the people do the very thing they had been asking for, namely, to worship the LORD. In addition to the people, permission was granted to take their small animals and cattle. Further abrupt imperatives ('take ... and go') indicate Pharaoh's wish to be rid of the troublesome people. But before Moses and Aaron depart, he sought a blessing from them – 'and also bless me'. 'Also' (*gam*) has no great emphasis here, as it simply notes that the request is additional to blessings that would accrue to the Israelites.[60] While previously Pharaoh's requests for prayer were granted, on this occasion there is no indication that a blessing was given.

vi) The Exodus (12:33-42)
33-34 The opening of verse 33 has been translated differently by the English versions. The verb used of the Egyptians' attitude to Israel (*châzaq*, Qal.) has been the one used earlier in Exodus of God's actions in hardening Pharaoh's heart (see 4:21; 9:12;

---

59. *DCH*, VII, p. 224.
60. For the use of *gam*, see *IBHS*, p. 301, §16.3.5b.

10:20, 27; 11:10, but the verbal theme is in these instances the Pi. form). While several versions have 'urged', 'prevailed over' makes good sense.[61] Sensing further calamities ('lest we all die'), the Egyptian people wanted a swift exit for the Israelites. The usual bread had not been fully prepared, and so they took the prepared dough in kneading troughs that were carried on their shoulders.

35-36 These two verses record the fulfilment of what had been said earlier in 3:21-22 (see the commentary on these verses). His people followed Moses' directions, and they asked specifically for things made of silver and gold, and also for clothing. God had made the Egyptians amenable towards the Israelites (lit., 'the LORD gave grace to the people in the eyes of Egypt'), so that they acquiesced to their requests. Most English versions of verse 36 say that the Israelites 'plundered the Egyptians'. It is true that the verb used (*nâtsal*, Pi.) can refer to a victor taking spoil, yet in view of the earlier part of the verse, it is better to opt for a softer expression here, such as, 'they took the [offered] spoil from the Egyptians.'

37-39 The long journey to Canaan began when the Israelites set out on the night of the Passover. Leaving Rameses (see 1:11), they went to Succoth, probably a settlement near the Bitter Lakes. The number of men is stated as 600,000 on foot, accompanied by dependants.[62] The large numbers in the Old Testament do create a difficulty and various attempts have been made to explain them.[63] However, no alternative explanation has been accorded universal support, and the figures here and in Numbers, though large, are not inconceivable, and they are clearly intended as real figures.[64]

---

61. DCH, III, p. 185.

62. The NIV says, 'besides women and children', but the MT only says 'except from little children', using the Heb. word *taf*, that normally denotes young children.

63. See the discussions by R. E. D. Clark, 'The Large Numbers of the Old Testament', *JTVI*, 87 (1955), pp. 82-92; G. E. Mendenhall, 'The Census of Numbers 1 and 26', *JBL*, 77 (1958), pp. 52-56; J. W. Wenham, 'Large Numbers in the Old Testament', *TB* 18 (1967), pp. 19-53; G. J. Wenham, 'Additional Note on the Large Numbers', *Numbers* (Leicester: Inter-Varsity Press, 1981), pp. 60-66; David M. Fouts, 'A Defence of the Hyperbolic Interpretation of Large Numbers in the Old Testament', *JETS* 40, 3 (September, 1997), pp. 377-87; Victor Hamilton, *Exodus*, p. 194.

64. For good explanation of how such numbers could have grown from the seventy who came down into Egypt (Exod. 1:5), see John Currid, *Exodus*, vol. 1, p. 226.

In addition to the Israelites, the exodus from Egypt involved 'many other peoples' (MT, *'êrev rav*). This expression points to a large 'mixed company' that also made their exit.[65] These people could have also been slaves, who took the opportunity to escape along with the Israelites. Intermarriage might have been involved as well (see Num. 12:1 in reference to Moses' second wife being a Cushite). Extensive holdings of cattle and small animals were taken with them, as well as dough that was ready for baking unleavened bread. It was an indication of the haste with which the Israelites had left Egypt. Their sudden expulsion gave no time for leisurely baking, as they could not linger[66] to carry out food preparation.

40-42 These verses form a significant note concerning the total length of sojourn in Egypt, with the number of years being given twice (vv. 41-42). The LXX and the Samaritan Pentateuch both add 'and in the land of Canaan', thus reducing the time in Egypt to about 215 years. But the text here agrees in general both with the predicted 400 years contained in God's words to Abraham (Gen. 15:13) and with Paul's reference to 430 years in Galatians 3:17. Hence, there is no need to emend the MT by the addition of these additional words. Once again the phrase 'this very day' (see comment on v. 17) gives the indication of time, and it is repeated in verse 51. All the Israelites marched out as the LORD's army (*kol tsiv^e'ôt yhwh*) to worship and serve their warrior God (see 15:3). A play on a word occurs in verse 42. Just as the LORD kept watch over the Israelites (lit. 'a night of watch for the LORD', *lêl shimmurîm layhwh*) on the night when the destroyer passed through the land (vv. 23, 27, 29), so Israel was to keep watch on the night of the annual celebration of the Passover. The word used here for 'watch' or 'vigil' (*shimmur*) is not the normal word for a night watch (*'ashmûrâh/'ashmoret*), though these words come from the same root. This was to

---

65. The word *'êrev* appears to be derived from the verb *'ārav*, 'to mix'. It occurs more often in the prophetical books of Jeremiah and Ezekiel, and also denotes the foreigners in postexilic Judah (Neh. 13:3). See the entry in *DCH*, VI, p. 551. The Targum Onkelos made a connection with Num. 11:4, where the Heb. text has *hā'safsuf*, 'a rabble'.

66. The NIV 'did not have time' represents the Heb. verb *māhāh*, Hitpalp., 'linger, delay'.

be a perpetual vigil in honour of the LORD for all generations to come.

vii) The Passover Regulations (12:43-51)
12:43-45 Further instructions were given regarding the Passover, especially concerning those who were to be excluded from it. Three classes of people were not permitted to join in the Passover celebration – 'the foreigner' (*nêkâr*), 'the temporary resident' (*tôshâv*), and 'the hired worker' (*sâkîr*). The 'foreigner' seems to mean much the same as the more common word, *gêr*, while the 'temporary resident' and the 'hired worker' both describe groups that were not well assimilated from the social and religious points of view. In contrast with these, a slave, after circumcision, was reckoned as qualified to participate in the Passover.

46-47 The Israelites knew already that they had to stay in their houses so as to escape the judgment coming on the land. This meant that the meal had to be eaten in the houses, and it was a communal meal for all Israelite families. The emphasis on 'one house' (v. 46) draws attention to the fact that the lamb was not to be divided between several homes. Rather, the eating of it in 'one house' denoted that the fellowship meal had to display the unity of these participants. In addition, the instruction that not a bone was to be broken was intended to show the difference between the Passover feast and an ordinary meal.[67] This was the LORD's Passover (vv. 11, 27, 48), and hence special regulations applied (see Num. 9:12 for the repetition of this instruction). John the Evangelist referred to this when he noted that the Scriptures were fulfilled when the legs of the crucified Jesus were not broken (John 19:32-36). The implication was that Jesus died as the perfect Passover sacrifice.[68]

---

67. Another explanation could be that the bones were often broken to extract the marrow. To forbid that would be further confirmation that this was a special feast, not an ordinary meal, and therefore breaking the bones was prohibited.

68. Sometimes reference is made to Psalm 34:20. This passage is concerned with God's care for His own, and the statement is made: 'he protects all his bones, not one of them will be broken'. However, this passage does not seem nearly as relevant as Exodus 12:46 in the case of Jesus. For further comment on John's account, see Leon Morris, *The Gospel of John*, rev. ed. (NICNT: Grand Rapids: Eerdmans, 1995), p. 727.

48-49 An essential qualification for males participating in the Passover was that they had been circumcised. If an alien (*gêr*) wanted to share in it, he had to ensure the circumcision of all under his authority. This complied with the original instruction to Abraham that all the males in his household, whether born in it or purchased by him, had to be circumcised (Gen. 17:13). In this regard, no distinction was to be made between the native born (*'ezrach*) and the alien (*gêr*) who had come to reside within the borders of the Israelite community. This law was reiterated later in the Pentateuch (see Lev. 24:22; Num. 15:29), while Leviticus 19:34 stipulated that since the citizen was once a stranger himself, he had to love the alien.

50-51 In terms almost identical to verse 28, it is recorded that just as the Lord had commanded Moses and Aaron, so all Israel carried out the instructions. As in verse 28, a slightly stronger translation is needed: 'Thus all the children of Israel did; as the Lord commanded Moses and Aaron, so they did' (NKJV). The statement in verse 51 repeats the information of verse 40 regarding the Lord's divisions leaving Egypt, though in this case one of the distinctive verbs for the exodus is used (*yâtsâ'*, Hi., 'brought out').

6

Exit from Egypt
(13:1–15:21)

1 Consecration of the Firstborn (13:1-16)

1-2 The LORD had already claimed the firstborn of Egypt, both human and animal (12:29). Now He was asserting His rights over the men and animals among the Israelites. The people were told to consecrate the firstborn to the LORD, the verb 'consecrate' (*qâdash*, Pi.) having the idea of setting apart for holy service. The law post-Sinai is given in Deuteronomy 21:15-17, where it is set down that the rights of the firstborn were due to a man's [procreative] power, i.e. the firstborn was a sign of man's ability to produce children.[1]

3 The command Moses gave to the people was that they were to 'remember' (*z^ekôr*) the day of their leaving Egypt. While this verb 'remember' may point to inner mental acts, it is often used in situations where remembering flows over into actions.[2] Clearly such was the case here. Recollection of the exodus events was to prompt the people in the future to observe the appointed annual celebration. The actual exodus is referred to in two different ways. From the standpoint of the Israelites, they 'came out' (*y^ets'âtem*), while from God's viewpoint He 'brought out' (*yâtsâ'*, Hi.) His people 'with a mighty hand' (*b^echozeq yâd*). This latter

---

1. A good discussion concerning the firstborn is given by J. N. Oswalt in *TWOT*, 1, pp. 109-10. For comment on the law of the firstborn here and in other Pentateuchal passages, see Victor Hamilton, *Exodus*, pp. 202-03.

2. For the varied uses of this verb, see *TWOT*, 1, pp. 241-43.

expression, and its related one, 'the outstretched arm' (*zerôa' netûyâh*), were already known in Canaan in the fifteenth century B.C. and applied to the conquering might of Pharaoh. Hence, this verse was a challenge to the Egyptian concepts and, in particular, a challenge to the power of Pharaoh.[3] The final sentence in this verse draws attention once more to the prohibition against yeast.

4-5 The month of Abib was marked out as a special month by the observance of the Passover. This was the month of 'ears [of grain]', identified later with Nisan.[4] The promises of God regarding exit from Egypt were now at the stage of immediate fulfilment. Several factors about the land of Canaan were again noted (see the comments on 3:7-8). First, it was a land about which God had already made promises. Secondly, it was not unallocated territory, but one in which Canaanites, Hittites, Amorites, Hivites, and Jebusites were living. Thirdly, it was a good land, a land 'flowing with milk and honey'. Corresponding to the idea that Israel was being brought *out* of Egypt is the idea of the LORD bringing them *in* to Canaan (*kî yᵉvî'ᵃkâ 'el*, 'when he brings you into ...').

6-7 Emphasis falls again on the prohibition on yeast for the seven days of the Passover celebration (for the previous passages, see 12:15, 18-20). The same two words for yeast are used as in 12:15, 19. In place of breads made with yeast, the people were to eat *matsôt*, the word that is still used in modern Hebrew and English for the flat unleavened bread used at Passover. The attempt had to be made to eradicate any yeast, for it was not even to be seen anywhere within the borders of land occupied by Israel.

8 The didactic aspect of the Passover was very real. Rather than just waiting for children to ask questions about it, the instruction was that the father had the responsibility of telling the redemptive significance of the festival: 'I do this because of what the LORD did for me when I came out of Egypt' (NIV). While the Passover had a communal aspect to it, yet the individual had to relate the significance of its personal side.[5]

---

3. See for further information, J. K.Hoffmeier, 'The Arm of God Versus the Arm of Pharaoh in the Exodus Narratives', *Bib* 67 (1986), pp. 378-87.

4. For discussion on the Israelite calendar, see D. J. Wiseman, 'Calendar', *IBD*, pp. 222-24.

5. From the Hebrew verb used at the beginning of the verse, 'you shall tell'

9-10 The annual Passover celebration is likened to someone who had literally a sign on his hand, and some mark on his forehead to remind him that the LORD had redeemed His people from slavery in Egypt. This idea is expanded further in Deuteronomy 6:4-9 immediately following the *Shema*' ('Hear, O Israel, …'). Some Orthodox Jews in the past, as well as down to the present time, have taken this instruction literally. That these things were practised in New Testament times is clear from Matthew 23:5 in reference to phylacteries. However, there are good reasons for taking the words here and in Deuteronomy in a non-literal way.[6] The LORD's law had to be part of their daily conversation, with it always being on their lips. There follows what amounts to a mini-confessional statement: 'For the LORD brought you out of Egypt with his mighty hand.' That in a nutshell was the account of the Israelites' escape from Egypt. What had transpired was not due to themselves. Rather, it was a sovereign act of God, a display of His mighty power.[7] Keeping this celebration was an obligation upon Israel. While the NIV has 'year after year' (Heb. *miyyâmîm yâmîmâh*), this phrase is better understood as 'once every year'. Literally it means 'from days to days', and on the basis of its use in 1 Samuel 1:3 and 2:19, it is better to take it in this alternative way.

11-13 Moses looked ahead to the situation that would exist when Israel was in possession of Canaan. Later, Israel's connection would be so strong with the land that the language of the people is called 'the lip of Canaan' (Isa. 19:18). The Israelites had God's pledged word that they would have possession of that land, something that had been promised to the patriarchs and repeatedly restated right down to this time.

God's claim was over the firstborn of the livestock. They belonged to Him. The use of the verb 'give over' ('*âvar*, Hi.) is a reminder of the previous use of the same verb to describe

---

(*nâgad*, Hi., 2 m. s.), comes the word *Haggada(h)*, the recital of the Passover events that is still used in modern Judaism.

6. I have discussed the Deuteronomy 6 passage, and also given reasons for a metaphorical interpretation in my commentary, *Deuteronomy: The Commands of a Covenant God* (Fearn: Christian Focus, 2007), pp. 94-95.

7. The expression 'with a mighty hand' (*b^eyâd chazâqâh*) is identical in meaning to the slightly different one in v. 3 (*b^echozeq yâd*).

how the angel of death 'passed over' the Israelite homes (12:13). Later, this verb will be used of the action of Israel in 'crossing over' the Red Sea (15:16). Two new provisions are now given. First, a donkey could be redeemed with a lamb, as it was an unclean animal and therefore could not be used in sacrifice. Later, the price of such redemption was set at five silver shekels (Num. 18:15-16). If the donkey was not redeemed, it was to be killed by breaking its neck so that it was unavailable for any use. Secondly, no firstborn child was to be killed, but rather redeemed. Israel was not to suffer what the Egyptians had to suffer when the angel of death swept through the land (12:29).

14-16 These verses are very similar to 12:24-27 and 13:8-10. Such repetition is common in the Pentateuch (cf. Deut. 6:4-9 with Deut. 11:18-21). The stress in them is on the fact of the divine power exhibited in the events surrounding the exit from Egypt. It was accomplished by the mighty hand of the LORD (vv. 14, 16), a graphic anthropomorphic phrase to describe divine power. God's response to Pharaoh's hardness of heart was the judgment that fell on the firstborn of Egypt, both man and animal. The explanation to be given to any inquiry by children was to be that the facts of God's judgment were the reason for this continual practice of sacrifice at the time of the Passover celebration (v. 15).[8] While the firstborn of animals would be sacrificed, the firstborn son was to be redeemed. This verse marks the first occurrence in the Old Testament of a verb meaning 'to redeem' (*pâdâh*). It is a verb whose meaning overlaps with another verb for 'redeem', *gâ'al* (used already in 6:6), and these verbs can be used in parallel (see Jer. 31:11 and Hosea 13:14). Here the idea is of man redeeming his son, but the wider concept of God the redeemer became extremely important in both the Old and New Testaments. Just as the Passover celebration was said to be 'a sign on your hand and a reminder on your forehead' (v. 9), so this sacrifice was to be 'a sign on your hand and a symbol on your forehead'. The NIV adds '*like* a sign', which is undoubtedly the meaning, though it does not represent any word in the Hebrew text. The point

---

8. The NIV's 'I sacrifice to the LORD' does not bring out the force of the Heb. participle used here, *zovêach* (*zâvach*, Qal active part., m. s.). It is a usage denoting a repeated action that takes place over time. See *IBHS*, p. 626, §36.6e.29.

is that here in Exodus 13:9, 16, as in Deuteronomy 6:9, these are metaphorical expressions that were not meant to be taken in a literal way. Instead of the phrase, 'a reminder (*zikkârôn*) on your forehead' in verse 9, here in verse 16 a different word is used (*tôtâfot*). This word always appears alongside *zikkârôn*, and always in the plural. Later Judaism took these words in a literal way to mean a sign of some kind on the forehead, and these 'frontlets' became standard practice, and remain so for extremely orthodox Jews. It was an ostentatious way of proclaiming obedience to the law, and called for a rebuke by Jesus in His ministry (Matt. 23:5).

Study Questions

1) Along with the Israelites, many others left Egypt with them. What implications does this have for later in Israel's history?

2) Not everyone could partake in the Passover celebration. How is this paralleled in regard to observance of the Lord's Supper?

3) Why were military terms used to describe the Israelites as they left Egypt (see 12:51)?

4) In 13:8 a principle is stated for teaching the children about the Passover: 'I do this because of what the LORD did for me when I came out of Egypt'. Can you think of other cases where God's example became the pattern for the believer?

2 Crossing the Red Sea (13:17-22)

17-18 These verses recount the actual exodus. Pharaoh's action in this was to 'let the people go'. God's action was to 'lead' the people 'around by the desert road towards the Red Sea'. The explanation is given that the choice of route was God's, and it was to avoid having the Israelites clash with the Philistines if they took the shorter route along the Mediterranean Sea. Hence they journeyed on the desert road towards the Red Sea (*yam-sûf*). Here, this Hebrew expression denotes a body of water the Israelites had to cross, possibly the Bitter Lakes, or Lake Timsah. Elsewhere the same term is used of the Gulf of Suez (Num. 33:10-11) and the modern Gulf of Aqaba (1 Kings 9:26). The reason for this choice was lest the Israelites turn back to Egypt if the Philistines confronted them. However, they were prepared for hostilities, as they went out 'armed for battle'. This fact ties in with the expression that has been used twice already, that the Israelites were to march out in their [military] divisions (12:17).

13:19 Before his death, Joseph made his people swear that when God came to their aid and visited them, then they would carry up his bones from Egypt to Canaan (Gen. 50:25). The narrative here in Exodus echoes that passage in Genesis as it relates the fulfilment of that solemn promise. This fact is important in both Old Testament and New Testaments as it is referred to several times (see, in addition to Exod. 13:19, Josh. 24:32; Acts 7:16; Heb. 11:22). There seems to have been an understanding that God's redemptive presence was going to be manifested in Canaan, and Joseph and his father Jacob (Gen. 49:29-30) both wanted their bones carried up for burial in the sworn land. Moses assured his people that God was indeed going to visit them (*pâqod yifqod*, NIV 'come to their aid'). The verb 'visit' (*pâqod*) can mean either to visit in judgment, or visit in blessing. Clearly the latter is the meaning here and in Genesis 50:25.

13:20-22 The narrative now picks up again on the account of the exit from Egypt, and specifically what happened when they left Succoth (see 12:37). The location of Etham is unknown, except that it is characterised here as being on the edge of the desert, i.e., it was on the very edge of the cultivated and irrigated Egyptian land. God's presence went with them, as symbolised in the pillar of cloud (*'ammûd 'ânân*) and the pillar of fire (*'ammûd 'êsh*). These signs were to encourage the Israelites as they were led and protected on their journey to Canaan, but they also served as a threat to their enemies (Num. 14:13-14). Israel never forgot this experience, for even after the exile they could still recount how by day God 'led them with a pillar of cloud, and by night with a pillar of fire to give them light on the way they were to take' (Neh. 9:12).[9]

---

9. For fuller discussions on the pillar and the cloud, see *NIDOTTE*, 4, pp. 1052-55.

3 At the Red Sea (14:1-14)

1-3 Moses was given strategic instructions regarding the movements of the Israelites. Four geographical areas are mentioned in the text, though none of them can now be identified with any certainty. The first, Pi Hahiroth, seems to be an Egyptian word, while Migdol and Baal Zephon (*ba'al ts^efon*) are certainly Hebrew words. 'Migdol' is the Hebrew word for 'a [watch] tower', and there may have been several places with that name. 'Baal Zephon' means 'Baal of the north'. This points to the presence of Baal worship in Egypt, suggesting that the followers of this religious devotion were active in propagating their faith. By his word to Moses, the LORD instructed the people to turn back from where they were at Etham and encamp by the sea. This was to make Pharaoh and his forces think that the Israelites were muddled in their thinking, and could be contained within a small area.

4 Another hardening of Pharaoh's heart was predicted, as he and his men pursued the fleeing Israelites. But the chase by the Egyptians would bring glory to God, as they would come to realise that the God of the Israelites was indeed the LORD (*yhwh*). The events that were going to unfold would be a further display of God's power, and in themselves they would be a way of bringing more glory to Him. Whatever doubts any of the people had (see the later section, vv. 10-14), at this stage they obeyed and acted in accordance with the message.

5-9 On hearing of the departure of Moses and the people, Pharaoh and his officials quickly realised what this meant, as his country had now been deprived of much of its workforce. The prospect of economic loss was the great motivator for their decision-making. Pharaoh's response was to assemble his troops, especially his chariots, and pursue the fleeing Israelites. The reference in verse 6 to his getting his chariot (*rikbbô*) ready may be to his whole force of chariots, not just his individual one. The assembled army was a large one, six hundred special (Heb. *bâchûr*, 'chosen') chariots, together with other unnumbered ones. The LORD's word to Moses was fulfilled, and Pharaoh's heart was hardened. Meanwhile, the Israelites were marching out 'boldly' (NIV; Heb. *b^eyâd râmâh*). This expression occurs in the parallel passage (Num. 33:3) and may well have had a military overtone to it. If that were so, the word 'triumphantly' would suit well as the translation here.[10] The Israelites were chased and overtaken[11] as they camped by the sea near Pi Hahiroth, and opposite Baal Zephon. The strength of the Egyptian force is emphasised by saying that 'all Pharaoh's horses and chariots, horsemen[12] and troops' pursued the Israelites. Pharaoh was clearly determined to prevent his slaves from escaping.

10-12 As the Israelites looked up, there was Pharaoh and his troops coming against them in military order. Fear gripped them and they cried out to the LORD. The same verb used here for 'cry out' (*tsâ'aq*) was used earlier of the Israelites crying out to God as they sought relief from their situation. Whether in Egypt, or during their wilderness journey, Israel had to look to the one true God who could deliver them. Moses' own people, though, raised the question that it would have been better for them to die in Egypt rather than in the wilderness. They went further by reflecting on their own arguments for staying in Egypt and not taking part in any attempt to escape. In their minds the option of staying in slavery to the Egyptians was preferable to going out to die in the desert. These verses help to explain later actions by the people, as clearly they had been arguing against Moses in Egypt, not wanting to take part in the escape from slavery. Service of the Egyptians was regarded as better than the service of the LORD (v. 12).

13-14 Moses responded by assuring the people that salvation (*y'shû'â*, NIV 'deliverance') was going to be provided by the LORD that very day. He and Joshua were merely leaders of the people, not their saviours. The people's fear had to be banished. The command, 'Do not be afraid', was the same word of encouragement given earlier to Abraham (Gen. 15:1) and Isaac (Gen. 26:24), and also the one to be given later to Joshua (Jos. 8:1). Instead, they had to set themselves

---

10. Cf. C. J. Labuschagne, 'The Meaning of *Beyad Rama* in the Old Testament', in W. C. Delsman, et al, *Von Kanaan bis Kerala: Festschrift für Prof. Mag. Dr. J. P. M. van der Ploeg O.P.* (Vluyn: Neukirchener Verlag, 1982), pp. 143-48.

11. This combination of 'pursue' and 'overtake' occurs elsewhere, so forming a verbal pair. See, e.g., Gen. 44:4; Deut. 19:6; Josh. 2:5.

12. NIV footnote says 'charioteers' because this word can designate not a rider but someone driving a chariot. See *DCH*, VI, pp. 787-88.

(Heb. *yâtsav*, Hitp.; cf. its use already in 2:4 and 8:20) to wait passively to see God's intervention on their behalf. The fear of the Egyptians pursuing them would only be temporary, since they were to lose their lives in the Red Sea. God was the warrior who would fight for His people (v.14). This concept comes to even clearer expression in the Song of Moses, the victory song following the triumph over the Egyptians (15:3-8). All that was required of the Israelites was to wait patiently and be quiet.[13] The translation can be strengthened by noting that the final clause is adversative, 'The LORD will fight for you, *but* you are to stay silent'.[14]

4 Through the Red Sea (14:15-31)

15-16 What was required was action, not more words or even prayers to the LORD. The first move on the way to Canaan was simply to commence the journey, and so Moses was told to issue the order for it. Moses' staff, already used in earlier events in this book (see 4:2, 4; 7:17, 20; 8:5, 16), was again employed as a symbol of God's power, stretched out over the water in order to create dry land on which the Israelites were to walk.

17-18 While mention was made earlier to the LORD hardening Pharaoh's heart, now the reference is to the hearts of the Egyptians being so hardened that they would follow the Israelites into the dry sea bed. The trap was laid for them. Victory over Pharaoh and his troops would result in glory to the LORD (see the earlier use of this expression in 14:4), with the double use of this expression drawing particular attention to the idea. The purpose of this was to demonstrate to the Egyptians that the salvation of the Israelites and the destruction of their army were indeed from God. They would come 'to know' that the LORD was God, i.e., to have experiential acquaintance with Him and His power. The declaration, 'I am the LORD' (*ʾanî yhwh*), began to take on special significance, not just as a self-assertion of God's existence, but more pointedly of His being 'the LORD', the covenantal, redeeming God.

---

13. NIV has 'be still' as the translation of the Heb. verb *chârash*, Hi. The better translation is 'be silent, cease speaking' (*DCH*, III, p. 323).

14. On this point, see *IBHS*, p. 172, §141.

19-20 The angel of God (synonymous with 'angel of the LORD') was earlier identified with the burning bush (Exod. 3:2). Now He is mentioned as having had a role in leading the Israelites as they left Egypt, and then as a defence at their rear, being joined there by the pillar of cloud that served as a barrier between Israel and the Egyptians. The latter part of verse 20 poses a problem, for though the general meaning seems clear, yet the syntax is difficult. A literal translation runs: 'And it happened, the cloud and the darkness, and it illuminated the night, and it did not draw near this to this all the night'. As early as the LXX translation (c. 250 B.C.) attempts were made to overcome the perceived difficulties. The LXX translators clearly read a different verb at the commencement of the verse, for they rendered it, 'And the night passed' (*kai diêlthen hê nux*). Another problem is that the antecedent of 'it' in verse 20 is 'the cloud', and hence the question arises as to how the cloud could have enlightened the night. These and other problems explain the differences between various versions at this point.[15] The main idea is that the glory of God seen in the cloud brought light and salvation to Israel, while bringing darkness and judgment to the Egyptians.

21-22 The whole contest between the LORD and Pharaoh and the gods of Egypt came to a climax at the Sea of Reeds (*yâm sûf*). The LORD's supremacy over Egypt was displayed in the destruction of the pursuing troops and in the salvation of Israel. As God had commanded, Moses stretched out his rod, and a strong east wind blew all night, and what had been water turned into dry land.[16] The Israelites were able to pass through with the water as a wall on the left and the right. Not surprisingly, this momentous event formed part of the hymnology of Israel. Psalm 78:13 reads: 'He divided the sea and led them through; he made the water stand firm like a wall', while Psalm 106:8-9 describes the same event: 'Yet he [the LORD] saved them for his name's sake, to make his

---

15. For further comment, see Victor Hamilton, *Exodus*, p. 213.
16. The word here for 'dry land' (*chârâvâh*) is not that in v. 16 (*yabbâshâh*). The two words do not seem any different in meaning, as is shown by the change to *yabbâshâh* in the next verse. However, the one here only occurs eight times in the OT, and, except for two cases (Gen. 7:22; Hag. 2:6), they all denote land made dry by God's direct command.

mighty power known. He rebuked the Red Sea, and it dried up; he led them through the depths as through a desert'.

23-25 The earlier references to the Egyptian pursuit of Israel (vv. 8, 10) are supplemented at this point with the graphic reference to all Pharaoh's troops following into the midst of the sea (*'el tôk hayyâm*). They were not just at the edge of the water, but right into it. The next morning God looked down on the situation, and caused havoc in the Egyptian camp. The wheels of the chariots became 'heavy' (*kᵉzêdut*),[17] and so the Egyptians were slowed up in their attempt to escape.[18] The reaction of the Egyptians was to get out of the dangerous situation with the utmost haste. They acknowledged the presence of Israel's God, the LORD (*yhwh*), who was fighting against them. There is no way of deciding how much understanding they had of the LORD, or of His ability to rescue His people. However, the fact that they clearly knew that Israel had left their country to serve the LORD would have been sufficient for them to make the connection between what they knew previously and their present experience.

26-28 The procedure set out earlier for parting the waters (v. 21) is now reversed. Moses stretched out his hand over the sea, and the waters returned as they had been previously. The Egyptians attempted to escape from it (see NIV footnote for v. 27) but by divine action they were swept into the sea. Israel had to learn that salvation was a work of God, not one the people themselves could perform. The account stresses the completeness of the victory, as Pharaoh's whole army (*kol chêl par'oh*) was destroyed, without a single chariot or horseman surviving. The Egyptians were routed completely. However, no mention is made of Pharaoh perishing, nor that every single Egyptian soldier died. The principle of divine judgment needed only representative numbers to display punishment on a disobedient people.

29-30 These verses contain the summary account of the crossing of the Israelites on the dry seabed, together with

---

17. This is a *hapax legomenon* from the root *kâvêd*, 'to be heavy'.

18. Most English translations are close to the meaning here, but often periphrastic like the NIV. The ESV rendering, 'threw the Egyptian forces into a panic, clogging their chariot wheels so that they drove heavily', is following the rendering of the Samaritan Pentateuch, the LXX, and the Syriac.

a theological comment concerning the nature of this event ('the LORD saved Israel'). Again, mention is made of the wall of water on the right and the left (cf. v. 22). What happened was a display of God's saving power, the verb 'save' (*yâsha'*, Hi.) being used for the first time here when God is the subject and Israel the object. He had saved His people so that they became known as 'a people saved by the LORD' (Deut. 33:29).

31 A later song rejoiced in the fact that God had saved His people at the Red Sea for His name's sake, and to make His power known (Ps. 106:8-9). Here, the text notes that Israel saw His 'great power' (NIV; Heb. *hayyâd hagg^{e}dolâh*, 'a mighty hand', cf. the earlier expression, *yâd châzâqâh*), feared God, and trusted in Him and His servant Moses. They were witnesses to the victory over the Egyptians, and this confirmed them in their assured confidence in the LORD and in His servant, Moses. But mingled with trust was fear as they assimilated in their minds all that had been promised through Moses and now fulfilled in such a powerful way.

Study Questions

1) What understanding did Joseph have of God's commitment to give Canaan to His people for him to insist that his bones be buried there (compare Gen. 50:25 and Exod. 13:19 with Heb. 11:22)?

2) Why was the earlier hardening of Pharaoh's heart not sufficient to stop him pursuing the Israelites (see 14:4, 8)?

3) After seeing all God's signs and wonders done in Egypt, why did His people want so soon to return as slaves?

4) Psalm 77:20 reads: 'You led your people like a flock by the hand of Moses and Aaron'. How does the account of crossing the Red Sea given in Exodus 14:21-31 confirm this statement of Moses' and Aaron's roles as shepherds of the flock?

5 The Song of the Sea (15:1-18)

The main part of this chapter is given to the Song of Moses, or the Song of the Sea as it is often called. It is a lengthy poem dedicated in praise of the LORD for Israel's deliverance from the Red Sea. It has no other parallels in Exodus, though embedded songs do occur in other books (e.g., Lamech's song, Gen. 4:23-24; the song of Moses, Deut. 32:1-43; Deborah's song, Judg. 5:1-31; Hannah's song, 1 Sam. 2:1-10). Several general observations need to be made about this poem at the outset.[19]

1. This song is set within the prose narrative of the exodus experience of Israel. Without the song, the narrative from Exodus 14:31 could almost be followed immediately by Exodus 15:19-21 (see later comment on these verses).

2. The song is in typical Hebrew poetic form exhibiting many of the usual features such as use of metaphors, assonance, and parallelism.

3. It is unusual in that it puts into poetical format the information already given in prose in chapter 14, enabling a comparison to be made of the two styles of communication of ideas. It reinforces the teaching by expressing theologically and poetically the truths about God's great redemptive work.

4. In the Near East there was a tradition of victory songs, some of which were in both prose and poetical versions. Hence this song fits in well to the cultural context of the time. The expressions in it have many parallels with later parts of the Old Testament, especially the psalms.[20]

5. It has three time frames – the immediate situation of the exodus from Egypt, the coming invasion of Canaan, and finally the establishment of a place of worship on Mount Zion.

6. This poem shows how fitting song is in forming a response to God's saving mercy. This includes poetic

---

19. There is considerable literature on Exodus 15. Two very helpful discussions, containing much bibliographical material, are by R. D. Patterson, 'The Song of Redemption', *WTJ* 57 (1995), pp. 453-61, and 'Victory at sea: prose and poetry in exodus 14-15', *BS* 161 (January-March 2004), pp. 42-54.

20. I have listed some of these in my article 'The Exodus and Sinai Covenant in the Book of Psalms', *RTR* 73, 1(2014), pp. 3-27.

passages in the prophetical books, many of the psalms, the songs of Mary and Zechariah (Luke 1:46-55; 68-79), and songs of the redeemed in the book of Revelation (Rev. 5:9-10, 12-13). Words and music combine to give memorable praise to the redeemer.

i) The Saving Power of the LORD (15:1-3)
1 Moses and his fellow Israelites joined together in a song addressed to their redeemer God.[21] The song commences with a declaration of praise to the exalted LORD; for He has overthrown the Egyptian chariots, hurling them into the sea. It is phrased as first person singular, 'I', which means that it was intended for the individual member of the community to use. Rightly, the song focuses immediately on the character of Israel's God. In this way it resembles the commencement of some psalms, such as Psalm 89:1: 'I will sing of the love of the LORD for ever; with my mouth I will make your faithfulness known through all generations'; or, Psalm 138:1: 'I will praise you, O LORD, with all my heart; before the "gods" I will sing your praise'.

2 The personal testimony continues with statements concerning 'my strength', 'my song', and 'my salvation', and all these relate to *Yah*, an abbreviated form of the divine name *yhwh*. This form occurs many times in the Old Testament but mainly in names such as Elijah, Isaiah, and Uzziah, where the English 'iah' represents the Hebrew *yah*, only appearing alone in Hebrew poetry as here. The thought in the first colon, 'The LORD is my strength and my song', is sharpened by the climactic statement in the second colon, 'he has become my salvation'. That explains why the LORD is His strength and His song. The conjunction of 'strength' and 'salvation' appears elsewhere (cf. Ps. 28:7; 62:7–8; 118:14). It has been suggested that the word 'song' (*zimrâh*) should be translated as 'refuge' or 'protection', but the evidence is not strong enough to compel such a change.[22] The experience of the exodus was a demonstration of God's strength, and, as a consequence,

---

21. The verb translated 'sang' (*yâshîr*) is actually an imperfect form of the verb 'to sing', not perfect. However, the insertion of 'then' ('*âz*) before it indicates that it is referring to past time.

22. See the lengthy note on this word in Victor Hamilton, *Exodus*, p. 222.

it became an object of praise, being incorporated into verbal acknowledgement of it in a song. Though the LORD had been the God of the patriarchs ('my father's God'), He also had become Moses' God as well. Past knowledge of the LORD was confirmed by personal acquaintance so that he confesses Him as 'my God', the one who is worthy of all praise. 'Exalt' is simply a way of saying that God will be treated with reverence and adoration.

3 In reflection on the LORD's actions in redeeming His people by overthrowing the Egyptian army, Moses referred to Him as a warrior, a description that some modern readers may find disturbing. However, it was a recognition that the LORD had fought on His people's behalf. It is simply putting in another way the truth that God had promised deliverance to His people by omnipotent power, and that He had also said He would fight for them (14:14). Because of the great victory that had been achieved over the Egyptians, Moses likened God to a victorious soldier. This imagery of God's might is pervasive in the Scripture, and many later passages take up this theme. They point to the ultimate battle when God will be victorious over the forces of evil (Rev. 19:11-21).[23] Earlier (3:14), God had declared that His name was indeed the LORD (*yhwh*), and now that is reaffirmed in the declaration, 'the LORD is his name'.

ii) Victory over Egypt (15:4-10)
The theme of the victory over Egypt is developed, first with mention of the overthrow of the army (vv. 4-5), and then in more general terms in verses 6-8 of the defeat of the Egyptians being an expression of God's anger.

4-5 The destruction of the Egyptian chariots is described in graphic language. The LORD hurled them into the sea, called again in Hebrew *yam sûf*, the Re(e)d Sea (see the earlier discussion on its name and location). It was not just the ordinary soldiers who died there, but also the best of

---

23. For discussion on the theme of the Lord as a warrior, see especially Tremper Longman III, 'The Divine Warrior: The New Testament Use of an Old Testament Motif', *WTJ* 44 (1982), pp. 290-307; 'Psalm 98: A Divine Warrior Victory Song', *JETS* 27 (1984), pp. 267-74; Tremper Longman III and D. G. Reid, *God is a Warrior* (SOTBT, 1995).

Pharaoh's military officials. Like stones, they dropped to the bottom of the sea and were drowned.

6 Up to this point in Exodus mention has been made of God's hand ('my hand', 3:20; 7:4), but now this song speaks of His 'right hand' as the agent of destruction, stressing it by the repetition of the phrase within the verse. The power of the LORD was majestic in shattering the enemy. As much as the earlier signs were displays of His power, the overthrow of the Egyptian army was an even greater one. In later Old Testament poetry God's right hand and holy arm are mentioned as working salvation (Ps. 98:1).

7 Victory over the Egyptians is described as an overthrow of opponents, and as anger that burns up even as fire consumes stubble. God had sent His anger on a mission to consume the enemy. Here is poetic language that draws together ideas both of God's majesty and His definitive action against those who try to hinder His sovereign purposes. None can stand before His might.

8-9 The reference in the prose account to the piling up of the water as walls is depicted as being accomplished by God's breath (*rûach*, 14:21). From His nostrils came the wind (*rûach 'âppêkâ*) that drove the surging waters into a firm wall, so allowing the Israelites to pass through unscathed. The Egyptians' boasting is expressed here in the first person: '*I* will pursue; *I* will overtake …; *I* will divide…; *I* will gorge…; *I* will draw my sword.' Proud Egypt thought that human might could intervene and frustrate divine purposes. That comes out strongly in the final words of verse 9. Egypt's puny hand was set against the mighty hand of the LORD. The contrast is emphasised at the beginning of verse 10: 'I will (x 5) … *but* you blew …' To God's breath is attributed the return of the waters (cf. 14:21, which attributes it to a strong east wind). Just as the drowning Egyptians were compared to sinking stones in verse 5, so now they are compared to lead.

iii) Confrontation with the Living LORD (15:11-16)
11-12 A change comes in the song at this point. Two rhetorical questions highlight the characterisation of God. The first one implies His incomparability with all the other gods, including those of Egypt. They had been vanquished by the judgment

inflicted on the night of the first Passover (see 12:12). The second question asked who could be like the Lord – 'majestic in holiness, awesome in glory, working wonders?' In Himself He was separated from His creatures by His holiness, while in the outworking of His purposes His glory was awe-inspiring. His deeds were indeed 'wonders' such as no one else could imitate. They were peculiarly His, since they were divine actions manifesting His eternal power. What happened to the Egyptians is said to have been caused by the Lord stretching out His right hand (cf. v. 6). The destruction of the Egyptians is likened to the earth opening up and swallowing them.

13 In parallel expressions the point is made that in God's unfailing love (Heb. *chésed*) He will lead His people to the place of His appointment. They were His redeemed people, who needed guidance on their way from Egypt to the 'sworn' land, where ultimately they would come to His holy dwelling. The same verb for 'redeem' has already appeared in God's response to Moses' puzzlement over the Lord's seeming lack of action to rescue His people (6:6). Later in this song (v. 17) this holy dwelling is called God's sanctuary. The reference is to the fact that the ark of the covenant would first be brought to Jerusalem, and then afterwards Solomon would build the temple there where the Lord would dwell among the Israelites and not abandon His people Israel (1 Kings 6:13). The way in which God would lead His people would be like that of a shepherd as He tenderly brought His people to Canaan (cf. the use of the same verb for 'lead', *nâhal*, in Ps. 23:2; Isa. 40:11; 49:10).

14-16 Not only did God show His power in bringing the people out of Egypt, but in bringing them into the land of Canaan as well. This combination of being 'brought out' and 'brought in' was a promise He made repeatedly (cf. 3:8, 17; 6:6-8). News of the exodus would reach surrounding nations, especially those whose territory lay in the path of the Israelite journey to Canaan, and they would fear. The Philistines were a problem for Israel for several centuries until David finally subdued them. Edom and Moab were going to be a thorn for Israel, and Deuteronomy 2:1-23 details the contact with them en route to Canaan. Then too Canaan will submit to the military prowess of Israel ('the power of your arm') until the people redeemed from slavery in Egypt pass by. In this song addressed to God, Israel is called 'your people', 'the people you bought'. Redemption was but a prelude to occupation of their own land. The verb used here is *qânâh*, which, while having a general meaning of 'acquire', can also be used as a synonym for 'redeem' (cf. the parallel between the two in vv. 13 and 16, and in Psalm 74:2).

iv) Worship on the Mount (15:17-18)
The final verses of the song look ahead, not just to the occupation of the land of Canaan, but also specifically to worship of the LORD there.

17 The thought is that Israel will be 'brought in' and 'planted' in Canaan. Later, a psalmist, employing this same imagery, pictured Israel as a little plant taken from Egypt and transplanted into the land (Ps. 80:8-11). The place where worship would take place is declared to be 'the mountain of your inheritance – the place, O LORD, you made for your dwelling.' David's capture of Jerusalem (2 Sam. 5:6-12) was followed by the moving of the ark of the covenant there (2 Sam. 6:1-23). From then onwards there was never any question as to where the LORD's dwelling place should be. Psalm 132:13-14 expressed it succinctly: 'For the LORD has chosen Zion, he has desired it for his dwelling; "This is my resting place for ever and ever; here I will sit enthroned, for I have desired it."' On that mountain a sanctuary would be built, a dwelling place for the LORD.

18 The song ends with a declaration of the LORD's kingship. A little later it will be clear that Israel was chosen as a kingdom of priests (19:6), but at this stage there is simply the assertion of God's kingly rule. The God who redeemed His people from slavery was indeed the everlasting king. The exact sentence here, 'The LORD will reign for ever and ever,' does not occur elsewhere. The nearest equivalent is Psalm 10:16: 'The LORD is king for ever and ever,' whereas the idea of God's eternal kingship is reasserted often.

6 A Summary of the Events at the Red Sea (15:19-21)
The narrative is resumed at this point with a short summary statement of what happened to the Egyptians and the

Israelites, followed by a note concerning Miriam and other women singing and dancing.

19 As in the fuller account (14:26-31), note is taken of the contrasting situations of the Egyptians and the Israelites at the Red Sea. By divine action the waters were brought back on the Egyptians – horses, chariots, and horsemen – while Israel went through on dry land. This verse draws on the language of 14:23, 28-29.

20-21 Miriam, Moses' sister, led the women in song with tambourines and dancing. She is called 'a prophetess' (*nᵉvî'âh*), one of a number of women in the Old Testament who are so designated (see for other examples Judg. 4:4-6; 2 Kings 22:14-20; 2 Chron. 34:22-28). The same term is used of a prophet's wife (Isa. 8:3). The song they sang was the first line of the Song of Moses. The song exalting the victory over the Egyptians was fittingly taken up and utilised by the women in this outpouring of gratitude and praise.

Study Questions

1) Why is the Song of Moses framed as a song for an individual to sing ('*I* will sing', '*my* God') rather than as a communal song ('*We* will sing', '*our* God')?

2) Compare the questions of verse 11 with Job 38:1-11 and Isaiah 40:25-31. How do such questions help to stress the character of God?

3) What experiences during the exodus prompted the people to sing so assuredly that God was going to lead them to Canaan?

4) The people were soon to have a tent of meeting where the ark of the covenant would be kept. Why did they need another sanctuary on the mountain of God's inheritance (v. 17)?

PART II
The Journey to Mount Sinai
(15:22–18:27)

7

The Waters of Marah and Elim
(15:22-27)

22-24 Moses' role is set in its correct perspective by the opening words of this verse. He '*led* Israel from the Red Sea', using the causative form of the verb 'to journey' or 'to travel' (*nâsa'*, Hi.).[1] He was the appointed leader who had the responsibility of being 'a servant in all God's house' (Heb. 3:5), and part of that role was to bring Israel to the land of God's choice. He led Israel into the desert of Shur, probably an area to the east of where the people crossed the Red Sea. The word *shûr* in Hebrew means 'a wall', and it may have been used to denote an area of Egyptian fortifications built to keep out Bedouin tribes. It is referred to in connection with Abraham (Gen. 20:1), and much later in David's time it was land occupied by Amalekites (1 Sam. 27:8). Seemingly it is to be identified with Etham (Num. 33:6-7).

When after three days they reached Marah, the water there was bitter, which gave the place its name. Just as the Israelites had earlier grumbled against Moses while they were still in Egypt (5:19-20), so again they complained specifically about the lack of water to drink. They had taken unleavened bread with them (12:39), and presumably some

---

1. The Hi. form of this verb is rare. It is used twice in Psalm 78 in description of God's actions in the wilderness experiences of Israel (Ps. 78:26, 52). The Qal form is the usual one in the Pentateuch to note that Israel journeyed further on their way, occurring almost ninety times in this sense in the book of Numbers.

water, but once that water failed they had to search for alternative sources.

25a After appeal to the LORD, Moses was shown a piece of wood that he threw into the water, and so purified it for drinking. No good purpose is served in trying to discover what sort of wood this was, because the incident is another instance of supernatural provision for Israel. In the MT a gap occurs in the middle of this verse, indicating that the Massoretes considered that a break in the narrative occurred here (the NIV, RSV and NRSV all make the break by starting a new paragraph at this point).

25b The new paragraph commences in Hebrew with the words *sham sâm*, 'there he put', with this and the following two verses having many other words with the s/sh sounds, at least seventeen of them. This phenomenon simply draws the attention of the reader of the MT and fixes the content even more definitely in the mind. What the text says is that God was testing His people in this experience, the verb 'to test' (*nisâh*, Pi.) being used again of God's relationship with Israel in 16:4, 17:2, and 20:20. Consequently God established a decree/law for Israel stemming from it, with no distinction to be made between these two words for a divinely given law, nor with 'commands' in the next verse.

26 The pledge was given that if obedience were shown in doing what was right in the LORD's eyes (as expressed in His decrees/laws/commands), then He would not bring on His people all the diseases (*kol mach^alâh*) He had afflicted on the Egyptians. While other passages refer to the 'diseases of Egypt' (Deut. 7:12-15; 28:60-61), yet in the context it is better to assume that this is a reference to the signs that had been performed, rather than some diseases specific to the Egyptians. Nowhere in Exodus are the signs called diseases, but in 1 Kings 8:37// 2 Chronicles 6:28 it does occur as the parallel of 'plague, sign' (*kol néga' kol mach^alâh*). They had earlier experienced the sign in Egypt when God so changed the water in the Nile into blood that the people could not drink it (Exod. 7:18, 21, 24). As they set out on their journey to Sinai, the Israelites experienced another divine intervention, this time on their behalf, when again water was made potable. The statement that concludes the promise, 'For I am the LORD your healer' (*kî 'ᵃnî rofekâ*), was not an assertion of personal medical care for every Israelite. Rather, it was an assurance to the nation that He was Israel's physician. God's desire for His people was that they would act in such a way that judgments like those inflicted on Egypt would not be put on them. This passage should be considered alongside the assurance given after the dedication of the temple in Jerusalem that, if the people sought the LORD and turned from their wicked ways, then He would heal the land (2 Chron. 7:14).

27 No mention is made of them leaving Marah (but cf. Num. 33:9, which also confirms the details given here) but only of their arrival at Elim, whose location cannot now be determined. The important point is made that in contrast with Marah, there was both abundant water (twelve springs) and food (seventy palm trees). On this occasion no miracle was required to satisfy the people as God's provision was already in evidence. Most probably additional food was available there, sufficient to provide sustenance for all the people.

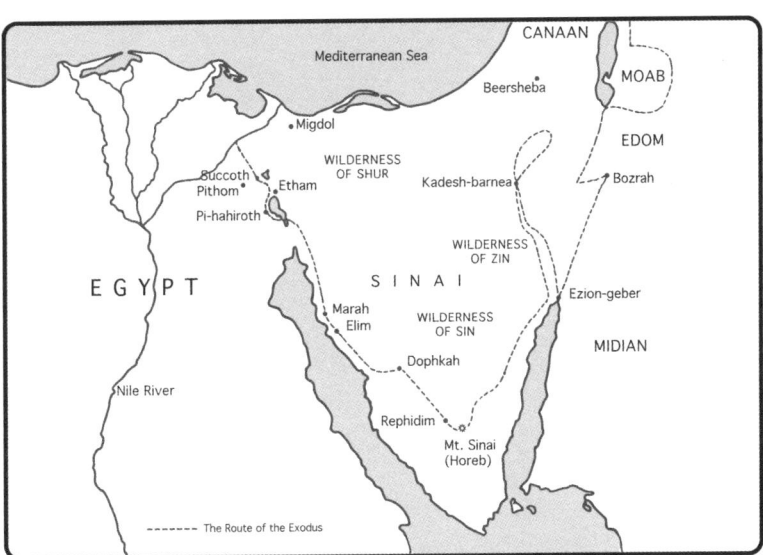

The Proposed Route of the Exodus

8

The Grumbling Community
(16:1-36)

This whole chapter dedicates its attention to the food that God provided for Israel. It also contains an account of the grumbling of the people against Moses and Aaron, that they rightly regarded as grumbling against the LORD (v. 8). The attitude of Israel to their experiences in their desert journey is picked up in some of the historical psalms. They accepted the miraculous provision of water, but queried whether food would be provided: They said: 'Can God spread a table in the desert? ... Can he also give us food? Can he supply meat for his people?' (Ps. 78:19-20; cf. Jude 5). This attitude was one of unbelief and disobedience (Ps. 78:21-22). In spite of receiving 'the bread of angels' and 'meat' from heaven, the people kept on sinning (Ps. 78:32). While the people forgot God, He did not forget them, 'for he remembered his holy promise given to his servant Abraham. He brought out his people with rejoicing, his chosen ones with shouts of joy' (Ps. 105: 42-43). The characters of God and of Israel are both delineated here with clarity.

1 The chapter opens with a note relating how Israel left Elim and came to the Desert of Sin.[1] This location is mentioned again in Exodus 17:1 and Numbers 33:11-12, but it cannot

---

1. This place (*midbar sîn*) should not be confused with the later Desert of Zin (*midbar tsin*, Num. 13:21), as the two words commence with different consonants.

now be identified with precision. The name may be derived from 'Sinai' but that cannot be confirmed. An additional note gives the time of this move as the middle of the second month after leaving Egypt. The exodus from Egypt had earlier been set as in the month of Abib (13:4). Abib roughly equates to March, and so this event was approximately six weeks later.

2-3 At the Desert of Sin Moses and Aaron were faced with rebellion on the part of the people as a whole ('all the congregation of the children of Israel'). A collective grumbling took place because of the lack of food.[2] They wished that the Lord had killed them in Egypt.[3] Reminiscing, they recalled the times they had eaten abundantly all that they wanted, while their present experience was going to mean their death through famine.

4-5 God's response was to promise a continuing supply of bread from heaven.[4] Each day the people were to go out and collect sufficient for that day. The testing of the people was twofold. On the one hand, they had to trust God for the gift of food. On the other hand, they had to trust that after gathering a day's supply, they could be assured that on the next day similar provision would occur. Conformity to God's law ('my law', *tôrātî*) was what was required. They also had to continue to observe the Sabbath by gathering sufficient food for it on the sixth day. The Sabbath was a creation ordinance (Gen. 2:2-3) that was kept even before it was formally incorporated in the prescriptive law for Israel (Exod. 20:8-11; Deut. 5:12-15).

6-7 The Lord's message was communicated to the people by Moses and Aaron. What was to happen about provision of food would be evidence that it was the Lord indeed who

---

2. The verb for 'grumbling' (*lûn*) only occurs in Exodus 15–17, Numbers 14–17, and Joshua 9:18. It may be close in meaning to 'rebellion' (see *DCH*, IV, p. 530), though the LXX uses *diagonguzō*, which occurs in the New Testament in Luke 15:2 and 19:7.

3. The form of expression is a Hebrew way of expressing a wish. Literally the expression means, 'who will give' (*mî yittēn*). For further information, see R. J. Williams, *Hebrew Syntax: An Outline* (Toronto: University of Toronto Press, 1984), p. 25, §122, pp. 91-92, §130; *DIHG~S*, p. 186, §155(b).

4. The Hebrew construction is the particle, 'look' (*hinnēh*), + the pers. pronoun 1 s., with the participle 'causing to rain' (*mamṭîr*, Hi. part. m.s., *māṭar*). The implication is that there will be a continuing supply.

redeemed them from slavery, and a demonstration of His glory. Evening and morning supplies were evidence that He had heard their grumbling and was responding to their need. Moses and Aaron were insignificant as compared with the LORD, and hence they indicated that by their question: 'Who are *we*, that you should grumble *against us*?' (v. 7).

8 The message of verses 6-7 was given again by Moses. Evening and morning a copious supply of meat and bread would completely meet their wants. This was God's response to their grumbling, and the words make plain what Moses and Aaron had already implied (v. 7).

9-10 Moses instructed his intermediary to call for the entire community to gather before the LORD. The terminology, 'draw near before the LORD' (*qir^{e}vû lif^{e}nê yhwh*), is part of the language of worship and service, and as 'before the LORD' (*lif^{e}nê yhwh*) appears in Leviticus 9:5 and 16:1 in connection with sacrifice, it may well have covenantal overtones here.[5] He had not finished speaking to them when they looked towards the desert and saw a revelation of God in the form of divine glory manifested in the cloud.

11-12 The visual manifestation of God was accompanied by words of explanation. Once more, God declared His knowledge of the grumbling of the Israelites (see vv. 8-9). The response was that He was making provision for their physical needs by providing meat in the evening and bread in the morning. This was emphatic confirmation that it was indeed the LORD (*yhwh*), the God who had delivered them from their slavery in Egypt, who was now meeting their daily needs.

13-14 These verses record the actual provision of food, though some of the Hebrew vocabulary is rare. Hence, English translations can differ quite significantly. First, the Hebrew verb *'âlâh* is used twice at the commencement of both verses 13 and 14. In verse 13 it means 'to go up', while in verse 14 it means 'to disappear', as in Genesis 17:22 and 35:13. Secondly, the word *s^{e}lâv* only appears here and in Numbers 11:31-32 and Psalm 105:40. It is generally accepted that it means 'quail' (Coturnix coturnix). Thirdly, the word usually translated 'layer [of

---

5. This is the argument of Paul Ferris, 'Manna Narrative of Exodus 16:1-10', *JETS* 18 (1975), pp. 191-99.

dew]' (*shikvat [hattâl]*) more often denotes 'falling', as in the expression 'falling of seed' (semen; Lev. 15:16, 32; 22:4), though here in this context 'layer' seems quite appropriate. Fourthly, the word *daq* appears twice in verse 14, 'fine flake-like thing', 'fine as the hoarfrost' (NASB). Its use in reference to dust in Isaiah 40:15 suggests an English word like 'fine' rather than the more common 'thin'. Fifthly, the word translated by the NIV as 'thin flakes' (*mᵉchuspas*) is a *hapax legomenon*.[6] Sixthly, 'hoar frost' (*kᵉfôr*) is also a rare word, only occurring here and in Psalm 147:16 and Job 38:29. But with all these unusual features the main sense of the verses is clear. God provided for His people both meat and bread. The latter was 'food from heaven' (v. 4; Ps. 78:24; John 6:33) and the 'bread of angels' (Ps. 78:25). There is no point in trying to identify some natural phenomenon to account for this gift of God. Further description of it is given in verse 31.

15-16 The sight of the manna in particular caused questioning among the Israelites. It was an unknown phenomenon and so they asked each other, 'What is it?'[7] Moses' answer to the question was that it was food given by the LORD. He also relayed to the people the LORD's instruction regarding gathering the manna. According to the head count, they were to gather just as much as each one needed.[8] The amount for each person was to be an omer, which was approximately two litres. The same measurement is given in verses 18, 32, 33, and 36.

17-18 The people followed the instructions that Moses gave, and this meant that some gathered more than others. Some gathered a lot (*marbeh*; Hi. part. m. s. of *râvâh*) while others gathered little (*mamʿît*; Hi. part. m. s. of *mâʿat*). But then the point is made emphatically that what was gathered was exactly appropriate to the needs of the individual so that there was no wastage at all. Paul quoted verse 18 when writing to

---

6. It is a passive participle of a rare and irregular verb, *châsaf* (Pualal, m. s. part.). Cognates in Aramaic and Arabic suggest it means something crackling or crisp.

7. The interrogative here is *mân*, whereas the normal word is *mâh*, as in the following sentence, 'what it was'. *Mân* could be an old particle, or else what we have here could be a statement, 'Manna it is'.

8. 'According to the headcount' represents the Hebrew *laggulgolet*. The word *gulgolet* means 'a skull'. Cf. Golgotha, 'the place of the skull' (Matt. 27:33; Mark 15:22).

the church at Corinth (2 Cor. 8:15) to reinforce the point that this served as an illustration of how Christians should share with one another when the need arose.

19-21 The LORD's instruction was that the people were to go out each day and only gather enough for that day (v. 4). However, even after Moses told them not to retain any of it overnight, this warning was disregarded. What was retained became infected with maggots and stank, and the people's disobedience incurred Moses' anger. The manna did not last all day, for when the sun was really hot, it melted away.

22-23 God's intention was that the people would gather a double portion on the sixth day of the week, as the manna was not to be provided on the Sabbath. This they did, and the leaders confirmed this to Moses.[9] He reiterated what God had already said about the seventh day. It was to be 'a Sabbath observance',[10] 'a holy Sabbath to the LORD' (*sabbat qôdesh layhwh*). Instructions were given concerning the necessary preparation of food for the Sabbath. Whatever cooking method was adopted (baking or boiling), after partaking of it for that day, the remaining amount was reserved for the next morning.

24-26 These verses record the result of Moses' instruction. There was no corruption of the manna, and hence no tainted smell from it (cf. v. 20). He encouraged the people to eat the remaining cooked manna from the previous day, again reminding them that no new manna was to be provided on the seventh day. The seventh day, the Sabbath, was marked as distinctive by the absence of a fresh supply of manna.

27-30 The NIV's 'nevertheless', though catching the spirit of the passage, is an unnecessary insertion, 'Nevertheless some of the people went out to gather'. The RSV, NRSV, and ESV all have 'On the seventh day some of the people went out to gather' (*vay^ehî bayyom hashsh^ev'î yâts^e'û min hâ'âm*

---

9. The word for 'leaders' (*n^esî'îm*) is used in the Old Testament for non-Israelite chieftains, but also, as here, for those in authority within Israel (see, in addition to this verse, Exod. 22:28; Josh. 9:15, 18). Its most frequent usage (over half of all appearances) is in Ezekiel for the future Davidic prince.

10. Heb. *sabbatôn*. This word can be used with wider reference than just to the Sabbath day. It is used, for example, of the day of atonement (Lev. 16:31), and the feast of trumpets (Lev. 23:24). The ending *–ôn* often marks out an abstract word in Hebrew. Cf. *pithrôn*, 'a solution'; *zikkârôn*, 'a memorial'. See *IBHS*, p. 92, 5.7b; *GKC*, p. 238, §85 u.

liqqot), which is a suitable translation of the Hebrew. Explicit command was met with disobedience. It was a fruitless search for manna on the seventh day, for none was provided. The LORD's message to the people through Moses was a question to them:[11] 'How long will you refuse to keep my commands and my instructions?' They were reminded that God was a generous giver, having *given* them the Sabbath, and then *given* them a double portion of food so that they would have sufficient food for the seventh day. No excursions outside the camp were to be permitted on the Sabbath, and as a consequence the people were able to enjoy its rest.

31 This verse picks up the name of the food, 'manna' (Heb. *mân*), mentioned already in verse 15 (see comment). Here reference to its colour and taste is added. It was 'white like coriander seed', and tasted 'like wafers made with honey'. Further particulars about the manna are given in Numbers 11:6-9.

32-36 The LORD gave a particular 'word' (*zeh haddâvâr ᵃsher tsivvâh yhwh*) concerning preservation of some of the manna. The instruction was that an omer of it was to be kept so that future generations could see the wilderness food that Israel ate after redemption from Egypt. It was the bread (*léchem*) that God caused the people to eat (*heᵉkaltî 'etᵉkem*), and so there was to be a memorial to that divine provision. Following the instructions, Moses saw to it that Aaron put the manna 'in front of the testimony'. This must have occurred later, as the building of the Tent of Meeting and the ark had not taken place at this time. The ark is variously designated in the Old Testament ('the ark of the covenant', 'the ark of the LORD', 'the holy ark'), and calling it 'the ark of the testimony' occurs thirteen times. The word 'testimony' ('*êdût*) is applied to God's testimonies, the tabernacle, and the ark, while in a few instances it stands alone to designate the ark (here in 16:34 and in 27:21; 30:36; Lev. 16:13). The final two verses, which may also have been added later than the main narrative here, note that the food of heaven was provided for a period of forty years, and that the size of an omer was one tenth of an ephah.

---

11. The Hebrew verb 'will you refuse' is 2 pers. m. pl.

The Grumbling Community 16:1-36

Study Questions

1) From the previous behaviour of the Israelites, could their grumbling about lack of food have been anticipated?

2) The Egyptians had to learn that the Israelites' God was the LORD (7:5). Why did the redeemed people need further convincing of the same truth (v. 12)?

3) Can you suggest any reasons why God gave a previously unknown food (the manna) rather than something with which the people were already familiar?

4) The law of the Sabbath was yet to be promulgated in the Decalogue (20:8-11). What did the people know about the Sabbath at the time of the giving of the manna?

9

Water from the Rock
(17:1-7)

The next section in this book (Exod. 17:1–18:27) continues the narrative of how Israel moved southwards towards Sinai. Three problems that the people faced are noted. First of all, they were again desperate for water (see the comments on the previous incident (15:23-27), and the LORD had to intervene for them. Secondly, this need was just satisfactorily met when, still at Rephidim, they had their progress impeded by the military strength of the Amalekites. Then thirdly, the burdens on Moses from excessive responsibility for legal decisions were to be met by the appointment of leaders who were able to exercise a legal role.

1 Moving on from the Desert of Sin (see 16:1), all of Israel travelled by stages just as the LORD had commanded. In Hebrew there is a close link between the verb 'to set out' (*nâsaʻ*) and the expression 'travelling from place to place'. This latter expression is an attempt to translate 'by their stages' (*lᵉmasʻêhem*), with the noun 'stage' (*massaʻ*) coming from the root verb, 'to set out'. There was orderly progression on the way as determined by the LORD, but when they reached Rephidim, no water was available for them. The location of Rephidim cannot be ascertained with certainty, but usually it is identified as being Wadi Refayid in southwest Sinai.

2 Moses again became the object of the people's displeasure, as they quarrelled with him, and demanded that he provide water for them. 'To quarrel' is a Hebrew verb (*rîv*) that later in the Old Testament became a technical term for God's challenges to His erring covenantal people (see, e.g., Micah 6:2; Amos 7:4; Isa. 3:13; Jer. 2:9). The word *rîv* is the basis for the word naming the place where this dispute took place, Meribah (Heb. *m^erîvâh*; see v. 7). In reply Moses asks why the quarrel is directed to him, while the actions of the people are in effect putting the LORD to the test. The tables were reversed in that in the earlier incidents it was the LORD testing them (15:25; 16:4), whereas now it was the people of Israel testing their God. This aspect is picked up in a significant way by the psalmists as they recount the wilderness experiences (Pss. 78:18; 106:14, 25, 29).

3 Thirst drove the people to complain further against Moses.[1] Their earlier hunger had caused them to long to be back in Egypt and eating the food to which they had been accustomed. On this occasion they complained that the result of Moses' leadership was that they, their children, and their cattle were all going to die because of thirst.

4 In view of the previous intervention of God, when He had responded to the complaints (16:9, 11), Moses voiced his complaint to Him. The same verb is used here of Moses as occurred earlier regarding the cry of the people to the LORD (Exod. 2:23, *zâ'aq*).[2] The LORD's servant was compelled to approach his Sovereign seeking direction on how to deal with the people at this juncture. His fear was that he was shortly going to be stoned by them. The NIV translation, 'They are almost ready to stone me', is a good idiomatic translation of the Hebrew text here (lit. 'still a little [time] and they will stone me'). Other ancient Near Eastern law codes embodied capital punishment, but never by stoning. In the Mosaic code, stoning could apply to animals (Exod. 21:29) and to humans (Deut. 13:10; 17:5).

---

1. The verb here is *lûn*, Hi., 'to murmur' or 'grumble at someone', and is not to be confused with *lîn*, that means 'to spend the night'.

2. This is the basic form of this verb, though the orthographic variant, *tsâ'aq*, occurs as well. The same variation appears with the nouns for 'cry': *z^e'âqâh/ts^e'âqâh*. For further discussion, see *TDOT*, IV, p. 114.

5-6 God's instruction to Moses was to go ahead of the people, and to take with him some of the elders.[3] Also, he had to have in his hand the staff with which he had struck the river Nile at the time of the second sign (7:20). There is a marked difference, however, in the two incidents. The first one concerned making the water of the Nile undrinkable (7:21), while this one related to the provision of water in a desert situation. Moses was to stand by the rock at Horeb, which was an alternative name for Mount Sinai. Presumably here in this passage it is used with a wider connotation to denote the general area. This also explains why it is said that the meeting was to be 'at the rock' (*tsûr*), not 'at the mountain' (*hâr*). The final stage of the journey and the arrival at the mount itself is related in 19:1-2. God declared that He would Himself stand before Moses at the rock. While the text does not specify in what form God was going to appear, it is most natural to think of an appearance of the glory cloud. In the presence of the elders as witnesses, Moses fulfilled the Lord's command to him, striking the rock so that water would flow. This supernatural event was remembered later in the poetry of Israel (see Ps. 105:41).

7 Moses gave to that place the names Massah ('testing') and Meribah ('quarrelling'), doubtless as a reminder that there they tested the Lord by quarrelling and by saying, 'Is the Lord among us or not?' These names were meant to be a reminder to Israel, in time to come, of what transpired there. Psalmists reminded the people of the nature of what happened at Meribah and the Lord's reaction to their sin.[4]

---

3. The Heb. *mizziqᵉnê yisrâ'êl* embodies a good illustration of the partitive use of the preposition *min*, '*some* of the elders of the people'.

4. For discussion on the two accounts of testing at Meribah, see Gordon Wenham, *Numbers*, pp. 149-51, and Andrew Hill, 'Massah and Meribah', *NIDOTTE*, 4, pp. 931-33.

10

The Amalekites Defeated
(17:8-16)

This passage relates the first incident in which Israel was involved in battle with another nation after leaving Egypt. It is the first of many such battles, and the lesson should have been learned – victory would not come through natural ability or acquired military skills. Israel's trust had to be firmly rooted in the Lord as the defender of His people. Amalek was Esau's grandson (Gen. 36:15-16). The bitter relationship between Jacob (later called Israel, Gen. 32:22-28) and Esau was replicated in later times (see, for the biblical record, the encounters with Saul, 1 Sam. 15:1-35, and David, 1 Sam. 27:8-11, 30:1-20). All of them draw attention to the message that divine assistance, not military prowess, achieves victory against God's foes.

8-9 An unprovoked attack was made on Israel by the Amalekites, while the camp was still at Rephidim. Moses instructed Joshua to go out and engage in battle with the Amalekites on the following day, while he remained standing on the top of the hill with God's staff in his hand. This is the first biblical reference to Joshua, who was later to be designated as the leader in succession to Moses (Deut. 31:1-8). Joshua's earlier name was Hoshea ('salvation') but Moses changed it to 'Joshua' ('the Lord saves'; see Num. 13:8, 16). He was from the tribe of Ephraim, one of the largest and most powerful of the twelve tribes.

10-13 Joshua was obedient to the directions that the LORD had given him. Along with Moses, Aaron and Hur, he went up to the top of the hill. Hur is mentioned later in 24:14 as associated with Joshua in judicial work. He is also noted as the grandfather of Bezalel, the chief workman responsible for building the tabernacle (Exod. 31:2; 35:30; 38:22). The Jewish tradition about him, that claimed that he was the husband of Miriam, was preserved by Josephus.[1] While Moses had his hand with the staff in it lifted up, Israel prevailed, but whenever he lowered it through tiredness, Amalek prevailed. The staff was a symbol of God's power and, when lifted up, it denoted that He was acting in power to enable Israel to prevail over Amalek. To assist Moses, Joshua and Hur seated him on a stone, and helped by holding up his hands. This continued right through the day until sunset, by which time it was clear that the victory had been achieved.

14 The record of what had happened that day had to be recorded in '*the* scroll' (not '*a* scroll', as most English versions have it). This suggests an existing, well-known document recording important events in Israel's history.[2] The NIV rendering of the next clause, 'and make sure that Joshua hears it', is rather free. The Hebrew text has: 'and set it in the ears of Joshua', which probably is better translated as 'and recite in the ears of Joshua'. The message was that Amalek would ultimately be destroyed completely (see also v. 16).

15–16 Moses constructed an altar, just as the patriarchs did. Abraham built an altar where God had appeared to him (Gen. 12:7), as did Jacob when he arrived at Shechem, calling it 'God the God of Israel' (*'êl 'ĕlohê yisrā'êl*). The name given by Moses to this altar was 'The LORD is my Banner'. The Hebrew word for 'banner' (*nês*) meant a standard or signal pole, especially one used to rally troops in battle. Moses' appearance on the top of hill acted like a banner, and it indicated the presence of God with His people. The purpose of the altar is not stated, but from the name it would appear that it was more than just a commemorative stone. The word

---

1. *Antiq.* iii.2, §4.

2. A comparison can be made with the account in 2 Kings 22:8 when Hilkiah reports finding '*the* book of the law' during Josiah's reign, that is, the well-known book.

The Amalekites Defeated 17:8-16

'altar' (Heb. *mizbêach*) denotes the place where sacrifices are offered, and so one like this could serve the dual purpose of remembering God's graciousness in giving victory over the Amalekites, as well as providing a suitable site for making sacrificial offerings.

The first part of what Moses said is difficult to translate and interpret, as it reads like cryptic poetry. A literal translation is, 'For a hand[3] against/towards the throne of the LORD' (*kî yâd 'al kês yâh*). The text does not speak explicitly about 'my hand' or 'hands', while the Hebrew word *kês* seems to be an abbreviated form of the normal spelling of 'throne' (*kissê*').[4] 'The LORD' represents Yah, the abbreviated form of the divine name *yhwh* (see comment on 15:2). A Jewish interpretation was followed by the AV, 'Because the LORD hath sworn', and this has been accepted by the NASB and NKJV. Another interpretation is that the text is speaking of the actions of the Amalekites in raising their hands against the LORD (see NIV margin, 'because a hand was against the throne of the LORD, the LORD ...'; also NLT and ESV). While this viewpoint is possible, the connection between verses 15 and 16 inclines towards acceptance of the NIV understanding that the hand(s) referred to are those of Moses, lifted up in prayer towards God's throne.[5] Help had been given in answer to prayer, with the assurance that this was not just an isolated case but represented the LORD's continuing attitude towards the Amalekites. They would reap the reward for their challenge to His authority, and His hostility would be maintained generation after generation. Chapters 15 and 30 of 1 Samuel describe the ultimate blotting out of the Amalekites.

---

3. A variation of this is the view that the words relate to an oath by Moses. See the REB translation: 'My oath upon it'.

4. Many scholars have suggested altering *kês* to *nês*, 'banner', which, though fitting in with the immediate context, does not have manuscript support. The emendation is followed in various versions including the RSV and NRSV.

5. While accepting the NIV understanding, it is best to take *yâd*, hand to be '[my] hand', as the plural 'hands' would require different orthography. For this point, see Douglas Stuart, *Exodus*, p. 401, n. 216.

11

Provision of Judicial Help
(18:1-27)

This chapter relates something that happened after the giving of the law at Sinai. However, it is inserted here because it ties in with the theme of the previous chapters. Such linking by subject matter rather than chronology occurs elsewhere in the Old Testament.[1] The story about Jethro must follow 19:1 chronologically, as at the end of chapter 17 Israel had not yet reached Mount Sinai. Moreover, the account dealing with a Gentile both complements Israel's praise of the Lord (15:1-21) and contrasts with the unbelief of Israel demonstrated in the incidents recorded in 15:22–17:7. It also contrasts sharply with the attempt of other pagan Gentiles (the Amalekites) to destroy Israel by force (17:8-16).[2] Clues are given early in the Old Testament that Gentiles – non-Jews – were going to be incorporated within God's people. Examples are the provision for foreign slaves to be circumcised (Gen. 17:12-14), and the

---

1. Examples include the placing of the record of David's battles in 2 Sam. 8:1-14 after the declaration that God had given him rest from all his enemies, 2 Sam. 7:1; or the positioning of Isa. 38-39, that chronologically precede chs. 36–37. This phenomenon, sometimes called 'dischronologized narrative', occurs with some frequency in the Old Testament. For an introduction to this feature, see W. J. Martin, '"Dischronologized Narrative" in the Old Testament', *VT Supplements* vol. 17 (1968), pp. 179-86.

2. For discussion on these points, see Ralph Davis, *The Word Became Flesh: How to Preach from Old Testament Narrative Texts* (Fearn: Christian Focus Publications, 2007), pp. 78-80.

place of Moses' second wife, a Cushite, in the family of Israel (Num. 12:1). Later, other examples are provided of Gentiles like Rahab, Ruth, and Naaman who showed believing faith in Israel's God.

Here, then, is a significant account of Reuel/Jethro (see comment on 2:18) that demonstrates that non-Jews could profess that the LORD was truly the saviour God (18:10-12). Placing the chapter here forms a fitting hinge between the preceding narrative (the unbelief of Israel and the Amalekite antagonism) and the following chapter that asserts the saving activity of Israel's God (see especially 19:3-6 and 20:2).

a) The Meeting with Jethro (18:1-12)
1 News of God's intervention on behalf of both Moses and the people of Israel reached Jethro, his father-in-law, in Midian. He was fully acquainted with what had transpired since Moses had returned from there to Egypt, and what 'God had done for Moses and his people Israel'. He also knew that the exodus was indeed a demonstration of God's power, for freedom from Egypt's yoke was not achieved by Moses but by the LORD.

2-4 The time when Moses sent his wife Zipporah back to Midian is not stated. She was last mentioned at 4:24-26 (see comment). While the Hebrew verb here ('sent', *shâlach*, Pi.) can later have the meaning of 'divorce', there is no need to import that meaning here. All that the text says is that at an unspecified time Zipporah and her two sons returned to Midian, where Jethro received them. Gershom's name was already given in 2:21-22, while the second son was given a significant name relating to salvation, Eliezer ('my God is helper'). In expanding on the name giving, Moses related it to the fact that his father's God had been his deliverer from the sword of Pharaoh. Again, name-giving is linked to a specific period of his life. Whereas 'Gershom' was a reminder of alienation in foreign territory, 'Eliezer' was a reference to the salvation from the hands of Pharaoh and his troops.

5-6 Moses and the children of Israel were encamped at the mountain of God. Accompanied by Zipporah and her two sons, Jethro came to Moses in the desert, though first probably sending him notice that they were coming. The

MT simply has, 'and he [Jethro] said', where the verb can be translated as a pluperfect, 'and he *had* said'. The NIV expands this to, 'and Jethro had sent word to him', which, while not a literal translation, may be a legitimate inference.

7-8 When Moses and Jethro meet again, Moses showed due deference to his father-in-law, bowing down and kissing him. The NIV paraphrases the words in the MT regarding greeting another. The Hebrew idiom for asking someone how they are is, 'Is it peace (*shâlôm*) with you?' Literally the Hebrew text reads, 'And they asked each other concerning peace', that is, they went through the normal ritual of greeting. In the tent Moses related three things to Jethro: first, what the LORD had done to Pharaoh and his people on account of Israel; secondly, the hardships they had experienced on the way, doubtless including the problem caused by the people's unbelief; and, thirdly, the LORD's saving activity. Redemption from Egypt was by the sovereign power of the LORD, and hereafter this became the model for God's salvation on later occasions.

9 Moses' account brought joy to Jethro as he heard of God's intervention on Israel's behalf, delivering them from the power of the Egyptians. Again, as in verse 4, the same Hebrew verb is used, though translated differently by the NIV (*nâtsal*, Hi.). Probably the reference to 'all the good things' God had done requires emphasis, as the term 'the good' (*hattôvâh*) was part of the covenantal language of Israel denoting the blessings bestowed by God.[3] In rescuing Israel from slavery God had fulfilled covenantal promises made long before (Gen. 15:13-15; Exod. 2:23-25).

10-11 These verses consist of a doxology that Jethro proclaimed. It is a declaration in honour of Israel's God (*yhwh*) who rescued (again in Heb., *nâtsal*) both Moses and the people from Pharaoh and the Egyptians. 'Praise be to the LORD' (*bârûch yhwh*) is a standardised form of adoration expressed to God, though often in the Old Testament, especially in the book of Psalms, there is added, 'Israel's God', (*'elohê yisrâêl*; see, for example, Pss. 41:13; 72:18; 106:48). Jethro went on to state his conviction concerning the superiority of the LORD over

---

3. See in particular, A. R. Millard, 'For He is Good', *TB*, 1966, pp. 115-17, and the literature he cites. Fuller discussion concerning the covenantal significance of *tôv* and *tôvâh* is found in P. Kalluveetil, *Declaration and Covenant*, pp. 42-50.

all other gods, for he had seen how the LORD had punished those who had treated His people in such a contemptuous and arrogant fashion.[4] Clearly there was deepening faith on Jethro's part and he had come to the point of confessing the exclusive claims of Israel's God. At some point, undesignated in the text, Jethro became a true follower of Israel's God.[5] The fact that his descendants went up with the people of Judah to live near Arad confirms his commitment (Judg. 1:16).

12 The priest of Midian then proceeded to bring (MT, 'took', *lâqach*) sacrificial offerings, 'burnt offerings and other sacrifices'. While the text does not explicitly say who actually performed the sacrificial ritual, if it was Jethro then this would be an indication that he had come to real faith in Israel's God, confirming the impression given in verses 10-11. The terms used of the sacrifices are well known from elsewhere in the Old Testament. Burnt offerings (*'olâh*) later denoted bringing an offering that was totally consumed on the altar. They were often offered on occasions of joy, usually accompanying another sacrifice. 'Other sacrifices' (*z^{e}vâchîm*) was a term often used in connection with peace offerings, but sometimes a distinction is drawn between them (Num. 15:8; Josh. 22:27). What followed was a meal, shared by Jethro with Aaron and the elders of Israel whom he brought with him. While there is no mention of a covenant, yet the account is very similar to what is related in Genesis 26:31 and 31:54, and it may be that there was a formal agreement between Jethro and the Israelites.[6] Likewise, Exodus 24:11 records how the elders of Israel 'ate and drank' with God on the mount, illustrating a regular practice associated with making treaties.

b) *Jethro's Advice (18:13-23)*

Moses' roles had come to be extensive. There is no recognition that he was formally appointed to the position of judge,

---

4. Another interpretation of the second part of v. 11 is that it refers not to the Egyptians but to the 'gods' just mentioned in the first part of the verse: 'for in the thing wherein they dealt proudly *he was* above them' (AV). This is a possible, but less likely, interpretation.

5. The case of another Gentile, Naaman, is significant, and he made a similar confession as Jethro had made. See 2 Kings 5:15.

6. See the comments of John Currid and the literature he cites, *Exodus*, vol. 1, p. 379.

as depicted in this section. It may be that the people were acknowledging that his Egyptian training qualified him to act in this way, as well as the fact that he had dynamic leadership gifts. Jethro, having confessed his faith in the LORD, was prepared to offer good advice to his son-in-law, which was taken up and acted upon by him.

13-14 On the next day, Moses took what appears to be have been his usual seat and engaged in judging. All day long, from morning till evening, the people were gathered around him. Jethro was watching and questioned him about the process: 'What is this that you are doing for the people? Why do you alone sit as judge, while all the people stand around you from morning till evening?' His concern, spelt out more fully a few verses later (see vv. 18-23), revolved around the fact that Moses was single-handedly exercising the judicial role among the people.

15-16 Moses' response was not a defence of his actions, but simply a statement of the practice in the patriarchal period of revelation. When people were in a dispute they needed to seek God's will. The normal ways of doing this was by going to a place of worship (Gen. 25:22; Num. 27:21) or to a prophet (1 Sam. 9:9; 1 Kings 22:8). Moses was fulfilling the latter role, determining cases and also giving instruction in 'God's laws and decrees'. This statement is important, for it shows that even before the giving of the law on Sinai, God's decrees were being brought into some coherent document (see the reference in 15:25-26), and from it Moses was able to teach the people. Judgment in disputes was not given arbitrarily, but on the basis of revelation.

17 Jethro's summary of the situation was in few words: 'What you are doing is not good'. He could see the weaknesses in the situation, and the following verses record the various reasons that lay behind this statement.

18 The first reason that Jethro gave was the task that Moses had taken on himself was too heavy a burden for him as well as for those who came to him. This may be saying that the people were wearied by their long wait for a hearing, so that judge and people were finding the current situation overly tiresome.

19-20 Jethro's proposal was recognition of Moses' role as representative of the people before God, and also of him as their instructor in relation to God's statutes and laws (*'et hachuqqîm v^e'et hattôrot*). His position was unique in Israel, for no one else had the relationship he had with God, who spoke to him face to face (Num. 12:7-8). In regard to this whole matter, Jethro expressed the desire that God would overrule so that His will would be done ('may God be with you'). An unusual word for 'teach' or 'instruct' is used in verse 20 (*zâhar*, Hi.). It occurs twenty-one times in the Old Testament, of which fifteen are in the book of Ezekiel in passages speaking of Ezekiel's role as a watchman. His task was to warn the people, pointing out to them the danger they were in. A comparison with 2 Chronicles 19:10, where the word is used of the task of the newly appointed judges to warn the people lest they incur God's wrath, suggests that a similar meaning is quite appropriate here (ESV, 'you shall *warn* them about the statutes and the laws'). 'Statutes' is a regular term for specific instructions and at times equivalent to 'covenant' (cf. Pss. 25:10; 132:12), while 'laws' covers a broader sweep of God's revelation.[7] The aim was to reinforce instructions on how to live ('the way in which they should go') and the duties they had to perform ('the work they should do').

21-22 The qualifications of those to be judges stressed the fact that they had to be morally upright in order to fulfil this role. They had to have innate ability (lit. 'men of worth', Heb. *cháyil*), be living reverently before God, be trustworthy, and not attempt to achieve dishonest gain by taking bribes. The concept of reverent living ('fearing God') becomes an important idea later in the Old Testament, especially in the Psalms and the book of Proverbs (see, Pss. 34:9; 111:10; 112:1; Prov. 8:13). These selected men were to be placed over a graduated series – over thousands, hundreds, fifties and tens. Their role was to serve as perpetual judges, but only dealing with less important cases, for anything more serious was still to be dealt with by Moses himself.

23 If according to God's will all this came to pass, then the people would be satisfied that justice had been executed fairly. They would go to their homes satisfied (lit. 'in peace').

---

7. For discussion on these terms, and others relating to revelation of God's word to man, see Willem van Gemeren, 'Reflections: The Word of God', 'Psalms', *EBC*, vol. 5, pp. 220-22.

No mention is made of the number of these judicial officials, but the same type of divisions in the nation operated after the entry into Canaan (Josh. 7:16-18).[8]

c) The Appointment of Judicial Assistants (18:24-27)

24-27 Moses' wisdom and humility showed in his acceptance of the advice that his father-in-law gave him, implicitly carrying out his plan to ease his burden while still providing efficient legal administration. The only difference in the distinction between the cases is that in verse 22 they are called 'the big matter' and ' the small matter', while in verse 25 they are described as 'the hard matter' and 'the small matter'. The chapter ends with a note that balances the opening of the chapter. There Jethro arrives with his family to meet Moses at the mountain of God (v. 5). Now his departure is noted (v. 27) as he returns to his own land.

Study Questions

1) The second miracle involving the provision of water is recorded in 17:1-7 (for the previous one, see 15:22-25). Why was such repetition necessary?

2) What is there in the narrative in 17:8-16 that points to the fact that Moses' action in lifting up his hands was prayer?

3) How much does Moses' names for his sons (18:2-4) tell us of his understanding of God's intervention in his life at this time?

4) How did Jethro's plan for the administration of law serve as a model for Israel later in Canaan?

---

8. For a chart, setting out the civil, judicial, and military groupings in Israel, see *NIDOTTE*, 2, pp. 1139-41.

PART III

The Covenant at Sinai
(19:1–24:18)

Introduction

In chapter 24, mention is made of Moses writing down 'everything the LORD had said' (24:4), and then that 'he took the Book of the Covenant and read it to the people' (24:7). These references raise various questions that have stimulated considerable discussion. The most common position is to say that the Book of the Covenant comprises 20:22–23:33, that is, the section following the Decalogue until the start of the passage describing the confirmation of the covenant at Sinai. As the text itself does not specify the contents, an exegetical decision has to be made as to what parts of the previous sections were incorporated in it.

First, though, a comment needs to be made on the Hebrew phrase in 24:7 (*sêfer habbᵉrît*). The translation of it into English has been 'the book of the covenant' at least as far back as the AV of 1611, probably drawing on the Latin Vulgate (*volumen foederis*) and the LXX (*to biblion tês diathêkês*). But the use of 'book' is an anachronism, since the earliest books were codices originating probably in the first century A.D. Sheets of papyrus were stitched so that various documents were bound together, and this format later developed into our present books. In translating the Old Testament text the Hebrew word *sêfer* should be rendered as 'scroll' or 'document'.

The content of the scroll of the covenant is uncertain, but serious questions must be asked about the common view that it only embraces material following the Decalogue. The reference in 24:4 to writing down all the words of the LORD must refer to the preceding verse ('When Moses went and told the people all the LORD's words and laws'), and in turn this must go back to 21:1: 'These are the laws you are to set before them'. But in 20:22 there is mention of God's speaking to Moses, and hence, in accordance with the common view, 20:22-26 are also to be reckoned as part of the covenant scroll. But the further question then arises: Can we look back even earlier than 20:22 to view material that could have been part of that scroll? In 24:7 it is said that in sprinkling the blood of the sacrifice on the people, Moses said: 'This is the blood of the covenant that the LORD has made with you in accordance with all these words'. That appears to indicate that the events of chapter 24 (the ratification of the covenant) were carried out in obedience to the full covenantal provisions, including the Decalogue. This means that what follows is the expansion and explanation of the basic principles asserted in the Decalogue. Hence, the Decalogue must be the foundation on which the following chapters are based, and must be regarded as an important part of the content of the scroll of the covenant.[1]

The issue of the content of the scroll needs also to embrace consideration of chapter 19. It is programmatic of what follows, for it is proclaiming the new relationship of Israel to the LORD – a priestly kingdom with access to the divine presence.[2] This means that the contents of chapter 19 link in with 24:1-11 almost as anticipation and realisation, with a very definite association between 19:3b-8 with 24:3-8.[3] Though not strongly supported in current discussions, if the main contents of chapter 19 are closely linked with the Decalogue and its exposition in 20:1–23:33, then it seems most probable that the scroll of the covenant should be viewed as

---

1. The position that the scroll of the covenant contains the Decalogue along with 20:22–23:33 has been argued by G. Ch. Aalders, *A Short Introduction to the Pentateuch* (London: Tyndale Press, 1949), pp. 148-49. He wrote: '... we venture to assert that the Decalogue must be considered as a constituent part of the covenant, even as a fundamental part (cf. also Ex. xxxiv.28; Dt. iv.13, ix.9f.)'.

2. See the discussion by John A. Davies, *A Royal Priesthood: Literary and Intertextual Perspectives on an Image of Israel in Exodus 19:6* (London: T. & T. Clark International, 2004), pp. 61-102.

3. ibid., pp. 113-24. The Jewish scholar, U. Cassuto, argued that is possible to understand chapter 19 as being part of the Book of the Covenant. While he opts for the position that the Book was probably a short general document, he wrote: 'If the Book of the Covenant was a written record of all the words of the Covenant, it would have been necessary to include not only the ordinances but also, and in particular, the essence of the covenant, namely, the proposals advanced in xix. 5-6, and the fundamental principles contained in the Decalogue'. *A Commentary on the Book of Exodus* (Jerusalem: Magnes Press, 1987), p. 312.

incorporating the place of Israel.[4] Hence, in the discussion that follows I will understand the content of that scroll to contain virtually all of God's revelation to Israel embodied in chapters 19–23.

---

4. One modern scholar who takes this position is William Kaiser, Jr. See his words in 'Exodus', p. 508: 'The Book of the Covenant contains in its narrowest meaning in scholarly use today words from 20:22 to 23:33 but more fully, here [24:7], the contents of chapter 19, the Decalogue of chapter 20, and the case laws of 20:22 to 23:33.'

12

At Mount Sinai
(19:1-24)

1 The Chosen People (19:1-6)

The narrative in this chapter is a continuation of the account given in chapter 17 concerning the period Israel spent at Rephidim. The time had come for the people to move on and reach Sinai where God was going to meet them in a special way. This chapter is notable for the description given of their exodus from Egypt and their new status as a kingdom of priests (vv. 4-6), a passage that is the foundation of Peter's description of the nature of the New Testament Christian community (1 Pet. 2:9-10).

At Sinai, God communicated with the people through Moses, the covenantal mediator. God's stated purpose in redeeming Israel from Egypt is highly significant, for it contains a combination of terms that encapsulates the teaching of Exodus relating to the new status of Israel before God. They were not just a collection of families but were now designated as a nation before him. At Sinai they would come under a new covenant that supplemented the earlier one to the patriarchs. The earlier one was not set aside, but to the promises given in it (the covenant with Abraham) was added the law given through Moses (the Sinai covenant). This is the explanation of the relationship between the two covenants set out by the apostle Paul in Galatians 3:15-21.[1] Exodus 19 is an important

---

1. Paul poses the question, 'Is the law, therefore, opposed to the promises of

part of the narrative in Exodus dealing with the covenant at Sinai. Its teaching is integral to the divine revelation that is contained from this point right through to Numbers 10, with a few narrative sections intervening.

1-2 Three months after leaving Egypt, the people of Israel left Rephidim and moved on to the wilderness of Sinai. The derivation of the name 'Sinai', and also its precise geographical location, are both uncertain. The traditional view, that Sinai is the present Jebel Musa, can be traced back at least to the fourth century A.D., when Christian hermits settled there. Jebel Musa is on the southern Sinai Peninsula, and it rises to a height of 7,500 feet (2,286 m). The word 'Sinai' by itself only appears five times in the Hebrew Bible, while it occurs more frequently in the compound 'mountain of Sinai', or, as here, 'the wilderness of Sinai'. The latter expression denotes the desert area at the base of the mount itself. There Israel camped, and to emphasise the significance of the location, the narrative takes note that it was the wilderness before the mountain of God. The people remained on the plain while Moses ascended the mountain to meet with God.

3 This is the record of the first of seven ascents of Mount Sinai by Moses. He went up seemingly of his own initiative, as no mention is made of a direct command to do so. However, he could have recalled the LORD's words from the appearance at the burning bush (Exod. 3:12). The divine voice called to him, 'Thus you shall say to the house of Jacob and tell the people of Israel'. The word 'thus' (Heb. *koh*) was later used consistently by the prophets as an indication that their messages were indeed revelation from God, and they were merely spokesmen for Him. The message was addressed to 'the house of Jacob' and 'the children of Israel'. The phrases are synonymous terms for the progeny of Abraham who came down into Egypt, the original seventy (Exod. 1:5) who had increased greatly during the Egyptian sojourn.

4 The first part of the message was a reminder of what had happened in Egypt immediately before the exodus. It was an open demonstration of God's power as He displayed His

---

God? Absolutely not!' (Gal. 3:21). This response is given in a very emphatic way in the Greek, *mē genoito* (lit. 'let it not be!').

signs and wonders against the Egyptians. Towards His own people God had acted like an eagle as He carried them out of their slavery in Egypt to meet with Him at Sinai. This is a beautiful simile, as the eagle is noted both for its power and also its meticulous care and protection of its young. The same illustration of God's care for His people occurs in the song that the LORD gave to Moses and Aaron to teach the Israelites just prior to their entry into Canaan (Deut. 32:11-12). The sovereignty of His actions is stressed by the repeated use of 'I': "what *I* did', '*I* carried you', '*I* brought you'. The initiative in covenantal formulation was with God.

5 The second part of the message ('Now if you obey me fully ...') has suggested to some interpreters that the covenant was conditional upon obedience being given by the people. However, it is plain from the text here and elsewhere that the covenantal relationship was already in existence, and what happened at Sinai was a continuation and amplification of the Abrahamic covenant. What was conditional was enjoyment of the blessings of the covenant, and the only fitting response of the people was to affirm their willingness to obey (see vv. 8 and 24:7).[2] The covenant is declared to be God's covenant ('*my* covenant'), which explains why He could demand total obedience (lit. 'if you will indeed obey *my* voice').

The special relationship of Israel was that she was to be the LORD's treasured possession, and also be to Him a kingdom of priests and a holy nation. These terms are highly significant. The Hebrew word (*s^{e}gullâh*) translated 'treasured possession' has strong connotations of a privileged position. It only occurs seven times in the Old Testament. In 1 Chronicles 29:3 it is used of special treasure belonging to David, which he was giving to God's temple. In Deuteronomy 7:6, 14:2, and 26:18 it occurs in almost identical expressions and in a similar way to that here in Exodus 19:5. It appears again in Malachi 3:17, while in Psalm 135:4 it is used alongside the verb 'to choose' (*bâchar*). The idea of a strong link between God's choice and

---

2. On issues relating to this covenant, see the very helpful discussion by John Murray, *NBD*, p. 266. Wider aspects of this feature are brought out by Richard Pratt, Jr., 'Were the Covenants with Abraham and David Conditional?' *God's Fiery Challenger for Our Time: Festschrift in honor of Stephen Tong*, ed. Benjamin Intan (Jakarta: Reformed Center for Religion and Society, 2007), pp. 137-67.

Israel being a treasured possession comes out clearly in this passage also.

6 The following expressions denote the relationship of Israel with the Lord, but also the responsibility she had of serving Him and being a light to the nations. Israel was to be a kingdom of priests, an expression that depends on the fact that the covenant formulated at Sinai was a proclamation of God's kingship over Israel. The role of the priests was both in the area of sacrificial worship and also in teaching the people (see Mal. 2:4-7). Perhaps the two ideas are combined here, for Israel was to be a worshipping community (with everyone being a priest), and also with the task of teaching others the ways of the Lord. Moreover, the redeemed people of God had to reflect God's own character in that they were called to be 'a holy nation'. They were to be holy, just as He was holy (Lev. 19:2), a principle of imitation of God that carries over into the New Testament, for the goal is that believers will ultimately be like God (1 John 3:2). Moses was commissioned to deliver this message to the people.

2 Consecration of the People (19:7-15)

7-9 Moses gathered the elders and passed on 'all these words that the Lord had commanded him'. Presumably they brought the community together, for the people gave a collective response: 'All that the Lord has spoken we will do'. This is one of the ways in which Israel showed acquiescence with the covenantal demands. On other occasions the response of the people was a solemn 'Amen' (Deut. 27:15-26; Josh. 8:30-35) or the taking of an oath (Ezra 10:1-5; Neh. 10:28-29). When the Lord heard Moses' report He gave an assurance that He was coming to meet with the people. What was promised was another theophany in the form of a thick cloud, though clearly not the pillar of cloud. As a full revelation of God is impossible (Exod. 20:19), He appeared in concealed form in a cloud (for other similar theophanies, see Exod. 40:34-38; 1 Kings 8:10-11; Matt. 17:5). The purpose was that the people, though not seeing God, could hear Him speaking with Moses, and this would serve as a confirmation for them of Moses' role as their covenantal mediator. The later account in Deuteronomy 5 notes how the Lord spoke on Mount Sinai, the people heard, and feared lest they would be consumed (vv. 22-27). Moses conveyed to God the people's words.

10-11 True worship of God necessitated both internal and external preparation. Earlier Moses had to obey God's instructions as he approached Him (3:5). Now the people as a whole had to take due care as they came near to the holy mountain. The first instruction for the people was that on that day and the next Moses was to consecrate the people. The verb 'consecrate' comes from the root 'to be holy' (*q-d-sh*). Here the form is the intensive theme (Pi.) and it conveys the idea of setting someone or something in a state of holiness, of separation to and for God. Later in this chapter the same verbal form is used of consecration of the mountain (v. 23; for other examples of the same use of this verb, see v. 14, Josh. 7:13, Job 1:5, and 1 Sam. 16:5). In the book of Leviticus there are repeated instructions regarding laundering and then bathing (see, for example, Lev. 14:8; 16:28; 17:15), but here there is no mention of bathing. The people had to make due preparation for a highly significant meeting with God that was going to take place 'tomorrow' (for other places with the same combination of 'consecrate' and 'tomorrow', see Num. 11:18; Josh. 3:5; 7:13). Approaching God required a consciousness that those coming to Him needed to be free of outward contamination, with the time interval important as denoting a period in which holiness was high on the agenda.

12-13 Boundaries were to be placed around Mount Sinai itself lest there be an unwarranted intrusion into the place where God was going to reveal Himself in His glory. No ill-prepared attempt was to be made to approach the holy God. Some markers were probably put in place to confine the Israelites to their camp and to indicate the limits of their movements. Anyone who heedlessly came near the mountain, or touched even the edge of it, was to be devoted to God, and hence suffer the death penalty. If an executioner even touched the transgressor, he too would be contaminated. This meant that any penalty had to be imposed without touching the victim, and so stoning or killing by shooting a dart was prescribed. The instruction ended with the prescription that the people should come up to the mountain when they heard a long blast of the trumpet. The trumpet (*yovêl*) was made from a ram's horn, and blowing it appears to have been used to indicate God's presence, either as saviour or destroyer (cf. Josh. 6:8 and Rev. 8:6). The trumpet was also used to denote the start of the year of remission, 'the jubilee' (Lev. 25:10, 11; Num. 36:4; the English word 'jubilee' derives from the Heb. *yovêl*).

14-15 Moses the mediator obeyed implicitly the instructions given him, going down from the mountain and sanctifying the people, while they carried out the ritual washing of clothes. He instructed the people to be ready for the third day just as God had commanded (v. 11). The final word of command was not to go near a woman. This is a case in which the verb *nâgash*, 'touch' (like *qârav*, 'draw near') is used of sexual relations. Why this restriction was made is unexplained. Sexual relations between spouses in themselves were not sinful, but on such an occasion it would render the couple ceremonially unclean, and also indicate that their own relationship took precedence over the relationship with their covenantal lord.

3 Meeting with God (19:16-24)

These verses record the divine theophany, a theophany that was to be continued after the giving of the Decalogue (see 20:18-21; Deut. 5:22-27). They also note the limitations placed on the people lest they approach too near to the LORD's presence. Such an event was a demonstration of God's might and His ability to control natural forces. A similar theophany occurred later when Elijah went to Mount Sinai (called by its alternate name, Horeb, in 1 Kings 19:8), where he was confronted by a mighty wind, an earthquake, fire, and most probably a strong voice (1 Kings 19:11-12).[3] The darkness and the earthquake at Jesus' death on Calvary is another example of this type of theophany (Matt. 27:45-54).

---

3. The traditional rendering in 1 Kings 19:12 of the Heb. expression *qôl d^emâmâh daqqâh* is 'a still small voice'. But the expression is difficult, and the context demands a translation like 'a thunderous voice'. This is the translation of Jeffrey Niehaus, *God at Sinai: Covenant Theology in the Bible and Ancient Near East* (Grand Rapids: Zondervan, 1995), p. 238. His translation is supported by David Howard, 'David's "Lamp" (1 Kings 11:26), and "A Still Small Voice" (1 Kings 19:12)', Part 1 of 4 Parts of 'My Favourite Mistranslations', *BS* 171 (January-March 2014), pp. 3-18.

16 On the morning of the appointed third day the theophany consisted of thunder, lightning, a thick cloud, and a very loud blast of the trumpet (here *shôfâr*, the more general word for 'trumpet', is used, not *yovêl*). These combined as a majestic appearance of God. All the forces of nature were at His disposal, while fire and cloud were specifically signs of His presence. This was so at the garden of Eden (Gen. 3:24), at God's appearance to Abraham confirming His covenantal promises (Gen. 15:17), and at Moses' experience at the burning bush (Exod. 3:2). The revelation by the cloud is one of the most distinctive features of the book of Exodus. It was the pillar of cloud that led the people out of Egypt (13:21-22), that protected them (14:19-20), and in which His glory was revealed (16:10). Not surprisingly the response of the people was one of awe, as they trembled before the LORD.

17-18 Moses led the people out to the foot of the mountain, as the prerogative of going to the top of it belonged only to Moses, Aaron, Nadab, and Abihu, and the seventy elders (24:9). There they stationed themselves. The mountain, the whole of it (*kullô*), was encompassed by smoke, like the smoke generated by a kiln. The whole mountain shook, the narrative using the same verb (*chârad*) as used in reference to the people trembling (v. 16). The stress in the narrative is placed on the fact that the whole mountain was involved in the theophany, not just a restricted part of it (*v^{e}yech^{e}rad kol hâhâr me'od*).

19-20 As God had already indicated, the trumpet blast was used as a signal, and it 'grew much louder and louder'.[4] The second part of verse 19 can be understood to refer to Moses' speaking as being the sound of the trumpet, to which the thunder was a reply. Alternatively, it can be taken as a conversation between Moses and God, and thus one of the occasions when God spoke with him 'face to face' (Exod. 33:11; Num. 12:8). God condescended to come down on to the top of Mount Sinai, and to that place Moses was called.

21-22 Moses was instructed to return to the people in order to warn them not to come too close. Curiosity was not to govern their actions, for attempts to view God would lead

---

4. The Hebrew idiom here uses the particp. of the verb *hâlak* in a metaphorical sense expressing progress (*hôlêk v^{e}châzêk me'od*). For this usage, see *DIHG~S*, Rem. 3, pp. 125-26.

to capital punishment. The verb used for this communication by Moses (*'ûd*, Hi.) is one that occurs elsewhere in legal and covenantal contexts. It may well carry that sort of overtone here, as Moses conveyed the sovereign's message to His people. It was a solemn warning to them lest they come too close to God. The priests also needed warning, lest they tried to come without formal consecration (the same verb is used as in verse 10 of the people as a whole). The threatened punishment in their case was that God would 'break out' (*pârats*) against them, i.e., God's judgment would not be constrained but burst forth upon them.[5] These priests could have been elders (3:18; 12:21; 18:12) or younger men (24:5).

23-24 The LORD had already indicated that the people as a whole were not permitted to come up the mount (vv. 12-13), and so Moses reminded Him of that previous instruction. Permission was given for Aaron to accompany Moses up on the mount, but priests and people were prohibited from coming up to the top of the mountain. The concept of 'breaking through' is continued in this verse, using the same verbs as in verses 21 and 22 (*hâras* and *pârats*), 'break through' and 'cause a breach'. If the people broke through, forcing their way to the top of the mount, then God would act in judgment against them.

---

5. For the use of both *pârats* and the noun *pérets* (a cognate accusative), see the case of Uzzah in 2 Sam. 6:8: *pârats yhwh pérets be'uzzâh*, lit. 'the Lord breached a breach against Uzzah'.

13

The Ten Words
(19:25–20:1-17)

This section is crucial, since it sets out the constitutional charter for Israel, the nation committed to the Lord by His sovereign choice. In chapter 24, reference is made to 'the book of the covenant' (*sêfer habberît*, 24:7), and this seems to be a term that includes chapter 19, the giving of the Decalogue, and the application of it that follows (20:22–23:33).[1] Clearly these two sections belong together, as they constitute two aspects of the same legal framework. The first, the Decalogue, contains the prescriptive law, while the section that follows is the descriptive version. In the one, there are direct instructions ('you shall/shall not ...'), while the other contains case law ('when/if ...').

Several facts about these covenantal requirements are important.

1. The pattern exhibited in the Mosaic covenant is similar to many extra-biblical treaties from the Ancient Near East. The pattern observable in Exodus, and in the renewals of this covenant made on either side of the Jordan (Deut. 29–30 and Josh. 24) show a correspondence with those from the second millennium B.C. The pattern of these treaties (preamble, historical prologue, stipulations, curses and blessings, and oath) is reflected here

---
1. See the earlier discussion on the scroll of the covenant, pp. 189-91.

in the Decalogue as it is in the renewal of the covenant forty years later, as described in Deuteronomy.

2. The intent of the Decalogue was not to introduce new ways of thinking about God and His demands on men. Rather, the principles underlying the Decalogue can be seen in the narratives in Genesis since their substance had been part of God's law from the beginning. To take the case of the Sabbath, it was clearly known and practised prior to the instructions concerning it given at Sinai (Exod. 20:8-11; 23:12). God had blessed the Sabbath (Gen. 2:3), the week of seven days was understood (Gen. 29:27), and the Sabbath observed during the early wilderness experience (Exod. 16:22-30).

3. It is clear that the covenant at Sinai was made in fulfilment of the covenant with Abraham (Exod. 2:24; 3:16-17). The same sovereign administration of grace prevailed as in the Abrahamic covenant (and its renewals to Isaac and Jacob).

4. The setting of the Decalogue in Exodus 20 is against the background of the redemption from Egypt. Its opening words, 'I am the LORD your God, who brought you up out of the land of Egypt, out of the house of bondage', summarise the narrative about God's redemption of Israel already narrated in earlier chapters of this book. The redemption was an expression of God's love for Israel (Deut. 7:8).

5. A corollary of the previous point is that the new aspects of the relation between God and Israel expressed in the Sinai covenant did not depend on obedience by Israel of God's demands. Israel's privileged position was based on God's grace, not upon works.

6. The so-called 'Ten Commandments' are never referred to in that way in the Hebrew text. They are called 'the ten words' (Exod. 34:28; Deut. 4:13; 10:4), and in two passages the implication is that they are equivalent to 'covenant'. The English term, 'Decalogue', has come into English from Greek and Latin, and is an accurate

reflection of the Hebrew expression. This point is significant, as the Decalogue does not equate to modern legal codes. It lacks the detail and the penalties that we associate with our laws. Rather, the Decalogue belongs to the broader concept of covenant.[2] In the discussion that follows, if the ten parts of the Decalogue are being referred to they will be designated by the use of a capital 'W' – Word(s).

7. Expressions used in the biblical text make explicit the link between the Decalogue and God's covenant with Israel. It is called 'testimony' (Exod. 25:16, 21; 40:20; cf. 2 Kings 17:15), while the tablets on which it was written are called 'the tablets of the covenant' (Deut. 9:9, 11, 15), or 'the tablets of the testimony' (Exod. 31:18; 32:15; 34:29), or even 'the covenant' (1 Kings 8:21). The ark in which the tablets were placed is called either 'the ark of the covenant' or 'the ark of the testimony'.

8. The manner in which the Decalogue was given emphasised its significance. It was given through Moses as the covenantal mediator (Exod. 21:1; Deut. 5:31; 6:1), and the law was written with 'the finger of God' (Exod. 31:18; Deut. 9:10). This was a recognition that the source of the law was God Himself, just as the magicians in Egypt had recognised that the plague of insects had come by 'the finger of God' (Exod. 8:19).

Nowhere in the Old Testament is any indication given as to how the Ten Words are to be divided. Three different systems are in operation. 1. The Protestants and Greek Catholics follow Josephus (*Antiquities* iii.5.5) in making verse 2 the preface and then it is followed by the Ten Words. On this enumeration exclusive worship of God is separated from the prohibition of idolatry. 2. Roman Catholics and Lutherans combine the first two Words together, and then, in order to

---

2. This point has been made decisively by Meredith Kline, in his book *The Structure of Biblical Authority* (Grand Rapids: Eerdmans, 1972), pp. 118-19: 'The revelation they [the tablets] contain is nothing less than an epitome of the covenant granted by Yahweh, the sovereign Lord of heaven and earth, to his elect and redeemed servant, Israel. Not law, but covenant—that must be affirmed when we are seeking a category comprehensive enough to do justice to this revelation in its totality.'

get back to the number ten, divide the tenth Word into two, separating covetousness of a neighbour's house from coveting a neighbour's wife and property. 3. Jewish scholars, from soon after the New Testament era, combined the so-called 'preface' with verse 3, the prohibition of worshipping any other God but the Lord. From that point the order follows the normal Protestant order.

The biblical text never suggests that verse 2, the 'preface', is not part of the Ten Words. Hence, it makes good sense to combine it with the traditional first word. The combined Word identifies the Lord as the redeemer God and then links this with His claim to exclusive worship.

19:25 The final verse of chapter 19 simply indicates that Moses fulfilled his commission, delivering the Lord's message for the people. However, it is important as it provides the link between the account of Moses' reception of the Ten Words and the actual transmission of them according to the divine instructions.

1 The First Word (20:1-3)

20:1 This section commences with the simple note that God spoke 'all these words', that is, the 'Words' that follow. This is important, as it points to the fact that God did not leave His people without clear revelation concerning both His character and His demands on His redeemed people.

2-3 Earlier, God had declared more than once that He was the Lord, the gracious God of the covenant (see 6:2, 6-8; 12:12). On stating in this formal way His demands on His children, he joined that declaration with His redemptive purposes expressed in bringing His people, Israel, out of bondage to the Egyptians. Having experienced this deliverance, Israel should readily acknowledge that His victory over the gods of Egypt indeed demonstrated that He was the only God (12:12). To Him exclusive honour and obedience was due. The God who claimed to be their God ('I am the Lord *your* God') could not permit worship of any alien god. He could not be replaced with a substitute. While other Near East communities had many gods, Israel had only one who was radically different from idols (Ps. 115:1-8). The God of redeeming grace claimed exclusive worship from His servants. The whole subject of

The Ten Words 19:25–20:17

idolatry and the uniqueness of the living God is expanded in Deuteronomy 4:15-31, and restated and forcefully presented by prophets such as Isaiah (cf. 43:8-13; 44:6-8; 45:5-6, 18-22; 46:9). The *Sh^ema'*, 'Hear, O Israel, the LORD our God, the LORD is one' (Deut. 6:4), was another restatement of God's uniqueness.[3] The final words in this Word, 'before me', or 'beside me', are an additional reason that should impel obedience to this command. The LORD's honour would be offended if any other objects of worship were set by His side.

2 The Second Word (20:4-6)

The Second Word does not forbid all forms of art, but only the use of human artistic skills to create either an image of God, or an idol that resembles anything of the created order, whether in the skies ('in heaven above'), on earth ('that is in the earth beneath'), or in the seas (' in the water under the earth'). The danger, if there was a representation of God, was that the image could be used as a magical token to try and manipulate events. This image would then in effect become a second 'god'. The expansion of this instruction in Deuteronomy starts with the premise that the people did not see a form when God spoke to them at Horeb. Therefore, there could be no visual representation of God, either male or female. Also, animals and the heavenly bodies were themselves created, and they could not provide a model for making an idol (Deut. 4:15-31). If such images were made or they came across them among the surrounding peoples, no one in Israel should prostrate themselves before them or vow allegiance to them. Their pledge of servitude was to the LORD alone. This Word had two reasons attached to it. The first related to God's character, while the second took into consideration the threats and promises that He made. The word used here for 'jealousy' (*qannâ'*) is most frequently used in the Old Testament of jealousy within marriage. God is the jealous husband who will not tolerate His bride, Israel, entering into a relationship with another

---

3. Several other translations are possible of these Hebrew words. See my discussion in *Deuteronomy: The Commands of a Covenant God*, pp. 92-93, where I opt for 'The Lord is our God, the Lord alone!'. This translation is grammatically acceptable, and it fits the context where the stress is on both the unity and the uniqueness of God.

so-called god. The threat was that those who hated the Lord would be punished, as would their descendants, down to the third and fourth generations. To the opposite class, those who showed genuine heartfelt love to the Lord and obeyed His commands, covenantal love towards them would be continued indefinitely. The older translation of this command used the expression 'to thousands' (*la'ᵃlâfîm*). This meant that there was an inconsistency in translation, for neither in verse 5 or verse 6 does the word 'generation' occur. Either it should be in both or in neither. Deuteronomy 7:9 helps at this point, because it echoes the same promise and specifically mentions that God keeps His covenant 'to a thousand generations' (*lᵉ'élef dôr*). The contrast ('to the third and fourth generation ... to the thousandth generation') highlights the abounding love and grace that God shows to His people who love and obey Him.

3 The Third Word (20:7)

The Third Word speaks of not taking the Lord's name in vain. The Hebrew verb 'to take' (*nâsâ'*) is never used elsewhere in reference to speech. It means to bear or to carry, and here its object is 'the name of the Lord'. To carry His name meant to carry His character or reputation. The way Israel could bear God's name was living as the people of God, showing by imitation of Him that they were a people of holiness. They had to carry His likeness. The adverbial phrase 'in vain' (*lashshâv'*) probably means something like 'hypocritically'. There could be no hypocrisy in His service. The covenantal curse was expressed against anyone who was living a false profession, for such a person would stand guilty before God.[4]

4 The Fourth Word (20:8-11)

The Fourth Word is the longest of them all. It deals with the structuring of time to follow God's own pattern, for He worked and then entered into His sabbatical rest. The opening word, 'Remember' could be interpreted to mean, 'remember the Sabbath that has already been enjoined upon

---

4. The interpretation I had offered here of the Third Word is spelt out much fuller in my article, 'The Interpretation of the Third Commandment', *RTR* 47 1, (1988) pp. 1-7. A similar interpretation has been followed more recently by Daniel I. Block, 'Bearing the Name of the Lord with Honor', *BS* 168 (2011), pp. 20-31.

you'. However, it is more likely that it means 'remember' in the sense of 'remember to keep'. The instruction is to sanctify, that is, to set aside as holy, the seventh day. The other six days are designated as days on which work is to be performed. On the seventh day all the family members, the servants, the aliens living in the community, and even the animals were to do no work. The reason given for this pattern is that the LORD made the heavens and the earth in six days, and then rested (*vayyânach*). This rest was not that of a weary workman, but the rest of satisfaction and joy in that the whole of creation corresponded to God's purpose. His own example was to be the motivating factor in Sabbath observance. The concluding statement of verse 11 is a strong echo of Genesis 2:3: 'So God blessed the seventh day and made it holy, because on it God rested from all his work that he had done in his creation' (ESV). The seventh day was special among the creation days, in that it was the only one that was consecrated by being set apart.[5]

The later description of the Sabbath as belonging to the LORD (*layhwh*, Exod. 31:15) indicates how significant the Sabbath was as a covenantal sign. When this Word was reaffirmed in the covenant made just prior to the entry of Israel into Canaan, the reason for observing the Sabbath was altered from creation to the redemption of Israel from Egypt (Deut. 5:15). Thus the observance of the Sabbath was meant to enable the people to remember 'the two great benefits of creation and redemption'.[6]

The Sabbath was important for other reasons also, for the sabbatical principle (six + one) was extended to the seventh year, the year for cancelling debts (Deut. 15:1-6), the release of bonded servants (Deut. 15:12-18), and allowing the land to lie fallow (Exod. 23:10-11). The last of these provides a significant link between the Sabbath and creation. The Sabbath is rooted

---

5. For further discussion on the Sabbath, see Gerhardus Vos, *Biblical Theology*, pp. 138-43; Willem VanGemeren, *The Progress of Redemption: The Story of Salvation from Creation to the New Jerusalem* (Grand Rapids: Academie Book, 1988), pp. 46-58; John Murray, *Principles of Conduct* (London: InterVarsity Press, 1956), pp. 30-35.

6. These words are from the answer to Question 121 in the *Westminster Larger Catechism*.

in God's blessing of it following His creative activity, and the sabbatical year allowed the ground to rest and be refreshed.

5 The Fifth Word (20:12)

The Fifth Word focuses on family relationships, and especially the respect for parents. This is the first commandment with a promise, as Paul wrote to the Ephesians (Eph. 6:2). The verb here, 'honour' (*kâvêd*, Pi.), has a variety of meanings. It is used of honouring and esteeming other human beings, but it is also used for the response of worship given to God (1 Sam. 2:30; Ps. 86:9; Prov. 3:9; Isa. 24:15). These Ten Words were addressed to adults, and this suggests that something more than just obedience of children to their parents is in view here. The latter part of this Word confirms this fact, in the reference to having long life in the land that God had sworn to give to His people. Long life would depend on obedience to God's instructions, and also by recognition of His appointed representatives, including parents, who would exercise His rule. The elders in Israel had an important role in maintaining good order, and the family was the primary means of passing on knowledge of the LORD (cf. Deut. 6:4-9; Ps. 78:1-8). Inherent in this Word is a warning. Failure to show respect to parents would amount to rebellion against God, and very abruptly, the people would be deprived of occupancy of the land. Ezekiel mentions disrespect for parents as one of the sins that caused the exile (Ezek. 22:7). As the New Testament makes plain, obedience to parents must be in recognition of their God-given role in the family, and yielded as unto the Lord Himself (Eph. 6:1-4; Col. 3:20).

6 The Sixth Word (20:13)

This Word is the first of three that have a common short formula: 'Do not + verb.' In Hebrew they consist of a negative particle (*lo'*) plus a verbal form. This is not the usual mode of negation in Hebrew, but a form reserved, in the main, for use in legal literature, particularly of divine commands.[7] Behind

---

7. The much more frequent negative command is formed by the particle *'al* followed by a jussive form of the verb. See, *IBHS*, p. 566, §34.2.1 b; *IBH*, p. 114; Page H. Kelley, *Biblical Hebrew: An Introductory Grammar* (Grand Rapids: Eerdmans, 1992), p. 173: 'When *lo'* is used with the imperfect, it expresses an absolute or categorical prohibition. It is used, for example, for the prohibitions of

this prohibition lies the biblical teaching on the image of God in man (Gen. 1:26-27; 9:6). The sanctity of human life had to be respected, for it was precious in God's sight. The verb used is not the most common one for kill (*hârag*) or put to death (*mût*, Hi.). Here the verb (*râtsach*) is one that can denote killing in general, or murder, or manslaughter. No object is stated for the verb, so the open expression could include both murder and suicide. Various exemptions were to apply. It was applicable to humans only, and it did not include capital punishment, defence of one's home (Exod. 22:2), accidental deaths (Deut. 19:5), or loss of life in wartime. This Word also makes no distinction between social classes of either the murderer or the victim. Deliberate and malicious action causing death is prohibited without any restriction excusing a particular group or class from its breadth.

7 The Seventh Word (20:14)

Another sanctity that had to be preserved was the marriage bond, that had to be guarded from sexual impurity. This Seventh Word stands in marked contrast to the infidelity and promiscuity of other religious life in the Near East. The verb here (*nâ'af*) is used of both men and women, though predominantly of men. It is employed of sexual intercourse of a man with another man's wife (Lev. 20:10), and of intercourse of a wife with a man, presumably a married man (Ezek. 16:32; Hos. 4:13). The general form of this prohibition is against sexual relationships between people, at least one of whom is considered as married to someone else. No distinction was intended between married women and those who were betrothed (Deut. 22:22-24). If this prohibition was breached, it was regarded as primarily a sin against God (cf. Joseph's words, 'How then could I do such a wicked thing and sin against God?' Gen. 39:9). In general, if the oneness established by God in the beginning is breached (Gen. 1:27; 2:18, 23-24), then adultery has taken place. The marriage bond was to be regarded as inviolable, and this may well have been for other associated reasons as well, especially in relation to the transmission of property to the following generation. The

---

the Ten Commandments'.

way in which the prophets link adultery with the worship of what are no-gods (*lo' 'ᵉlohîm*, Jer. 5:7) demonstrates how seriously this prohibition was regarded. The same word as used here for 'commit adultery' is also employed in reference to Israel's breach of covenantal fidelity in introducing idolatry (Isa. 57:3-13; Jer. 3:6-9; Ezek. 23:36-49).

8 The Eighth Word (20:15)

A further sanctity that had to be preserved was possession of property and, more widely, the preservation of relationships that can be so easily disrupted by theft. Individuals and society as a whole have rights that must be respected. For the third successive Word, a verb is used without an object, giving this prohibition the most general setting possible. The verb itself is speaking of acts of theft done secretly, without the knowledge or consent of the owner. It relates to both stealing and kidnapping (Exod. 21:16). God was the owner of all (Ps. 24:1), but He entrusted His gifts to human beings, and the use of property had to be respected. Even those in debt, who were forced to sell their property (or themselves as slaves), saw it returned to them in the sabbatical or jubilee years (Exod. 21:2-4; Lev. 25:23-34; Deut. 15:1-11). Clearly practices that are not so openly breaches of this Word were included, including holding back the wages of a worker (Lev. 19:13), dishonest business practices (Lev. 19:35), or charging exorbitant rates of interest (Lev. 25:16). Life in community must be protected, and abuse of property rights distorts seriously the functioning of society. Even the highest levels of society were not exempt from this Word, as was demonstrated in the case of Ahab's misappropriation of Naboth's vineyard (1 Kings 21:1-29). Justice was a significant issue in Israel, and there is frequent condemnation by the prophets of injustices perpetrated in particular by the nobility and wealthy (cf. Isa. 1:21-23; Amos 5:12-17).

9 The Ninth Word (20:16)

In legal cases there was another sanctity that had to be respected, and that was the sanctity of truth. Any false speech (lying) and any false actions (stealing) were both practices that were to be set aside by believing Israel (see Lev. 19:11).

The primary reference here is to a court scene in which a member of the Israelite community bears false witness against another member (*rê'a*) who was on trial. That the concept was far broader than just a law court situation is shown by the alteration in Deuteronomy 5 of 'false, fraudulent' (*shéqer*) to 'nothingness, emptiness' (*shâv'*). In both Exodus and Deuteronomy there are passages that expand this Word to prohibit lying in general (Exod. 23:1-3; Deut. 17:6; 19:15-21; 22:5, 13-21).

10 The Tenth Word (20:17)

The tenth and final Word is different from the preceding ones in that it deals with an issue that may never express itself in an outward way, or even lead to another sin. It prohibits having a desire to obtain possession of what belongs to one's neighbour, something known only to the person concerned and to God. In view are inward motives, not outward actions. Here, the Hebrew verb for 'covet' (*châmad*) occurs twice, while in the reissuing of the Ten Words in Deuteronomy, the second verb is changed to another verb meaning 'crave' or 'desire' (*'âvâh*, Hitp., Deut. 5:21). This latter verb is more neutral as it is used elsewhere of legitimate, good desires. As the final Word, this one, in one sense, summarises all the others. Illicit desire was the root from which all other sins would spring. Both Old and New Testaments teach that coveting comes from the heart (Prov. 6:25), and ultimately it expresses itself in an outward action (Jas. 1:14-15). While the list in this Word (house, wife, male and female servants, ox, and donkey) is typical of similar lists in the Ancient Near East), yet the final clause ('or anything that is your neighbour's') points to it indicating objects of desire rather than being a comprehensive list of what a man owned. Though not necessarily an outward sin, the seriousness of coveting is reinforced by Paul's equation of it with idolatry (Col. 3:5).

14

The Theophany
(20:18-21)

These verses continue to describe the theophany that took place on the occasion of the giving of the Ten Words. It has to be understood in the light of the description given in the previous chapter (Exod. 19:16-25) and the fuller account in Deuteronomy 5:22-31, and also the reference to the events after the giving of the law in Deuteronomy 9:7-12.[1] Several facts emphasise the uniqueness of what happened on Mount Sinai. It involved dramatic visual and audible effects (cloud, thunder, lightning, smoke, the trumpet sound). The difference between the Ten Words and their subsequent exposition in both Exodus and Deuteronomy is marked by the statement that God added nothing further to them (Deut. 5:22), and by the way in which they were recorded on tablets of stone by the finger of God (Exod. 24:12; Deut. 5:22; 9:10). It is clear from Exodus 34:28 that what was on the stone tablets was indeed 'the Ten Words'.

18-19 The exposition of the Ten Words in the Book of the Covenant that follows (20:22-23:33) is preceded by a description of the reaction of the people to the theophany. The opening words of verse 18 ('the people *saw* the thunder ... and the sound of the trumpet') may seem strange to Westerners

---

1. I have commented on these two passages in *Deuteronomy: The Commands of a Covenant God*, pp. 83-87 and 120-22.

but the Hebrew verb 'to see' (*râ'âh*) has a range of extended meanings that include 'perceive' and 'become aware of'.[2] The use of the participle (*ro'îm*) conveys the idea that the people 'were perceiving' over a period of time, and thus implying that this perception included the divine revelation in chapters 19 and 20. The response of the people was that 'they saw and trembled'.[3] The repetition of the idea of seeing simply reinforces the point that the people were well aware of the extended theophany.[4] The effect on the people was that they shook with fear (cf. the use of the exact same verb [*vayyânû'û*] to describe the doorposts shaking in Isaiah 6:4), and retreated to a position far away from the mountain. They did not want any direct communication between themselves and God, lest that caused their death. Instead, they wanted the mediator, Moses, to be the one who made known to them God's messages.

20-21 Moses' response to the people's fear and his acceptance of his role as mediator is to command them not to be afraid. His explanation is given in two parallel clauses, both of which use the preposition 'in order that' (*ba'ᵃvûr*).[5] The first explanation is that God had come to them in order to test them (*nasôt 'etᵉkem*), that is, to ascertain how they reacted to His presence and His verbal revelation in the Ten Words. The second was that fear of God might keep them from sinning. The expression here, 'fear of God', is a precursor of the later 'fear of the LORD' that denoted the heart-felt devotion of a servant to the will of the sovereign Master. The people had to understand that God had manifested Himself in glory, and their duty was to respond in obedience to His demands

---

2. *CHAL*, p. 328; *NIDOTTE*, 3, p. 1008.

3. Many of the early versions (LXX, Samaritan Pentateuch, Vulgate) translate the Hebrew *vayyar' hâ'âm* by 'and the people feared'. The two Hebrew verbs 'to see' and 'to fear' are very similar, but here the more difficult reading is to retain the rendering 'saw'. The rendering 'and they feared' involves assuming that the MT should be altered from *vayyar'* to *vayyîr'û*.

4. The Hebrew verbs alternate between plural and singular in this verse. The first verb is a plural participle (*ro'îm*), the second a singular *vav* consecutive (*vayyar'*), while the third (*vayyânû'û*) and fourth (*vayya'medû*) are plural *vav* consecutives. The switch to singular is because the subject, 'the people' (*ha'âm*), is singular, and there is no need to make the second verb conform to the other plural forms.

5. *CHAL*, p. 262.

The Theophany 20:18-21

upon them. They had been confronted by God's presence in the theophany, and now, conscious of their covenantal relationship with Him, they are called to refrain from sinning against Him. The people retained their distance from God, while Moses then approached the thick darkness (*ᵃrâfel*) where God was. The word used of God in verses 18-21 (as in v. 1) is not 'the LORD' (*yhwh*) but *ᵉlohîm*, possibly to draw attention to His majesty.

Two descriptions of this experience of Moses and the people are significant. In Deuteronomy 4:11, Moses reminded the people how they 'came near and stood at the foot of the mountain while it burned with fire to the heart of heaven, wrapped in darkness (*chóshek*), cloud ('*ânân*) and gloom (*ᵃrâfel*) (ESV)'. Then, much later, the writer to the Hebrews contrasted the experience of Israel at Sinai, coming to 'a blazing fire and darkness and gloom and a tempest' (Heb. 12:18), with the experience of Christian believers coming 'to Mount Zion and to the city of the living God, the heavenly Jerusalem' (Heb. 12:22). Moses, in addition to all the people, was so filled with awe that he declared: 'I tremble with fear' (Heb. 12:21).[6]

---

6. These words of Moses set down in Heb. 12:21 (*ekfobos eimi kai entromos*) are not recorded in Exodus. The nearest to them is when he reminded the people how he interceded for them after the incident of the golden bull: 'For I was afraid of the anger and hot displeasure (LXX *kai ekfobos eimi dia tên orgên kai ton thumon*) that the Lord bore against you' (Deut. 9:19).

15

Worship Regulations
(20:22-26)

Prior to setting out the implications of the Decalogue for daily living, these verses set out two significant features of Israel's worship. The first relates to idolatry, while the second concerns the place of sacrifice, the altar. The first of these reinforces the second Word (20:4), while the second anticipates fuller instructions that follow later (27:1-8).

22 The LORD gave Moses explicit instructions to pass on to the people. 'Thus you shall say to the people of Israel' (*koh to'mar 'el bᵉnê yisrâ'êl*) specified that the communication was to be exactly as God told him. The message commenced with reference to the knowledge the people had that God had indeed spoken to them from heaven. The reference to 'seeing' ('you *have seen* for yourselves') does not imply actual sight of God, for the verb 'see' is used, as in verse 18, of perception of a certain fact, not necessarily physical sight.

23 Nothing could be a substitute for the living God. The prohibition relates to any physical representation of Him. The MT is awkward in that it has no object for the verb 'make': 'You shall not make alongside me (*lo' ta⁽ᵃ⁾sûn 'ittî*)'. Something is needed and so the NIV adds 'any gods', while another suggestion is 'anything to be'.[1] This meaning is made explicit

---

1. This is the suggestion of Victor Hamilton, *Exodus*, p. 362. *IBHS*, p. 195, notes that 'the object of *'t* may also be an addition ("besides, alongside of, in addition to…")'.

in the following clause: 'do not make for yourselves gods of silver and gods of gold'.

24 The prohibition in verse 23 is stated as a plural (*lo' ta'ªsûn*), whereas in this verse the instruction is narrowed down to the individual (*lo' ta'ªseh*). Limits were placed upon the type of altar that Israel could use. Here it is specified that it was to be of earth, while in verse 25 one of undressed stones was permissible, whereas in 27:1 it is said that it could be of acacia wood. At Arad in southern Israel, an earthen altar has been discovered, having the same measurements as those set out in 27:1. This altar is dated from the period of Solomon. Clearly, they were temporary places of sacrifice, that resembled the altars that had been used in the patriarchal period (see Gen. 12:7; 13:18; 22:9). These altars were for burnt offerings and fellowship offerings. The first (Heb. *'olâh*) was the whole-burnt offering, while the second was the accompanying sacrifice that was eaten by the worshipper(s). The location of altars is described as being wherever the LORD caused His name 'to be honoured' (*'azkîr 'et sh^emî*). This has been the common understanding of this verb (*zâkar*, Hi.), but more probably it means 'to invoke God's name'.[2] Liberty was given to Israel to build and use altars in addition to the one at the central sanctuary, this explaining Elijah's reference to the many altars in existence in his day (1 Kings 19:10, 14).

25 To the instruction that altars were to be built of earth was added the concession that they could be made of undressed stones, for it would be defiled if a tool had been used. The tool is referred to as a *chérev*, a sword, a word that is used, at times, for any sharp instrument. The same prohibition occurs in Deuteronomy 27:5 and Joshua 8:30-31. The reason was probably twofold. Firstly, the Canaanites had altars built of dressed stones, and secondly, any tool used in the process could easily become an object of veneration and worship. Hence, the need for Israel to avoid a contemporary heathen practice and possible false worship of the tool used in shaping the stones.

26 The final instruction here regarding these provisional altars was that they should have no steps, so there could

---

2. See *TWOT*, 1, p. 242, and note this usage in Exodus 23:13.

be no indecent exposure of the bodies of the priests. Later, steps were permitted, but the priests had to wear linen undergarments (Lev. 6:10 [MT 6:3]; 9:22; Ezek. 44:17-18).

Study Questions

1) The Ten Words *follow* the redemption of Israel from slavery in Egypt. What significance does that have?

2) In Exodus 20:11 the reason for keeping the Sabbath is God's pattern of resting at creation, while in Deuteronomy 5:15 it is Israel's deliverance by God's mighty hand and stretched out arm. How do these two reasons blend together?

3) A theophany was a revelation of God's power and majesty. Why did it occur again at Sinai in Elijah's experience there (1 Kings 19:11-13)?

4) Were the altars now permitted for Israel (20:24-26) any different from those that the patriarchs had been using (see, for example, Gen. 22:9; 26:25; 33:20)?

16

The Laws
(21:1–23:33)

A transition takes place at this point. Whereas in chapter 20 the Decalogue is called 'the Words', the instructions that follow in this section are referred to as 'laws' (*mishpâtîm*). The Decalogue and these chapters are distinguished by the use of different Hebrew forms of speech (the Decalogue, 'do/do not ...'; 'the laws', 'if ...'), as well as their difference in content. The one has prescriptive covenantal laws, while the other has descriptive laws that both explain the Words but also apply them to a particular societal setting.

Various attempts have been made to ascertain if there is a correlation between these chapters and the order of the Decalogue.[1] There does seem to be an order, but not exactly as in the Decalogue. It can be tabulated in this way:

Exodus 21:2-11	4th Word
Exodus 21:12-36	6th Word
Exodus 22:1-15	8th Word
Exodus 22:16-27	7th Word
Exodus 22:28	5th Word
Exodus 22:29-31	3rd Word

---

1. For some examples see J. G. Murphy, *A Critical and Exegetical Commentary on the Book of Exodus* (Edinburgh: T. & T. Clark, 1876), pp. 239-33; Edward Robertson, *The Old Testament Problem: A Re-Investigation* (Manchester: Manchester University Press, 1950), pp. 103-04.

| Exodus 23:1-9 | 9th Word |
| Exodus 23:10-19 | 4th Word |

Other use of the Decalogue in Scripture shows the same sort of variation in the order of the Ten Words. For example, in Matthew 19:18-19, the order is 6, 7, 8, 9, 5, plus the command to love one's neighbour, while in Mark 10:19, the order is 7, 6, 8, 9, 5, plus between the 9th and 5th the command, 'Do not defraud', is inserted. Luke 18:20 has the order 7, 6, 8, 9, and 5, while Paul, in Romans 13:9, uses the order 7, 6, 8, 9, 10, with the observation, 'And whatever other commandments there may be, are summed up in this one rule: "Love your neighbour as yourself."' Clearly the order was not sacrosanct, for the Ten Words were presented in whatever order the context demanded.

1 Slavery (21:1-11)

1 The transition to the descriptive law is marked by this verse, which contains God's words to Moses. He was instructed to set these laws before the people for their benefit, and so they could see the way in which the Decalogue made demands on so many different aspects of their lives.

2 The opening case study is one that expands on the sabbatical principle of the Fourth Word and applies it to the situation of Hebrew slaves (cf. the similar laws in Deut. 15:12-18). Particular laws relating to non-Hebrew slaves are given elsewhere (Lev. 25:44-46). It needs emphasising that while slavery was a social institution in the Old Testament, and therefore tolerated, it should not be equated with more modern forms of slavery such as the transportation of African slaves to the Caribbean or North America. That infringed the prohibition of kidnapping (Exod. 21:16) and also meant intergenerational slavery. What is referred to here is debt or temporary slavery, by which a debtor is able to pay his debt by working for his creditor.[2] The slave was the property of his master, but he retained rights as a human made in God's image. The clauses are introduced by 'when' (*kî*), with 'if' (*'im*) being used in subsidiary clauses.[3] In

---

2. For an excellent discussion on slavery in the Old Testament, see Andrew Sloane, *At Home in a Strange Land: Using the Old Testament in Christian Ethics* (Peabody: Hendrikson Publishers, 2008), pp. 99-113.

3. Several English translations do not observe the difference between kî and

the sabbatical year (the seventh) he was to be released without any payment being made. The term used to describe the freed slave is *chôfshî*, one that is almost exclusively used in the Old Testament for freed slaves. Deuteronomy 15:13-14 indicates that in addition to being freed, a slave had to be provided with sustenance, or perhaps fuller provision to give him economic viability. This release was to take place in the seventh year. Some have suggested this refers to the general sabbatical year, but if so, some slaves would serve much longer periods than others. Most probably, the six years of service started when the slave began to serve his master.

3-4 Two 'if' clauses follow. If the slave came into this bonded relationship by himself, he was to go out alone. However, if he was already married when that bonded relationship to his master began, then both husband and wife were to go free. The situation was different if his master gave a wife to the slave. In that case, the wife, and any children born to them, were to remain as the possession of the master. This seems harsh to us, but it was typical of other Ancient Near East cultures.

5-6 The continuation of voluntary servitude was a possibility. If the slave expressed his willingness to remain in the bonded relationship because he loved his master, then a particular ceremony to give effect to that was necessary. His master had to take him before 'God' (*'el 'ᵉlohîm*), and against a door or doorpost and pierce his ear with an awl. Various questions arise here, relating to the translation of *'ᵉlohîm*, and whether there are two stages in the process (indicated by the double use of the verb, *vᵉhiggîshû*, ESV 'his master shall bring him to God, and he shall bring him to the door'). While it is correct that *'ᵉlohîm* can refer to judges (cf. Exod. 22:7-8; Ps. 82:1, 6), it is best to retain the rendering 'God' here, and suggest that what is intended is, first, bringing the slave to the sanctuary, and then taking him to have his ear pierced.[4]

'im, translating both of them the same, 'when'. The particle kî introduces the general law, while 'im introduces specific applications of that law. The three best translations in this regard are RSV, NRSV, and the ESV.

4. This interpretation is following the discussion by J. Robert Vannoy, 'The Use of the Word *hâ'ᵉlôhîm* in Exodus 21:6 and 22:7, 8', John H. Skilton, ed., *The Law and the Prophets: Old Testament Studies Prepared in Honor of Oswald Thompson*

Coming to the sanctuary may have involved an oath of some kind, while the ear-piercing could be performed by the slave owner. The slave would then be indentured to his master for life. The MT says that he shall serve his master *l^e'olâm*, a phrase that is often translated as 'for ever', but in contexts such as this clearly means for the term of his natural life.

7-11 These verses state an exception to the rule concerning release of slaves. They are concerned with the case of a woman who is sold to become the wife (or perhaps, concubine) of a man or, more probably, his son. While it is not stated explicitly in the text, the probable scenario is a case where a family were in debt, and in order to cover that debt, 'sell' a daughter to another family. The man accepting the arrangement would have a double advantage from it. He would cover the debt he was owed, and also he would find a wife for his son. While the woman was regarded as a female servant (Heb. *'âmâh*), she had rights that had to be respected. If she did not please her new master, she could be redeemed by her own family (v. 8). This provision uses the word for 'redeem' (*pâdâh*) that is used elsewhere of God's redemption of His people from slavery in Egypt (Deut. 15:15; 24:18). This is another indication of how the concepts relating to the redemption of Israel from slavery in Egypt are applied in various ways to Israel, not least in using that redemption as the motive for particular actions on the part of God's people. Rejection of the woman could not lead to selling her to foreigners, while selection of her for his son meant that she then had the rights of a daughter (v. 8). In a situation in which the son married another woman, she would not suffer deprivation, retaining three things in particular. The first two, 'meat' (= food, *sh^e'êr*) and 'clothing' (*k^esût*), are clear, but the third one (*v^e'onâtâh*) is uncertain. It is a *hapax legomenon*, and various translational possibilities have been proposed – 'marital rights', 'dwelling', 'ointment'.[5] Another alternative is to take the reference to 'three' to refer to refer back to the three scenarios that have been described in the preceding verses, and to take the expression here as

---

Allis (Nutley, N.J.: Presbyterian and Reformed Publishing Co., 1974), pp. 225-41. In addition, see F. C. Fensham, 'New Light on Exodus 21:7 and 22:7 from the Laws of Eshnunna', *JBL* 78 (1959), pp. 160-61.

5. See *DCH*, VI, pp. 501-02.

being a comprehensive term following the words 'food' and 'clothing', 'and [that is], her upkeep'.[6]

The laws regarding slaves conclude with the provision that if the 'purchaser' of the woman does not do 'these three [things]' she can go free without any payment of money. The understanding of 'these three' depends upon the interpretation of the previous verse. The traditional view would be that they refer to 'food', 'clothing' and 'marital rights'. If the alternative view is adopted, then 'these three' refers back to the three possible scenarios described above. On either interpretation, the woman is to be released from any further bond, and without any exchange of money (Heb. *chinnâm 'ēn késef*, 'without compensation, no silver') she goes out from the relationship.

2 Homicide (21:12-17)

Human life was indeed precious, because men and women had been made in God's image (Gen. 1:27). Hence to attack a fellow human being was in essence an attack upon God himself (Gen. 9:6). So serious were certain crimes in Israel that the death penalty was the appropriate punishment. Four homicides and the case of kidnapping are set out in verses 12-17, and they are expanded later in Deuteronomy 21:1-9; 24:7; 27:24-25.

12-14 Whether or not a killing was intentional was an important consideration. While the verdict of death for manslaughter is given in verse 12, the following verse indicates that if the death was not one of premeditated murder, then there could be a place of safety for the murderer. The expression covering lack of intention to murder is unusual: lit. 'and God allowed to happen (*'innâh*) to his hand'. The verb is rare (only here and in 2 Kings 5:7; Ps. 91:10; and Prov. 12:21) but the meaning seems to be as the LXX translated, 'but God did not give into his hands'. In such a case, the murderer could flee for safety to the place God had provided. Before Israel crossed into Jordan, three cities were designated as cities of refuge (Deut. 4:41-43), while three other cities were appointed later on the west bank (Deut. 19:1-13). The idea

---

6. This is the view proposed by Victor Hamilton, *Exodus*, p. 370.

was clearly that anyone killing someone unintentionally could as quickly as possible get to these cities, but the practice is only referred to in the Old Testament in 1 Kings 1:50-53 and 2:28-34. However, where deliberate and malicious intent was involved, no safety was afforded by going to the altar, for from there the murderer was to be taken and executed.

15 An attack upon parents was a breach of the Fifth Word ('Honour your father and your mother ...'), and such disrespect would amount to rebellion against God. The reason for this was confirmed by the promise of long life in Canaan on condition of obedience to God's commands (20:12). Parents were appointed as representatives of God, exercising His rule in the family circle. The word used for 'strike' (*makkêh*) may well have the stronger meaning of 'strike fatally' or 'kill' (see NIV footnote).[7]

16 Kidnapping was an affront to human dignity by overlooking another person's status before God, and also by treating him/her as mere property. Theft was a serious matter, but even more serious was theft of a human life, since that person had been made in God's image. There was to be no human trafficking, and if the perpetrator of the offence still had the victim with him when caught, he was to be put to death.

17 Alongside the offence of striking (or killing) a parent (v. 15), cursing father or mother was also punishable by death.[8] The verb 'to curse' (*qâlal*, Pi.) has the basic idea of making small or insignificant, and hence the very opposite of the demand for honour stated in the Fifth Word (20:12). It was doubly serious because it was an attack upon God's image-bearer, and also an act of defiance against God's authority delegated to parents. Later, in the New Testament, that line of authority is recognised in the instruction to fathers to bring up their children in 'the training and instruction *of the Lord*' (Eph. 6:4). The New Testament also instructs that verbal cursing of another is something that should not occur, as humans have been made in God's likeness (James 3:9).

---

7. The entries for this meaning are given in *DCH*, V, p. 685.

8. The LXX changes the order of the verses to place vv. 15 and 17 in the MT alongside one another, but the Heb. manuscripts do not support any alteration.

3 Bodily Injuries (21:18-32)

18-19 Injury inflicted after a quarrel is covered by the provision that if the victim does not die but recovers from a blow, the one who caused the injury will not be held responsible for it. However, he must pay compensation for the loss of the victim's time (and money), and also ensure that he is completely healed. Should the victim die, then the provisions of verse 12 would apply.

20-21 Another scenario is depicted in these verses. A distinction is made between two types of injury caused by the beating of slaves. If it causes the slave's death, then due punishment must be meted out (cf. v. 12). Otherwise, a couple of days walking around would demonstrate that the victim had not been fatally injured. While the explanation is given that the slave belongs to the master by right of purchase (lit. 'for he is his money', *kî kaspô*), yet humane considerations enter into the legal provisions. These are in marked contrast with Roman law that permitted an owner to kill a slave with impunity.

22-25 The next case is that of a pregnant woman intervening in a quarrel between two men, who then gives birth prematurely (or else, has a miscarriage) as a result of 'injury' (Heb. *'âsôn*).[9] The Hebrew verb here for 'fighting' (*nâtsâh*, Ni.) seems to imply the on-going nature of this quarrel, with the combatants trading blows with one another. Even though both mother and child survive, an appropriate sum of money would have to be paid. In this case, the woman's husband would propose the amount and have it ratified by the elders sitting in judgment (*bip*ᵉ*lilîm*).[10] However, if there is injury, presumably either to the mother or the baby, then the *lex talionis* would apply: 'eye for eye, tooth for tooth, hand for hand, foot for foot, burn for burn, wound for wound, bruise for bruise'. Deuteronomy 19:21 has a slightly abbreviated list, omitting 'burn', 'wound' and 'bruise', and Leviticus 24:19-20 has some variation in restating it as 'fracture for fracture, eye for eye, tooth for tooth'. The intention was to ensure that

---

9. This noun only occurs five times in the MT, three of these in the narratives of Genesis in which Jacob's concern for Benjamin is in view. See Gen. 42:4, 38; 44:29.

10. Coming from the root *p-l-l*, the noun *pâlîl* is used of the officials who determined the amount of money paid in injury cases.

the punishment fitted the crime, and that no punishment exceeded the hurt committed. This rule prevented harsh vengeance, and instead guaranteed justice.[11] Our Lord contradicted a very legalistic interpretation of this rule that the Pharisees had adopted, and rejected any idea of personal vengeance (Matt. 5:38-42).

26-27 Physical injury to a slave caused by a master's abuse of corporal punishment could not go unnoticed and unpunished. Two examples are given of how the *lex talionis* would apply. If an eye were seriously damaged and sight destroyed, then compensation had to be paid. Likewise, the loss of a tooth also required compensation. In both cases, the penalty to the master was that the slave would go free (Heb. *chofshî*; cf. its use already in vv. 2 and 5). The formula is identical in both cases: 'To freedom he shall send him away on account of the eye [tooth]'. For unplanned injury to a slave, a master had to reckon with economic consequences. He would lose the financial gain of having the slave working for him. This was a strong deterrent against any physical abuse of slaves.

28-32 The final case of personal injury concerns being gored by an ox. The distinction is drawn between an unexpected event and one that could have been predicted. The first is the case of an ox suddenly goring a man or a woman. Immediately the provision of Genesis 9:4-6 comes into play, in which God required the life of man or animal that took human life. He had said: 'I will demand an accounting from every animal. And from each man, too, I will demand an accounting for the life of his fellow man' (v. 5). Hence, the flesh of that animal was not to be eaten, but the owner would not suffer any other penalty. He would be innocent (*nâqî*), i.e., free from punishment. The second case relates to an ox with the known habit of goring. If the owner does not guard it (*v^{e}lo' yishm^{e}rennû*), and it then gores a man or a woman, both the ox and the owner are to be put to death. The same law applied if the ox gored a son or daughter of the household (v. 31). However, there was a way in which

---

11. For a discussion of some of the exegetical problems in these verses, see W. C. Kaiser Jr., *Toward Old Testament Ethics* (Grand Rapids: Zondervan, 1983), pp. 102-04.

the owner could escape the death penalty in these cases, and this involved the payment of ransom money (*pidyon*). Since Numbers 35:31 states that no ransom could be paid for the life of a murderer, this means that while the owner of the ox was negligent, he was not technically a murderer and so a ransom was permissible. Presumably the ransom price was set in a way comparable to what has been described in verse 22. The life of male and female slaves was valuable, and their rights had to be protected. They were not in the same privileged position as family members, but if gored, the ox was killed and thirty shekels of silver was paid to the slave's master.[12] This may have been the standard figure for the redemption of a slave.

4 Property Matters (21:33–22:15)

The focus shifts, at this point, as the laws now address property matters. In essence, this section is setting out the principles that flow out of the Eighth Word (20:15), and applying them to various settings.

33-34 The first of five cases involves the situation in which a person may negligently fail to cover a pit. A neighbour's animal wanders on to his property, falls into the pit, and dies. The outcome is that the dead animal belongs to the man who owns the pit, but he is required to pay an appropriate amount to recompense the owner for the loss he has sustained. Careless actions that had consequences for men or animals had a financial penalty imposed (for humans, cf. Deut. 22:8).

35-36 Damage to, or death of, an animal because it was attacked by a neighbour's animal has monetary consequences. The live animal is to be sold, and the money from the sale and the body of the dead animal are to be divided between the two owners. Both suffer loss, but that financial loss is shared equally for the common good. Like the earlier provision regarding fatality caused by an unwatched ox (21:28-32), so now provision is made for the case where an animal with a history of attacking humans does so again. In this case, the owner of the bull that attacked the other one had to accept

---

12. At this period the shekel was a weight (approx. 11-13 gm), not a coin. Judas was paid 30 pieces of silver for betraying Jesus (Matt. 26:14), but no direct connection with this passage is involved.

full responsibility for the accident. Payment had to be made, and then the dead animal was his.

22:1[13] This verse commences a series of five scenarios, all of which relate to theft. Stealing animals, whether cattle or sheep, was probably one of the easiest forms of theft, as there was no breaking and entering into premises. While animals were out grazing, one could be stolen to be eaten, or else sold to someone else. A different price had to be paid for the larger animal. For an ox, five times was required, while for a sheep four times. This differential was probably related to the work involved in caring for the ox and sheep respectively, or the time, trouble, and cost in replacing a dead animal.

2-4 Three cases are cited regarding a thief caught in the very act. While killing a thief who was breaking into a property at night was not punishable, to attack and kill in daylight was to make the killer guilty of bloodshed. Even a thief had rights that had to be protected. By daylight such a thief could be identified, caught, and made to pay restitution. If when caught he did not have the stolen goods, and has no means of making an appropriate payment, he must be sold into slavery (see comment on debt slavery on 21:2). The third case involves a thief who is caught red-handed with a living animal – whether ox, or donkey, or sheep – and he would have to repay double. Thus the person from whom the theft was made would get back the equivalent, and more to compensate for what had happened, making clear the unacceptable behaviour of the thief.

5 Three aspects about taking care of someone else's possessions are dealt with in verses 5-15. Not only was having private possessions a right, but recognition of the same rights for others was also important. Straying herds or flocks could easily cross on to a neighbour's land and graze,[14] and the resulting deprivation of crops could not be fixed easily.

---

13. The MT includes 22:1 in the previous chapter, so that chapter 21 has 37 verses.

14. The verb *bâ'ar* is a homonym, and may have up to four different meanings (see *DCH*, 2, pp. 242-43). It occurs in the following verse with the meaning of 'burn', and this meaning has been suggested for this verse also. However, on the basis of the LXX rendering by *kataboskein*, 'to feed', and the almost unanimous testimony of the Heb. manuscripts, it is best to take the verb here and in the next verse to mean 'graze'.

Negligence like this had to be recompensed by using the owner's best quality crops, an action of generosity on his part, and also an assurance of the quality. This provision is looking ahead to the time when Israel would be settled in Canaan, and such boundary disputes would become more common.

6 The next case relates to letting a fire burn out of control, and thus destroying much of a neighbour's property. A fire that started in a thorn bush could easily spread to surrounding properties, devouring all the grass set aside for feed for animals. Suitable restitution had to be paid to the farmer to cover the cost of the lost crops.

7-9 At the next stage of the regulations comes the question as to the procedure when articles left on deposit with someone else are stolen. These could be 'silver' (*késef*) or 'goods' (*kêlîm*). If the thief is caught, then he must pay a double amount. A different procedure was set in place if there was any suspicion that the one keeping the valuables took them for himself. If no thief was discovered, then the person must 'draw near to God' (*vᵉniqrav 'el 'ᵉlohîm*). While *ᵉlohîm* was translated as 'God' in 21:6 (see comments), here it is more probable that the judges are in view. The actual procedure is not set out, but probably it involved a solemn oath of some kind, whereby the man under suspicion declared his innocence. The full oath is not given, but the words 'whether not' (*'im lo'*) at the beginning of verse 8 are often used elsewhere in the Old Testament as an oath formula. If there was disputed ownership with two saying, 'This is mine' (v. 9), both parties had to come before the judges who would make a determination in the matter. The losing party would then have to pay the equivalent of double the value for the missing items.

10-13 Further instructions follow in relation to an animal (donkey, ox, sheep or any other animal) that is left in a person's custody, and it dies, or is injured, or is stolen when no one was watching. The contending parties had to appear before the LORD[15] and an oath sworn that no hand had been raised against the lost animal, and the owner had to accept this declaration. No restitution money was required.

---

15. The use of LORD (*yhwh*) here confirms the translation 'God' in v. 8.

However, if the animal was stolen from the neighbour, then he had to make restitution. If a wild animal tore it to pieces, then, on production of the remains, the person was absolved from any payment.

14-15 The final case of property responsibilities is that of borrowing or hiring an animal. It concerns injury or death of an animal under three conditions. The first is when the owner is not present, and so the borrower is responsible for making restitution. The second is when the owner is present, and he, not the borrower, has to accept responsibility. The third is when hiring has taken place, rather than borrowing, and if there is injury the owner has to bear the loss.

5 Social Responsibilities (22:16-31)

Further implications for life of commitment to the covenantal God are spelt out in this section. God's holy people (v. 31) had to reflect His character in every sphere of life, and in so doing they had to be distinguished from the Canaanite people amongst whom they would be living ultimately.

16-17 The first situation dealt with concerns of the seduction of a virgin. These verses have to be considered alongside Deuteronomy 22:28-29, that follow close after directions regarding how to deal with a case of rape (Deut. 22:25-27).[16] The provision here is that if an unpledged virgin is seduced and sleeps with a man, he has to marry her, paying the customary 'wedding price' (*mohar*). This is a rare word, only occurring in two other places in the Old Testament (Gen. 34:12; 1 Sam. 18:25), while the verb 'pay' (*mâhar*) only occurs here.[17] Probably the 'wedding gift' was in addition to the compensatory money given to the girl's family. However, if the girl's father rejected the marriage proposal, he was still required to pay the 'wedding price', for the sin involved had be acknowledged.

18 Sorcery was anathema to the Lord, it being one of the Canaanite abominations that Israel was to shun (Deut. 18:10).

---

16. The Heb. verbs point to the difference between 'rape' and 'seduction'. In Deuteronomy 22:25 'seize' (*châzaq*, Hi.) is used of 'rape', while in 22:28 a different verb (*pâsâh*) is used, that, while it can mean 'seize', is also used of seduction (cf. Gen. 39:12). Here in Exodus 22:16, the verb is *pâtâh*, Pi. See *DCH*, VI, p. 798.

17. The only other place where *mâhar* may occur is in Psalm 16:4, but more likely it is *mâhar* I, 'to multiply'.

It was an attempt to manipulate the future through use of potions and herbs (the noun here may be from a verb 'to cut'). There is no indication why the feminine form 'sorceress' (*mᵉkashshêfâh*) is used instead of the masculine 'sorcerer' (*mᵉkashshêf*). In Deuteronomy 18, sorcery is condemned, but here the verdict is that a sorceress must not be allowed to live (*lo' tᵉchayyeh*). No difference from the more common 'be put to death' is apparent.

19 Another Canaanite practice that was forbidden was having sexual relations with animals. The practice of bestiality with some animals was condoned among the Hittites, while permitted with others.[18] It is condemned here and in Leviticus 18:23, 20:15-16, and in Deuteronomy 27:21. Bestiality is a sin because it transgresses boundaries put in place by God between humans and animals, and so is a rejection of God's purposes in creation. In some cultures people practised it because they thought they could obtain union with the deity symbolised by the animal. This may explain why it comes in this context in conjunction with the prohibition of sacrifice to any pagan god in the very next verse (22:20).

20 Sacrificial activities were to be performed for the LORD alone. This exclusivism is spelt out more fully in Deuteronomy (see, for example, Deut. 4:39), and the concept of being devoted to destruction is also developed further (Deut. 3:6; 7:2; 13:16; 20:15, 17). This is the first occurrence of the verb that means devoted to destruction (*châram*, Hi., and passive, as here, Hof.).[19] To be under the LORD's curse was to be devoted entirely to Him, being at His exclusive disposal. This usually meant destruction, though in some cases humanitarian considerations had to be taken into account (see, Deut. 20:10-15).

21 Israel's own experience in Egypt was to be the motivation for the treatment of non-resident foreigners living with them. Just as they had been aliens there, so they had now to have special regard for those in a similar position. The verb used for 'ill-treat' (*yânâh*, Hif.) means 'to do wrong' to

---

18. Hittite law prohibited practice of bestiality with horses or mules, but not with sheep, cows, or goats. See ANET, pp. 214-15.

19. I have discussed the verb *châram*, and the related noun, *chérem*, in *Deuteronomy: The Commands of a Covenant God*, pp. 102-03.

someone, and when it is used in Leviticus 19:33-34 in enforcing the same principle its opposite is 'to love as yourself.' Israel's experience of Egypt, the great oppressor, should move them to ensure that no similar experience would happen to aliens within their borders. This instruction is repeated with some slight variation in Exodus 23:9, while other passages show the same concern for the alien (see Lev. 19:9-10; 23:22; Deut. 14:28-29; 16:11-14; 24:17-22; 26:11-13).

22-24 The most vulnerable in society in ancient Israel were widows and orphans, as they lacked the normal protection afforded by a husband and father.[20] The verb used in relation to mistreatment of these classes ('*ânâh* II, Pi.) has various meanings, but basically in the Old Testament it denotes humiliating or humbling someone.[21] The consequence of such an action (vv. 23-24) is spelt out in a form that draws attention to its seriousness. Firstly, it is introduced by the particle 'if' (*'im*) that regularly is used in oaths (with, or as here without, any introductory formula).[22] Secondly, the threat is stated using the first person singular, '*I* will certainly hear', '*my* anger', '*I* will kill you'. God presents Himself as the one who will personally protect those who are most vulnerable, if they 'cry out' to Him, using again the same Hebrew verb as was used of Israel in Egypt (*tsâ'aq*, as in Exodus 3:7). Thirdly, the threat is stated in terms of the second person plural, 'your wives' (*n^{e}shêkem*), 'your sons' (*b^{e}nêkem*), that brings home sharply the consequences for any of the people who perpetrated such crimes. God declares the punishment: 'I will kill you with the sword'. This could refer to death in warfare, or else be a metaphor indicating more generally death in a violent form.[23]

25-27 Regulations regarding taking interest occur in several parts of the Pentateuch (see, in addition to this passage,

---

20. Widows, orphans, and aliens are often linked together in the Old Testament, and treatment of them grouped together. See Deuteronomy 16:11, 14; 24:19-22; 26:13; and Psalm 94:6.

21. For the range of meanings, see *DCH*, VI, pp. 495-96.

22. On the use of *'im* in oaths, see *DIHG~S*, pp. 186-87.

23. Translation of the Hebrew noun for 'orphan' (*yâthôm*) in these verses in English versions is interesting. The AV uses 'fatherless' in both v. 22 and v. 24. While the RSV had 'orphan' in v. 22, it used 'fatherless' in v. 24. The NIV has the same as the RSV, but ESV has reverted to the AV position. Certainly 'fatherless' is a more emotive word than 'orphan'.

Lev. 25:35-38; Deut. 23:19-20). The principle is stated that a fellow Israelite was not to be charged interest. The reason is clear enough here from the fact that he was a fellow member of the covenantal community (notice the reference by God to 'my people', *'ammî*). This is expanded in Leviticus 25:35-38 by reference to redemption from Egypt and possession of the land of Canaan by Israel. The picture in verse 26 is of a very poor man to whom his pledge had to be returned each sunset so that he could sleep in it (see Deut. 24:12-13). The implication is that he had nothing else to give as security, while the return of the pledge each morning would have been a constant reminder of the debt. An extra-biblical text found south of Tel Aviv refers to a farm worker who complained to the governor that his cloak had been kept overnight. If denied the return of the cloak, the man could cry to God (again the verb *tsâ'aq* as in v. 23) who would hear, because He is the merciful God (*kî channûn 'ânî*). This declaration of God's character is enlarged later in what became a basic credal statement for Israel: 'The LORD, the LORD, the compassionate and gracious (*channûn*) God, slow to anger, abounding in love and faithfulness' (Exod. 34:6).

28 Respect for God Himself, and for the human officials who represented Him in society, was essential. Hence there could be no cursing of either. Different verbs are used in the two clauses in this verse (*qâlal*, Pi., and *'ârar*), but in meaning they are very close. The first of these has already been used in reference to parents in 21:17. The word used for 'ruler' (*nâsî'*) was earlier employed of the leaders of the people in 16:22. All authority structures in Israel depended on delegation by God, and so respect had to be given both to Him and to His deputies in society.

29-30 These verses enunciate the principle that, as all the good things of life came from God, offering of first-fruits was an acknowledgement of this fact and an act of thanksgiving on the part of covenant servants. The instruction was not to withhold for a time[24] offerings 'from your granaries (*mᵉlê'âtᵉkâ*) or your vats (*dim'ᵃkâ*)'. Both the words for 'granaries' and 'vats' are exceptionally uncommon, the former occurring only twice elsewhere (Num. 18:27; Deut. 22:9), while the latter

---

24. The verb used here (*'âchar*, Pi.) means to delay in giving, not refusing to give.

is a *hapax legomenon*. The commitment of the first-born son to God has already been set out in 13:2. The same principle was applied to cattle and sheep, which, on the eighth day, were presented to God, just as the male child was circumcised on the eighth day.

31 Rather than the normal command to be holy, the distinctiveness of God's people is described as being 'men of holiness' (*'an^eshê qódesh*). Commitment to the redeemer had to be expressed in outward behavioural patterns that matched inward trust in Him. One example of such behaviour is cited. Rejection of the meat of an animal killed by wild beasts was necessary, first, because the wild beast could be an unclean animal, and, secondly, because the blood would not be treated in the appropriate manner.

Study Questions

1 Quite a few of the cases cited in chapters 21–23 concern underprivileged people in Israel (slaves, aliens, widows and orphans). Why should they have been singled out for such attention?

2 In 21:13 reference is made to those who killed someone unintentionally fleeing to a place that God would designate (see the provision of the cities of refuge, Deut. 4:41-43; 19:1-13). Did this have any theological significance, or was it just to protect human life?

3 How difficult would it have been for someone in Israel to take the illustration in this section and apply it to other situations in daily life?

4 Why was cursing a ruler (22:28) put on the same level as cursing God?

6 Relationships with Others (23:1-9)
1 In legal cases no slander was permitted, whether only a single person was involved or many.[25] Nor should one join

---

25. The NIV's 'do not spread false reports' goes further than the MT: 'do not take up a false report', as the prohibition could embrace just a single action, as well as more widespread defamation of someone.

oneself with a wicked man (Heb. *'al tâshet yâdekâ 'im râshâ',* lit. 'you shall not set your hand with a wicked man'). The intention of such a relationship was that the person would become 'a malicious witness'. 'Malicious' translates a Hebrew word (*châmas*) that denotes 'violence', almost always sinful violence. The impact of its use is to highlight the fact that no testimony was permissible that would do serious harm to the other person. Basically, the same prohibition occurs in Deuteronomy 19:16-19 and Psalm 35:11.

2-3 There was always the danger that a witness would side with the vast majority (Heb. *rabbîm,* 'the many', 'the crowd'). The double mention of this danger (NIV 'do not follow the crowd', 'siding with the crowd') points to the danger of going with the majority. That could easily result in 'tilting'[26] the case in a way that distorted the legal process. The prohibition of showing favour to a poor man in a law case might seem odd, as we would expect it to apply to a rich man. However, the point is that, whatever the social standing of anyone, the law was to be administered fairly.

4-5 With regard to animals that were wandering off or collapsing under a heavy load, the relationship of the one helping the owner of those donkeys was not to be decisive when assistance was needed. Even if they belonged to someone who was an enemy (v. 4), or who showed animosity (v. 5), help was to be given. The direction in both cases is stated in an emphatic way: 'Be sure to take it back', and 'be sure you help him'.[27] These regulations are amplified and extended in Deuteronomy 22:1-4.

6-7 The case of a poor man is taken up again, this time by the instruction that there must be no perversion of justice (Heb. lit. 'you shall not turn aside justice'). The same idiom is also found in Deuteronomy 16:19, 24:17, 27:19, and 1 Samuel 8:3. A poor man must neither be favoured (v. 3) nor prevented from

---

26. This is the translation of Victor Hamilton, *Exodus,* p. 423. The verb *nâtâh* occurs twice in v. 2, first as the Qal inf. constr. (*lintot*) and then at the end of the verse as the Hi. inf. constr. (*lᵉhattot*).

27. In both cases 'be sure' in the NIV is an attempt to translate the inf. absol. + cognate finite verbal forms: *hâshêv tᵉshîvennû, 'âzov taᵃzov.* While this is a common way of translating this construction, it can be done in other ways, such as the ESV 'he shall'. See *DIHG~S,* §101, pp. 123-24.

obtaining justice (v. 6). One way in which justice would be denied was by stating what was not true. Hence verse 7 directs that one must stay far off from lying, a direction that could apply to anyone involved in a legal case, even a defendant himself.[28] The worst possible case of lying is when someone does so with the result that an innocent or honest person is put to death. The case of the death of Naboth is a notable example from the biblical text of violation of this principle (1 Kings 21:8-13). Once again (cf. 22:22-24), it is God Himself who will dispense justice ('*I* will not acquit the guilty').

8 In addition to the aspects of the administration of justice already mentioned, bribery was not to have any place in the life of God's people. This was because they were expected to pattern themselves on God Himself, who was not partial and who took no bribes (Deut. 10:17). The reasons given for this instruction are that a bribe blinds those who are clear-sighted and subverts the cause of those who are in the right. In Deuteronomy 16:19-20, the same injunctions of not perverting the cause of justice (v. 6) and not taking bribes (v. 8) occur in almost identical language. The case of Samuel shows us both faithful adherence by him of the principles set out here and the abuse of them by his sons (1 Sam. 8:3).

9 This section of the text concludes by affirming again the motivating principle behind observance of these laws. The Israelites' own experience in Egypt had to compel them to act fairly to aliens in their midst. The wording in this verse differs slightly from that in 22:21 as it speaks of knowing how it feels to be an alien (Heb. *yᵉdaʻtem ʼet néfesh haggêr*, lit. 'you know the soul [or, life] of the stranger'). This expression points to the understanding that the Israelites had of the limitations placed upon aliens.

7 The Sabbath Principle (23:10-13)

The law of the Sabbath (20:8-11) is explained in these verses and the principle behind it is extended to include the sabbatical year. Fields, vineyards, and olive orchards were

---

28. For an interesting application of this to modern cases of 'plea bargaining', see Douglas Stuart, *Exodus*, p. 527, n. 220. Stuart holds to the position that a defendant can engage in plea-bargaining as long as the crime admitted is part of the original charge.

all embraced in the application of the rule regarding rest. Obligation to God and humanitarian concerns were included in observance of the sabbatical year.

10-11 The sabbatical principle in regard to land was that after six years of cropping it was left fallow in the seventh year. This was not just to allow the land to rejuvenate but also so that the poor among the people could eat from the produce of that year, and what they left could provide fodder for beasts. The same principle applied to vineyards and olive orchards. How this principle worked out in practice is unclear. There could have been a nationwide observance of it every seventh year, but this would mean the poor had very little food in other years. Most probably, individual farmers had the right to set their own sabbatical year, and so at all times there would have been some fallow ground about, on which the poor could rely.[29]

12 Immediately following the regulation concerning the sabbatical year, the law relating to the weekly sabbath is given, which in no way could be neglected. Rather, the Fourth Word (20:8-11) is repeated as it was a sabbath to the LORD (31:15). The emphasis is placed on the need for oxen and donkeys to rest, and also that any slave born in the household (*ben ʾaʾmâtᵉkâ*, lit. 'son of your maidservant') and any alien could be refreshed by a sabbatical rest. The verb for 'refresh' (*nâfash*, Ni.) is very rare, only occurring here and in Exodus 31:17 and 2 Samuel 16:14. It appears to be a verb made up from the word *néfesh*, which among other meanings can indicate 'breath' or 'life'.[30]

13 This section closes with an instruction to observe carefully all that the LORD had told the people to do, and a warning not to recite the names of other gods. Everything (*bᵉkol*) was important, and the people were encouraged to take good care that they kept what was required. The verb used here (*shâmar*, Ni.) is often employed in contexts in which giving careful attention to the obligations of the covenant is in view. The gods of the peoples they were going to meet

---

29. It is possible that other laws relating to the landless poor meant that they would have enough sustenance even if the fallow year were observed over the whole land at the same time. See *NIDOTTE*, 4, p. 157.

30. For the wide range of meaning of *néfesh*, see *DCH*, V, pp. 724-34.

in Canaan were lifeless idols (see the description of them in Psalm 115:4-7), and not even mention of them was allowed.

8 Three Annual Festivals (23:14-19)

These verses contain the preliminary reference to the three annual pilgrimage festivals, with later passages giving more detailed information about them (see Exod. 34:18-26; Lev. 23:4-44; Num. 28:16-29:40; Deut. 16:1-17). The account here is preliminary since more detailed specification would only be necessary after Israel was established in Canaan. In the first case (the Feast of Unleavened Bread), the actual month is mentioned in which the festival took place. The names also underwent some adjustment later.[31] Here, the connection with the exodus is only specified in the first case (v. 15), whereas later passages make the connection for the other two feasts (Deut. 16:12 and Lev. 23:43 respectively). These annual pilgrimages were meant to be joyous occasions (Ps. 42:4) as the tribes went up 'to praise the name of the LORD' (Ps. 122:4).

14 Two significant words occur in the MT of this verse. The instruction is directed to every individual ('you', s. m.) in Israel that three times (*re gâlîm*) every year they are to celebrate a festival (*tâchog*) to the LORD (*lî*, 'to me'). The word *re gâlîm* is the plural of *régel* that means 'foot', and one of its extended usages is to denote 'a [number of] times'.[32] The verb indicating celebrating a festival is *châgag*, while the noun for a festival is *chag*, with the corresponding Arabic noun *hajj* being current in English to denote the pilgrimage of Muslims to Mecca.

15 The first of the feasts, that of Unleavened Bread (*chag hammatstsot*), has already been noted in 12:14-20. It involved using only unleavened bread for seven days, with the festival taking place in the month of Abib, the month when Israel left Egypt. In a modern calendar this is from about mid-March to mid-April. The attached specification, 'No one shall appear before me empty', states an important principle. In coming

---

31. For a chart giving names and dates, see R. K. Harrison, *Leviticus: An Introduction and Commentary* (London: Inter-Varsity Press, 1980), p. 214.

32. See *DCH*, VII, pp. 412-14. Cf. the way in which in Hebrew *pa'am*, 'a step', is similarly an element in expressions of time, and, significantly, it is used in v. 17. The root *r-g-l* also provides the verb 'to spy' (go about on foot) and the adjective meaning 'on foot' (*raglî*).

before God no one was to come empty-handed. This gift was an acknowledgement of the source of all bounty and of the LORD's liberality to His redeemed people. The same instruction is repeated in Deuteronomy 16:16-17.[33]

16 Mention is made for the first time of two further festivals. The first, the Feast of Harvest (*chag haqqâtsîr*), that is called the Feast of Weeks (*chag shâvû'ot*) in 34:22, consisted of presentation of the first-fruits of crops that had been sown in the fields. Further details about it are given in Leviticus 23:15-22 and Deuteronomy 16:9-12. It was to be celebrated fifty days from the opening of the barley harvest, and therefore, under the influence of the Septuagint, it became known as Pentecost (Gk. *pentêkonta*, 'fifty'). The second festival is the Feast of Ingathering (*chag hâ'âsîf*) that marked the end of the agricultural year. Here, and in Exodus 34:22, the same name is given to this festival, whereas in Leviticus 23:34 and Deuteronomy 16:13, 16 it is called the Feast of Tabernacles. The Hebrew word for 'ingathering' (*'âsîf*) only occurs three times in the Old Testament, two of them in the list of religious festivals (Exod. 23:16 and 34:22). However, it occurs in an important extra-biblical text, the Geza calendar,[34] while the verb 'to gather' (*'âsaf*) is used for the harvesting of summer fruit, grapes and olives (Lev. 25:3; Deut. 28:38; Jer. 40:10, 12).

17 The instruction of verse 14 is repeated with some variation and additional information. Three times a year (cf. v. 14 and footnote) every male was called upon to present himself at the sanctuary before 'the Sovereign LORD' (NIV). This is the way chosen by the NIV translators to render the Hebrew *'âdon yhwh*, whereas the ESV has 'the Lord GOD'.[35] Presumably, as

---

33. The principle is stated by E. W. Hengstenberg, 'The Sacrifices of Holy Scripture', in *Commentary on Ecclesiastes, with Other Treatises* (Edinburgh: T. & T. Clark, 1860), p. 369: 'Godliness ... is driven by an irresistible impulse to seek its origin and source, and knows that so certainly as man is created in the image of God, even so certainly may he not appear empty before his Creator: its feeling is, that man cannot refuse to bring back in loving devotion what God has bestowed, that he cannot refuse to make sacrifice, without denying the true dignity of his nature...'

34. The text of the Geza calendar can be found in J. C. L. Gibson, *Textbook of Syrian Semitic Inscriptions, volume 1 Hebrew and Moabite Inscriptions*, p. 2.

35. The difficulty is that *yhwh* is often rendered by 'LORD'. When a combined expression like *'âdon yhwh* occurs, it would be confusing to render this in English as 'Lord LORD'. Hence, alternative phrases are used in various English versions.

seen in 1 Samuel 1:1-8, this instruction to appear three times annually before the LORD meant that whole families were to participate in these journeys.

18 While there is some ambiguity about this regulation, the best interpretation is that it refers to the Passover offering and prohibits killing the lamb if there was still leaven in the house. Alternatively, it could refer to using blood as an ingredient in bread.[36] Clearly, the prohibition was important since it is repeated in 34:25. The second prohibition in this verse concerns keeping the fat of an animal overnight, thus endorsing a principle rather like not retaining manna overnight except for that gathered for the Sabbath (see 16:4-5, 17-30). The principle is given fuller expression in Leviticus 3:16-17 that indicates that the fat was to be burnt on the altar, for 'all the fat is the LORD's'. This meant that the LORD's offering had to be made, not even retained for use the following morning.

19a The first-fruits have already been referred to in verse 16 in relation to the Feast of Harvest. The instruction to Israel was to bring 'the first' (*rê'shît*), i.e. 'the best', of the first-fruits to 'the house of the LORD your God'. No such 'house' existed at that time, but this, and a similar instruction in Deuteronomy 23:18 (MT v. 19), must be pointing ahead to the tent and temple. The term 'house' is used in relation to both.

19b The reference to cooking a kid in its mother's milk appears also in Exodus 34:26 and Deuteronomy 14:21b. There does not seem to be anything intrinsically wrong with the practice, but rather it was a heathen practice that had to be avoided. Outside the Bible the nearest parallel is in a text from Ugarit/Ras Shamra in northern Syria that contains the line: 'cook the kid in milk, the lamb in butter'.[37] However, this Ugaritic text is problematical and should not be used to come to any definitive understanding of this verse.[38] It looks as if

---

36. This is the position of Douglas Stuart, *Exodus*, pp. 537-38, who considers the wording of the prohibition deals with mixing blood and yeast, not simply conjoining blood and yeast for use at the same time.

37. For the text, see J. C. L. Gibson, *Canaanite Myths and Legends*, 2nd ed. (Edinburgh: T. & T. Clark, 1978), p. 123.

38. Gibson says in a footnote that the proposed translation of the Ugaritic is unsuitable, and that the Heb. text in v. 19 says 'slaughter', not 'cook'. It also adds 'of its mother' after 'milk'. Ibid., p. 123, fn. 11.

the Canaanites did practise a ritual that was forbidden for the Israelites. Possibly it involved a fertility rite in which the milk in which the kid was cooked was then sprinkled on the fields.[39] This verse remains relevant for Orthodox Judaism to this day as it provides the rationale for not eating meat and milk products at the same time.

9 Promises and Warnings (23:20-33)

Danger lay ahead for the people of Israel. They were going to face severe trials as they progressed towards Canaan. Protection was to be provided by an angel, but they had to be careful they were not enticed by foreign gods. The boundaries of the 'sworn land' were restated by Moses (v. 31) and the warning was given that the conquest was not going to be accomplished all at once. This note is important, for in the book of Joshua the record of the conquest clearly shows that this is what happened. In principle, the land was fairly quickly conquered; in reality, the total conquest did not come until David and his men captured Jerusalem (2 Sam. 5:6-10).

20-21 The introductory particle 'See' (*hinnêh*) draws attention to the very significant announcement that was made. No precise identification is given of the angel, but his prerogatives and mission link him with the revelation of the angel of the LORD (see comment on 3:2). The first part of his mission was to guard the people on their journey and to bring them to Canaan, the place that God had designated for them (Gen. 12:6-7; 15:18-21; 26:3; 28:13). The verb used of God's action regarding the land (*kûn*, Hi.) is stronger in meaning than just 'prepare', for it carries with it the overtones of divine certainty. To rebel against the angel would be to rebel against God. This is made clear by the reference to the angel not forgiving rebellion, and the fact that God's name dwelt in him. In a similar way, God's name resided on the tabernacle (Deut. 12:5, 11) and the temple (1 Kings 8:29). In spite of such a clear direction, Israel did rebel in the wilderness as noted in Psalm 78:17, 40, 56, in each case using the same verb for 'rebel' as here (*mârar*).

---

39. For more extensive discussions, with good bibliographic references, see Douglas Stuart, *Exodus*, pp. 539-40, and Victor Hamilton, *Exodus*, pp. 431-32.

22 Two aspects in this verse are related to covenantal formulation. First, the words, 'If you listen carefully and do all that he says', is an example of a formula that is analogous to ones in the extra-biblical texts, when a superior was speaking to an inferior.[40] Implicit obedience was required of covenantal servants. Secondly, the promise was that obedience to the LORD would mean He would be an enemy to Israel's enemies and oppose those who opposed them. One of the features of many of the extra-biblical treaties in the Near East was the assurance that the superior would defend his vassals if attacked. This is precisely what the LORD says He will do for Israel.[41] Defeat of Israel's enemies was based on obedience (see Lev. 26:7; Deut. 6:19), while defeat of Israel was to be a mark she had departed from God (Lev. 26:17, 25, 32; Num. 14:42; Deut. 1:42).

23 The role of the angel in leading the people to the sworn land is reiterated (cf. v. 20). The land to which they were headed was occupied by a variety of tribal groups – Amorites, Hittites, Perizzites, Canaanites, Hivites and Jebusites[42] – but the assurance was that God would destroy them.[43] The verb used for this action (*kâchad*) basically means to hide, but came to denote non-existence or effacement. It is used a few times in the Old Testament of annihilation of Israel's enemies (Exod. 9:15; 2 Chron. 32:21; Zech. 11:8). Other passages deal with the detestable practices of the Gentiles in Canaan, and the need for their total destruction. God's ultimate judgment on sin and unbelief found a preliminary fulfilment in the process of the conquest of Canaan.[44] Eventually not all the Canaanites

---

40. Examples are given by Paul Kalluveettil, *Declaration and Covenant*, p. 153.

41. This is the only occurrence of a non-participial use of the verb *'âyav* in the OT, where it means 'to be hostile to', 'to treat as an enemy'. The common participial form, *'oyêv*, appears in this verse also ('your enemies').

42. The land of Canaan was inhabited by ten population groups, and they are listed ten times in the Pentateuch, but never with the full number in any list. See Exod. 3:8, 17; 13:5; 23:23, 28; 33:2; 34:11; Num. 13:29; Deut. 7:1; 20:17. For information on most of these groups, see Alfred J. Hoerth, Gerald L. Mattingly, and Edwin M. Yamauchi eds., *Peoples of the Old Testament World*.

43. The MT has 'I will destroy *him*', clearly regarding the group of names as a single identity.

44. For the concept of God's intrusive judgment as displayed in the destruction of the Canaanites, see M. G. Kline, 'Intrusion and the Decalogue', *WTJ* 16 (1953-54), pp. 1-22, especially pp. 15-16.

were obliterated, and the remainder became slaves under Solomon's reign (1 Kings 9:20-21), except for the Gibeonites whose treaty with Joshua was honoured (Josh. 9:1-26).

24 One of the problems for Israel entering Canaan was going to be the attraction of heathen gods. No worship was to be rendered to them, nor service given to them. 'Serve' can have a wide meaning, though it is better to retain the translation 'serve' (ESV) rather than change to 'worship' (NIV). Neither should there be any imitation of heathen practices, while their sacred stones were to be broken in pieces. The 'sacred stones' (*matstsêvot*) were cultic pillars that had to be destroyed, while Israel was told later not to follow this pattern, as such objects were things hated by God (Deut. 16:22). The thrust of this verse is expanded in Deuteronomy 4:15-31 and 7:12-26.

25-26 The negative command regarding worship of false gods is followed in verse 25 with the positive command. Israel's devotion was to be to the LORD alone. God's providence was to overrule every aspect of their lives, including food, water, health, fertility, and longevity. These promises were not given irrespective of obedience to the LORD, but like all the other promises were conditional upon faithful adherence to the terms of the covenant. The later announcement of covenantal blessings covered the same general areas as here (Deut. 28:1-6). There does not seem to be any real difference in meaning between 'In your land, I will give you a full lifespan' and 'that you may live long in the land the LORD your God is giving you' (20:12).

27 The LORD's 'terror' (*'êmâh*) has already been referred to in the Song of the Sea (15:16), while the verb 'throw into confusion' (*hâmam*) was used in the describing what the LORD did to the Egyptian forces after the people of Israel had crossed the Red Sea (14:24). As strong encouragement to Israel in heading towards Canaan, God assured them that He would confront their enemies so that they would be like the Egyptians. Rather than facing Israel, they would display their backs as they fled. Divine assistance would come to Israel's aid as they confronted belligerent opponents.

28-30 The reference to 'a hornet' (*tsir'âh*) is uncertain. This probably rests on the LXX translation (*sphêgias*), but the major dictionary of biblical Hebrew lists four possibilities.[45] Even if 'hornet' is correct, yet rather than adopting a literal interpretation, it is possible that this is a use similar to the way that 'fly' and 'bee' occur in Isaiah 7:18 to depict the Assyrian army. This understanding would mean that God was promising some intervention to help in the process of removing the Hivites, Canaanites and Hittites from the path of Israel. On the other hand, it could refer to dejection on the part of the enemies, who having heard of what happened at the exodus from Egypt would be fearful of meeting the large contingent of Israelites. The occupation of Canaan was not to be a speedy process, since rapid expulsion of the inhabitants would result in vacant fields and the incursion of wild animals. This is confirmed in the later historical references (see especially Judg. 1:27-36). Only 'little by little' ($m^{e\text{'}}at\ m^{e\text{'}}at$) would Israel enter into the full occupation of the allotted territory.[46]

31-32 The book of the covenant concludes with reference to the extent of the sworn land and warnings regarding relationships with the existing inhabitants. Treaties between Israel and these peoples were forbidden, as were any approximation to their worship practices. The boundaries of the land that God had in store for Israel are set out in verse 31, being given in a form slightly different from other passages dealing with the same territory. Here, 'the sea of reeds' (*yam suf*) is mentioned, referring, not to the Red Sea, but to the upper portion of the Gulf of Aqaba, as in 1 Kings 9:26. 'The Sea of the Philistines' was the Mediterranean, this being one of the various expressions used to describe it.[47] To the south 'the

---

45. *DCH*, VII, p. 163. The possibilities are 'hornets', 'terror', 'dejection', and 'pestilence'. Other suggestions have been made, including J. F. A. Sawyer's that *tsir'âh* should be linked with *tsara't*, 'leprosy'. See his article, 'A Note on the Etymology of *sâra'at'*, *VT* 26 (1976), pp. 241-45.

46. In Biblical Hebrew, the same word can be repeated to indicate intensity of some form, e.g. 'year year', 'heap heap', 'gold gold'. For comment on the grammatical point, see *GKC*, p. 396, §123.e, and *DIHG~S*, §39 (e), Rem. 4, p. 42.

47. Other ones include 'the great sea' (Num. 34:6), 'the western sea' (Deut. 11:24), and 'the sea of Joppa' (Ezra 3:7). The last case could be translated as in the NIV, 'by the sea of Joppa', but the translation 'the sea of Joppa' is certainly possible: 'The Hebrew could be translated "to the sea of Joppa", which could then mean near the anchorage at Joppa; cf. 2 Chr. 2:16)', L. H. Brockington, *Ezra, Nehemiah, and Esther* (Century Bible New Series: London: Thomas Nelson and

desert' was the limit, probably meaning the Negev area, while in the north-east the boundary was set as the Euphrates River. The variation in descriptions of the land God swore to give to Israel points to the fact that it was a broad concept, rather than territory that could be surveyed and pegged with minute precision. The inhabitants were also to be given over to Israel, so that they could dispossess them. No treaty arrangements were to be made with them or with their gods. The usual verb for initiating a covenant arrangement (*kârat*) is used, though with a different preposition than normal (*l^e* instead of *'im* or *'et*). The reference to 'gods' is significant, as often the lives of people and their gods were so closely intertwined that it was hard to make a difference between them (cf. the judgment not only of the people, but also of the gods of Egypt, 12:12).

33 The continuing presence of Gentiles in the land would easily become a snare to Israel. Their idols would be prominently displayed, and their religious practices could easily appeal, especially as they had altars and offered sacrifices. Separation was a divine demand on the LORD's redeemed people.

Study Questions

1) Are the laws in 23:1-9 simply isolated regulations, or is there some unifying factor present?

2) The Sabbath principle was central to Israel's life. Do any of the laws in 23:10-12 have any reference for how Christians observe the Lord's Day?

3) How does Isaiah 63:8-9 explain further the promise of God's gracious care of Israel (23:20-23)?

4) How did the reference to occupation of Canaan work out in actual historical circumstances as described in the book of Joshua?

Sons, 1969), p. 69.

17

Ratification of the Covenant
(24:1-18)

1 The Formal Covenant Ceremony (24:1-11)

At the conclusion of the scroll of the covenant (chs. 19–23) comes the formal ratification ceremony of the Sinai covenant. The occasion involved all the people, and all the twelve tribes. This is made plain by the repeated affirmation from the people that they would keep all that the LORD had said to them (vv. 3 and 7), and also by the setting up of twelve pillars to represent the twelve tribes of Israel (v. 4). Sacrifice was involved, with the blood sprinkled on the altar and on the people. The covenant was sealed in a sacred meal on the top of Mount Sinai, where God's glory was manifested in the cloud that descended on the mount.

1-2 Moses was again directed to come up on to the mountain, along with Aaron, Nadab, and Abihu, and with seventy of the elders of Israel. While Aaron had been introduced in the earlier part of this book, he is now mentioned with his sons. They along, with their brothers Eleazar and Ithamar, are later mentioned as priests (28:1). The wording in verse 1, 'Then he said to Moses' (Heb. 'and to Moses he said', *vᵉ'el mosheh 'âmar*), marks off these words as directed to the mediator of the covenant, whereas the earlier revelation was to the people as a whole: 'And the LORD said … Tell the Israelites this' (20:22). No explanation is given of the choice of 'seventy elders'. It cannot relate to the tribes of Israel, because if this was the case, seventy-two would be expected. Most probably it is a number that is associated with the seventy mentioned in 1:5 who constituted the whole family. The clause 'you are to worship at a distance' may mean that there was to be worship by the whole group on the approach to the mountain. However, it was Moses only who was permitted to draw near to the Lord. This requirement is emphasised by the pointed reference to 'Moses alone' (*mosheh l^evadô*), and by the repeated instruction that the others (MT lit. 'they') must 'worship at a distance' and that 'the people 'must not come up with him'.

3-4a Moses went and related to the people what had been said by the Lord, recounting His words and all the judgments. They responded by pledging themselves to keep all His words. The language here is so very close to that in 19:8 (preserved in the NASB translation):

> 'All that the Lord has spoken we will do' (19:8)
> [*kol 'asher dibber yhwh na'aseh*]

> 'All the words which the Lord has spoken we will do' (24:3)
> [*kol hadd^evârîm 'asher dibber yhwh na'aseh*].

In both instances the people respond to the divine initiative, and both immediately precede a theophany. Moses proceeded to write down 'all the words of the Lord' (*kol divrê yhwh*), using the same description of God's revelation as in the preceding verse. The spoken revelation became also written revelation, to be preserved and observed by the people. Earlier written records were referred to in 17:14.

4b-7 Early in the morning Moses got up and built an altar near the base of the mountain, presumably in accordance with the prescription in 20:24-26. He also set up twelve pillars to symbolise the twelve tribes of Israel. On later occasions, twelve stones were used to memorialise God's great acts on behalf of His people and as a sign for future generations (see Josh. 4:4-7, and also 1 Kings 18:31). Young men were appointed to offer sacrifices, both burnt offerings and fellowship offerings, as mentioned in 20:24. The choice of these young men appears to have been Moses', though soon afterward such priestly ministry would be the province of the

Levites. The blood of the slain animals was divided in half. One half was reserved in basins for later use in sprinkling the people, verse 8, while the other half was sprinkled over the altar. Until the fuller symbolism of the tent of meeting was provided, the altar represented the presence of God. The verb used for 'sprinkling' (*zâraq*) is mainly of sprinkling in religious ceremonies, and indicated here that atonement had been made for the people's sins.

7-8 The writing of the document already referred to in verse 4 is now called 'the covenant scroll' (*sêfer habb^{e}rît*, see on page 189 for comment on this term). Moses took the scroll and read from it to the people. Such public reading of a covenantal document was part of the ratification of a treaty in the ancient Near East.[1] The effect of the reading was to obtain a suitable response from the people. Their united response was in the same terms as in verse 3 (*kol hadd^{e}vârîm 'asher dibber yhwh na'^{a}seh*), though they now added a pledge of obedience ('and we will obey', *v^{e}nishmâ'*). Then Moses took half the blood and with it sprinkled the people, making the pronouncement: 'This is the blood of the covenant that the LORD has made with you in accordance with all these words'. Two very important things come out in this verse (v. 8). The first is the reference to 'the blood of the covenant', a reminder of how important blood was in covenant-making.[2] The blood symbolised expiation of sin. The second is the assertion that the confirmation of the covenant was 'in accordance with all these words', a phrase that immediately ties in with 19:8 and 24:3, 7. The initiator of the covenant (the LORD) and His oath-bound servants (Israel) were both obliged to fulfil the terms of the covenant ('all these words'). At times 'word(s)' could be used as a synonym for 'covenant', either the covenant itself or the stipulations.[3]

9-11 The larger company of men (Moses, Aaron, Nadab and Abihu, and the seventy elders, v. 1) went up and '*saw* the God of Israel' (*râ'âh*), a statement repeated using a differing verb for 'seeing' in verse 11 (*châzâh*). It is inconsistent

---

1. For an example, see *ANET*, p. 151.

2. Cf. O. Palmer Robertson's definition of covenant in *The Christ of the Covenants* (Phillipsburg: Presbyterian and Reformed Publishing Co., 1980), p. 4: 'A covenant is a *bond in blood sovereignly administered*' (italics his).

3. For examples, see Paul Kalluveettil, *Declaration and Covenant*, pp. 33-34.

with all the warnings concerning approaching God to think that somehow God in person was literally seen. The general biblical teaching is that God cannot be seen (Exod. 33:20; John 1:18; 1 Tim. 6:16), and this agrees with Moses' own words that when God revealed Himself, he only saw His 'form' or 'shape' (*tᵉmûnâh*, Num. 12:8). Here the men were presented with a theophany, though the words that follow in the MT are difficult to translate and interpret, as the variety of English translations indicate. Under God's feet was something like a pavement of *sappîr*, and it was like the bone of the heavens (*kᵉ'étsem hashshâmáyim*) for clearness (*lâtohar*). *Sappîr* should not be translated as 'sapphire' but as *'lapis lazuli'*, a blue precious stone much sought after in the ancient world.[4] The Hebrew word for bone, *'étsem*, can have a wider meaning almost like 'self' or 'substance', and so a translation such as 'the very heavens' (NKJV) is good.[5] The noun *tohar* is used in the Old Testament especially of the tent of meeting, temple, and priests' clothing. It appears in the sense of 'clean' or 'pure', and in Exodus is applied to the gold used in the ark (25:11), the mercy seat (25:17), the table (25:24), the lamp stand (25:31), the plate (28:36), and the incense altar (30:3). The vision of God was majestic in beauty and holiness, indicating something of the purity of heaven itself. This revelation of God to the elders of Israel did not result in their expulsion from His presence, for they were not intruders there. Rather, they, as representatives of Israel, were welcome guests. The word used for elders (*'ᵃtsîlîm*) is only employed here in this sense. Normally it means a 'joint' of the hand or arms.[6] These leaders were privileged to eat and drink before the LORD, a solemn meal that probably involved the use of the fellowship offerings mentioned in verse 5.

2 The Revelation of God's Glory (24:12-18)

The final section of chapter 24 is concerned with further revelation of God, including the gift of the law and the commands in

---

4. *DCH*, VI, p. 181.

5. *DCH*, VI, p. 537, gives 'heaven itself, the very heavens'.

6. *DCH*, I, p. 363. For a longer note on the Heb. word *'âtsîl*, see W. C. Kaiser Jr., 'Exodus', p. 451.

written form. God's glory was revealed in the cloud and in the fire. While Joshua was privileged to accompany Moses to the mountain, it was only Moses who was allowed to enter into the cloud where he stayed for forty days and forty nights.

12 The invitation was given to Moses to come up again to the mountain in order to receive 'the tablets of stone', containing 'the law and the commands'. A tablet (*lûach*) was normally wooden, but in this case God specified that they were to be stone tablets. Because of their content, they are later described as 'tablets of the testimony' (31:18), and for safekeeping they were placed in the ark of the covenant (Deut. 10:5), just like other ancient documents that were preserved in the temples of a people's god.[7] The divine origin of the law is stressed by the later reference to the fact that what was written on the tablets was done by the finger of God (31:18). The content of the writing is 'the law (*hattôrâh*) and the commandment (*hamittsvâh*)', an unusual phrase that seems to refer specifically to the Ten Words. This means that the *vav* before the combined phrase is one of explanation ('*that is*') rather than being simply a conjunctive *vav* ('*and* the law and the teaching'). This written revelation was designed for instructional purposes. That is to say, the written law was not only to be a record admired from a distance, but a living word in the hearts and minds of God's people (Deut. 6:5-9).

13-14 Further instructions are related as to who was to accompany Moses on to Mount Sinai. Joshua, his servant (already introduced in 17:8-13), was with him, and although the biblical text does not state this explicitly, he must have gone part of the way up the mountain, where he remained, while Moses went further up. The fact that Joshua stayed somewhere lower down on the mountain is confirmed by comparison with 32:17. Mount Sinai is called here 'the mountain of God' (*har hâ'elohîm*; cf. the use of this phrase in 3:1, where it is also called Horeb), the place of His own self-revelation. The elders (referred to now by the more normal word, *zâkên*), were instructed to remain where they were.[8] Meanwhile, Aaron

---

7. See *ANET*, p. 205.

8. The MT has *bâzeh*, which means 'in this [place]'. Hence, as in Genesis 38:21 it is equivalent to *poh*, 'here'.

and Hur (see 17:10-13) were given delegated responsibility for settling disputes that might arise in Moses' absence.[9] The reference to Hur is puzzling, as he is not mentioned later in connection with the episode with the golden bull (32:1-35).

15-18 Moses was the obedient servant who did as his master had directed. He went up into the cloud that was covering the mountain. There the glory of the LORD was 'dwelling' (*shâkan*), and after six days the LORD called to Moses from the midst of the cloud. The appearance of the glory of the LORD was like flaming fire to the Israelites. The MT expression is 'devouring fire' (*'êsh 'okélet*), but this seems to be a way of describing a blazing fire without any stress on the action of continuing to consume objects in its path. Fire was a fitting medium through which God could reveal Himself (cf. the revelation at the burning bush, 3:1-6). 'Glory' became almost a technical term for God's presence, so that Israel's rebellion could be described as exchanging 'their glory' for an idol (Ps. 106:20), language that is echoed by the apostle Paul in Romans 1:23. From the vantage point of the elders of Israel, Moses went up into the cloud, and continued there for forty days and forty nights. No explanation is given of why 'forty' was the appropriate time, but in 34:28 it is repeated with the indication that Moses was supernaturally provided for while on the mount ('he neither ate bread nor drank water'). The same time frame reappears in the narrative of Elijah's journey to Horeb (1 Kings 19:8), while Jesus fasted for forty days and forty nights (Matt. 4:2). Probably, two things were in mind. First, this period of forty days was a time of testing, but secondly, it was also a time of strengthening of their faith.

Study Questions

1) Twice in chapter 24 the people of Israel solemnly promised to do everything the LORD had said (vv. 4, 7). Was this a promise of genuine obedience?

---

9. 'Anyone involved in a dispute' is the NIV translation of 'who[ever] [is] a master of words/matters'. For a note on the translation issues here, see Victor Hamilton, *Exodus*, p. 444.

Ratification of the Covenant 24:1-18

2) Are there similar motives behind the erection of twelve stones recorded in Joshua 4:8-9 and 1 Kings 18:30-33 as in Exodus 24:4?

3) Why was the blood (vv. 6-8) such an important part of the confirmation ceremony of the covenant?

4) The glory of the LORD was manifested at the conclusion of the formal giving of the law and the commandments. It was also manifested after the Tent of Meeting was built (40:34-38). Did these two revelations of God differ at all?

PART IV

Instructions Regarding the Tent of Meeting
(25:1–31:18)

Introduction

The previous chapter has described how the priestly kingdom of Israel had responded to God's claims upon them with a pledge of full obedience (24:3, 7). Then the representatives of the people, Moses and the other leaders in Israel, had gone up and communed with God on the mountain and the covenant had been ratified by a communal meal (24:11). The concept of God's presence with His people is now taken up and detailed attention paid to the symbol of that presence, the Tent of Meeting, and the accompanying diagram will show the its general layout.[1]

The term 'Tent of Meeting' is preferable to the traditional one, 'tabernacle', that comes from the Latin word for 'tent'. Continuing to use it conceals the significance of God's dwelling in a tent like His people (see point 2 below). It is a confusing term for modern readers who do not know what 'a tabernacle' is, and it also causes problems for New Testament translators. If 'tabernacle' has been used in the Old Testament, then it should be used in various passages in the New Testament for the sake of consistency, even though the Greek word for 'a tent', *skênê*, is translated elsewhere in the same version by its normal English equivalent.[2]

---

1. The diagram of the Tent of Meeting on p. 382 draws upon three presentations. The first is that of A. R. S. Kennedy, 'Tabernacle', *A Dictionary of the Bible*, IV, pp. 657. The second is D. W. Gooding, *The Account of the Tabernacle: Translation and Textual Problems of the Greek Exodus* (Cambridge: Cambridge University Press, 1959), diagram following p. 114. The third is Vern Poythress, *The Shadow of Christ in the Law of Moses* (Brentwood: Wolgemuth & Hyatt, 1991), p. 17.

2. The NIV uses 'tabernacle' in the book of Hebrews when the reference is to the Tent of Meeting (Heb. 8:2, 5; 9:2, 8, 11, 21; 13:10), but not for other tents (Heb. 11:9). This is in keeping with its use of 'shelter' to translate *skênê* in Matt. 17:4; Mark 9:5; and Luke 9:33, and 'tent' in Acts 15:16. At times it employs 'dwelling [place]' (Luke 16:9; Rev. 13:6; 21:3), while 'shrine [of Molech]' appears in Acts 7:43-44.

Before detailed discussion on the text, some general comments may help to prepare the way.[3]

1. The narrative concerning the Tent of Meeting is not an irrelevancy, but rather a very significant section of the book of Exodus consisting of chapters 25–31 and chapters 35–40. In between these two sections are the accounts of the gross sin of the people in reverting to idolatry, the breaking of the covenant, and its renewal (chs. 31–34). The tent mentioned in 33:7-11 is not the tabernacle but a temporary place of meeting for this interim period (see the comments on this passage). The narrative in Exodus is vitally important as it sets out how Israel had to approach the living God by the means that He appointed. It symbolised God's heavenly dwelling, and the appointment was for His people to meet with Him there.

2. The people of Israel were living in tents, and God Himself chose to come among them *in a tent*. It was an expression of His love and concern for them that He should, in an act of self-humiliation, assume such a dwelling place among them.[4] That Israel desired this to happen is shown by the fact that the freewill offerings of the people provided the materials out of which the tabernacle was made.

3. The Tent of Meeting is referred to by several different names:

    - A dwelling place (*mishkân*)
    - A tent (*'ohel*)
    - The tent of testimony (*'ohel hâ'êdut*)
    - The dwelling place of testimony (*mishkân hâ'êdut*)
    - The Tent of Meeting (*'ohel mo'êd*)
    - A holy place (*miqdâsh*)

---

3. Two discussions by O. T. Allis in relation to the Tent of Meeting should not be overlooked. The first is a general summary of the significance of the tent in *God Spake by Moses* (London: Marshall, Morgan & Scott, 1951), pp. 81-94. The second is his commentary on Leviticus in *The New Bible Commentary*, edd. D. Guthrie *et al* (London: Inter-Varsity Press, 1970), pp. 140-167.

4. Cf. the words of Geerhardus Vos, *Biblical Theology*, p. 149: 'For, since the Israelites lived in tents, the idea of God's identifying His lot with theirs could not be more strikingly expressed than by His sharing this mode of habitation.' See his whole discussion, pp. 148-55.

Introduction

The multifaceted nature of the Tent of Meeting meant that one name could not encompass all its aspects. Three main ideas are conveyed by these names. (1) The use of 'dwelling' and 'tent' point to God's graciousness in condescending to draw near to His people, to live symbolically in a tent with them. (2) The expressions that use the word 'testimony' or 'witness' point to God's self-revelation of His character and will for men, and this is reinforced by the use of the term 'sanctuary', 'the holy place'. His holiness had to be respected, and special provision was made for an unholy people to be ceremonially cleansed from sin. (3) 'The Tent of Meeting' can be understood in two ways. It could refer to the gathering of the people together before God, but more probably it refers to the fact that this was God's appointed place for meeting with His people. It was the place where God drew near in grace and communed with them. He approached them and conversed with them.[5]

4. Our understanding of the significance of the tabernacle must flow from the biblical text itself. Some early Jewish writers, such as Josephus and Philo, thought that the tabernacle in some way represented the whole universe. Christian writers like Cocceius believed that the tabernacle represented the church of Christ. But these explanations are very remote from the biblical teaching. The biblical text points the way in both Old and New Testaments. In the holy of holies was the ark, and it contained the tablets on which was written the Decalogue. That fact alone points to the tabernacle as being intimately connected with the covenant that was confirmed on Sinai (24:1-18). God said: 'Then have them make a sanctuary (*miqdâsh*) for me, and I will dwell among them' (25:8). The sovereign God,

---

5. In his significant discussion on 'the tabernacle', Bishop W. F. Westcott referred to the Puritan writer, John Howe, who spoke of God's 'conversableness'. The phrase seems to refer both to the manner of God's approach and His interaction with them. Perhaps 'revelatory approachableness', or some similar expression, comes close to what both Howe and Westcott were meaning. See Westcott's *The Epistle to the Hebrews: The Greek Text with Notes and Essays*, pp. 235-42. The reference to Howe is his work, *The Living Temple*, vol. 1 (chap. 6, §1).

who had entered into a covenant with Israel, indicated that He would dwell with His people in the manner indicated by the tabernacle. The fullest discussion of the significance of the Tent of Meeting in the New Testament is in Hebrews 8–10. However, the exposition of it given in Hebrews indicates that it was intended to teach Israel, and in so doing to point to the fulfilment of the typology in Christ.

5. The point should be made that the exposition in Hebrews deals only with some of the main items of the tabernacle, not with every detail (Heb. 9:5). That should indicate that caution is needed in trying to work out the significance of each part mentioned in the Exodus accounts. The tabernacle had to fit together, and stand in all sorts of weather conditions. It also had to be disassembled, carried, and erected in the next place of pilgrimage. Many of the details relate to these aspects, and as such have no typological significance. Another example of lack of detail concerns the cherubim, of which no description is provided. All this means that the Tent of Meeting has to be considered as a unit, and interpreted as such. The fact that many of the details are not incorporated in the later temple also points to the need to interpret it as constituting a unified structure without attempting to find symbolical significance in every part.[6]

6. Despite the many details recorded about the Tent of Meeting, yet there are problems in understanding exactly how it was constructed. This is so, for example, in regard to the covering, which may have been horizontal, or draped over a pole. In either case, no slats

---

[6]. For a discussion making this same point see W. H. Gispen, *Exodus*, p. 251: 'When we consider the meaning of this chapter [Exod. 26] for us as Christians, we must stay with what the Scriptures, and especially the New Testament, say, and look at the tabernacle as a whole, rather than seeing a "deeper" meaning in every loop, clasp, and crossbar'. In reference to the interpretation in the Epistle to the Hebrews, note the comment by Elmer A. Martens, *God's Design: A Focus on Old Testament Theology*, 2nd ed. (Grand Rapids: Baker Books, 1994), p. 100: 'The author of Hebrews views the tabernacle as such as a type, but he does not see individual parts of it as having typological significance.'

or batons to prevent it from sagging are mentioned. Difficulties such as this explain the variations that occur when attempts are made to draw it, or to attempt a reconstruction. God told Moses: 'Make the tabernacle and all its furnishings exactly like the pattern I will show you' (25:9). The New Testament confirms that Moses was shown a pattern (Acts 7:44; Heb. 8:5; 9:23). In addition to the verbal instructions, he had other revelation to guide him.

7. The principles defined by the tabernacle were to come to greater expression in the building of the temple in Jerusalem. The close connection between tabernacle and temple is shown by the fact that the measurements of the temple were exactly double those of the tabernacle. Whereas the tabernacle was a temporary and moveable sanctuary, the temple was intended as a more permanent and substantial one that was located by God's deliberate choice on Mount Zion (Ps. 132:13-14). Even that temple was not the ultimate one, as both tabernacle and temple pointed forward to the Son of God taking on human flesh and 'tenting' with us (John 1:14). In that passage John uses, not the normal Greek word for 'dwelling', but *skênoô*, 'to pitch one's tent', 'to live temporarily'. The significance of the Old Testament sanctuary was fulfilled in the incarnation, as Jesus took on human flesh and in so doing revealed His grace and glory.

8. The measurements of the tabernacle are significant. The inner room, the holy of holies, was a perfect cube, measuring 10 cubits by 10 cubits by 10 cubits. The outer room, called the holy place, measured 10 cubits by 20 cubits by 10 cubits. The outer court had dimensions of 50 by 100 by 5. These figures show that the innermost room had the perfect measurement, while the other rooms became progressively less perfect.[7] When the

---

7. See the discussion by Vern Poythress, *The Shadow of Christ in the Law of Moses*, pp. 15-18. Note especially his comment: 'The dimensions clearly become less perfect as one moves outward. The inner room is a perfect cube. The outer room is not, but deviates from perfection simply by multiplying one dimension by two. The courtyard is still less perfect, inasmuch as all three dimensions are different. But

temple was erected, it was basically an enlarged tent, two rooms and an outer courtyard, with the horizontal measurements being doubled.

9. The importance of the Tent of Meeting is shown by the extraordinary amount of details that are given to it, as well as the repetition that occurs. The pattern was first shown to Moses (25:9), and then seven chapters describe its various parts (chs. 25–31). The account of the building of the tent takes up almost five chapters (35:1–39:32), with a summary in 39:33-43. The final chapter deals with the setting up of the tent and the coming of the cloud as a sign of God's indwelling presence (40:1-34).[8]

---

the dimensions still have simple ratios to one another, expressing a kind of limited balance and perfection. Thus each of the three areas is a kind of lesser image of the preceding one' (p. 15). Another modern discussion on the Tent of Meeting, with good bibliography, is by R. E. Averbeck, *Dictionary of the Old Testament: Pentateuch*, edd. T. Desmond Alexander and David W. Baker (Downers Grove: InterVarsity Press, 2003), pp. 807-27.

8. Two lists are provided by Victor Hamilton to show the important elements in the accounts of provision for, and the building of, the Tent of Meeting. See his *Handbook on the Pentateuch* (Grand Rapids: Baker Book House, 1982), p. 232, Table 7, and *Exodus*, pp. 452-53.

18

Contributions for the Sanctuary
(25:1-9)

The people had already pledged themselves to the LORD by spoken words of commitment (24:4, 7). Now the opportunity is afforded to them to do so by the way of gifts of precious metals and other materials that were to be incorporated in the Tent of Meeting.

1-2 While still on the mountain, Moses received detailed instructions in relation to the construction of the Tent of Meeting and associated matters. The first thing was the source of the materials to be used in its construction. These were to be mainly voluntary contributions that were to be heart-felt offerings to the LORD. The word here for 'offering' (*t^erûmâh*) is used in general of what is taken and set aside as a special contribution. Such a gift was to be made with a willing heart, not under compulsion (cf. the New Testament expression of this principle in 2 Cor. 9:6-12). The only exception to the norm of voluntary gifts was the census tax, by which a half shekel of silver was contributed by everyone aged twenty and over (30:11-16).

3-7 These verses list the items that were needed for the sanctuary or in connection with the priestly ministry there. They are almost all known from other sources and were available either in Egypt or in the Sinai Peninsula. Many of the items were included in the things given to them by the Egyptians as they left Egypt (3:22; 11:2; 12:35-36). The objects can be classified in various groups:

Metals:	gold, silver, and bronze.
Vegetable:	blue, purple, and scarlet [yarns]; fine linen; spices.
Animal:	goats' hair, goats' skins, skins of rams, skins of sea cows.
Forestry:	acacia wood, olive oil.
Precious stones:	onyx, stones for setting on the high priest's ephod and breastplate.

A few of these need some explanation. Blue dyes were obtained from shellfish in the Mediterranean, while purple was derived from the eggs and carcases of worms (*coccus ilicus*). Fine linen (*shêsh*) is a loan word from Egyptian, and almost all its occurrences in the Old Testament are in connection with the Tent of Meeting or with priestly attire. 'Sea cows' is a provisional translation of a Hebrew word (*tachash*) that may be the name of a marine animal such as a porpoise or a dolphin, or it may be the designation of a special leather.[1] 'Acacia' is probably *Acacia seyal*, from which hard timber was obtained, and which was impervious to insect infestation.[2] 'Spices', such as myrrh, cinnamon and cassia, were mixed with oil to create a special anointing oil (30:23-24). The '[other] gems' are given in detail later (28:17-20), and they were used for 'filling' the ephod and breastplate of the high priest.[3] 'Onyx' translates a Hebrew word *shoham* that cannot be identified with absolute certainty. It was used on the high priest's breastplate and ephod, and was included among the precious stones that David accumulated for building the temple in Jerusalem (1 Chron. 29:2).

8-9 After the specification of all the objects needed for making the Tent of Meeting, the command to do so follows. The instruction was to make 'a sanctuary' (*miqdâsh*), literally, 'holy place'. From one point of view, the making of the Tent of Meeting was a re-creation of the Garden of Eden. That

---

1. See the entry in *DCH*, VIII, p. 621.

2. For *shittâh*, the LXX renders it *xula asêpta*, 'incorruptible wood'. Various place names in Palestine carry the name of this wood: Shittim (Num. 25:1; Josh. 2:1; 3:1); Abel Shittim (Num. 33:49); Beth Shittah (Judg. 7:22); Nahal Hashshittim (Joel 3:18).

3. 'Filling' (*millu'îm*) comes from the root *mâlê'*, 'to be full'. This Heb. word is used of the consecration of the priests (29:22) in addition to its use here.

had been God's garden (Ezek. 28:13), and now He was again promising His presence: 'And I will dwell among them.' God's symbolic presence was to be shown by the Tent of Meeting and its associated furnishings. No liberty was given in regard to the construction of the tent. It had to be made exactly in accordance with all God had revealed (v. 8), this being further defined as following the pattern (*tavnît*) that He had shown to Moses. This element is stressed in the epistle to the Hebrews, where the writer refers to this passage, quoting God's words: 'See to it that you make everything according to the pattern shown you on the mountain' (Heb. 8:5).

19

The Ark of the Covenant
(25:10-22)

Central to the sanctuary was the ark of the covenant, an oblong box that originally contained the two tablets of the covenant, a pot of manna, and Aaron's rod that budded. However, when the ark was placed in the temple in Jerusalem it only contained the tablets (1 Kings 8:9). The Hebrew word used for it is *'arôn*, which simply denotes a box or a chest. It should not be confused with the word used for Noah's ark, or for the container in the Nile in which his mother put Moses. In these cases, the word used is *têvâh*. The covering of the ark was the 'mercy-seat', with cherubim at either end. It was there that God was to meet with His people, and this fact explains the references to Him as 'the dweller of the cherubims' (1 Sam. 4:4; Ps. 99:1). On one occasion the expression 'between the cherubims' is used (Exod. 25:22). The prophet Jeremiah spoke about the time coming when the ark of the covenant of the LORD would no longer be needed: 'It will not be missed, nor will another one be made' (Jer. 3:16). Once the Word was made flesh (John 1:14), there was no need for the symbolism of the ark any longer.[1]

---

1. One of the best discussions on the ark is M. H. Woudstra, *The Ark of the Covenant, from Conquest to Kingship* (Nutley, NJ: Presbyterian and Reformed Publishing Co., 1965). A summary of his discussion is contained in his article, 'Ark of the Covenant', in *The Encyclopedia of Christianity* (Wilmington: National Foundation for Christian Education, 1964), vol. 1, pp. 401-04.

1 The Nature and Use of the Ark (25:10-16)

10-11 A chest was to be made of the acacia wood provided by the people's offerings. It was to be two and a half cubits long, a cubit and a half wide, and the same measurement in height. If the cubit was approximately 44 cm (17.5 inches), then the ark measured 110 x 66 x 66 cm.[2] Inside and out it was plated in pure gold, and it had a golden moulding around it.

12-15 The Tent of Meeting was a movable sanctuary. Hence, provision had to be made for it and its various elements to be carried from place to place. Golden rings were to be made and attached to the chest, into which poles, with gold overlaid on them, were inserted. These poles were the means whereby it could be carried, and even left in place when stationary in a specific location. This would be a constant reminder that God had no permanent dwelling place. Even when the ark was finally put in the Solomonic temple in Jerusalem, the poles remained in place in the holy of holies, but were visible from the holy place immediately adjacent (1 Kings 8:8). No symbolic meaning is attributed to the poles, which merely served a utilitarian purpose.

16 One major intention was that the chest would be the depository for 'the testimony' (*hâ'êdût*), one of the alternative terms for the Decalogue. Coming from the verb 'to testify' (*'ûd*), the word 'testimony' can be used to indicate the Decalogue, or more broadly the covenant.[3] Hence, the expressions 'the ark of the testimony' (25:22; Num. 4:5; Josh. 4:16) and 'the tent of the testimony' (Num. 9:15; 17:7-8) occur. Here, 'testimony' is employed in the narrow sense of the Decalogue, which was to be formally given to Moses on behalf of the people of Israel (see the later comments on 34:27-28). The book of the law (probably the whole of Deuteronomy) was placed beside the ark after the covenant was renewed prior to entry to Canaan (Deut. 31:26).

---

2. The standard study is R. B. Y. Scott, 'The Hebrew Cubit', *JBL* 77 (1958), pp. 212-14.

3. Cf. the words of Paul Kalluveettill, *Declaration and Covenant*, p. 31, that *'êdût* 'refers to stipulations of covenant and sometimes stands by metonymy for covenant itself'.

2 The Lid of the Ark (25:17)

A lid or cover of the same measurements as its length and width was to be placed over the ark, called in Hebrew, *kapporet*. Many English translations use 'mercy-seat', but this is not suitable as no suggestion is implied in the text here or elsewhere that the ark was God's seat or throne. The word *kapporet* comes from the verb *kâfar*, which in the Piel theme, *kippêr*, means 'to make atonement [for]'. It is probably best to opt for translations like 'place of atonement' or 'place of expiation'. The LXX translated it by *to hilastêrion*, and this is used in Hebrews 9:5 when the writer is describing the cherubim which were 'overshadowing the atonement cover' (NIV; RSV, NASB, NKJV, ESV all have 'mercy seat'). On the day of atonement, the high priest had to spread the blood of the sacrificed goat over and in front of the atonement cover 'to make atonement for the holy place' (Lev. 16:16).

3 The Cherubim (25:18-20)

Two golden cherubim were to be placed at the ends of the lid. No description is given of them, except that their wings were to be spread upward (v. 20). They faced each other so that their wings overshadowed the lid. The only other reference to cherubim, other that relating to the Tent of Meeting, is in Genesis 3:24, where the narrative tells of the positioning of cherubim so that Adam and Eve were prevented from attempting to approach the tree of life. The cherubim are throne attendants, fulfilling the mission given them by God, and are probably similar to the seraphim that appear in Isaiah's vision of God (Isa. 6:2-7). In Revelation 4:8, 9, they, by their presence and praise, extol God's majesty.

4 Atonement and Revelation (25:21-22)

The lid was to be placed over the ark, and in it Moses was commanded to place 'the testimony' (see v. 16). At that place, 'from above the atonement cover, from between the two cherubim that are over the ark of testimony', God promised to meet with Moses and to speak with him. 'To meet' (*yâ'ad*, Hi.) implies not a random meeting, but one by appointment, and it is the verb from which '[tent of] meeting' (*mô'êd*) comes. The place of atonement was to be the place of revelation.

Further teaching was going to be communicated to Moses, and through him as mediator transmitted to Israel.

20

The Table
(25:23-30)

This is the first of the instructions concerning the fittings that were to be placed in the holy place, the restricted area outside the inner shrine, the holy of holies. The table was smaller than the ark, being two cubits long, a cubit wide, and a cubit and half high. Like the ark, it was made of shittim wood, and it was also overlaid with gold. It had both a moulding and a rim. The moulding was probably on the top of the table, whereas the rim may well have been lower, fitting around the top of the legs. Close to the rim were four golden rings to hold the poles by which the table would be transported. Even they had to be of shittim wood with a gold overlay.

The table from the second temple was taken by Antiochus Epiphanes in 167 B.C. (1 Macc. 1:23), and a replacement was made by Judas Maccabeus (1 Macc. 4:47-51). Following the fall of Jerusalem in A.D. 70, the table was removed by the Romans. It is shown on the inscription on Titus' Arch in Rome.

The vessels to be made of pure gold were plates (*qeʻârâh*, pl. *qeʻârot*), ladles (*kaf*, pl. *kappot*), pitchers (*qasvâh*, pl. *qesâvot*), and offering bowls (*menaqqît*, pl. *menaqqîyyot*). The plates were for the bread (Lev. 24:5-6), while the ladles were for holding incense (Lev. 24:7). Wine for drink offerings was kept in the pitchers, from where it was poured into the offering bowls (Num. 15:1-10).

Unleavened bread was put on the plates, and it is designated here, and elsewhere, as 'bread of the presence' (*léchem [hap] pânîm*, 1 Sam. 21:6). This has often been interpreted as meaning that the bread was a symbol of God's presence. However, the context here, literally, 'put on the table the bread of the presence before me continually', suggests that this bread was an offering brought to the place where God symbolically was present. The reference to 'continually' (*tâmîd*) indicates that this was to be the regular custom, as the loaves were eaten by the Levitical priests (Lev. 24:9), and then replaced with fresh bread. This led to the term 'continuous bread' (*léchem hattâmîd*) being used as an alternative description of it (Num. 4:7). In addition to it being an offering, indicating Israel's dependence on God, it also pointed to the fact that God provided for and sustained His people. For details concerning the bread, Leviticus 24:5-9 should be consulted.[1]

---

1. Our Lord, when challenged by the Pharisees over His disciples plucking corn on the Sabbath, answered by reference to the incident concerning David recorded in 1 Samuel 21:1-6. When David came to Nob with his men he asked the priest, Ahimelech for bread. The only bread available was 'the consecrated bread', which Ahimelech handed over. See Mark 2:23-28.

21

The Lampstand
(25:31-40)

The provision of light for the holy place was by a lampstand (*mᵉnorah*) that was to be kept alight from evening until morning. It was the task of the priests to ensure that this was done (27:20-21). The lampstand was a stylised almond tree, and as such it was one of the few parts of the Tent that, in addition to a utilitarian purpose, had aspects that were purely decorative. The tree-like menorah may well have suggested that this was part of a new Garden of Eden. It is impossible to try and re-create a lampstand according to the directions given, as, like other parts of the sanctuary, it was made in accordance with the pattern shown to Moses on the mount (25:40). A lampstand from the second temple was also taken when Jerusalem fell to the Romans in A.D. 70, and it is depicted on the Arch of Titus in Rome (see comment on the table, v. 23). Some of the translation and interpretation of this section is difficult because words are used in a different way than elsewhere in the Old Testament.[1]

31-33 Once again pure gold is specified as the material out of which an item was to be made, and immediately mention is made of decorations that were to be part of the lampstand – 'flower-like cups, buds and blossoms shall be of one piece

---

1. Examples are the case of the Heb. word *qânâh* that is translated as 'shaft', but also is used for 'reed' or 'stalk', and *yârêk* that is translated as 'base' but often means 'upper thigh'.

with it' (v. 31). The lampstand had a base, a central shaft and six branches, three on either side. Three cups like almond flowers were on each branch, while the central shaft had four. The description of the lampstand in Zechariah 4:1-7 is clearly based on the one in the Tent of Meeting, but it passes over many points and changes others to fit in with the main intent of the vision, e.g. the reservoirs on the lampstand are fed automatically with oil from the adjacent olive trees.

37-40 The central shaft had a lamp on it, and so did each of the six branches. To enable the lampstand to function efficiently it needed wick trimmers and trays, and they were also to be made of pure gold. The specification is given in verse 39 (and in 38:24) that a talent of gold was required 'for the lampstand and these [accessories]'. This would amount to 34 kg of gold. The final verse in this section is a repetition of the instruction regarding the lampstand that it had to be made according to the pattern being shown to Moses on the mount. Visual and oral revelation combined to give the complete picture. The opening word in verse 40, 'and see' (*ûrᵉʾêh*, imper. 2 m.s.), is virtually equivalent to 'behold' (*hinnêh*), and it functions to draw specific attention to what follows.

22

The Dwelling Place/The Tent
(26:1-37)

The narrative at this point picks up with the mention in 25:9 concerning the *mishkân*, 'the dwelling place', a word that was translated in the Vulgate by *tabernaculum*, and hence into English (via Luther) as 'tabernacle'.[1] Sometimes the term *mishkân* can refer to the whole sanctuary, but here it is used more strictly in reference to the ten curtains that had the cherubim woven into them. The outer perimeter of the surrounding courtyard is described later (27:9-19). The curtains were placed over frames (vv. 15-29), and then there was a triple covering of goats'-hair curtains, rams' skins, and finally, seal (or, porpoise) skins.

1 The Linen Curtains (26:1-6)

The main covering of the Tent consisted of ten curtains made from twisted linen and coloured yarn – blue, purple, and scarlet. Images of the cherubim were worked into them. The size of the curtains was uniform – twenty-eight cubits long (1232 cm), and four cubits wide (176 cm). They were joined together in two sets of five, which were then linked by means of loops on the end-curtains, with gold clasps holding them in position so that the *mishkân* was a single unit (lit. 'and the

---

1. The Latin Vulgate uses *tabernaculum* as the translation of both Hebrew nouns, *'ôhel* ('tent') and *mishkân* ('dwelling').

mishkân was one'). These linen curtains were, in effect, the inner lining of the tabernacle.

2 The Goats'-Hair Curtains and the Two Additional Coverings (26:7-14)

Over the linen was a covering made from goats' hair. Eleven curtains were required, and each was twenty-eight cubits long and four cubits wide. This meant that these curtains were two cubits longer than the linen covering. These curtains were joined in a similar way to the linen ones (cf. vv. 3-7 with 9-11), but with bronze clasps and not golden ones. The eleventh curtain was folded double at the entrance. The larger size of this curtain meant that it more than covered the linen curtains on each of the four sides. The final verse in this section (v. 14) notes that three additional coverings were provided as well. One was made from rams' skins that were dyed red. As with other references to colour, no indication is given of any specific significance of the colour 'red'. There was a fourth item as well, 'a covering of hides of sea cows'. The exact nature of this final covering is uncertain, as the variety of translations in the English versions testify. The Hebrew word (*tachash*) may refer to a sea animal (dolphin, or porpoise) or to a specific kind of leather made from animal skins. In the Old Testament, it is used only for the covering of the Tent of Meeting, or for the making of sandals (Ezek. 16:10).[2] No mention is made of any supports for the covering to prevent it sagging. It is possible that there was some form of ridgepole resting on pillars, or else the two top covers (rams' skin and hides of sea cows) were longer and so could be pulled tightly and pegged to the ground. No measurements are given for these two coverings.

3 The Frames and Crossbars (26:15-29)

Having described the curtains, the text now sets out the framework of wood that was required on which the various coverings could be placed. The traditional rendering of the Hebrew word for 'frames' (*qᵉrâshîm*; cf. the very similar word for 'clasps', *qᵉrâsîm*) is 'boards', but it is much better to understand them as consisting of two longer pieces of

---

2. See the entry in *DCH*, VIII, p. 621.

wood with cross-bars. This would have produced a ladder-like construction over which the various coverings could be stretched. They were to be constructed of acacia wood, and were to be stood upright (MT lit., 'and make for the *mishkan* [of] acacia wood standing'). Each frame was ten cubits long and a cubit and a half wide. Twenty such frames were needed for both the south and the north sides, this being the first indication of the orientation of the Tent of Meeting. The fact that forty silver bases were to be provided, with two bases for each frame (v. 19), suggests that the ladder-like picture of the frames is correct. Six frames were needed for the western end, plus two frames for the corners, possibly for additional support. Since there was only one single ring at the top this may mean that the frame was narrower there than at the bottom. Again, gold was to be used as overlay on the frames and crossbars, as were the rings to hold the crossbars. All these components of the Tent of Meeting must have been of considerable weight, and the Merarite clan of Levites was allotted the task of transporting them (Num. 3:36-37; 4:29-32).

4 Confirmation of the Building Plan (26:30)

This verse confirms the instruction already given in 25:9: 'Make this tabernacle and all its furnishings exactly like the pattern I will show you' (see also v. 40). However, the terminology differs in that instead of 'the pattern' (*tavnît*), Moses was told to build it according to the *mishpât* shown him on the mountain. The word *mishpât* normally means 'a judgment' or a 'legal decision'. However, it is used in 1 Kings 6:38 in noting that the temple in Jerusalem was built according to its 'specifications' or 'plan', and this meaning fits well here.[3] This statement is a re-iteration of the command to build just as was revealed on the mountain, and the New Testament statements confirm that the Tent of Testimony was built according to a divinely given pattern (Acts 7:44; Heb. 8:5).

5 The Veil (25:31-35)

To separate between the Holy Place (*haqqódesh*) and the Most Holy Place (*qodesh haqqodâshîm*) a veil (*pâroket*) was

---

3. So *CHAL*, p. 221: 'conformity'; 'building plan'.

placed between them. The purpose of the veil was to create a marked division between the two (v. 33), for only the high priest could penetrate the veil and appear in the Most Holy Place (Heb. 9:1-7). It was composed of 'blue, purple and scarlet yarn and finely twisted linen', though no indication is given of the significance of the colours. The same instruction as was given concerning the curtains of the tent (26:1) is repeated, with skilled craftsmen to incorporate cherubim worked into it. Once the veil was in position, hanging on four posts of acacia wood, the ark was to be placed in the Most Holy Place, with the atonement cover on it (cf. 25:17-22). The table was then to be put on the north side of the Holy Place and the lampstand opposite on the south side. The innermost sanctuary, the Most Holy Place, had no artificial light (cf. Solomon's reference in relation to the temple, 1 Kings 8:12), but later was filled with the light of God's presence (40:34-38).

6 The Curtain at the Entrance of the Holy Place (26:36-37)
The final instruction regarding the Holy Place concerned the curtain that was placed at the entrance. Only the priests entered in beyond it: 'the priests entered regularly into the outer room to carry on their ministry' (Heb. 9:6). It is designated by a different Hebrew word (*mâsâk*) than the veil at the entrance to the Most Holy Place (*pâroket*). Like the veil, this curtain was also of blue, purple and scarlet yarn and finely twisted linen, but no cherubim were worked on it. Instead of silver bases as with the curtain separating the Holy Place from the Most Holy Place, for this curtain bronze bases were sufficient. This was another expression of the principle that the most special metals (gold and silver) were used in connection with the Most Holy Place, and then progressively moving outward from it the less precious ones.

Study Questions

1) Liberality was encouraged among the Israelites when it came to the construction of the Tent of Meeting (25:1-2). Is Paul's teaching on generous giving in 2 Corinthians 8 and 9 any different from this?

2) Why do you think so many different terms are used to describe the contents of the stone tablets given by God to Moses – the Ten Words, the Testimony, the words of the covenant?

3) Was there any significant difference between having some of the manna in the Most Holy Place (16:34) and the bread of the Presence on the table outside (25:30)?

4) The curtain guarding the entrance to the Most Holy Place was made of blue, purple and scarlet yarn (26:36). Could this have been to represent the colours of the heavens shielding God from view?

23

The Altar of Burnt Offering
(27:1-8)

Provision had already been made for temporary altars of earth or undressed stone (20:22-26), but additional instructions were needed to make provision for the altar that would be placed in the courtyard of the Tent of Meeting. It had to be sufficiently durable for the burning of sacrificial animals, but light enough to be transported. It was a very significant part of the Tent of Meeting as the sacrifices offered on it pointed forward to Christ's sacrifice. He was the Passover lamb of God (John 1:19; 1 Cor. 5:7) who came to offer Himself once and for all 'to bear the sins of many' (Heb. 9:26-28).

1-3 The altar was made of acacia wood, it was a square of five cubits (2.20 m), and it was three cubits high (1.30 m). While the word 'horn' (*qéren*) often meant the horns of animals, it assumed the specialised meaning of a projection on the altar's four corners. A number of examples uncovered by archaeological investigations (such as those at Arad and Beersheba) have confirmed the general structure of altars complete with horns.[1] The horns may have been designed to help in attaching the sacrificial animal, and though grasped by those seeking asylum (cf., for two contrasting cases, the respective results for Adonijah [1 Kings 1:50-53] and Joab

---

1. See e.g. Yohanan Aharoni, 'The Horned Altar of Beersheba', *Biblical Archeologist* 37 (1974), pp. 2-6.

[1 Kings 2:28-34]), they do not appear to have had greater significance than any other part of the altar. To protect the wood, bronze was used as an overlay. Various utensils were necessary for the sacrificial rituals, and these were also to be made of bronze.

4-7 These verses relate to some parts of the altar that are difficult to describe with any certainty. The first one is called in Hebrew a *mikbâr*, a word that only occurs six times in the Old Testament, all of which are in the Exodus accounts of the Tent of Meeting (27:4; 35:16; 38:4, 5, 30; 39:39). It appears to mean something that is intertwined, and hence 'a grating'.[2] The next one is called an *réshet*, a common term for nets for catching fish or birds. Here it is used for 'network' that had four bronze rings in its corners, into which were inserted poles for transportation (vv. 6-7). This grating and network were attached to the altar under the top ledge so that the network extended half way down (v. 5).

8 It is made plain that the altar was not of solid construction. Rather it was 'hollow' (*nevûv*), a word that only occurs four times in the OT (Exod. 27:8; 38:7; Job 11:12; Jer. 52:21), but its meaning is confirmed by the LXX's use of *koilon* in translating it (cf. in the NT, *hê koilia*, 'body cavity', 'belly'). Even though the wood of the altar had a bronze overlay, the intense heat must have been a problem, and thus it is possible that the hollow interior was filled with earth to prevent any damage to the structure of the altar. Another section ends at verse 8 with the reminder that in regard to the altar, no deviation from the pattern shown to Moses on the mount was permissible. No mention is made here of the altar of incense that was positioned in the Holy Place (see 30:1-10).

---

2. *Mikbâr* seems to be a noun created from the verb *kâvar* II, See *BDB*, p. 460; *DCH*, V, p. 266.

24

The Courtyard
(27:9-19)

The most outward part of the Tent of Meeting was the courtyard (*chatsêr*), which was an open area into which any worshipper could enter. It was also the place of sacrifice, where, after a layman killed the animal, a priest offered it on the altar. Parts of the description are difficult to interpret, and it is not surprising that from the time of early Jewish writers, such as Philo and Josephus, various attempts have been made to work out how the whole tent fitted together.[1] These discussions concern matters such as the number of posts and whether the corner ones were counted twice. Many writers have insisted that the space between the posts was identical, but nowhere in the text is this asserted.

9-11 A boundary was set around an area measuring a hundred cubits long by fifty cubits wide. This courtyard was enclosed with finely twisted linen curtains, held in place by twenty posts on each side. These fitted into bronze bases with silver hooks and bands. No measurement is given for the height of the curtains until verse 18.

12-19 The west end (lit., 'the one towards the [Mediterranean] Sea') was fifty cubits wide, having curtains, ten posts,

---

1. Of the older writers, the discussion by A. R. S. Kennedy, 'Tabernacle', *A Dictionary of the Bible*, IV, pp. 653-68, is very detailed, though strongly influenced by critical thinking. In replying to critical discussions, A. H. Finn, *The Unity of the Pentateuch* (London: Marshall Bros., n.d., approx. 1915), pp. 255-93, has provided good information, though not in an attractive format.

and ten bases. Similar provision was made for the one facing the east (lit. 'the one towards the sunrise'). A variation in terminology occurs in this chapter in reference to the curtains and posts. Whereas, in describing the curtains and frames around the holy places chapter 26 uses *yᵉrî'ôt* and *qᵉrāsîm*, here in chapter 27, when setting out the particulars of the courtyard area, the terms are *qᵉlā'îm* ('hangings') and *'ammudîm* ('pillars') respectively. Fewer bases are specified for these curtains, and there is no mention either of the type of wood needed or if they were overlaid with any metal. While the curtains were to be of blue, purple and scarlet linen (as in 26:1, 31), yet they were not decorated with cherubim, marking again a distinction between the inner holy places and the outer court. Provision was made for an entrance into the courtyard, a curtain of twenty cubits, with four posts and four bases. While it is normally assumed that this screen was placed in line with the other curtains, this does not necessarily follow. It could easily have been placed either outside or inside the line of the other curtains, creating a double entry. This can be diagrammed in this way:[2]

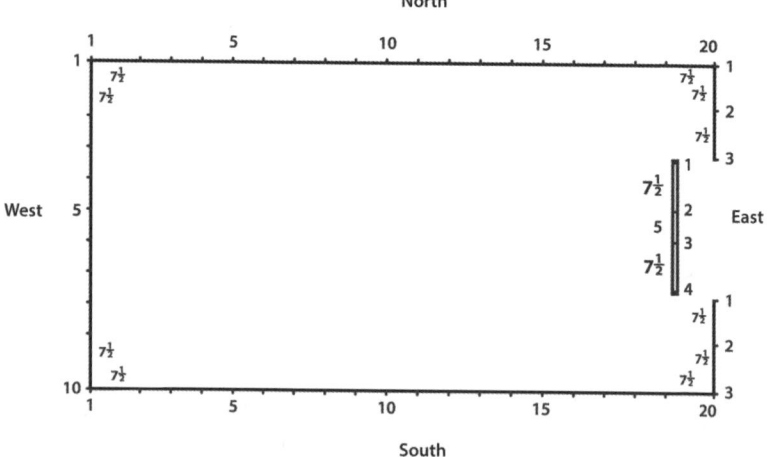

Proposed Entrance to the Tent of Meeting

---

2. I am following the suggestions of A. H. Finn, *The Unity of the Pentateuch*, p. 259, whose view seems to have been adopted by David Gooding in his articles, 'The Tabernacle', *NBD*, pp. 1231-34, and in *IBD*, 3, pp. 1506-11. He does acknowledge that adopting the idea of a recessed gate 'gives very awkward measurements for the spaces between the pillars' (p. 1510).

Mention in verse 19 of the utensils of 'the dwelling' (*mishkân*) seems to be a reference to the tools used in its construction, rather than for continuing use as part of the sacrificial rituals.[3] Also included for the first time were the pegs (*y^{e}thidôt*), presumably used, somewhat like modern tent pegs, to fasten securely all the side panels that formed part of the Tent of Meeting. The consistent pattern of the use of bronze, when further removed from the holy places, is continued with the specification of the metal to be used for these utensils.

---

3. The NIV translation of this verse is rather free. The ESV is tighter: 'All the utensils of the tabernacle for every use, and all its pegs and all the pegs of the court, shall be of bronze.'

25

Oil for the Lampstand
(27:20-21)

The golden lampstand has already been described in 25:31-40. Not only were its details important, but also the perpetual nature of its use was to be stressed. The oil to be used in it was specified ('you shall command the children of Israel …') and it had three characteristics – it was to be olive oil (*shémen zayit*), pure (*zâk*), and beaten (*kâtît*). That is, the oil had to be unadulterated and beaten, not pressed, in order to produce the clearest and finest oil for the purpose. The lampstand was to be placed outside the curtain that hid the contents of the Most Holy Place, and Aaron and his sons were to keep the lamps burning from evening till morning (cf. 1 Sam. 3:2-3). It is possible that a single lamp was kept lit during the day, so that the other ones could be lit from it at night without the need for kindling a new flame. Though the prescription was that this practice of illuminating the Holy Place each night was a perpetual obligation on Israel (v. 21), yet there were times later when it was not observed in the period of the first temple. Such a time occurred just prior to Hezekiah's reforms (see 2 Chron. 29:7).

26

The Priests' Garments and Their Consecration
(28:1–29:46)

Having explained the setting up of the Tent of Meeting, it is not surprising that the following narrative concerns the dress of the priests, in general, and especially of the high priest. Some of the ornateness of the Most Holy Place is replicated in the breastplate and turban of the high priest. The significance of the priestly dress does not lie in each individual part, nor does the import of the priest's role depend on each individual action they performed in Israel. The exposition of that role in the epistle to the Hebrews must guide the interpretation. The priestly role was to serve the LORD, and 'to offer gifts and sacrifices for sin' and 'to deal gently with those who are ignorant and are going astray' (Heb. 5:1-2). The priests also had responsibilities relating to the law, for they had to read it to the people and remind them that as covenant servants they had duties to perform (Deut. 31:9-13; Neh. 8:2-3).

1 The High Priestly Garments (28-1-5)
1-2 While the text does not say so explicitly, this chapter deals mainly with the dress of the high priest, though there is some mention of the other priests as well. The most frequent designation of the high priest, at first, was simply '*the* priest'

(*hakkohên*), while later he is referred to as 'the great priest' (*hakkohên haggâdol*, Num. 35:25, 28), or less often as 'the first priest' (*hakkohên hâro'sh*, 2 Chron. 19:11). Just as it was later prescribed for the kings and prophets (Deut. 17:15; 18:15), the priests had to be from Israel itself, not imported from other nations. Aaron had already served as Moses' prophet (Exod. 4:10-16), while his sons, Nadab and Abihu, had been associated with the elders of Israel in worship of the LORD (24:1). Now two other sons, Eleazar and Ithamar, were to be set aside as priests as well. The LORD indicated three times in this section that the task of these men towards Him was 'to serve as a priest' (*l^{e}kah^{a}nô lî*, vv. 1, 3, 4). It is not the usual verb for 'serve' that is used here but a verb made up from the noun 'priest' (*kohên*).[1] Aaron in particular was to be clothed in sacred garments (lit., 'garments of holiness') 'for glory and for honour' (*l^{e}kâvôd ûl^{e}tif^{e}eret*). The high dignity of the office had to be reflected by the wearing of suitable garments.

3 Specific men were chosen by God, and endowed with His spirit, for the task of making the Tent of Meeting and the garments worn by the priests (31:1-11). They were given the spirit of wisdom, later referred to as a filling with the Spirit of God (31:3; 35:31). The leaders of this group were Bezalel and Oholiab (31:2, 6).

4-5 Six specific items of dress were specified, two of which, the ephod (*'êfôd*) and the breastpiece (*chóshen*), are described in much fuller detail in verses 6-14 and 15-30 respectively. Of the others, the robe (*m^e'îl*) is also given further treatment in verses 31-35, while the woven tunic (*k^{e}tonet tashbët*) is discussed in verses 39-41. The turban (*mitsnéfesh*) features in verses 36-38, while the sash (*'avnêt*) is described in verses 39-40. All these items are called 'holy garments' as they were designed for special use at the Tent of Meeting. They separated the priests from the rest of the community, and their colours (gold, blue, purple and scarlet) tied them in explicitly with the colours of the Tent of Meeting.

2 The Ephod (28:6-14)

Since there is no exact equivalent in English of the Hebrew word *'êfod*, it is almost universally transliterated as 'ephod'.

---

1. For information on denominative verbs, see *IBHS*, pp. 373, 410-14.

Several other ephods are mentioned in the Old Testament in addition to that of the high priest dealt with in these verses ('*êfod shêsh*). The rest of the priesthood wore something that was less elaborate (called '*êfod bad*, 1 Sam. 2:18). Some replica ephods were venerated (see e.g., Judg. 8:27; 17:1-5).[2]

6-8 The ephod was a close-fitting garment with sleeves, extending from the shoulders to the hips, and held together by two shoulder pieces (*k^etêpot*). It was made of yarn and linen, with an integrated waistband of the same composition and colours.

9-14 The representative nature of the high priest's role is emphasised by the further provision concerning the engraving of the names of the twelve tribes on stones. Two onyx stones were needed, with six of the names on each one, and listed according to their birth order.[3] These stones were placed in an appropriate jewellery setting before being attached to the shoulders of the ephod. The word for 'jewellery setting' (*mishb^etsôt*) only occurs in the passages in Exodus dealing with the high priest's garments, except for Psalm 45:14, where it seemingly means 'embroidered garment'. The significance of these stones is brought out by the repeated mention in verse 12 that they were 'memorial stones' (*'avnê zikkârôn*). Together with the names on the breastplate (see v. 21), these signified that when the high priest ministered in the Holy Place he was fulfilling a mediatorial role for Israel.

3 The Breastpiece (28:15-30)

The breastpiece was not purely decorative.[4] It served a function in the judicial processes of Israel, for it held the Urim and Thummim (see comment on v. 30). The names of sons of Israel on it contributed to the intercessory ministry of the high priest.

15-21 The breastpiece was similar in composition to the ephod, yet distinct from it. Square in shape, it had four rows

---

2. For further discussion on the various ephods, see C. Van Dam, 'Priestly Clothing', *Dictionary of the Old Testament: Pentateuch*, pp. 643-46.

3. The MT says: 'according to their generations'. This Heb. word for 'generations' (*tôledôt*), while normally meaning 'generations', can have wider connotations such as 'family history', 'descendants', and here apparently 'order of birth'.

4. The etymology of *chóshen* is uncertain, though suggestions have been made linking it with Arabic, Aramaic, and Egyptian words.

of precious stones (with three in each row) set in the same sort of embroidered settings as used for the stones attached to the shoulders (cf. vv. 6-14). On each stone was the name of one of the twelve tribes. The significance of the reference to using it to make decisions (v. 15, *chóshen mishpât*), as well as the note regarding the names of the tribes, are both brought out later (see vv. 29-30).

22-28 Detailed instructions were given as to how the breastpiece was to be attached to the ephod. When folded, the ephod served as a pouch or container for the Urim and Thummim. It had gold rings at the corners, and gold cords that tied it to the engraved gems on the shoulders. The lower rings enabled a blue cord to be tied to the breastpiece and thus to connect it with the waistband of the ephod. The reason for this was that 'the breastpiece will not swing out from the ephod' (v. 28). In other words, the breastpiece was to be held tightly against the ephod.

29-30 The purpose of the breastpiece was twofold. On the one hand, it was a reminder or memorial of the people of Israel, in addition to the memorial stones worn on the shoulders of Aaron. As the High Priest entered into the Holy Place he carried in a double way the names of the tribes he represented before the LORD. He carried them 'over his heart' (*'al libbô*, vv. 29-30), an expression that may be more than just a physical description, as the same Hebrew phrase is used by Jeremiah when describing the new covenant being written on the hearts of God's people ('on their hearts', *'al libbâm*, Jer. 31:33). It may denote the devout feelings of the high priest and his sympathy for those whom he represented. The second important function of the breastpiece was that it contained the Urim and Thummim. Twice in this chapter the expression is found that the breastpiece was used for making decisions for the Israelites (v. 15, 'breastplate for making decisions', *chóshen mishpât*; verse 30, 'Thus Aaron will always bear the means of making decisions', *v^enâsâh 'ah^aron 'et mishpât ... tâmîd*). The nature of the *urim* and *thummim* has never been revealed, and the derivation of these words is uncertain. The traditional meanings, 'lights' and 'perfections' (from Heb. *'ûr*, 'light', and *tôm*, 'perfection'), still seem more convincing than more recent suggestions. The two were something tangible, probably stones (in addition to the ones with the names of the tribes of Israel), and were entrusted to the Levites (Deut. 33:8). However, they could not have been stones providing only 'yes' and 'no' answers. When revelation was sought, the answer was given in terms of divine revelation, so that prophetic speech seems to have been involved (cf. Judg. 1:1-2; 1 Sam. 14:36-42). In the biblical text, there is no mention of the use of *urim* and *thummim* after the time of David, possibly being replaced by the ministry of the prophets.[5]

4 Other High Priestly Garments (28:31-39)

Further features of the high priest's dress are now given, including a robe worn under the ephod, pomegranates and bells for around the hem of the robe, and a plate on the turban on which was written, 'Holy to the LORD'.

31-35 Under the ephod a robe of blue cloth was to be worn (see Lev. 8:7-8). It had an opening with a woven edge for the head, much like the modern poncho. The hem was edged with blue, purple, and scarlet imitation pomegranates with golden bells between them. The pomegranates seem to have been purely decorative, as they were also on the tops of capitals in the Solomonic temple (1 Kings 7:18). Wearing this robe was compulsory for Aaron. Various explanations, encompassing more than one idea, have been given of the bells, whose sound would be heard when Aaron entered the Holy Place. It was a way of announcing the fact that he was appearing before the LORD on behalf of Israel, and the continuing sound of the bells would reassure the people that he was alive and still ministering.

36-39 A further necessary part of the High Priest's dress was a plate of pure gold attached by a blue cord to the turban so that it could rest on his forehead. As the Hebrew word for the 'plate' (*tsîts*) really means a 'blossom' or 'flower', the 'plate' may have been decorated with floral designs or else have been in the shape of a flower. Hence, 'ornament' may be a better translation. On it was engraven the words 'Holiness

---

5. Two discussions by Cornelius Van Dam are very helpful. The first is his monograph, *The Urim and the Thummim: A Means of Revelation in Ancient Israel*, 2 vols. (Winona Lake, IL: Eisenbrauns, 1997), and his summary discussion in *NIDOTTE*, 1, pp. 329-31. See also *TWOT*, 1, pp. 26-27.

to the LORD'. This meant that in addition to the High Priest representing the people as a whole by carrying their names on the breastplate, he also represented God. The words on the ornament signified the fact that God was holy, and only by grace could His people appear before Him. The text goes on to say that the High Priest will bear the guilt involved in the sacred gifts (*nâsâ' 'et 'awôn*). While the Hebrew expression, 'bear the guilt', can be used of 'bearing one's punishment', yet it can also mean 'remove one's iniquity'. It is the second meaning that appears here. Any guilt attaching to the failure to fulfil all the requirements of the laws concerning offerings could be removed when the High Priest represented the people as a whole before the LORD.

5 Dress of the Ordinary Priests (28:40-43)

The regular priests also had to wear special clothing, though not nearly as elaborate as that required by the High Priest. However, the motive for their dress was the same as for him, 'to give them dignity and honour' (v. 40; cf. v. 2).

40-41 The ordinary priests were to be clad in a fine linen tunic, with a turban made of the same material. These turbans are described using a different word (*migbâ'ôt*) than was used earlier for the High Priest's headdress (*mitsnéfet*, vv. 4, 39), presumably indicating something less ornate and without the plate mentioned in verses 36-38. They too were to wear an embroidered sash, which seems to have been wound around the chest and left hanging down to the ankles. When duly clothed the priests were to be formally installed in office. Three terms are used concerning this appointment: 'anoint' (*mâshach*), 'fill their hands' (*mâlê'*, Pi.), and 'consecrate' (*qâdash*, Pi.). Anointing was a formal way of separating an individual off for God's service, whether it be priest (as here), or king (e.g., 1 Sam. 15:17; 2 Sam. 12:7). 'Filling the hand' was first carried out in connection with Aaron and his sons (Lev. 8:33). The English verb 'ordain' is not the best word to translate the Hebrew idiom, as it carries later connotations of Christian ordinations. A more neutral term like 'install' is preferable. The 'filling' could have arisen from a practice in which something was placed in the hands of the person being installed, or that it was a reference to the fact that they were going to offer sacrifices to the LORD provided by others, and that such sacrifices were to be their means of sustenance.

42-43 All the priests were instructed to wear linen undergarments. This reinforces what is stated in 20:26 in regard to indecent exposure when in service as priests. Whenever they came into the Tent of Meeting, and especially when ministering at the altar in the Holy Place, they could not expose themselves. This may be a command that expressly draws a distinction between Canaanite religious practices in which sensuality was prominent, and the worship of the LORD, the redeemer of Israel. That the practice was to be taken seriously is stressed by the threat, 'so that they will not incur guilt and die'. The final part of verse 43 either relates only to this last instruction, or, more probably, to all the prescriptions regarding priestly dress. These belong to Aaron and his sons as 'a lasting ordinance' (Heb. *chuqqat 'ôlâm*). As in other places the use of the Hebrew word *ôlâm* does not necessarily imply an eternal priesthood, but one that is long-lasting (cf. its use in Exod. 12:14 and Joel 2:26-27). It was to be superseded by the priesthood of Christ.

6 Installation of the Priests (29:1-46)

This chapter is concerned with the detailed provisions for setting apart Aaron and his sons to serve as priests to the LORD. It flows on from the preceding section that was devoted to the garments to be worn by the priests as they carried out their duties. The Tent of Meeting and the altar also had to be consecrated (v. 44). It was God's intention that He would dwell in the midst of His people and that they would acknowledge Him as the God who had redeemed them out of Egypt (v. 46).

i) Preparation of the Priests (29:1-6)

1-3 Instructions were given as to how the formal installation of the priests was to take place, and these are repeated in Leviticus 8:1-5. There was to be a consecration of them. The verb used here (*qâdesh*, Pi.) is one that has already been employed in 13:2 regarding the setting apart of the firstborn. The prescribed animals for this sacrifice were a young bull and two rams, and they had to be 'without defect' (see comment on 12:5). Along with the sacrifices three kinds of bread comprised the fellowship offerings—unleavened bread, 'cakes mixed with oil, and wafers spread with oil'. When the sacrificial animals were being presented, these breads, placed in the one basket, were to be offered as a fellowship offering. This was the first of the preliminary steps before the actual installation of the priests.

4 The second preliminary was that Aaron and his sons were brought to the doorway of the Tent of Meeting and there ceremonially washed. Before putting on the garments the priests had to be symbolically cleansed so that they could fulfil the role allotted to them. No indication is given here of how much of the body was to be washed, while later hands and feet are specifically singled out (30:19, 21). Presumably the basin for washing, the specifications for which are given in 30:17-21, was already in place.

5-6 The third preliminary was Moses' investiture of Aaron with his distinctive dress as the high priest. All the various items that have already been described in chapter 28 were put on him—the tunic, the robe of the ephod, the ephod itself, the breastpiece, and the turban on his head with the diadem attached. With all these being worn, Aaron was ready for his formal installation to office.

ii) The Priestly Anointing (29:7-9)
7 Moses was instructed to take the anointing oil (*shémen hammishchâh*) and pour it on Aaron's head and so 'anoint him' (*mâshachtâ 'otô*). The verb 'anoint' (*mâshach*) principally occurs in sections like this dealing with the Tent of Meeting and the priesthood, and later in regard to the inauguration of the kingship under Saul, David, and Solomon. It signified setting aside something like the altar (29:36), or someone like the priests (as here and in 40:15), from ordinary to divine service. This is why anointing and solemn installation (NIV 'consecration') are joined together. The oil is not only called 'the oil of anointing' but also 'the sacred anointing oil' (*shémen mishchâh qódesh*, 30:25 2x). Such anointing conveyed special status and special responsibilities.[6]

---

6. For further information on anointing, consult the article by J. N. Oswalt, *NIDOTTE*, 2, pp. 1123-27.

8-9 Aaron's sons were also to be dressed in their tunics and headbands (see 28:40). The High Priest and his sons were invested with their sashes. No sash for Aaron has been mentioned up to this point, but it is referred to again in Exodus 39:29 and Leviticus 8:13. Two further notations are made concerning the priesthood. The first reiterates the words of 28:43, in designating the instructions regarding the priesthood as 'a lasting ordinance' (see explanation on 28:43). The second note is the one with which verse 9 closes, a direction to Moses 'to fill the hand of Aaron and the hand of his sons'. This idiom has already been used in 28:41 (see comment, and v. 22). The Aaronic priesthood was to be formally inaugurated by fulfilling all God's instructions.

iii) The Removal of Defilement (29:10-28)
An important step in the process of the inauguration of priesthood was the sacrificial offerings that accompanied it. These were three-fold: a sin offering (vv. 10-14); the ram that was a burnt offering, a pleasing aroma to the LORD (vv. 15-18); and finally, the fellowship offering (vv. 19-34). This section is also important in that it describes the process by which sacrificial offerings were made.

7 The sin-offering (29:10-14)

10 Setting aside of the bull has been noted in verse 1. The first action when the bull was brought to the front of the Tent of Meeting was highly significant. Aaron and his sons had to 'lay their hands on its head'. The verb used here for 'lay' (*sâmach*) is a technical term for laying hands on an animal about to be sacrificed. The clearest use of it is in the passage dealing with the Day of Atonement in which transference of sin was symbolised by this action (Lev. 16:22). The same meaning appears present here and in other similar cases.[7]

11-12 Moses had to slaughter it (*shâchat*), a verb that in the Old Testament most often occurs in Leviticus of killing animals for sacrifice (35 out of 84 times). Nowhere does the biblical text indicate the method of slaughter, though later rabbinic sources indicate that the swiftest and most painless

---

7. I have discussed the use of this verb in *NIDOTTE*, 3, pp. 270-71.

way was adopted.[8] Some of the blood was smeared on the horns of the altar (see comment on 27:2), while the rest was poured out at its base. This use of the blood was most important, for 'it is the blood that makes atonement for one's life' (Lev. 17:11).

13-14 The most select parts of the animal, the fatty parts around the liver and kidneys, were burnt on the altar, while the flesh, hide and offal were burnt as a sin offering outside the camp. This offering was for the removal of the guilt of unintentional transgressions and for purification from defilement. The writer to the Hebrews draws upon this practice to make the point that Jesus died outside the camp 'to make the people holy through his own blood' (Heb. 13:12), and hence we should similarly be prepared to suffer reproach for His sake (v. 13).

8 The Offering of the First Ram (29:15-18)

15-16 A similar procedure was necessary in connection with one of the two unblemished rams. After the priests' hands had been placed on its head, it was slaughtered, and blood was sprinkled all around the altar. The verb for 'sprinkle' (*zâraq*) and its synonym *nâzâh* (see its use in v. 21) are both used of the ritual of sprinkling blood in connection with sacrifice.

17-18 As distinct from the treatment of the bull, this ram was to be burnt *totally* on the altar. The dismembered pieces were burnt, so becoming 'a burnt offering to the LORD, a pleasing aroma, an offering made to the LORD by fire'. These three expressions used to describe the one sacrifice are significant. 'The burnt offering' ('*olâh*) was distinguished by the fact that all of it was consumed on the altar. As other offerings were also burnt, it would have been preferable if this had been designated in English as a 'whole offering'. 'A pleasing aroma' is an attempt to translate a Hebrew phrase (*rêach nîchôach*) that occurs forty-three times in Genesis-Numbers and Ezekiel, all in connection with burnt offerings. It is an anthropomorphic expression coming from the verb 'to rest' (*nûach*), and so indicates that the offering

---

8. The LXX rendering of this verb is *sphazo*, a verb used four times in Revelation to describe Jesus as the 'slain' lamb: Rev. 5:6, 9, 12; 13:8.

is restful.⁹ The third term, an offering of fire (*'ishsheh*), is used of any of the offerings—the whole offering, the grain offering, fellowship offerings—that were wholly or partly consumed by fire.

9 The Offering of the Second Ram (29:19-25)

19-20 The initial procedure with the second ram followed that of the first (laying hands on the head and then slaughtering it), but the next actions were new and distinctive. Blood was taken and put on the lobes of the right ear, the thumbs of the right feet, and the big toes of the right feet of Aaron and his sons. No indication is given in the text as to why these parts of the body were chosen, but they do represent the extremities of the body,¹⁰ and as such were representative of the entire body. The mention of toes is interesting as it is probable that the priests ministered at the sanctuary bare-footed, as no description of any footwear is given here or elsewhere. The remaining blood was to be sprinkled against the altar.

21 The formal installation of Aaron and his sons also included the provision that they themselves and their clothes were to be sprinkled with some of the blood already on the altar. No matter how little blood was there, it was essential. For both Old and New Testaments state that without the shedding of blood there was no forgiveness of sins (Heb. 9:22). This blood had to be mixed with the special anointing oil (see 30:22-33) before being used. This anointing was the official act of consecration (*vᵉqâdash hû'*, 'set apart as holy', NLT).

22-25 Certain parts of this ram were to be set aside as a whole offering (*'olâh*; see comment on v. 18). These were mainly fatty portions, but included also the kidneys and the right thigh. This ram is called 'the ram of filling' (see comment on 28:41). That is to say, it was the one that was partly burnt as a sacrifice, and partly to serve as the priests'

---

9. Cf. the comments by John N. Oswalt: 'Because a sacrifice is offered in faith, God's anger is put to rest. It is ironic in Ezek. (where NIV somewhat unaccountably translates, fragrant incense), instead of causing God's anger to subside through the offering of a pleasing aroma, the ones sacrificing actually provoke him to greater anger because they are offering it to the idols (Ezek 6:13; 16:19; 20:28)'. *NIDOTTE*, 3, p. 58.

10. See the comments on this matter by Douglas Stuart, *Exodus*, p. 624. Note also that in Hebrew, the thumb and big toe are both called the *bôhen*.

portion, and which was a specific item in the installation ceremony for the priests. In addition, some bread, cake and wafers (see 29:2-3) were also included as part of an offering to the LORD. All these things, which formed a special kind of fellowship offering, were to be placed in the hands of Aaron and his sons, and waved 'before the LORD as a wave offering' (*vᵉhênaftâ 'otâm tᵉnûfâh lifᵉnê yhwh*). This verb (*nûf*) and the cognate noun (*tᵉnûfâh*) are used a considerable number of times in connection with sacrificial ritual. Clearly the objects in the hand were raised and possibly moved from side to side. Because they are used of the offering of the Levites themselves (Num. 8:11), the expression 'to wave a wave offering' seems to have come to mean 'present a contribution' rather than always literally 'to wave'. It was part of the ritual of sacrifice where the contents of an offering were conspicuously displayed.[11] After all the items had been publicly displayed, they were to be totally dedicated to the LORD as an offering. The same three terms are used to describe it as were used in verse 18 of the first ram.

10 The Future Priests (29:26-30)

Instructions concerning the installation of Aaron and his sons also needed directions regarding the on-going appointment of priests in the future. Succession arrangements were in place, and these involved contributions from the people for the priests' livelihood.

26-28 The breast of the second ram (NIV, 'the ram for Aaron's ordination') was retained as Moses' share. Provision had to be made in addition for the future operation of the priesthood. The description of the priests' portion is marked out by the repetition of the word 'contribution' (*tᵉrûmâh*) four times in these verses (see the earlier use of it in 25:2-3). It was to be a perpetual statute (*lᵉchoq 'ôlâm*) setting out the way that the people of Israel were to support the priests. Parts of certain sacrifices were to be set aside in order to provide sustenance for the priests and their families (see further, Lev. 10:14). This was one of the purposes of the fellowship

---

11. For further discussion on the wave offering, Richard E. Averbeck, *NIDOTTE*, 3, pp. 63-67.

offerings, and they had to be regarded as an offering by the people to the LORD ('*their* fellowship offerings', *tᵉrûmâtâm*).

29-30 Aaron's special garments were intended for his successors as well. They had to be passed down, generation after generation, so that each new high priest could be anointed (*lᵉmoshchah*) and installed (lit. 'for the filling in them of their hand'; see earlier comment on 28:40-41). The new high priest had to wear the garments for seven days when he first approached the Tent of Meeting in order to minister at 'the holy [place]'. In later legislation 'the holy [place]' is defined as "the courtyard of the Tent of Meeting' (Lev. 6:26). The idea of 'seven days' (*shivʿat yâmîm*) most probably indicated 'completion'.[12]

a) The Covenant Meal (29:31-34)
Meals were very important in ratification ceremonies (cf. 24:11). The instructions for eating parts of the installation offering and the bread resemble the fellowship offerings (Lev. 7:15-16).

31-32 The remainder of the installation ram (29:1, 15) was to be cooked 'in a sacred place' (*bᵉmâqom qâdôsh*), i.e., somewhere in the forecourt area of the Tent of Meeting. After being cooked, the ram was to be eaten, along with the bread that was already placed in the basket (29:2, 23). This procedure was only followed when successive priests were being installed, not during the normal course of sacrifices from day to day.

33-34 These fellowship offerings were the ones that had been made both for purposes of atonement (*kuppar bâhem*) and for setting apart the priests for their distinctive role (*lᵉqaddêsh ʾotâm*). Because of the nature of these offerings, their use was restricted to the priests. No non-Levite (*zâr*) was permitted to eat of them. This word *zâr* can refer to non-Israelites, but it is also used, as here, in reference to someone who cannot legitimately take part in worship activities. The provision in verse 34 for destroying any food remaining is the same as for the fellowship offerings in general (cf. Lev. 5-6).

b) Details of the Priestly Installation (29:35-37)
The installation of priests could not be hurried. It was to take a whole week, something mentioned both in verses 35 and

---

12. On the symbolical use of the Heb. word for 'seven', see *TWOT*, 2, p. 898.

37. On each day of this week an atonement offering was to be made (see v. 14 for prior reference to the sin offering). Even inanimate objects like the altar had to be cleansed and set apart for worship of the LORD. They were not intrinsically sinful, but belonged to the sphere of what was common, and hence had to be ritually 'cleansed'. The verb used here (*châtâ'*, Pi.) in its basic form means 'to sin', but in the *Piel* form it points to the removal of sin.[13] Seven days' offerings would result in the altar being declared 'most holy' (*qodesh qᵉdâshîm*, lit. 'holy of holies'). The NIV rendering of the final words of verse 37, 'and whatever touches it will be holy', can be better translated as the NKJV does, 'and *whoever* touches it must be holy'. That it is to say, only those who had been consecrated to the LORD for service at the Tent (i.e., the priests) were to come near and touch any of things appointed for the worship there.

c) The Regular Offerings (29:38-43)

38-41 The regulations for the perpetual daily sacrifices follow these instructions regarding the consecration of the priests. Twice in this passage it is stated that these offerings were to be made 'continually' (*tâmîd*, vv. 38 and 42). Every day, two year-old lambs were sacrificed, morning and evening. Even in times of apostasy these offerings were made (see 2 Kings 16:15). The fact that they were for *all* Israel shows that *quantitatively* the daily offerings did not place excessive demands on the people. The expression denoting evening (NIV 'twilight') in Hebrew is 'between the evenings' (*bên hâ'arbâyim*), the same expression used earlier in 12:6 in the passage explaining the Passover. Along with the lamb a tenth of an ephah of fine flour (about two litres) was offered, mixed with a quarter of an hin of oil (about one litre), and also the same amount of wine as a drink offering. Only a handful of the mixed flour and oil was put on the altar, with the rest being allotted to the priests (Lev. 2:2-3). The same regulations applied to the morning and evening sacrifices, and they were called 'a pleasing aroma, an offering made to the LORD by fire' (see 29:18 for comment on these terms).

---

13. The majority of the Piel forms of this verb occur in passages describing a cleansing or purification ceremony (see, e.g., in addition to this passage, Lev. 14:29, 52; Num. 19:19; Ps. 51:7).

42-43 These burnt offerings were not to be made at a gathering of all Israel, but by the priests at the entrance to the Tent of Meeting. It was not the place for communal worship, but rather where God met by appointment with His people. This is brought out here by the use of the expression 'Tent of Meeting' (*'ôhel mô'êd*) and the two verbal forms 'I will meet' (*'ivvâ'êd*, v. 42; *no'adtî*, v. 43). Such meetings were not accidental, but by divine appointment. There God communicated His word, firstly to Moses ('to you', s. m.), and then to the people (lit. 'to the sons of Israel') via the priests. The final words of verse 43 simply say, 'and it shall be sanctified by my glory'. Many English versions take this to mean 'the place' (NIV, 'the place will be consecrated by my glory'; ESV, 'and it shall be sanctified by my glory'). It is better to interpret this as meaning that 'Israel' would be sanctified. After propitiatory sacrifice the people were considered as holy before God.[14]

d) Concluding Summary (29:44-46)
The long section dealing with the installation and consecration of the priests is rounded off by three summary verses. These bring the reference to the Tent, the altar, and Aaronic priests together, with a renewed statement of God's intention to dwell in the midst of Israel.

44 Both the place of meeting with God and its contents were set apart for their intended purposes. In addition, Aaron and his sons were consecrated for their priestly ministry. It is significant that the orientation of their ministry was not to the people but to God ('to serve *me* as priests').

45-46 These verses pick up a theme that was stated back in 6:6-7. The redeemer God rescued Israel from slavery in Egypt so that He might dwell in their midst. By past experience of His grace and His continued presence with them, they would be assured that He was indeed the LORD their God (*yhwh ᵉlohêhem*). The statement concludes with a self-declaration that their God is indeed the LORD (cf. 6:8).

---

14. Three ancient versions – the LXX, the Syriac, and the Targums – all render it as 'and I shall consecrate myself by my glory'. No Hebrew manuscript evidence supports this variation.

Study Questions

1) The main altar was placed in the courtyard into which the people could come to present their sacrificial gifts. What details about it suggested it was markedly different from the Holy and Most Holy Places and could be entered by other than priests (compare 27:19 and 38:1-20)?

2) What details in chapter 28 point to the representative role on behalf of all Israel that the High Priest had to perform before the LORD?

3) Can we explain how the Israelites could have understood, that though 29:9 asserts that the details concerning the priesthood were to be a lasting ordinance, yet Hebrews 7:11 says that perfection could not come through it?

4) How do the words in 29:44-46 reinforce the covenantal relationship between the LORD and Israel?

27

The Altar of Incense
(30:1-10)

The fact that the altar of incense was very significant comes from its placement in front of the curtain that separated the Holy Place from the Most Holy Place. The particulars concerning it were similar to those for the bronze altar (27:1-8), except it was smaller in size and was overlaid with gold, not bronze. Some of the regulations concerning it are added at this point, making clear how only authorised incense was to be permitted.

1-3 Like the bronze altar, the incense altar was made of acacia wood, but it was much smaller, being only a cubit square and two cubits high. Its horns were integrated into the body of the altar, and the whole coated with gold. Like the table on which the shewbread was placed, it had a border around it (cf. 25:24, 25).

4-5 Again, like the bronze altar, provision had to be made for transporting this altar from place to place. The golden theme was continued, as, under the border, rings of gold were attached so that the wooden poles, coated with gold, could be inserted.

6 The position of the incense altar was in front of the curtain that separated off the Holy of Holies. The ark is again called here 'the ark of the Testimony' (for previous occurrences, see 25:22; 26:33, 34; 27:21), and the promise is renewed that this was where God would meet, by appointment, His servant

Moses, who was also the representative of the people. No mention is made of the significance of the incense, but references such as Psalm 141:2, Luke 1:10, Revelation 5:8 and 8:3-4 indicate that the incense symbolised the prayers of God's people.

7-8 The high priest's duties extended to offering up incense twice a day. When he was tending the lamps morning and evening he had to offer incense to the LORD. Prayer was a necessary part of the life of Israel, and hence the provision was made for the incense offering to be part of their life in perpetuity.

9 No incense other than the duly prescribed one could be offered. The content of the incense is set out later in this chapter (30:34-38). What was proscribed was 'unauthorized incense' (ESV; Heb. *qᵉtoret zârâh*, lit. 'foreign' or 'illegitimate incense'). Nor could the golden altar be utilised for any other type of offering – whole burnt offering, grain offering, or drink offering. This was an altar dedicated to only one use, and any other type of offering would mar its intended purpose.

10 Once a year the high priest had to take blood from the sin offering and put it on the horns of the incense altar. Further particulars are stated in Leviticus 16:19, where the direction is given that the high priest had to sprinkle blood on the horns seven times in order to cleanse it from any uncleanness of the people. Also, when a sin offering was presented for the high priest or the congregation, the same procedure had to be followed (Lev. 4:7, 18). This altar procedure was also to be followed in perpetuity, and the regulations concerning it end with the affirmation that the incense altar was most holy to the LORD (*qódesh qodâshîm hû' lyhwh*). This meant that it was reckoned just as holy, and thus separated for the LORD's use alone, as the bronze altar was (29:37), or the furniture of the Tent of Meeting was (30:29).

28

The Census Tax
(30:11-16)

The regulations that now follow concern a tax that had to be paid by each Israelite after a census was conducted. The fact that this payment was applicable to rich and poor alike was an assertion of the principle that no one in Israel could serve the LORD without a ransom being paid.

11-12 This census differed from other ones mentioned in the Old Testament. Those done by David (cf. 2 Sam. 24:1-17) were for purposes of war, while this one seems most probably to have been in order to have a register for public duties. The tax was called a *kófer*, a term used alongside one of the verbs meaning 'redeem' (*pâdâh*) in Psalm 49:7, and so indicative of a ransom process. Payment of this amount ensured that 'the plague' (*négef*) would not touch them. This word normally indicates a divine punishment.

13-15 The Israelites were mustered and then counted. As each person crossed over to the gathering of those who had already been counted, they were required to pay a half shekel, according to the shekel of the sanctuary. At least three different shekels were in use among the Israelites. There was one in common use, as well as a royal shekel (see 2 Sam. 14:26), and the one mentioned here. This one was equivalent to twenty gerahs (probably less than half an ounce, or about 15 gm), and it constituted an offering (*tᵉrûmâh*) to the LORD, a fact emphasised by the double mention of it in successive verses

(vv. 13 and 14). This term has already been used in reference to the contribution for building the Tent of Meeting (25:2). The regulation applied to everyone over the age of twenty, both rich and poor.

16 It was specified that the purpose of this contribution was to maintain the Tent of Meeting, presumably meeting the initial cost and then the maintenance of it. It is called here 'a memorial' (*zikkârôn*), as it served year after year as a remembrance of the events of the Exodus. The final sentence of this verse repeats the wording at the end of the previous verse concerning the role this offering was to have in being a substitute for lives.

29

The Bronze Basin
(30:17-21)

Provision had to be made for purification of the priests as they performed their ritual tasks. Mention was made earlier that Aaron and his sons had to wash with water before they put on their priestly garments (29:4). In the directions given here no details are provided regarding the size of the basin, the source of the material, or the actual shape of the basin. On the latter point, 38:8 notes that the basin and its stand were made 'from the mirrors of the women who served at the entrance to the Tent of Meeting'.

17-18 Revelation continued regarding other necessities for the worship of Israel. Both the basin and its stand were to be made from bronze, and its position was between the altar and the Tent of Meeting, and it contained water.

19-21 The purpose of the basin was for ritual washing by Aaron and his sons, both hands and feet. Nowhere in the narrative regarding the Tent is there any mention of footwear for the priests. Apparently, they served at the Tent bare-footed. On each occasion the priests came to present an offering at the altar, or before entering the Tent, washing at the basin was necessary. The threat is added that they were to carry out these washings 'so that they will not die' (cf. the use of this threat in 28:35). It was a symbolic act pointing to the need of the priests to remain holy and pure in their service of the LORD. This ordinance was not to be seen as something temporary, for it was established as a lasting ordinance for Aaron and his descendants throughout future generations.

30

Anointing Oil
(30:22-33)

In 25:6 provision was made for the anointing oil and fragrant incense. Then the instructions on how to make these two items were given. The former was used to anoint the priests and also the various parts of the Tent of Meeting and its utensils used in the sacrificial system, while the latter was the material burnt on the incense altar (see 30:1-10 for the instructions regarding the building of that altar).

22-24 Specifications for how the oil was to be made were set out. The major ingredients were 500 shekels of myrrh (the sap of the balsam bush), 250 shekels of fragrant cinnamon (bark from the cinnamon bush), 250 shekels of fragrant cane (sweet calamus, the pith from the root of a reed), and 500 shekels of cassia (dried flowers of the cinnamon tree). These measurements were all to be according to the temple shekel (see v. 13). The base for the anointing oil was a hin of olive oil (about 3.8 litres).

25-29 These ingredients were to be blended together by someone skilled in the task. The purpose was to produce an anointing oil that was distinctive and appropriate for its use in setting apart all the items connected with the Tent of Meeting. Presumably only a few drops of this oil were actually placed on any of the furniture or on the priests. All of the items listed in verses 25-28 had to be designated as holy, and formally set apart for service of the covenant God. This is the meaning of 'consecrate' in verse 30. The NIV rendering in verse 29 suggests that holiness was obtained through simply touching any of these objects ('whatever touches them will be holy'). It is better to understand the clause to mean 'whoever touches them must be holy' (NKJV). Only those who were specially consecrated were permitted to touch any of the equipment connected with the sanctuary.

30 The priestly family was singled out for special mention. Aaron and his sons had to be anointed in order that by this ceremony they were fit to take their place in the ministry of sacrifice. They were servants of the LORD in order to fulfil a priestly service to Him.

31-33 Moses had to tell the people about this sacred anointing oil, and in particular inform them that this oil was to be prepared for generations to come. While it is not spelled out here, the presumption is that in addition to an annual act, every time the Tent of Meeting was set up afresh the anointing would take place. This special oil was not to be confused with other oils, and hence not used to anoint other than priests. Moreover, it was not to be considered something they could make for common use. No anointing oil using the same formula was allowed, for it was indeed holy (lit. 'you shall not make like it; it is holy; holy it shall be to you'). The seriousness of any departure from this regulation is spelt out in verse 33. If anyone made anointing oil with the same formula, or used it on people other than priests, then they would face the death penalty. The expression here, 'to be cut off from his people', does not mean excommunication from Israel, but rather execution (see the parallel expressions 'put to death' and 'cut off from his people' in 31:14).

31

Incense
(30:34-37)

34-35 Just as sacred anointing oil was needed, so was special incense. Equal amounts of four substances were required – gum resin, onycha, galbanum, and pure frankincense. Gum resin came from a shrub, while onycha was part of a shellfish. Galbanum was a type of gum, while pure frankincense was from the bark of a tree. How special these ingredients were is shown by the fact that some of them could only be obtained outside of Israel, such as the pure frankincense that was either produced in Sheba or it came via Sheba.[1]

36-37 The various ingredients were to be ground together, and then placed in front of the Tent of Meeting, where God met his people by arrangement. Like the anointing oil, it was regarded as particularly holy (lit. 'holy of holies'). Also, it was not to be produced for any other purpose, again in similarity with the anointing oil. Once more the penalty of death is expressed against anyone who made this incense just to enjoy its fragrance.

---

1. For further details on the ingredients of the anointing oil, see Douglas Stuart, *Exodus*, pp. 646-47.

32

Bezalel and Oholiab
(31:1-11)

Not only was direction given concerning the products needed to construct the Tent of Meeting and all associated with it, but God also chose the workmen to oversee the whole task. Special skills, divinely imparted, were necessary.

1-5 The LORD drew attention to the special appointment of Bezalel by His opening word ('see' instead of 'behold' as in v. 6), and by the way in which He refers to His favour resting on Bezalel. He 'called him by name' (*qâr'âtî bᵉshêm*), indicating a very personal and deliberate action. The choice of the main artisan was Bezalel, from the tribe of Judah. His name means 'in the shadow of God', and in the Old Testament he is only mentioned in Exodus and Chronicles (Exod. 31:1-11; 35:30-35; 1 Chron. 2:20; 2 Chron. 1:5). The references to him in Chronicles appear to be making the point that there was a close connection between the Tent of Meeting and the temple in Jerusalem. He received a special gift of the Spirit, so that he possessed wisdom, understanding, and knowledge to complete the complex task ahead of him. God uses those with special skills and gifts in His service, but He further endowed Bezalel to completely fit him for the work. Being 'filled with the Spirit' meant being given the necessary ability to do God-given tasks. No evidence is provided that this endowment was permanent. It related to 'all kinds of craft' (v. 3; the NIV translates the same Hebrew phrase by 'in all kinds of craftsmanship' in v. 5). His role was particularly in relation to the use of gems, stone, and wood.

6-11 The appointment of Oholiab (the name means 'the father [God] is my tent') is stated in different terms from that of Bezalel: 'And I, behold, I have appointed with him Oholiab'. This seems to indicate that Oholiab had a subordinate role to fulfil, and that he was a helper to Bezalel. Others were appointed as well, and verses 7-11 specify all the objects that have been mentioned in detail in chapters 25–30 in connection with the Tent of Meeting, and also the garments needed by Aaron and his sons for their priestly duties. The final command (v. 11) specifies that there could not be any deviation from the Lord's plan for the Tent of Meeting. Just as God commanded, so Moses was to do.

33

The Sabbath
(31:12-17)

The Sabbath law has already been dealt with in 16:22-31, 20:8-11, and 23:10-13. It is introduced again at this point because of the link between observing the Sabbath and worship at the Tent of Meeting. Weekly worship that was acceptable to God could only take place if the people kept the Sabbath as laid down by Him. Two aspects are added here to the earlier laws – the perpetuity of the requirement to observe the Sabbath and the punishment for failure to keep it correctly. While it is not stated, it could be an implication that even during the period of the construction of the Tent of Meeting the Sabbath had to be kept meticulously.[1] It is also significant that the law of the Sabbath is reasserted here at the conclusion of the instructions for building the Tent of Meeting, and then again in 35:1-3 before detailing its actual construction.

12-13 The LORD continued to speak to Moses about further instructions to be transmitted to the entire community, the children of Israel. The Sabbath command is introduced by an emphatic adverb (*'ak*) that means 'surely' or 'certainly', and it needs to be brought out in translation: '*Indeed* you shall keep my Sabbaths.' The plural 'sabbaths' appears quite regularly in the Old Testament (see, e.g., Lev. 19:3, 30; 26:2; Isa. 56:4;

---

1. For expansion of this view, see W. H. Gispen, *Exodus*, p. 290.

Ezek. 20:12-13), and this usage fits in with the requirement that the Sabbath be observed throughout the generations to come. The Sabbath was a sign (as was the rainbow and circumcision) of God's covenantal relationship with His people, a statement repeated in verse 17. A further word of explanation follows in that God indicates that keeping the sign of the Sabbath would confirm the knowledge that He was indeed the LORD who sets His people apart as holy.[2]

14 The observance of the Sabbath is enjoined in the same way as it is in Deuteronomy 5:12 (using the verb 'keep' or 'guard'), whereas Exodus 20:8 employs 'remember'. Keeping the Sabbath was a sign of being 'holy', being set apart for God, and displaying in this way loyalty to Him and His requirements. The penalty for disobedience was severe, as 'to be cut off' is synonymous in this context with the expression being 'put to death' in the next verse.

15 This verse repeats the demand stated in 20:9-10 that six days of work were to be followed by the seventh day being a Sabbath of rest. No work was permissible on the Sabbath, since it was to be a Sabbath festival, using the same word (*shabbâtôn*) that was already used in 16:23. Any breach of this requirement made an offender liable to capital punishment. While there is one case of application of this law in the Pentateuch (Num. 15:32-36), no indication exists of how often the punishment was applied.

16-17 The divine pattern of six days of work and then rest was to be followed by the people of Israel. The covenantal people had to imitate their covenantal LORD, and the fact that it would be a sign of a lasting covenant between the two is reiterated (see v. 12). Life was to have a rhythm of work followed by cessation of labour, and then rest and refreshment. The perpetuity of this is made even stronger than in the earlier reference in verse 12 ('a sign between you and me for the generations to come') by calling it 'a lasting covenant' (*b*e*rît 'ôlâm*) and one that was a sign lasting 'for ever' (*le'ôlâm*).

---

2. The NIV translation of the last clause of v. 13, 'who makes you holy', is acceptable if it means 'set apart as holy', but not if it is understood as inducing holiness in a subjective way.

34

Concluding Summary
(31:18)

The completion of God's oral communication to Moses was followed by the presentation to him of the two stone tablets. These have already been referred to in 24:12 as being 'the tablets of stone, with the law and commands' that God wrote for the people's instruction. Here it is said that there were two tablets, and they are described as being the tablets of the Testimony, written by the finger of God. 'The Testimony' refers to the Ten Words that were written on it, utilising both sides (see 32:15-16). In keeping with contemporary Near Eastern practice, these were most probably duplicate copies. Whereas in extra-biblical treaties these tablets were placed in the temples of the respective parties to the treaty, in Israel's case they were both put in the ark of the covenant. Stone tablets were doubtless chosen because of their durability, and though no measurements are given, they had to fit into the ark that measured 110 cm x 66 cm x 66 cm. The description that the tablets were 'inscribed by the finger of God' is an anthropomorphic expression denoting that by His power He produced this written and permanent copy of His law. God gave the law, and by some unseen divine power it was produced in written form.

Study Questions

1) Why were the poor not exempt from paying the atonement money (30:15)?

2) Other uses of the sacred anointing oil and the incense (30:31-33, 37-38) do not, at first sight, seem worthy of death. Why were these actions so reprehensible?

3) Does the New Testament have the concept of endowment for a particular work of God that parallels the endowment of Bezalel and his associates for constructing the Tent of Meeting?

4) Have you any explanation of why the ideas of the Sabbath and the sanctuary are conjoined here (see 31:12-17), and also in 35:1-3 and the narrative that follows?

PART V

Rebellion and Restoration
(32:1–34:35)

Introduction

A discrete part of the book of Exodus commences with 32:1 and proceeds until 34:35. The lengthy section dealing with the revelation to Moses on Mount Sinai (chs. 25–31) is followed by the account of the sin of Israel while he was still on the mountain. The preceding section has much to say concerning *holiness*, but now the narrative focuses on the *unholiness* of the people. While Moses was receiving the tablets of the covenant, the people were already breaking the covenant. The fullest account of this incident is contained in Deuteronomy 9:9-21, when Moses reminded the people of events in their past history that had to be avoided.[1] The significance of the rebellion of Israel is repeatedly referred to later in Scripture (see, e.g., Deut. 9:15-21; Ps. 106:19-23; Acts 7:38-43; Rom. 1:22-23).

---

1. I discuss this passage in *Deuteronomy: The Commands of a Covenant God*, pp. 121-22.

35

The Golden Bull
(32:1-6)

1 The children of Israel did not know how long Moses would be absent on the mountain. The elders had been told that in Moses' absence people were to look to Aaron and Hur; Hur was probably fulfilling a subsidiary role as Aaron's assistant (24:14). In Moses' prolonged stay on the mount, the people decided to seek a substitute object of worship instead of showing continuing allegiance to the Lord. Two different constructions can be placed on the words 'the people gathered around Aaron'. They could mean simply that the people gathered together and surrounded him. However, the Hebrew text (*qâhâl* Ni. + *'al*) can also be taken to mean that they gathered *against* him, and this is the preferred translation.[1] Moses' question later put to Aaron (v. 21, 'What did this people do to you?') supports this interpretation. The threat of force was used against Aaron, and while this does not excuse him for his part in the events that transpired, yet it casts another light on what he did. Fear for his own safety influenced his decision to acquiesce in their demands. What they wanted was a replacement for the living God who had redeemed them from their slavery in Egypt. Instead of the Lord continuing to lead them, they wanted another god to go before them. They spoke of Moses in a very derogatory way:

---

1. See the same usage in Num. 16:3; 16:42; 20:2.

'as for *this Moses*, the man who brought us up out of Egypt'.² Respect should have been shown to the one who under God had been their deliverer and leader. They claimed not to know what had happened to him because of the interval between his going up on the mount and the time when they were speaking.

2-4 Materials out of which an idol could be made had to be obtained. Hence Aaron called for the golden earrings worn by the people to be surrendered for this purpose. They obeyed and Aaron fashioned a golden bull from the gold. While most English translations use 'calf' here, the Hebrew word (*'êgel*) means a young mature bull, and it should be translated accordingly. The corresponding feminine form (*'eglâh*) is used in Genesis 15:9 of a three year old heifer. Nothing in the text suggests an idol of diminutive size. The amount of gold contributed would have been far greater than what was necessary for a small idol, and Psalm 106:19-20 refers to this incident in which the people exchanged their Glory for the image of a bull (*shôr*).³ Bulls were worshipped in Egypt, and this seems to have been an adaptation by the Israelites to this practice.⁴ We have to assume that not every single woman among the people had to give up her golden earrings, for sufficient could be provided without full participation. The exact meaning of the Hebrew words '*êgel massêkâh* ('an idol cast in the shape of a calf' NIV) is uncertain. Most probably, it was a wooden image shaped like a young bull with the gold overlaid (see v. 20 for the reference to its being burnt). This was an act of direct disobedience, for the Second Word (20:4-5) had prohibited the making of images. The finished idol was presented to the people as the saviour that had brought them up out of Egypt, which statement in itself was a parody on the opening of the Ten Words (see 20:2). The same

---

2. The phrase, 'this Moses' (*zeh mosheh*), contains a rare usage of the demonstrative *zeh before* a personal name. For other possible examples, see Ezek. 5:5 ('this Jerusalem') and Ps. 68:8 ('this Sinai'). For discussion on the use of *zeh*, see *DIHG~S*, p. 6.

3. This position was accurately set out over one hundred years ago by A. R. S. Kennedy, 'Calf, Golden Calf', *A Dictionary of the Bible*, vol. 1, pp. 340-43. The same translation will apply to Jeroboam's golden bulls (1 Kings 12:26-33).

4. For the worship of bulls in Egypt, see John Currid, *Ancient Egypt and the Old Testament*, p. 111.

claim was made much later in history when King Jeroboam, having set up two golden bulls, called upon the people to come and worship the gods who brought the people up out of Egypt (1 Kings 12:28-29). The text does not define who is the subject of the verb 'said' in verse 4 ('Then *they* said'). The best explanation is that they were the leaders of Israel (cf. v. 1, '*they* gathered').

5-6 Aaron was the leader in Moses' absence, and he proceeded to build an altar, and also to call for a sacrificial festival to the Lord on the following day. This was probably an attempt to see that the people did not turn away completely from the Lord. He did not know how far their apostasy would lead them. The next morning, the people got up early, sacrificed burnt offerings, and brought fellowship offerings. This was to be the standard practice in Israel, as the fellowship offerings were subsidiary to the burnt offerings. The people were purportedly worshipping the Lord, but in reality they were worshipping an idol. Instead of exclusive worship of their saviour, Israel under Aaron's leadership was engaging in religious syncretism. They sat down to eat and drink and 'got up to indulge in revelry'. Their actions in this regard were more typical of Near Eastern idol worship that true worship of their God. The NIV translation, 'to indulge in revelry', is the translation of a Hebrew verb (*tsâchaq*, Pi.) that can carry sexual overtones. However, there is nothing in the context to suggest that the revelry was anything other than the singing and dancing to which Moses later referred (see v. 19).

36

The LORD's Verdict
(32:7-10)

7-8 On Mount Sinai Moses received the Lord's instruction to go down to the people. He was told of their rapid descent into idolatry, contrary to His express command. They had bowed down and sacrificed to the idol they had made, claiming that it was their redeemer god.

9-10 The LORD's words to Moses continue, with a description of the people that indicated that there would be no change in their character or of His judgment on them, even if Moses should intercede for them. The verb 'see' (*râ'â*) carries the sense of 'know' or 'be aware of.' The people are characterised as being 'stiff-necked' (*qᵉshêh 'óref*), a frequent description of humans as being like rebellious oxen. Several times in this section of Exodus the people are referred to by the same term (in addition to v. 9, see 33:3, 5; 34:9), and long after this incident Israel was still characterised as having a rebellious spirit (see Deut. 9:6; 10:16; Judg. 2:19; 2 Kings 17:14; Neh. 9:16; Acts 7:51). The LORD asked that no more requests be made to Him concerning the matter, in order that His anger would be expressed against them and that they would be destroyed.[1] Thus the threat expressed to the Canaanites of complete annihilation (see Deut. 7:24) was now directed to Israel. If

---

1. The Heb. verb here is *kâlâh*, Pi., and it means 'to finish' or 'use up', and from that it came to mean 'destroy', 'exterminate'. About 32 times in the Old Testament it has this meaning. See *DCH* IV, pp. 416-18.

that happened, it would call into question the patriarchal promises of a great family,[2] but instead God promised to fulfil His purposes of having a large family through Moses ('I will make *you* into a great nation').

---

2. See the reference to the patriarchal promises in v. 13.

37

Moses' Intercession
(32:11-14)

1-12 The account here of Moses' intercession is not repeated in the account in Deuteronomy 9:9-21, the narrative there moving from the threat of extinction for Israel (v. 14) to Moses' descent from the mountain (v. 15). Moses implored God ('sought the favour of' NIV) to relent.[1] He put to the forefront the fact that the children of Israel were God's people ('why should your anger burn against *your* people?'). These were the people whom God had rescued from Egypt 'with great power and a strong hand'. This phrase became a standard expression to express the wonder of God's redemption of His people from the power of Pharaoh and the Egyptians. The next reason on which Moses based his request was that destroying Israel would give the Egyptians grounds for mockery. They would attribute to God an evil plan of bringing the Israelites out of Egypt only to kill them in the mountains, doubtless referring to the region of which Sinai was a part. Egypt, argued Moses, should not be given the occasion to gloat about their former slaves. The request was that God's anger would be turned away, and because

---

1. The verb is *châlâh* II, Pi., that has the same consonants as *châlâh* I, but is a distinct verb. It occurs 16 times and on every occasion it has as its object 'the face of.' Usually it occurs when God is entreated to show mercy or to rescue his people. The LXX translated the clause here, 'And Moses prayed before the Lord God' *(kai edeêthê Môusês enanti Kuriou tou theou)*.

God relented, disaster would be averted for His people. The only other joint occurrence of the Hebrew verbs for '[re]turn' (*shûv*) and 'relent' (*nâcham*, Ni.) is in Psalm 90:13, a psalm attributed to Moses. Other passages in the Old Testament speak similarly of God changing His mind (1 Chron. 21:15; Jer. 18:8; 26:3, 19; Amos 7:3, 6; Jonah 3:10). From a human point of view it appears that God's purposes had changed.[2]

13-14 Moses' prayer continued with an appeal to God to 'remember', another anthropomorphic expression. What he wanted was for God to fulfil the promises He had given to Abraham, Isaac, and Israel,[3] and had confirmed to them by an oath that He swore by Himself (cf. Gen. 22:16 and Heb. 6:13-18). There could be no higher form of oath-taking, and no greater certainty of its fulfilment. Moses referred to two of the main promises to the patriarchs, a large family and a land in which to live. The family had become a large group of people (cf. the opening words of this book, 1:1-12), and they could also look ahead to having a place in which to live, an inheritance that would be theirs if they continued in the way of the Lord. The result of Moses intercession is recorded in verse 14, on which Psalm 106:23 gives the verdict: 'So he [God] said he would destroy them – had not Moses, his chosen one, stood in the breach before him to keep his wrath from destroying them.' What is not recorded here in Exodus is the fact that Moses pled for Aaron's life (Deut. 9:20), and his request was granted.

---

2. For discussion on the question of the idea of God changing His mind, and the relation of this to the doctrine of God's immutability, see especially John Frame, *A Theology of God's Lordship, vol. 2, The Doctrine of God* (Phillipsburg: Presbyterian & Reformed, 2002), pp. 559-70.

3. The name 'Israel' occurs here in place of 'Jacob'. Some Heb. mss. and the LXX have made it conform to the normal pattern and changed it to 'Abraham, Isaac, and Jacob'.

38

The Broken Covenant and Its Curse
(32:15-29)

15-16 Moses' audience with the LORD on Mount Sinai being complete, he turned and went down, carrying the two tablets that had already been given to him (see 31:18). Their content is again called 'the Testimony' (see 25:21), and in keeping with known practices, they were inscribed on both sides. In verse 16, the making of the tablets and the writing on them are both ascribed to God. As in 31:18, the content of the Testimony was so important that God Himself inscribed it on the tablets.

17-18 No mention of Joshua has occurred since it was stated in 24:13 that Moses and Joshua his assistant arose, and Moses went up the mountain. The phrasing there may suggest that Joshua only went part of the way and then waited for Moses to descend. As they came near the camp it was Joshua who heard the 'noise' in the camp, as the people shouted. He said to Moses: 'There is the sound of war in the camp.' The word for 'sound' (*rêaʻ*) comes from a verb 'to shout' (*rûaʻ*) that is often used in military contexts, and hence Joshua's comment follows on from what he thought he was hearing. To him the indications were that battle was taking place. But Moses quickly disabused him on the matter, telling him that the sound was not of battle but of the people singing. His answer formed three lines of poetry:

> It is not the sound of victory,
> it is not the sound of defeat;
> It is the sound of singing that I hear.

It is possible that some or all of this poem was already known to the children of Israel, and its antiquity may explain some of the difficulty in translating and interpreting it.[1] Its point is that Moses denied that the sounds they heard were connected with battle at all. Instead, he recognised that they were associated with revelry. While he had been on the mountain with the Lord, the religious life of the people had degenerated, and this singing and dancing were outward expressions of the inward change of heart.

19-20 Moses' words to Joshua were confirmed when they came near the camp. When he saw the bull that Aaron had made and the dancing, he was angry. This was hardly surprising, as the LORD had already expressed the desire that His anger would burn hot and consume the people (v. 10). The next action of Moses, throwing down and breaking the tablets, should not be looked upon as a fit of pique on his part. It was a deliberate action to show that the covenant was already broken because of the people's sin. No other step could have indicated so profoundly the breach of the covenant that had taken place, and this was a public demonstration of the fact (see Deut. 9:17, 'breaking them to pieces before your eyes'). Breaking the tablets was to lead on to other consequences. The Tent of Meeting could not be constructed while the relationship between the Lord and His people was in disarray (see comment on 33:7-11). Moses took the bull, burned it and then ground it to powder. The idol they had made was most probably wooden with a golden overlay, and hence it could be reduced to powder by burning. Afterwards it was scattered on the water, and the Israelites were forced to drink it.[2] While elements of a practice like this are known

---

1. For detailed information and reference to bibliographical information on this verse, see Douglas Stuart, *Exodus*, pp. 675-76, and Victor Hamilton, *Exodus*, pp. 541-42.

2. In Deut. 9:21 it is stated that the dust was thrown into a 'stream that flowed down the mountain'. This may not contradict v. 20 as the stream could have been the source for all their drinking water.

from Ugaritic documents,[3] not sufficient comment is made on it in the biblical text for absolute certainty regarding its purpose. It has similarities to the trial of an unfaithful wife (Num. 5:12-31), and the fact that all the people had to drink of it may have been an admission of guilt on their part.

21 Interrogation of Aaron was intended to bring out the reasons that led up to the incident. The implication is present that the people put pressure on Aaron (see v. 1); yet it was he who brought upon Israel this great sin (*kî hêvê'tâ 'âlâv ch^{a}tâ'âh g^{e}dolâh*; see the double reference to this sin in vv. 30-31). This question highlighted both the role played by Aaron and also the real nature of the offence. He deliberately led them to commit a crime of such magnitude against their covenantal God, and this was why Moses had to make intercession specifically for him (see Deut. 9:20).

22 Aaron offered several excuses. His first one was that he was dealing with a people who were bent on evil. Committing sin was indeed a natural inclination of Israel, and various incidents have already been cited in chapters 15–18 to show their nature as covenant breakers. However, to place this emphasis here minimised the lack of leadership on his part. Israel failed because he failed.

23-24 Verse 23 accurately reports what has already been stated in verse 1, but a change comes in verse 24. Aaron's explanation is that the gold he was given by the people was thrown into the fire and miraculously came out as the bull! Even if this interpretation is set aside as too condemnatory of Aaron, yet his explanation is very general, and it lacks mention of the specific role he played in making the golden bull.

25-26 The meaning of verse 25 is difficult to determine because of two exegetical problems.[4] The first relates to the expressions describing what the people were doing ('running wild', 'out of control' NIV). The Hebrew verb in question (*pâra'*) seems to have the basic meaning of 'letting loose', such as letting one's hair down, and thus could be applied to unconstrained

---

3. See J. C. L. Gibson, *Canaanite Myths and Legends*, p. 77.

4. For detailed discussions of the Hebrew of v. 25, see Victor Hamilton, *Exodus*, pp. 549-50, and Douglas Stuart, *Exodus*, p. 680.

behaviour. This could have been sexual in nature.[5] The second concerns especially the word translated in the NIV as 'a laughing stock'. This word (*shimtsâh*) only occurs here in the Old Testament (it is preceded by the Hebrew preposition *l*ᵉ, 'for'). A similar word appears in Job 4:12 and 26:14 with the idea of 'a whisper'. What adds to the uncertainty here is that the following word, rendered by the NIV as 'their enemies', is not the normal word for an enemy. Rather, it is a participle of the verb 'to arise' (*qûm*), which can at times mean those who rise up to oppose (see Exod. 15:7; 2 Sam. 18:31). On balance, when all the possibilities are considered, it is best to take the verse to mean that because of the people's actions any potential enemy would hold them in derision. They were so embarrassingly out of control that this fact could only be mentioned in whispers.[6] Seeing the situation, Moses decided that he had to bring about a division among the people to see if any were committed to the LORD. Hence he stood at the entrance to the camp (called here 'the gate'), and cried out: 'Who[ever is] for the LORD – to me!' The absence of a verb in the first clause is quite typical Hebrew, though the absence of one in the second is unusual. It is a very abrupt call, though most English translations insert 'Let him come', or 'Come'. The reference to 'all the Levites' coming to Moses is probably a generalisation, for Deuteronomy 33:9 seems to indicate that not all the Levites were spared the judgment of God.

27-29 The instruction to the Levites to kill, though mediated through Moses ('*he* said to them'), was specifically a command of 'the LORD, the God of Israel'. It was divine retributive justice against impenitent transgressors. The command was to go back and forth throughout the camp and kill, whether the victim was brother, friend, or neighbour. Presumably the Levites made enquiries of the people, and any who showed a repentant attitude were spared, for the number killed was

---

5. The Latin Vulgate rendered the word by *nudatos*, 'nude'. The AV follows this: 'And when Moses saw that the people *were* naked; (for Aaron had made them naked unto their shame among their enemies)'. Walter Kaiser Jr. has taken the view that what happened was 'a type of religious prostitution connected with the people's worship of the golden calf' (Kaiser, 'Exodus', p. 541).

6. This is in line with the first of the options that Douglas Stuart, *Exodus*, p. 680, puts forward.

about three thousand (v. 28). The later incident at Baal-Peor (Num. 25:1-18) provides a parallel situation to this one, but there it is expressly stated that the idolatry was accompanied by sexual revelry (Num. 25:1, 6-8). This is one of the numerous passages in the Old Testament in which the ethics of the final judgment intrudes into God's administration of His rule in Israel.[7] Because of the faithfulness of the Levites that day (i.e., they did not spare their own sons and brothers), the Lord instructed them to set themselves apart for Him.[8] The choice of the Levites had already been made by God (see 27:21; 28:1), but their faithfulness at this juncture served as confirmation of their priestly role (cf. the appointment of Phinehas and his descendants to a perpetual priesthood after the incident at Baal-Peor, Num. 25:10-13).

---

7. For discussion of this principle, see Meredith Kline, 'Intrusion and the Decalogue', *WTJ* 16 (1953-54), pp. 1-22.

8. The MT has 'consecrate [yourselves]' but the LXX, Vulgate, and Targum all take the verb as a past tense, the NIV following this tradition with its rendering: 'You have been set apart'. The ESV renders it: 'Today you have been ordained'. For comment on the technical expression for 'consecrate' (lit. 'filling the hand'), see comment on Exodus 28:41.

39

Vicarious Atonement
(32:30-35)

30 The following day Moses indicated that he was going to return to the LORD on Mount Sinai. The purpose is stated as being to make atonement for the 'great sin' of the people, something with which he charged them (Heb. lit. 'you [pl.] have sinned a great sin'). The use of the word 'perhaps' must be understood in reference to what Moses suggested ('make atonement') and what he proposed ('but if not, then blot me out of the book').[1] He was raising the question as to whether there was a way whereby the Lord would accept his life as a substitute for the people. But no sacrifice, no matter who made it or what it was composed of, could atone for this sin (cf. Ps. 49:7: 'No man can redeem the life of another or give to God a ransom for him').

31-32 Moses returned to the LORD and confessed to Him the sin of the people. It was indeed a great sin, in that they had substituted the worship of their guide and saviour in favour of manufactured gods of gold. He posed an alternative with the LORD, in an impassioned plea. Either He forgave the sin of Israel, or else blotted Moses' own name out of the book of life. This is one of several Old Testament references to a book

---

1. The use of the particle 'perhaps' (*'ûlay*) plus the Pi. 1 s. coh. of the verb *kâfar*, yields the translation: 'Perhaps I can make atonement for you.' This is an example of an optative construction with the speaker's will involving doubt, and hence an indefinite potentiality. See *IBHS*, pp. 573-74.

of remembrance (see Pss. 69:28; 139.16), and the idea carries over into the New Testament (see Rev. 3:5; 13:8; 20:12). It is an anthropomorphic concept to highlight the certain knowledge that God has of His own children. The comparison should rightly be made with Paul's statement that he could wish himself cursed and cut off from Christ for the sake of his Jewish brothers (Rom. 9:3).

33-34 The divine reply was confirmation of God's judgment expressed already in verses 9-10, as well as a gracious refusal to accept Moses' offer. Those who had sinned against God in the incident of the golden bull must accept the punishment that was the consequence of their sin. The instructions to Moses relating to the blessing of the land was reinforced, as he was commanded to lead the people to the place of God's choice. This, in itself, was a reassurance, as it indicated that the covenant would continue, and the promise of the land of Canaan would stand. However, the warning of punishment was given, that would occur in the time of God's visitation of His people. The Hebrew verb used twice at the end of verse 34 (*pâqad*, 'to visit') can denote visiting either for good or evil. There is no doubt that here it marks out a visitation in judgment. No escape was possible for those who participated without remorse in the worship of the golden bull.

35 The ultimate punishment on Israel for rebellion against God was going to be expulsion from the land of Canaan, as Moses later predicted (Lev. 26:31-33 and Deut. 28:65-68). However, as an interim judgment Israel was going to be smitten (using the same verb, *nâgaf*, as is used of God's smiting of Egypt, Exod. 7:27 MT). No mention is made of the precise nature of the punishment for 'what they did with the calf Aaron had made'. Some have suggested that there is absence of chronological order here, and this statement refers to the 3,000 deaths recorded in verse 28. It is probably better to think of some sickness that afflicted them as a sign of the ultimate full judgment of exile that awaited them much later.

Study Questions

1) Twice it is mentioned that the people declared that the idol they had made was the god who had led them out of

Egypt (vv. 4, 8). How could they confuse an idol for the God who had redeemed them?

2) Can you think of other occasions when God relented and did not proceed with announced judgment?

3) Is the reference to the names in God's book (vv. 33-34) only an expression of God's complete knowledge, or does it relate to an actual written record?

4) Compare Moses' prayers in verses 11-13 and 31-32. Are there lessons here for us concerning the essential nature of prayer?

40

The Call to Move from Sinai
(33:1-6)

This next section flows on from the conclusion of chapter 32, as it is a continuation of the narrative of events at Mount Sinai. The time had come for Israel to move away from Mount Sinai and go to a place that had been promised to the people long before. The sin of the people in connection with the golden bull was still to the forefront and special provisions had to be put in place both for their journeying and for their meetings with the LORD.

1 The command was given for the people of Israel to move away from Sinai towards the land that God had sworn to give them. This had been promised to Abraham (Gen. 15:18-21), confirmed first to Isaac (26:3-5) and then to Jacob (Gen. 28:13-15).

2-3 The rebellion of the people almost brought about their destruction (vv. 3 and 5). Hence, instead of God going with them, He provided an angel to lead and to protect them. No suggestion is given in the text that this was *the* angel of the LORD. The description given of Canaan matches those mentioned earlier in the book, both in regard to the nations inhabiting it and also the reference to its being a land of milk and honey (see earlier comments on 3:8). God's attitude to the people was a direct result of the fact that they were stiff-necked (see comments on the first use of this phrase in 32:9). Though God had promised that His presence would go with the people (23:23), yet because of the people's rebellion that promise was temporarily withdrawn.

4-6 Realisation on the part of the people of their sin brought with it deep grief of spirit. They mourned, and as an act of penitence (like putting on sackcloth) they did not put on any ornaments. Reference is made in verse 5 to the previous words of the LORD to Moses accusing them of being stiff-necked.[1] This description of people as 'stiff-necked' is found much later in the Old Testament (see Jer. 17:23; 2 Chron. 30:8; 36:13), and even in the New Testament (Acts 7:51). The threat is that if God went with the people even for a moment, a blinking of the eye (*réga'*), He might even destroy them. An outward display of inward repentance had to be shown by the removal of their ornaments (cf. also Ezek. 26:16). No later mention of the ornaments occurs. Most probably they were not worn again, or at least for some considerable time.

---

1. There are some issues of translation in v. 5, especially regarding what tense to use in English for the verb *vayomer*. It is probably best to agree with the NIV and the ESV that the verb is a pluperfect, 'and he had said'. For the contrary opinion, see W. H. Gispen, *Exodus*, p. 304.

41

The Temporary Meeting Place
(33:7-11)

The sin of the people was so serious, and the covenant having been broken (see 32:15-20), a special place of meeting had to be provided for them. It could not be the true Tent of Meeting because of the lack of holiness on the part of the people. What was provided was an alternative meeting place outside the camp. It was only when the covenant was renewed (see 34:10-28) that the real Tent of Meeting could be constructed and used (see 35:30-35; 40:1-33).

7 Moses' practice was to pitch a tent outside the camp whenever a new site was selected. This was to be far off from the main camp, emphasising how estranged God and His people were at this time. The name given to it, 'the tent of meeting', contained an element of hope, for it suggested straightaway that God was still prepared to continue to deal with the people in spite of their wilful sinfulness. When anyone had a particular matter on which guidance was needed, then they would go outside and receive help at the tent of meeting.

8-10 These verses spell out the procedure that took place whenever Moses went out to 'the tent of meeting'. The rest of the Israelites were spectators, not participants. They stood at the opening of their tents, watching until Moses entered into 'the tent of meeting'. On each occasion, something happened that links in with the earlier reference in 13:21 regarding the pillar of cloud that went before Israel, leading them on their way. While Moses was in the tent, the pillar of cloud descended during the time he was speaking with the Lord. This was a symbolic happening to show that the Lord had condescended to meet with His servant Moses. The sight impelled the people who were watching to remain at the entrance of their tents and there to worship.

11 The friendship that Moses had with the Lord was special. The Lord spoke with him 'face to face', a statement that is repeated in slightly different words in Numbers 12:8. It was a unique relationship that Moses, the covenantal mediator, had with the Lord, one that could not be paralleled with anyone else. He spoke with him 'as a man speaks with his friend', an expression that points both to the nearness of the fellowship but also to the freedom with which the communication took place. When the revelation was over, while Moses returned to the camp, Joshua stayed there. No explanation is given of Joshua's role, but it seems that he was there as a guardian of the tent of meeting.

42

Moses and the Glory of the Lord
(33:12-23)

God's revelation of His own glory has already been referred to on several occasions in Exodus (see 16:7; 24:15-18; 29:43). Now another incident is related in which Moses received a special manifestation of that glory while hidden in a rock at Sinai. The description contains anthropomorphic terms (God has 'a face', 'a hand', and 'a back'), but the resulting revelation, and the declaration accompanying it, was a supreme manifestation of God's character (34:5-9). Moses' request for God to be with the people in their journeying (vv. 13-16) received an abundant answer.

12-13 Moses had already been told that God was going to send His angel before the people (23:20), but he wanted confirmation of this in the announcement of the name of the person. He was anxious as to how God was going to deal in the future with His people who had sinned so seriously over the golden bull. He recognised that he was in a special relationship with the Lord, for God 'knew' Moses and His grace had reached out to him. The concept of knowledge (Heb. verb *yâda'*) is important in these verses, occurring six times in verses 12-17. The verb is used here in accordance with its common usage of knowledge of God by humans, and also His knowledge of them. Moses was known by name (i.e., chosen for a special purpose), and he asked for a revelation to him of God's ways in order that he might be assured that

God's grace had brought him into a special and favoured relationship with the LORD. Psalm 103:7 is a comment on this request, as it affirms that God did make His ways known to Moses. A further consideration that Moses pressed on the Lord was that Israel was 'his people', those who had been brought up out of Egypt.

14-16 God's response was in terms of what is recorded in 23:20-21. Literally, the Hebrew has 'my face (*pânay*) will go'. This seems to have been an assurance that God's essential being would accompany Moses on the way to Canaan. The phrasing appears to differentiate between Moses and the rest of Israel, for the statement is second person singular: 'My presence will go [with you], and I will give *you* (2 m. s.) rest.' One of the ways that the Old Testament describes the blessing of Canaan is by speaking of 'rest' in the land. That rest would be important in itself, but it would also send the message that migration was over for Israel, and the people now could look forward to a sedentary pattern of life. The language may reflect God's attitude to His sinful people, and also the unique intimacy that Moses had with Him (cf. also the very rare use of the phrase 'to find favour in God's sight', one used too of Noah in Gen. 6:8). The way ahead, as far as Moses was concerned, depended on the divine presence being with them. It would have been better to stay where they were if they were to be bereft of that presence. Another argument put forward by Moses was that the presence of the LORD was going to be proof of the fact that God had chosen Israel to be His own people. Israel was differentiated from all other people groups by divine election.[1]

17 The Lord's response to Moses' request was an assurance that He would carry it out. The NIV rendering of the clause, 'because I am pleased with you', obscures the fact that the Hebrew here ('to find favour in the eyes of someone') is the same as has already occurred in verse 12. It is preferable to retain the same idiom in the English of both verses (as is done in many other English translations, including the AV, NASB,

---

1. The Heb. verb 'will distinguish' (NIV) in v. 16 is *pâlâ'*, most frequently used of God's actions in the sense that God's works mark Him off as divine. This, however, is one of the rarer secular uses of this verb denoting something marked off from something else.

NKJV, RSV, and ESV). The final sentence of the verse, 'and I know you by name,' is also a repetition of what was said in verse 12. It is a reminder of the close relationship forged between God and His servant Moses.

18-20 A further request of Moses was for a revelation of God's glory. The promise was given that God would cause 'all his goodness' to pass before him. It is hard to be sure whether 'goodness' (*tûvâh*) has its full covenantal significance here, namely, of the things promised in a covenant,[2] or whether it is used in a general sense of the many blessings that flow from God's presence. The former is the more likely as mention is made of the proclamation of God's covenantal name, the Lord (*yhwh*; see comments on 3:13-15). To declare His name meant a revelation of His nature and character, just as Jesus later was to manifest God's name to those whom He had been given out of the world (John 17:6). The answer to Moses' prayer is given in the following chapter (34:5-7). The words that follow are an emphatic assertion of God's prerogatives in relation to showing mercy and compassion. He could show mercy to His erring people because it was sovereignly dispensed. The apostle Paul took up this quotation in Romans 9:14-15 as he wrote about the possible injustice of God, seen in the election of Jacob and not Esau. To the question, 'Is God unjust?', he answered with the strongest negative, 'Not at all (*mê genoito*)!' before going on to quote Exodus 33:19. The point was that God's mercy was not a matter of justice at all. Rather it was determined by free and sovereign grace. In Exodus 33, this reference to the sovereign bestowal of mercy is followed by God's reminder to Moses that no one can see His face, for looking at His glory in that way causes death. The revelation of His glory was going to have this one restriction – there was to be no seeing of His face. The New Testament makes it clear that part of the significance of the incarnation of Jesus is that He is the revelation of the Father whom men could see and yet not die (John 1:18; 6:46; 1 John 4:12).

---

2. See the information on the use of the root *tûv* in covenantal settings in Paul Kaluveettil, *Declaration and Covenant*, pp. 42-47. Robert Gordon refers to cognates of the root *tûv* in Aramaic and Akkadian documents with the meaning of 'covenant', *NIDOTTE*, 2, p. 356.

21-23 These verses record further details about the impending revelation of God's glory. Moses is to draw near to God (lit. 'with me', *'ittî*) and to station himself on a rock. He is to be hidden in a cleft of the rock (*beniqrâh hatstsûr*) while God's glory passes by.³ While 'face' and 'hand' are used quite commonly of God, this is the only place in the MT where God refers to His 'back'. The idea is that God will so protect His servant that, in experiencing His presence and seeing some manifestation of His glory, Moses will not die as a result. While in English translation we need to retain 'my back' (as the translation of *'achorây*), yet we can understand it as indicating '"the after-effects" of his radiant glory'.⁴

Study Questions

1) Why was the promise of the land such an important element in the covenant with Abraham, Isaac, and Jacob?

2) Why did Moses occupy such a special position before God so that he was different from others, in that God spoke to him 'as a man speaks with his friend' (v. 11)?

3) Moses asked to see God's glory (v. 18). How do we know that God has once and for all manifested His glory in the person of His Son, the Lord Jesus?

4) Compare the accounts of Moses (vv. 18-23) and Elijah at Sinai (1 Kings 19:8-18). How were their experiences similar?

---

3. The word 'cleft' (*neqârâh*) only occurs here and in Isa. 2:21 in the MT. When the discouraged Elijah went 'to the mountain of God, [to] Horeb, he came there to *the* cave' (1 Kings 19:8-9). The use of the definite article (in Heb. but not translated in most English versions) seems to point to a well-known location, and it is probably to be identified with the cleft of the rock here in Exodus 33. Elijah is the 'second Moses', both in respect to the location and to the theophany he experienced there.

4. W. C. Kaiser Jr., 'Exodus', p. 546; and *Hard Sayings of the Old Testament*, pp. 81-84.

43

Preparation for New Revelation of God's Glory
(34:1-4)

Before coming to the verse-by-verse exegesis of this chapter some orientation is needed for this significant section, especially as it deals with the renewed covenant at Sinai and highlights the theme of God's presence with His people.

1. The background has been set in the description of the rebellion and apostasy of Israel, resulting in the breaking of the covenantal document, the two tablets written with the finger of God (32:16). In preparation for the renewed covenantal bond, Moses had to prepare two new stone tablets, which he carried to the top of Mount Sinai (34:1-2, 4).

2. Moses' pleas for his people resulted in the LORD dealing with them graciously, not because of merit on their part, but because of Moses' mediatorial actions. God's character was revealed in the manifestation of His glory (see Moses' request in 33:18), and the declaration of Himself as the compassionate and gracious God (34:6-7). This declaration became a virtual creed for Israel, and it is cited in many later Old Testament passages (see, e.g., Num. 14:18; Neh. 9:17; Pss. 86:15; 103:8; 145:8; Joel 2:13 14; Jonah 4:2).

3. Moses pled for the continued presence of God, even though he acknowledged that Israel was 'a stiff-necked people' (34:9), the fourth time this expression is used in chapters 32–34 (32:9; 33:3, 5; 34:9). This expression is only used elsewhere in Deuteronomy 9:6, 13 in a passage reflecting on the golden bull incident.

4. The regular formula for making covenants ('to cut a covenant') is used of this renewed relationship (34:10, 27). In addition, the content of the covenantal document is given the same designation as in the first covenant at Sinai, 'the Words' rather than 'the commandments' (cf. 20:1 with 34:27), though here the fuller designation is used, 'the Ten Words' (34:28).

5. The renewed covenant contained instructions regarding the provision God was going to make of the land for them and the need for the people of Israel to keep themselves separate from Gentile nations (cf. 23:23-30 with 34:10-16). Heathen idols had to be shunned, and no cast images (*'elohê massêkâh*) were permitted (34:15-17). This latter instruction is a pointed reference back to the bull the people had made (*'êgel massêkâh*, 32:4).

6. The section setting out the required feasts (34:18-26) outlines the divinely ordained festivals, not like the substitute one that Aaron had created (32:5).

7. The thought of God's presence that dominates chapters 32–34 comes to a climax in 34:29-35. Moses' face reflected the glory of God 'as he spoke to the people all the commands that the Lord had given him on Mount Sinai' (34:32). The restored presence of God could then be further symbolised by the building and use of the Tent of Meeting (as recorded in chapters 35–40). The temporary tent (33:7-11) was no longer necessary, for God could now symbolically dwell in the midst of His people. The Tent was placed at the very centre of the camp, with the Levites' tents surrounding it (Num. 1:51-53).

1-4 Before the revelation of God's glory could take place, certain preparations were necessary. Hence Moses was instructed to chisel out fresh stone tablets to replace the ones he had broken (32:19). On these God recorded the same words that had appeared on the first tablets. There is no discrepancy with the statement in verse 28 that simply says, 'he wrote on the tablets the words of the covenant, the Ten Words'. The subject in the MT is 'he', but in the context, 'the LORD', who had just been mentioned in the earlier part of the verse, must be in view. On the next morning, Moses alone was to ascend Mount Sinai again (for at least the seventh time) and stand before the LORD.[1] This differed from the earlier experience, when the elders, along with Aaron, Nadab, and Abihu, together with Joshua, went a certain way up the mount, probably to the edge of the cloud (24:9-14). The proscription of any animal being on the mountain is a repetition of what was forbidden in 19:12-13. The final verse recounts the obedience of Moses to the divine directions. He cut the new tablets, and early in the morning took them in his hand as he ascended the mountain. The theme of faithful adherence to the LORD's commands runs through the remaining narrative in this book (see 35:1, 4, 10; 36:1, 5; 39:1, 5, 7, 21, 26, 31, 32, 43; 40:16, 19, 21, 23, 25, 27, 29, 32). God was to be worshipped and served only in the way He appointed.

---

1. No explanation is given of the delay until the next day. It is very likely that Moses had to accomplish ritual cleansing before he again ascended the mountain.

44

God's Glory Revealed
(34:5-9)

5 As He did previously (see 24:15-16), God appeared in a cloud on the mountain. The following words do not indicate who is the subject of the verbs 'stood' and 'proclaimed'. While there are grammatical features that suggest both subjects should be Moses, yet it is probably best to take these verbs as referring to 'the Lord'. The verb 'stood' (*nâtsav*) is the same verb that has already been used of Moses in 33:21 and 34:2, though here it appears in a different theme (*nâtsav*, Hitp., instead of Ni.). This change of theme suggests that it is the LORD who is described in this action. If that is so, then the next verb is also to be understood as having 'the LORD' as its subject. While the expression used is 'to proclaim in the name of the LORD' (*qârâ' beshêm yhwh*), which is one more commonly used of humans making a declaration in the LORD's name, yet here the context does suggest that it was the Lord Himself who made this declaration. This then can be considered a summary statement of what follows in verses 6-7.[1]

6-7 In a wonderful way, God passed by in front of Moses so that he only became aware of 'the after-effects' of this

---

1. The English versions, as a whole, use 'he', that is, Moses, as the subject of both verbs. The exceptions are the REB and the NLT, which have Moses as the subject of the first verb (REB 'as Moses stood there in his presence, he proclaimed the name "the LORD"'; NLT 'Then the LORD came down in a pillar of cloud and called out his own name, "the LORD", as Moses stood there in his presence').

divine revelation (see comments on 33:23). The declaration of His character began with the repeated 'Lord, Lord' (*yhwh yhwh*). The repetition was unusual, yet concentrated attention on the fact that this was the covenantal God of Israel who was making known His own character to Moses. He was both merciful and gracious (*rachûm v^echannûn*), terms that highlighted God's unfailing compassion. The following phrases spell out these initial characteristics by saying that the Lord is 'slow to anger, abounding in love and faithfulness'. He does not react quickly to the transgressions of His people, but manifests extravagant love, while remaining utterly faithful to His promises. One of the best ways to help understand these expressions is to see how they are used in Psalms such as 86:5, 15 and 103:8-10. Passages such as those amplify the significance of the phrases here in Exodus 34.

Recollections of the Second Word (20:4-6) occur in verse 7. Firstly, though the wording is slightly different, the idea of continuing to love to the thousandth generation was again part of God's revelation of His own character.[2] The duration of His love is without a limit. Secondly, as a jealous God, the Lord ensures that the guilty are not allowed to escape the consequences of their sin, and this punishment will extend to the third and fourth generations. In between these two thoughts is the statement that God will forgive 'wickedness, rebellion, and sin'. These three expressions form a comprehensive summary of sin, as they view it from the perspectives of wilful transgression, treachery against God, and missing the mark. The same combination of terms for sin occurs in Psalm 32:1-2, as does the same assurance of the possibility of forgiveness. The expression here for 'forgiveness' (*nâsâ' 'âvon*) is not the most common one but it does appear elsewhere with God as the subject (cf. Num. 14:18; Pss. 32:5; 85:2; Hosea 14:2).

8-9 Moses' response was speedy, as he bowed to the ground and worshipped. He then made further intercession for the people, the fourth occasion on which he had done so (see 32:11, 31; 33:13). It is somewhat surprising that he addresses

---

2. For discussion on the expression 'to the thousandth [generation]', see the comments on 20:4-6.

God's Glory Revealed 34:5-9

God as 'Lord' (*ᵃdonay*), not as 'Lord (*yhwh*). The non-use of the covenantal name may be because Moses' perception of God was now focussed on His sovereign greatness. His first request was for the divine presence to accompany the people, providing God's grace had been extended to him ('if I have found favour'). His second request was a plea for God's forgiving grace to come to a 'stiff-necked people', using the same description of them as already used in 32:9, and 33:3, 5. It is significant that Moses identifies with the people, for he refers to '*our* wickedness and *our* sin'. Although he had not taken part in the rebellion, he still prayed as if he was one of those who had participated in making the golden bull. This same attitude continued in his final petition, asking that God would make 'us', that is, Moses and the whole community of Israel, His inheritance. This concept had already been stated in different words in 19:5, when God had assured His people that they were His 'treasured possession'. Inheritance conveyed the thought of continued possession, and it became part of Israel's confident belief that God would not abandon His inheritance (Ps. 94:14).

45

The Renewal of the Covenant
(34:10-28)

The beginning and end of this section confirm that what is recorded was a covenantal formulation ('I am making a covenant', v. 10; 'I have made a covenant with you and with Israel', v. 27). The exclusive nature of this renewed covenantal bond is illustrated by the call for obedience to the Lord's demands and the due recognition of His exclusive claims. This section is sometimes called 'the ritual decalogue', as it can be divided into ten sections that constitute the core of the relationship (and is so marked in the NIV text of vv. 15-26). There is a remarkable similarity between verses 10-26 and 23:21-33.[1]

10 The opening words must have been very comforting to all in Israel, as they gave the reassurance that God was again binding Himself and them in a covenantal bond. The declaration, 'I am making a covenant',[2] is preceded in the MT by the word *hinnêh*, which is left untranslated by the NIV. This particle often introduces significant statements, and it should be translated in some way in this verse, perhaps to emphasise that the making of this covenant was occurring right at that time (cf. the rendering in the REB, 'here and now

---

1. Victor Hamilton, *Exodus*, p. 582, gives the listing of the comparisons.
2. The words 'with Israel' in the NIV are not in the MT, and are an unnecessary addition.

I am making a covenant'; see also the RSV, NASB, NKJV, and ESV for fairly literal translations of the Hebrew text).[3] The reference that follows this opening statement, 'before you', is ambiguous, as it could refer to Moses or to all the people. Most probably the NIV and ESV are correct in taking this 'you' here as the people, and then consistently throughout the rest of this narrative. The assurance was that dramatic wonders would be performed before them such as had not occurred before, thus eclipsing in greatness those they had already seen performed in Egypt.[4] The verb here for 'never done before' is 'to create' (*bârâ'*, Ni.), the verb best known for its use in Genesis 1 to describe God's creative work. The power seen at creation was also demonstrated in the LORD's wondrous deeds on behalf of His people. Israel's neighbours in Canaan would observe divine interventions on Israel's behalf that they would find awesome.

11 The LORD's commands had to be followed explicitly. This theme of obedience is expanded in Deuteronomy 8:1-20, 10:12-22, and 11:13-32. A close relationship with the people who inhabited Canaan at the time of the Israelite invasion was not to be encouraged. Long before, Abraham had been promised that the land occupied by these various tribes would become Israel's (Gen. 15:18-21), and much more recently the Lord had again told of how these Gentile nations were to be driven out (Exod. 23: 28-33).

12-16 The detailed instructions that commence with verse 12 are in the main a repetition of 23:12-33, though not always in the same order. The command not to enter into treaty arrangements with the Gentile nations is a repetition of an instruction already given in 23:32. Having close links with Gentiles would constitute a constant snare for Israel. Hence, the heathen sites of worship and devotion – altars, pillars, and carved images representing the Canaanite goddess Asherah[5] – were to be destroyed entirely. The reason for such

---

3. For this use of *hinnêh*, see T. O. Lambdin, *Introduction to Biblical Hebrew* (New York: Charles Scribner, 1971), pp. 168-69.

4. 'I will do wonders' (*'e'eseh niflâ'ot*) alludes to miraculous actions that God alone can perform. He is a God who is described as 'awesome in glorious deeds, doing wonders' (Exod. 15:11, ESV); cf. the same idiom in Pss. 72:18 and 86:10.

5. No actual description of what the Asherim were like is given in the biblical

decisive action was because there could only be worship of one God, the Lord. No worship of another god (*'êl 'achêr*) was permitted. This is the only time that this expression is used in the Old Testament, as normally the expression is in the plural, no 'other gods' (*'elohîm 'achêrîm*), as in 20:3. What was meant by 'another god' is spelt out in Psalm 81:9, where worship of 'a foreign god' (*'êl zâr*) or 'an alien god' (*êl nêkâr*) is proscribed. The LORD is further defined as having the name 'Jealous', and as being 'a jealous God'. This is simply an emphatic way of expressing the truth brought out in the Second Word (20:4). Verse 15 is much more closely connected with the preceding verses than is suggested by the NIV ('Be careful not to make a treaty ....'). The continuity in thought is shown by the fact that the verse commences with *'lest [pen] you make a covenant with the inhabitants of the land'*. The preceding instructions were given to guard against the specific sins enumerated here. This explains the repetition of the command not to enter into covenantal arrangements with the Gentiles because that would bring them into close contact with their heathen worship and its associated practices. The men of these nations are depicted as lusting after their gods, and offering sacrifices to them.[6] When they invited Israelites to share in their sacrificial feasts, then they would probably accept. A further stage of syncretism would involve marriages between heathen women and Israelite men resulting in the men lusting after the foreign gods.

17 Making gods of metal was again forbidden (cf. 20:4, 23). This prohibition had special relevance for that time, as the golden bull made by Aaron was a molten image (32:3-4).

18-20 The first of the feasts again ordered was the Feast of Unleavened Bread (see 12:14-20 and 23:15 for earlier passages relating to it). For seven days the people had to eat unleavened bread as a memorial to the exodus from Egypt. This celebration was held on the fourteenth day of the first month, Abib. The instruction in verse 19 is a repetition of 13:2,

---

text. Clearly, they were not natural objects but some man-made aid of devotion to Asherah.

6. This, and Numbers 25:1, are the only two places in the OT where the subject of the verb 'prostitute' or 'whore after' (*zânâh*) is 'men'. Normally, it is used to refer to illicit heterosexual intercourse of women.

with the added specification that it applied to all animals, oxen and sheep/goats from the flock.[7] The first part of verse 20 is like 13:13, while the second part echoes 23:15 (see comment on that verse). The principle was that there had to be an acknowledgement of God's bounty, with the same instruction being repeated in Deuteronomy 16:16-17.

21 The Fourth Word dealing with the Sabbath was given in 20:8-11, reiterated in 23:12, and now restated yet again. To the earlier instructions is added a direction regarding the two very busy periods of the agricultural year, ploughing and harvest. Even at those times the sabbatical principle had to apply and the due rest taken on the seventh day. Work on food supplies did not take precedence over the Sabbath rest.

22-24 The two feasts mentioned in verse 22 have already been described in 23:16 (see comments of that verse). The one main difference between the two passages is the different name used here, 'the Feast of Weeks,' instead of 'the Feast of Harvest'. The other feast, 'the Feast of Ingathering,' is known by this title in Exodus (23:16; 34:23), whereas in Leviticus and Deuteronomy it is called 'the Feast of Sukkot' (Lev. 23:34; Deut. 16:13, 16). The thought of these festivals leads into the requirement that all males had to make the journey to Jerusalem three times every year (v. 23). The wording is the same as in 23:17, except that in addition to the words 'all your males shall appear before the Sovereign LORD' (*'êl pᵉnê hâ'âdon yhwh*) is added 'the God of Israel' (*'ᵉlohê yisrâ'êl*). This places emphasis on the expression by appending the most characteristic name for God in the Old Testament. The absence of reference to women going to the pilgrimage feasts should not lead to the conclusion that women were prohibited from joining in such worship. Other passages (such as 1 Sam. 1:1-2:11; 1 Sam. 9:11-14; Neh. 8:1-11) show that women were participants in worship and covenantal meals. Also, the pattern prevailing in the New Testament was carrying on an established practice (see the references to Anna, and the presence of Jesus' mother at the temple, Luke 2:36-38, 41-51). In view here is the situation that would

---

7. The word in v. 19 for 'flock' (*seh*) can include sheep and goats, as can the other common word for 'flock', *ts'on*.

prevail once occupancy of the land of Canaan was obtained. God was going to drive out the heathen nations and enlarge Israel's territory. Assurance was given that those going to Jerusalem would not be disadvantaged by others laying claim to their land while they were away.

25 The NIV rendering of this verse suggests that drinking blood was only forbidden when bread made with yeast was offered. However, the point was that no blood, and no bread containing yeast, were to be offered.[8] The provision regarding not letting what was left of the Passover feast remain till the next morning reinforced what was said in 23:18. Prompt offerings and speedy consumption of the Passover meal were required.

26a This is an exact reproduction of 23:19a. The first-fruits were to be dedicated to God as recognition that He, after redeeming His people from Egypt, had given them the land of Canaan. Deuteronomy 26:1-11 sets out the procedure to be adopted at the first harvest, and probably to be repeated annually.

26b This is another exact repetition from the earlier regulations in 23:19b (see the comment on that verse).

27-28 The section setting out the renewed covenant closes with a short statement that serves as a corollary to the opening statement in verses 10-14. Both specify that what took place after God's revelation of His glory (vv. 5-9) was the making of a covenant, a renewed bond that was a sovereign gift of God to His people. The emphasis is on God's initiative in making this covenant, as it was with earlier covenants such as the Noahic (Gen. 9:8-17) and the Abrahamic (Gen. 12:1-3; 15:12-21). The wording here is significant for another reason, as a literal translation brings out: 'I have cut *with you* (*'itt^ekâ*, you sing.) a covenant and with Israel.' The wording suggests that the relationship between God and Israel may still have been regarded as strained, and the mediatorial role of Moses was also given priority.[9] The instructions to Moses were to write down all 'these words', that is, all the words that God

---

8. See Douglas Stuart's translation: 'Do not offer the blood of a sacrifice to me, nor, likewise, anything containing yeast' (*Exodus*, p. 732, fn. 222).

9. This is following the comments of John Currid, *Exodus, vol. 2, Chapters 19–40*, p. 320.

had spoken but not including 'the Ten Words'. While the Ten Words had been referred to as 'words' before (20:1), this is the first occurrence of the phrase 'the Ten Words'. The difference between the general words and the specific 'words of the covenant' were marked by the different methods of recording them. Moses had to record in writing the general words, but it was God Himself who wrote the Ten Words on the new stone tablets. The concluding words of verse 28 may seem to leave open the possibility that Moses wrote on the tablets, yet 'the Lord' is the grammatical antecedent, and this then confirms what God had earlier said (34:10). Moses spent forty days and forty nights on the mountain, neither eating nor drinking, which replicated his earlier experience there (Deut. 9:9-12). He prostrated himself before the Lord and pled for Aaron and the people, and his prayers were answered (Deut. 9:19).

46

Moses' Radiant Face
(34:29-35)

The final description, completing the narrative concerning the renewal of the covenant, concerns Moses' appearance when he emerged from the LORD's presence. He who had asked to see God's glory (33:18) reflected that glory when he came to the Israelite community to tell them what had been commanded.

29-30 For the second time, Moses came down from Mount Sinai with two tablets in his hands. They are called here 'the two tablets of the Testimony'. The word 'testimony' ('*êdût*) refers to unspecified commands of God, and occurs in parallel with 'law' (*tôrâh*) in Psalm 78:5. The meaning of the expression here is clear from the context as the tablets contained 'the words of the covenant' (v. 28), and in Deuteronomy 9:9, 15 reference is made to 'the tablets of the covenant'. As he descended from the mountain Moses was unaware that his face was 'radiant' because he had spoken with the Lord. The verb in question (*qâran*) means 'to shine, send out rays', and it only occurs in verses 29, 30, and 35 in the Old Testament.[1] The LXX does not help greatly as it says that Moses' face was 'glorified'. In verse 30 the narrative says that when Aaron and all the people saw Moses, behold (*hinnêh*), his face shone. This 'behold' is significant

---

1. Because a cognate noun *qéren* means a horn, the Latin Vulgate misunderstood the meaning. This explains why medieval artists often portrayed Moses as having horns.

and should be translated (see RSV, NASB, NKJV, and ESV), as it draws attention to a remarkable phenomenon. Moses' appearance was such that when Aaron and all the people saw him they were afraid, and did not want to approach him.

31-32 Aaron and the other leaders were reassured by Moses' invitation to them, and they returned to listen to him. Afterwards all the people approached Moses and he related all that the Lord had commanded. This is a summary statement that should not be taken to mean that, at that time, everything was communicated, for chapters 35–40 show that the divine instructions for assembling the Tent of Meeting came later.

33-35 On finishing speaking to the people, Moses put a covering over his face. The word for covering (*masveh*) is a *hapax legomenon*, which the LXX translated as a 'veil' (*kalumma*), a translation carried over in Paul's use of this passage in 2 Corinthians 3:7-18. Moses' habitual practice was to remove the veil when he entered the Lord's presence, and not to replace it until he had told the Israelites what he had been commanded. While speaking to the people, his face was radiant, but then the veil was replaced until he again went in to speak with the Lord. God's glory and God's word were conjoined. After delivering the divine commands Moses covered his face, as the Israelites could not continue to look on the glory that represented God Himself. Most probably that revelation of God's glory reminded them of His holiness but also of their own sin and rebellion. Paul's use of the passage is where he is contrasting the era of the old covenant and that of the new, showing that believers in Christ have a new freedom through the Spirit.[2]

Study Questions

1) How do Paul's words in Romans 11:22 form a summary of God's declaration in verses 6-7 of His own character?

---

2. Simon Kistemaker, *2 Corinthians* (Grand Rapids: Baker Academic, 1997), p. 116 says: 'The present section [3:12-18] is no doubt one of the most difficult to understand in all Paul's epistles. This passage has spawned numerous interpretations and views; consequently, the literature on this particular segment is vast.' See his full discussion on pp. 116-32.

2) In what ways did Israel ever disobey the command regarding not making a covenant with the people of Canaan?

3) No one was to appear before God empty-handed (Exod. 23:15; 34:20; Deut. 16:16). Does the principle behind this instruction still govern our attendance at worship today?

4) How does Paul use the account of Moses' shining face in 2 Corinthians 3:7-18, and what point is being emphasised concerning the new covenant?

PART VI

Building the Tent of Meeting
(35:1–40:38)

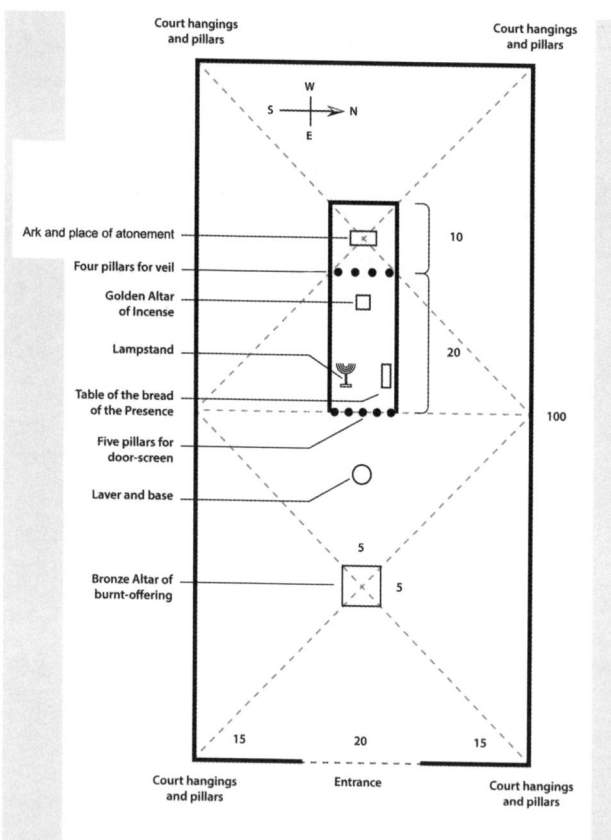

Diagram of the Tent of Meeting

Introduction

Some readers of this final section of the book of Exodus may think it superfluous, as it largely consists of material that has already been given in chapters 25–31. However, there are good theological reasons to view it differently. The specifications for the Tent of Meeting could not be utilised immediately by the people because of their sin with the golden bull. But when their sin was forgiven, and a renewed covenant made, the way was open for the building of the special place in which to meet with the Lord. This section, and the whole book, comes to a striking conclusion in 40:33-38. When Moses finished the work committed to him, God's glory filled the tent, a fact so significant that it is mentioned twice in 40:34-35.

The second book of Moses finishes on the note that God's presence with His people was signified in a tangible way, so that all Israel could see the cloud and rejoice in His abiding presence with them. Later, the glory of the Lord was manifested by the cloud in the temple in Jerusalem (1 Kings 8:11), while Ezekiel prophesied of a new Jerusalem whose name will be 'the LORD is there' (*yhwh shâmmâh*, Ezek. 48:35). The partial displays of God's glory will come to ultimate revelation when the new Jerusalem is seen to be the dwelling of God with men, and God declares that He will live with His people and be their God (Rev. 21:3).

This is an account of what actually happened, not simply instructions how to proceed with the construction of the sanctuary. Naturally, there are some changes between this section and the earlier ones about the Tent of Meeting (chs. 25–31).[1] The finite verbs in this second account describe what

---

1. Walter Kaiser Jr., 'Exodus', p. 301 give a convenient listing of the order in the command and fulfilment sections.

happened ('brought', 'received', 'made', 'fashioned'), rather than the imperatives in the first account ('make', 'set up', 'build'). Also, whereas the order in the instructions proceeded from the ark outwards, here the order seems to have been determined by time of manufacture of the various elements.

47

The Call to Build
(35:1-29)

1 The Sabbath Regulations (35:1-3, cf. 31:12-17)

1-2 The earlier account containing the instructions for building the Tent of Meeting ended with a note concerning the Sabbath (31:12-17). Now, the instructions for its construction begin with an abbreviated direction concerning its observance. There was an intimate connection between the Sabbath and the sanctuary, for worship on the seventh day at the appointed place was part of God's claim upon His redeemed people. The Sabbath law was not to be set aside during construction of the Tent. After assembling the people, Moses reminded them that what he was now commanding them to do was what God had earlier revealed to him (chs. 25–31). The death penalty was prescribed for anyone who worked on the Sabbath.

3 The instruction not to light a fire on the Sabbath was not contained in the earlier regulations, though it was implied by the direction to cook the manna and the quail on the eve of the Sabbath, and not on the Sabbath itself (16:23). While some Jews have considered this to forbid any fires on the Sabbath, most have taken the view that fires for comfort are permissible. In this context, the prohibition probably applied most directly to the use of fire by those involved in metalwork. By the language here (*'your* [2 masc. pl.] dwellings'), God's visible dwelling place was exempt, so that sacrifices requiring fire could proceed on the Sabbath.

2 Materials for the Tent of Meeting (35:4-19, cf. 25:1-9)

These instructions relate to the materials that had to be provided by the people in order for the sanctuary to be built, and they follow fairly closely the earlier section in 25:1-9.

4-9 These verses are a repetition of 25:1-7, with stress again on the voluntary nature of the gifts from the people (25:2, 'the offering for me from each man whose heart prompts him to give'; 35:5, 'everyone who is willing to bring to the LORD an offering'). What is not repeated here is the instruction to build according to the heavenly pattern shown to Moses (25:9, 40), though clearly that is presupposed.

10-19 A change comes in verse 10, as the invitation to take part in the work is widened from Bezalel and Oholiab to 'all who are skilled'. The Hebrew simply calls these people 'wise of heart' (*ch^akam lêv*). In verse 18, 'ropes' are mentioned for the first time, though earlier the note concerning 'tent pegs' (27:19) implied the use of ropes.

3 The Liberality of the Israelite Community (35:20-29, cf. 31:1-11)

These verses record the willingness with which the whole community participated in the task of building the Tent of Meeting and everything associated with it. This list is more extensive than the earlier ones (25:1-7 and 31:1-11).

20-21 The voluntary nature of the gifts is emphasised again. Though expressions used here are a little different and fuller than those in 25:2 and 35:5, yet the main idea does not change. The gifts did not come from a reluctant community who were forced to give. Rather, there was a spontaneous response to the call for materials, and later Moses had to restrain the people from bringing more (36:3-7).

22-24 In addition to the males in the community, the women were also involved in the presentation of gifts. While it is not recorded in the text, we have to presume that some of the precious metals and jewellery were part of the objects acquired from the Egyptians at the time of the Exodus (Exod. 12:35-36). These gifts were designated as offerings to the LORD, being referred to as 'wave offerings to the LORD' (vv. 22, 24; see the earlier comments on the wave offering on 29:24). Sacrificial language was applied to the gifts for the Tent of Meeting.

25-26 The women had a special role to play in addition to presenting jewellery and ornaments (see v. 22). Those who had the skill (v. 25) and were willing (v. 26) spun yarn or goats' hair to be used in making the curtains. This shows that the construction of the Tent of Meeting was not something that happened overnight, for time was needed to make all the necessary preparations, including those mentioned here.

27-28 The leaders were responsible for the provision of the precious stones for the ephod and breast-piece, and also for the oil for the lampstand and for anointing. This may have been just for the initial supply of oil at Sinai, as later in Leviticus 24:2 the instruction is for 'the Israelites', i.e., all Israel, to present the oil. Probably the latter became the regular practice.

29 The section ends with a summary statement of the generosity of many within the Israelite community. It reinforces what was already said in verses 20-21.

48

Bezalel and Oholiab
(35:30–36:7, cf. 31:1-11)

30-35 In the earlier instructions the work set out for Bezalel and Oholiab came near the end, whereas in this account of the actual making of the Tent of Meeting, it comes near the beginning. What transpired was accomplished by God's sovereign choice of workmen whom He endowed with His Spirit. The importance and necessity of this endowment is emphasised by the fact that the Hebrew root denoting wisdom (*ch-k-m*) occurs on sixteen out of eighteen appearances in Exodus in the passages relating to Bezalel and Oholiab. Extraordinary skills were needed, and this only came through God filling them with His Spirit (note the references to this in vv. 31 and 35). Another manifestation of this endowment was the ability of these men to teach others (v. 34). This was implied in 31:6, but now becomes explicit. The verb used (*yârâh*, Hi.) appears elsewhere in the Old Testament in practical contexts such as giving directions (Gen. 46:28) and parental instruction to children (Prov. 4:4, 11). From this verb comes the noun *tôrâh*, 'instruction' or 'law'. It does not preclude the possibility that a period of training somewhat like an apprenticeship could have been involved.[1]

---

1. See note in Douglas Stuart, *Exodus*, pp. 758-59, with the helpful comparison with Paul's discussion on spiritual gifts in Romans 12 and 1 Corinthians 12. He comments that these passages never deny 'gifts can be gradually obtained and/or improved with practice over time' (p. 759).

36:1 The chapter division is not helpful, as there is no break in the flow of the narrative here. This verse is a summary statement. It notes that all those involved in the work, from the leaders, Bezalel and Oholiab, down to all those others to whom the Lord had given ability, carried out their work precisely in accordance with His directions. There was no scope for deviation from the pattern set out by divine revelation.

2-7 When the time had come for the work to commence, Moses summoned all those whom the Lord had chosen for the task. Once more the qualifications of those people are emphasised: 'every skilled person to whom the Lord had given ability and who was willing to come and do the work.' Supernatural gifts were required, together with a willing heart (see the earlier references to this in 35:31 and 36:1). The gifts from the people were handed over by Moses to these men to be used in their work. The liberality was such that they had to come to Moses and request that the flow of gifts be curtailed, as they had more than enough for their tasks. Moses acted on the request, and men and women in the community were prevented from giving further gifts for the building.

49

The Progress of the Work
(36:8–39:31)

1 The Dwelling Place (36:8-38, cf. 26:1-37)

At this point the account of how those constructing the Tent of Meeting carried out their commission begins. The narrative varies from the earlier instructions in that a different order is followed.

8-19 The narrative commences with a statement that echoes the earlier instruction ('make ... then make', 26:1) by stating twice over that the work was completed ('made ... made them', NASB, NKJV).[1] This first verse of this section is longer and more detailed than the corresponding clauses in succeeding paragraphs, that simply read 'and he made' or 'and they made'. The verb 'made' (Heb. *'âsâh*) features prominently in chapters 25–40, as these chapters relate how the Israelites carried out the instructions they were given.[2] At the start of the book the Israelites had to build 'storehouses' (*miskênôt*) for the Egyptians, while at the end they build 'a dwelling place' (*mishkân*) for the Lord. Some

---

1. This is pointed out well by Douglas Stuart, *Exodus*, p. 762. One difficulty is that the final statement in the verse follows the singular subject of the instruction and has simply '*he* made them'. Either, the subject Bezalel has to be imported (as in the NASB), or else the subject is regarded as a collective singular, the group of men. This applies to all the verbs from v. 10 onwards, which are all singular.

2. The occurrences of *'âsâh* in these chapters amount to 236 out of a total of 323 for the whole of the book of Exodus.

slight differences are apparent between the account here and the earlier instructions in 26:2-11, such as the omission of 26:9b and part of 26:11.

20-37 This section also shows some small deviations from the account in chapter 26, as it narrates how the frames for the Tent of Meeting were constructed.

38 Here clarification is made of the instruction in 26:37.

2 The Ark (37:1-9, cf. 25:10-22)

The making of the ark of the covenant is covered in these verses, though the fact that there was an atonement cover (25:21) is not mentioned. Neither is there comment on placing the testimony in the ark (25:16, 21), as both had to take place after the dwelling place had been set up. The important task of making the ark was not delegated to a junior person but reserved for Bezalel himself (37:1, and then the repeated third person, 'he', in verses 2-8).

3 The Table (37:10-16, cf. 25:23-30)

Minor variations occur in these verses as compared with 25:23-30, such as the omission of reference to the bread, for that comes in the later narrative (40:23). All the verbs in this section are third person singular, 'he', referring to Bezalel. This should not be pressed to mean that he did all the work personally, but that he was responsible and oversaw the construction of the table. This is clearly the view adopted by the NIV translators, for, while acknowledging in a footnote that the verbs in this section are third person singular, they have inserted the third person plural, 'they', in the translation.

4 The Lampstand (37:17-24, cf. 25:31-40)

These verses are essentially a repetition of the earlier instructions, except that there is abbreviation of 25:37b, 40, and 25:40 is not repeated.

5 The Altar of Incense (37:25-29, cf. 30:1-5)

No significant alteration is apparent here, as compared with the earlier instructions, though there are some differences between 30:1-2 and 37:25. There is also a slight adjustment in 37:27 as compared with 30:27.

6 The Altar of Burnt Offering (38:1-7, cf. 27:1-8)

Of the differences between the two accounts, the most significant is the addition of the name given to the altar, 'the altar of burnt offering'. Some abbreviation has occurred (cf. v. 27:8b with 38:7).

7 The Bronze Basin (38:8, cf. 30:17-21)

This verse is a cryptic reference to the source of the bronze from which the basin was made. Several interpretative issues are involved here. The first is why the bronze mirrors owned by the women were used, when ample bronze had already been contributed. Secondly, the service of the women at the entrance to the Tent of Meeting is uncertain as there is no indication of the number involved, or their duties. Thirdly, the Tent of Meeting cannot be the one erected later (40:2), but an earlier one. Clearly the use of the bronze constituted a gift in addition to the contribution for the sanctuary. The fact that it was bronze mirrors that were utilised again emphasises the use made of precious objects that had been taken from Egypt and that were applied in the construction of the sanctuary. The reference to the women is unusual as it can be translated as 'serving women who served' (*hatstsov^e'ot '^{a}sher tsâve'û*).[3] The only other Old Testament reference to these serving women at the door of the Tent of Meeting is in 1 Samuel 2:22, which may point to a practice that continued right on until the temple was built. Their number and their role cannot be determined owing to lack of further biblical references. The tent in question cannot be the tent yet to be made, but rather the temporary tent that Moses established outside the Israelite camp (see the comments on 33:7-10).

8 The Courtyard (38:9-20, cf. 27:9-19)

As with other sections detailing the manner in which the sacred place was built, some details are added here concerning the courtyard. It was the necessary enclosure within which all the

---

3. The root of both the participle and finite verb here (*tsâvâ'*) has the idea of military service, and then of service in connection with ritual worship (see, for example, in addition to this verse and 1 Sam. 2:22, Num. 4:3, 23; 8:25). This explains why some commentators translate as Cassuto does, 'the mirrors of the women in array who stood in array at the door of the tent of meeting', *Exodus*, p. 466.

other main items for worship and sacrifice were placed. It was positioned at the very centre of the camp, and surrounded by the Levitical families (Num. 2:17) whose responsibilities extended to the whole congregation of Israel (Num. 3:7). In addition to the earlier instructions in 27:17, a note is added concerning the silver overlay on the tops of the posts (v. 17), while verse 18 may suggest that the curtains were composed of squares measuring five cubits by five cubits (lit. 'five cubits high in width').

9 The Costly Materials Used (38:21-31)

These verses detail the materials employed in making the dwelling place and their cost. The word translated 'the amounts of' in verse 21 of the NIV ($p^eq\hat{u}d\hat{e}$) is a *hapax legomenon*, and rather than this type of translation (cf. 'sum' in the RSV, and similar expressions in other versions) what is really being detailed is the cost. The total amounts, irrespective of whether we can reckon them in any modern equivalents, were clearly very significant. A problem that this passage and similar ones create is that the evidence points to varied systems of weights being used in ancient Israel.[4] The fact that they were a wave offering has already been referred to in 35:22. It is important to notice the term used here for the dwelling place. It is specifically designated 'the dwelling place of the testimony' (*mishkan hâ'êdût*), a reminder of how important the tablets of the covenant were. In 25:16, what was placed in the ark is simply called 'the testimony' (*hâ'êdût*), a synonymous term for the central document of the covenantal relationship between God and Israel. The formal appointment of the Levites does not come until Numbers 3, but Ithamar was already mentioned (Exod. 6:23), and later he had a leadership role among the Gershonites and the Merarites (Num. 4:28, 33).

10 The Priestly Garments (39:1-31, cf. 28:1-42)

The opening verse of this chapter practically serves as a superscription, with mention yet again of the colours of blue, purple and scarlet. These were associated with royalty, and

---

4. For discussion on weights and measures in the OT, see the excellent summary article by D. J. Wiseman, *The Illustrated Bible Dictionary*, vol. 3, pp. 1634-39.

hence were entirely appropriate for the vestments of those who served the Great King (cf. the use of this phrase for the Lord in passages such as Ps. 48:2). The description that follows is similar to the instructions in chapter 28, though it should be noted that on four occasions in this chapter (vv. 2, 7, 8, and 22) the NIV renders 'they' whereas the MT has 'he', referring clearly to Bezalel.[5] As in other verses these references are doubtless to the principal role that Bezalel played in the whole process. One significant addition as compared to chapter 28 is given in verse 3, where it is stated that gold was hammered into thin sheets and then cut into strands so that it could be interwoven with the other materials. This was an Egyptian practice of which Bezalel and others had knowledge.

Another feature of this section is also notable, and that is the number of times it is specified that all be done 'as the LORD commanded Moses' (vv. 1, 5, 7, 21, 26, 29, 31). Divine directions had to be followed explicitly since these were aspects of worship that were highly significant and concerning which no human variations were permitted. Also, the record points to God's delight in the obedience of His people, something that is noted on other important occasions as well (cf. the cases of Hezekiah [2 Kings 18:6] and Josiah [2 Kings 23:1-3]).

---

5. The Samaritan Pentateuch and the Syriac Peshitta both have 'he' in these verses, but there is no evidence that they were following a Hebrew text at this point.

50

Moses' Inspection of the Tent
(39:32-43)

The final section of this chapter begins and ends with the same theme, the completion of the specified work on what is called twice the Tent of Meeting (see vv. 32 and 40). The account has mention at the beginning and at the end of the completion of the work in exactly the way specified by the Lord, thus forming an *inclusio*. Several features of this section resemble Genesis 1–3.[1] The reference to completion of the task immediately reminds the reader of Genesis 2:1-2, that notes God's completion of His creative work. In addition, just as God had looked over all His creation with approbation (Gen. 1:31), so Moses had to look over all the workmanship now ready for installation (vv. 33, 43). This appears to be deliberately intended as a re-creation account, as parallels with Genesis match the earlier one in Exodus 1:7. God again is to dwell in the midst of His creatures, and by special provisions meets with His people and communicates with them (see Gen. 3:8-13). The connection with the creation account is also accentuated by the concluding words of the chapter, 'So Moses blessed them' (v. 43; cf. Gen. 2:3, 'And God blessed the seventh day and made it holy'). These words are ambiguous as 'them' (*'otâm*) could linguistically refer either

---

1. W. J. Dumbrell, *Covenant and Creation*, pp. 136-37, develops the concept of the links between Genesis 1–2 and the account of the building of the Tent of Meeting.

to the objects that Moses has just inspected, or to the people who had carried out the work ('they had done', *'âsû*). The second is most probable, as Moses invokes a divine blessing on those who had acted with such dedication to the work and done it precisely in accordance with God's demands.

51

Setting up the Tent
(40:1-33)

As the book draws to a close and the instructions for the completion of the Tent of Meeting and all associated items having been fulfilled, these verses set out the manner in which the elements came together to form the central worship system of Israel. Several factors are important.

1. Not only had the LORD given the directions to Moses and his associates regarding the making of the various items, but He also proceeded to instruct regarding setting up of the individual items.

2. Anointing marked the setting apart of the items and of the formal institution of the priesthood. In its religious usage, the verb 'anoint' (*mâshach*) designated the separation of something or some person for God's service. God was the authorising agent, even though some intermediator performed the action, as Moses did here.[1]

3. The note as to the timing of these happenings is significant. Twice it is written that it was set up on the first day of the first month [in the second year] (vv. 2 and 17). This means that the construction work had taken approximately half a year. The Israelites had

---

1. For the wider questions relating to the religious significance of anointing, see the article by Victor Hamilton, *TWOT*, pp. 530-32.

arrived at Sinai in the third month after leaving Egypt (19:1). About nine months had elapsed between that time and the first day of the second year when the work was handed over to Moses. If the days that Moses spent on Sinai (24:18; 34:28) and the time for giving the law (19:1-24:11) are deducted, that leaves about six months for the construction work itself.[2] There is no mention of how long it took to assemble the whole sanctuary. The reference to finishing it on the first day of the first month seems to be a deliberate echo of Genesis 8:13 that records the drying up of the ground after the flood. The dates both marked the commencement of new eras in the life of God's people.

4. The obedience of Moses to God's directions again features prominently, with the repetition of the refrain eight more times (see vv. 16, 19, 21, 23, 25, 27, 29, and 32). In contrast to the earlier rebellion against the LORD's commands (chap. 32), complete obedience occurred. Precise fulfilment of the requirements was necessary, both because they were divine instructions and because they pointed forward to the blessings to come under the new covenant. They were 'external regulations applying until the time of the new order' (Heb. 9:10).

5. This section marks the institution of the whole system of worship under the Sinai covenant. Features specifically mentioned are: the shewbread (v. 23); the lampstand (v. 24); the golden altar (v. 26); the altar of burnt offering (v. 29); the ritual washings (vv. 30-32); and the courtyard (v. 33). All these were to function from this time until the destruction of the temple by the Babylonians in 586 B.C. (cf. 2 Kings 24:13; 2 Chron. 36:18-19; Ps. 74:1-8). Undoubtedly there were periods when worship was in abeyance or corrupt, but from this point onwards the covenantal requirements were in operation.

6. The point made earlier regarding the connection with the creation account in Genesis is reinforced by the

---

2. This calculation is following that of C. F. Keil, *Biblical Commentary on the Old Testament*, vol. 2 (Grand Rapids: Eerdmans, reprint 1975), p. 256.

final words of verse 33: 'And so Moses finished the work' (*vay^{e}kal mosheh 'et hamm^{e}lâkâh*). This is so close to the description of God's creative actions: 'By the seventh day *God had finished the work* he had been doing' (*vay^{e}kal '^{e}lohîm ... m^{e}la'ktô*). Eden had been God's sanctuary, as had Sinai. Now a movable shrine became the place where God met with His people, to be replaced later by the temple that Solomon would build. At each stage the relationship between God and His people was marred by human sin. The ultimate fulfilment will be when there is no temple in the new heavenly Jerusalem because the Lord God Almighty and the Lamb will be its temple. No impure person will enter in, for this will be the final dwelling place of God and His redeemed people (Rev. 21:3-4, 22-27).

52

The LORD's Glory
(40:34-38)

The book of Exodus reaches its conclusion with reference to the visible signs of God's presence with His people. On their journey to Sinai the cloud had led them (Exod. 13:21-22), it had descended on Mount Sinai (Exod. 19:9, 16; 24:15-16), and on the temporary place of meeting outside the main camp (Exod. 33:9-10). Now it covered the Tent of Meeting, as it stood ready for use. It was also going to fulfil a similar function as the journey to Canaan continued with many new arrangements for worship and service in place.

34 This verse continues on from the final sentence of verse 33. As Moses' work was completed, so the cloud came down on the Tent of Meeting in confirmation of this. The dwelling-place, the Tent of Meeting, the sanctuary, whatever precise term is used in any passage, denoted not just the symbolic presence of God but contained it. It was His house, and to it His people were invited on specified occasions as guests.[1] The 'glory' is not defined but was probably some awesome glow in daylight, but it appeared as fire by night (cf. Exod. 13:20-22; 14:24).

35 At this very preliminary stage, even Moses was prohibited from entering the tent. What had now transpired was God's response to his request in 33:15-16. Later records

---

1. See the discussion on this by Geerhardus Vos, *Biblical Theology*, p. 154.

show how the priestly ministry functioned from this point onwards. The manifestation of God's glory was testimony to His acceptance of the completed sanctuary and the subsequent worship that would be carried out there.

36-38 The book of Exodus began with the Israelites seemingly bereft of God's presence and His help in their slavery. The conclusion is so different. They now had the visible sign of His presence, not just apparent to the priests but to the people as a whole (v. 38, 'in the sight of all the house of Israel'). God's glory was manifest, with the assurance that His presence was on-going. The decision to move camp was not a human decision, but a divine one, and this applied whether the stay at any place was short or long (see Num. 9:15-23). Some details of matters before the setting up of the sanctuary, and some later ones, are recorded in the following books of the Pentateuch. However, what is so significant is that Exodus ends with the God of glory present with His redeemed people, Israel. He had brought them out of Egypt with a mighty hand and an outstretched arm, and now confirmed His approval of the construction of the sanctuary and the assurance of His abiding presence. Later biblical history will record not only the repeated sinfulness of the people but also the continuing faithfulness of their covenantal LORD.

Subject Index

Aaron
 birth of 58
 genealogy of 99-102
 and golden bull 337-8, 339,
  346-7, 352, 373
 and grumbling of the
  Israelites 173, 174-5, 178
 and Israelites freedom
  from slavery 142
 mission to Pharaoh............ 87-9, 91-2,
  101, 103, 104
 on Mount Sinai 209, 210, 259
 and Passover 141, 146
 priesthood of 299, 302, 304,
  305, 306, 307, 308-9,
  311-12, 313, 315, 321-2, 324
 and ratification of covenant 259,
  263-4
 and rebellion of Israel 29, 344,
  346-7, 364
 and renewed covenant............. 377-8
 role of 78-9, 85-6, 102
 and signs/miracles/
  wonders of God 107-8, 110,
  112, 113, 114, 116,
  119, 125-8, 133, 136
Abihu... 259, 302
Abraham 74, 83, 146, 154, 186,
  204, 209
 covenant with God 47, 49, 64,
  65, 67-8, 73, 77, 96, 98,
  140, 144, 173, 203, 205,
  212, 344, 355, 372, 375
Adam.. 281
Adonijah 293
adultery 219-20

Ahab 220
Altar of Burnt Offering .. 293-4, 393, 400
Altar of Incense 317-18, 392
altars 186-7, 227-9, 259, 260-2,
  293-4, 295
Amalek/Amalekites 28, 169, 181,
  185-7, 189-90
Amminadab 101
Amram 57, 101
angel of the Lord 66, 84, 156, 253-4
Anna 374
anointing/anointing oil 276, 306,
  308-9, 311, 313,
  323-4, 325, 387, 399
Antiochus Epiphanes, King 283
Arad 228
Arch of Titus 283, 285
ark of the covenant 163, 164, 178,
  213, 263, 271, 279-82,
  318, 331, 392, 394
Asherah 372
atonement 281, 310, 314, 351-2
Augustine 74
authorship of Exodus 28-32

Baal 69, 153
Baal-Peor 349
Baal Zephon 153, 154
Babylon 116
bells 305
Benjamin 48
bestiality 243
Bezalel 28, 186, 302, 327-8,
  386, 389-90, 391n, 392, 395
Bilhah 48
Bitter Lakes 128, 143, 151

405

Subject Index

blood 78, 85, 109-11, 119, 135, 136-7, 140, 170, 259, 260-1, 310-11
Boaz 97
boils 118-20
Book of the Law of Moses 29, 30-1
breastpiece 302, 303-5
bribery 248
Bright, John 37
broken covenant/
  covenant curse 346-7, 357, 363
bronze basin 321-2, 393
burning bush 65, 66-7, 66n, 69, 73, 94, 95, 156, 204, 209
burnt offerings 129-30, 192, 228, 260, 293-4, 309, 310-11, 314-15, 318, 339, 393, 400

C

Canaan 34, 37, 47, 48-9, 65, 74, 97-8, 140, 360
  God's judgment on 254-5, 257, 341, 372-3, 375
  and Israelites' exit
    from Egypt 148-9, 152, 163-4
  as 'land of milk and
    honey' 69, 148, 355
  population/borders of 69-70, 148, 254, 254n, 355
  promises and warnings
    from God 253-6
  and social responsibilities
    of Israelites 242-3
canonical status of
  Pentateuch 29-30, 32
capital punishment/death
  penalty 137-8, 182, 207, 210, 219, 235, 239, 324, 330, 385
Carmel 65
cattle 117-18
census tax 275, 319-20
cherubim 272, 279, 281, 287, 290, 296
circumcision 83, 84-5, 99, 145, 146, 189
cloud imagery 27, 34, 152, 156, 183, 206, 209, 259, 264, 358, 367, 383, 403
Cocceius 271
courtyard (Tent of
  Meeting) 287, 293, 295-7, 313, 393-4, 400
covenant meal 313
coveting 221

creation 49-50, 107, 174, 217-18, 243, 372, 397, 400-401
'crying out' 63, 70, 89-90, 113, 132-3, 154, 182, 244, 245
cursing 236, 245
curtains (in Tent of
  Meeting) 287-8, 290, 295-6, 317
Cyrus, King 126

d

darkness 128-30
date of the Exodus 36-8, 38n
David, King 101, 163, 164, 185, 205, 253, 308, 319
Deborah 159
Decalogue 27-9, 41, 199-200, 211-21, 223-4, 227, 263, 271, 280, 331, 338, 364-5, 374, 376
  and descriptive laws 231-57
defilement, removal of 309
descriptive laws (of
  Decalogue) 231-57
Desert of Sin 173-4, 181
diseases 170

e

ear-piercing 233-4
Ebal 29
Eber 53
Edom 163
Egypt
  defeat of 157-8, 161-3
  first attack on Israelites 50-3
  God's judgment on 105-7, 109-33, 136-7, 142, 150, 157, 162-3, 191-2
  Hyksos invasion of 50-1
  increased Jewish
    population 47-50, 51, 52, 53, 55, 88-9
  Israelites' exit from 147-50, 151-3
  and Israel's rebellion
    against God 343
  Moses' mission to
    Pharaoh 71-2, 74-5, 79, 80-3, 85-6, 87-92, 99, 100-101, 102-3, 104
  oppression of
    Israelites in 47-56, 68, 70, 89-92
  pursuit of Israelites 153-5, 156-7
  second attack on Israelites 53-5
  third attack on Israelites 55-6

Subject Index

Eighth Word 220, 239-42
Eleazar 259, 302
Eli.....................................36
Eliezer 81, 83, 84-5, 190
Elijah 208, 228, 264
Elim..................................171, 173
Elisheba 100, 101
ephods 302-3, 304, 305
Esau...................................54, 185
Etham..........................152, 153, 169
Euphrates River..........................257
Eve....................................281
Ezekiel.......................194, 218, 383
Ezra 30-1

Feast of Harvest 251, 252, 374
Feast of Ingathering..................251, 374
Feast of Sukkot 374
Feast of Tabernacles 251
Feast of Unleavened Bread...............138, 250-1, 373-4
Feast of Weeks 251, 374
fellowship offerings...........228, 260, 262, 308, 309, 312, 313, 339
Fifth Word..........................218, 236
fire imagery................66, 152, 209, 264
first ram, offering of.................310-11
First Word 214-15
'first-born' status 82
first-fruits................82, 245, 251, 252, 375
flies 115-17
forced labour........................51-3, 61
foremen...........................89-92, 93
Fourth Word 216-18, 232-5, 249, 374
frames and cross-bars (in Tent of Meeting)........................288-9
frogs 111-13
'frontlets' 151
future priests........................312-15

Garden of Eden.............209, 276-7, 285, 401
Gentiles.....................139, 189-90, 254, 257, 364, 372-3
Gershom.....................63, 81, 83, 84, 190
Gershonites 394
Gibeonites 255
gnats.................................113-14

goats' hair curtains (in Tent of Meeting)..............288, 295
God
 anger of...........78, 133, 161, 162, 244, 341, 343-4, 346
 assurance of..............170-1, 206, 255, 360, 369, 371, 404
 attempts to kill Moses................84-5
 back of....................................359, 362
 blessing of.....................152, 191, 205, 218, 255, 397-8
 breath of...162
 and choice of Moses....65-70, 359-60
 as cloud 27, 34, 152, 156, 175, 183, 206, 209, 259, 264, 358, 367, 383, 403
 commands of...........49-50, 67, 103-4, 208, 216, 365, 372, 377-8
 compassion of 132, 245, 361, 363, 368
 concern of 63, 64, 103, 270
 consecration of Israelite firstborn...............147, 149-50, 246
 covenant with Abraham..........47, 49, 64, 65, 67-8, 73, 77, 96, 98, 140, 144, 173, 203, 205, 212, 344, 355, 372, 375
 covenant with Isaac.....63-4, 67-8, 77, 97, 98, 344, 355
 covenant with Israel.................28, 30, 32-3, 64, 72, 96-7, 98, 199-201, 203-7, 211-13, 214, 216, 217, 225, 254, 259-64, 269, 272, 304, 330
 covenant with Jacob....63-4, 67-8, 77, 97, 98, 355
 and creation...............49-50, 107, 174, 217-18, 243, 372, 397, 400-401
 'crying out' to.........63, 70, 89-90, 113, 132-3, 154, 182, 244, 245
 and Decalogue see Decalogue
 defeat of Egypt.......157-8, 161-3, 214
 deliverance of............27, 58, 63, 68-9, 74-5, 93, 95, 97-9, 105, 115-16, 134, 161, 190, 214
 demands of......27, 206, 212, 224, 398
 disobedience of Israelites 173, 177-8

Subject Index

dwelling place of 163, 164, 269, 270-2, 273, 274, 277, 279, 287-90, 307, 364, 383, 391-2, 397, 401, 403
face of 359, 360, 361, 362
faithfulness of 68, 97, 160, 245, 368, 404
father/son relationship with Israel 82, 97-8
fear of 54, 55, 68, 122, 123, 158, 224, 224n
finger of 106, 114, 213, 223, 263, 331, 363
forgiveness of 368-9
and fruitfulness of Israelites 49-50, 52
glory of 27, 34, 58, 153, 156, 163, 175, 207, 209, 224, 259, 262-4, 315, 359, 361-2, 363, 364-5, 367-9, 375, 377, 378, 383, 403-4
grace of 27, 64, 74, 78, 115, 212, 214, 216, 271, 359, 361, 363, 368, 369
and grumbling of the Israelites 173-5, 182
hand/hands of 75, 95, 103, 121, 123, 147-8, 162, 163, 343, 359, 362, 404
hearing of 63, 68, 70, 97
holiness of 66, 163, 206, 207, 246, 262, 271
image of 219, 232, 235-6
inheritance of 369
and Israelites' exit from Egypt ... 147-8, 149-50, 151-3
jealousy of 215-16, 368, 373
judgment of
  upon Canaan 254-5, 257, 341, 372-3, 375
  upon Egypt 103, 105-7, 109-33, 136-7, 142, 150, 157, 162-3, 191-2
  upon His people 210, 341, 343-4, 348-9, 352
kingship of 164, 206
knowing/
  knowledge of 64, 109, 359
laws/decrees of 193-4, 199, 213-21, 231-57, 263, 331
  see also Decalogue
light of 129, 290

love of 28, 68-9, 122, 160, 163, 212, 216, 245, 270, 368
mercy of 68, 159, 245, 361, 368
and midwives 54-5
and Moses' mission to Pharaoh 71-2, 74-5, 79, 80-3, 85-6, 87-8, 89-90, 92, 102-4
name of 34, 58, 67, 71, 72-3, 88, 93-9, 121, 160, 161, 187, 216, 228, 361, 367, 369
obedience to 54, 102, 104, 121, 170, 205, 212, 214-15, 216, 218, 224, 236, 254, 255, 269, 330, 372, 395, 400
omnipotence of 75, 77, 94, 113, 161
plan of 52, 64, 121
power of 53, 67-8, 75, 82, 109, 112-13, 119-20, 121-2, 125, 128, 149, 150, 153, 155, 156-8, 162, 163, 186, 190, 191, 204-5, 343
praise of 160-1, 250
presence of 34, 71, 74, 94, 125, 152, 208-9, 225, 261-2, 264, 269, 274, 284, 355-6, 360-1, 363, 364, 369, 377-8, 383, 403-4
and promised land 69-70, 74, 97-8, 140, 148-9, 163-4, 253-7, 352, 355, 360, 372-3, 375
promises of 28, 34, 73, 74, 93-5, 97, 191, 253-7, 342, 344
provision of food 173-8
purposes of 65, 72, 82, 94, 101, 122, 162, 163, 214, 217, 342, 344
ratification of covenant ... 259-64, 269
rebellion against 86, 236, 253, 264, 335, 341, 343-4, 346-7, 351-2, 355-6, 357, 359, 363-4, 369
redemptive actions of 28, 33, 52, 65, 67, 68-9, 115-16, 149-50, 152, 159, 160, 163-4, 212, 214, 234
relenting of 344
remembering of 63-4, 97, 344
and renewed covenant 363-5, 371-6, 377-8, 383

Subject Index

revelation of 30, 35, 65-7, 71-2, 73, 79, 93-9, 102-3, 113, 125, 175, 194, 201, 204, 207, 214, 260, 262-4, 271, 281-2, 359-62, 364-5, 367-9, 375, 378, 383
salvation of 34, 97, 137, 154, 155-8, 160-1, 162, 190-1
signs/miracles/
  wonders of 71-2, 77-8, 79, 81, 85-6, 103, 105-34, 106n, 136-7, 142, 156-7, 163, 170
and slavery of Israelites .. 68-70, 74-5
sovereignty of 64, 66, 67, 78, 82, 100, 102, 103, 115, 120, 132, 205, 361, 369
strength of 160-1
submission of Israel to 27
tests His people 170, 182, 264
and theophany 122, 206, 208-10, 223-5, 260, 262
transmission of His deeds 125
trust in 158, 174, 246
uniqueness of 214-15
as warrior 155, 161
will 193, 194
Word of 28, 35, 79, 199, 213, 214-21, 279, 315, 378
worship of 164, 175, 207, 214-15, 218, 227-9, 260, 339, 365, 373, 400
golden bull 264, 337-9, 341, 346-7, 352, 355, 359, 364, 369, 373, 383
Gomorrah 116
Goshen 115, 120, 122, 129
Gulf of Aqaba 128, 152, 256
Gulf of Suez 128, 152

H

Habiru 53
hail 120-5
Hannah 36, 159
Herod, King 55-6
Hezekiah, King 52, 134, 299
high priestly garments
  (for Tent of Meeting) 301-6, 313
Hilkiah 30
honouring 218
Horeb 65, 71-2, 183
hornets 255-6
Hur 186, 264, 337

Hyksos 50-1
hyssop 140

I

Idolatry 214-15, 220, 221, 227-8, 249-50, 255, 257, 337-9, 341, 346-7, 349, 351, 352, 364, 372-3
incense 317-18, 325
injury, bodily 237-9
Isaac 63-4, 67-8, 77, 97, 98, 154, 355
Isaiah 64, 78, 215, 281
Israel/Israelites
  and broken covenant/
    covenant curse 346-7, 357, 363
  consecration of 206-8
  consecration of firstborn 147, 149-50, 246
  covenant with God 28, 30, 32-3, 64, 72, 96-7, 98, 199-201, 203-7, 211-13, 214, 216, 217, 225, 254, 259-64, 269, 272, 304, 330
  cross the Red Sea ... 151-2, 155-8, 255
  disobedience to God 173, 177-8
  exit from Egypt 147-50, 151-3, 163-4
  father/son relationship
    with God 82, 97-8
  freedom from slavery 33-4, 74-5, 142-4, 154, 234
  God's love for 68-9, 122, 212, 216
  God's provision of food 173-8
  God's salvation of 34, 97, 137, 154, 155-8, 160-1, 162, 190-1
  and golden bull 337-9, 341, 346-7, 352, 355, 359, 364, 369, 373, 383
  grumbling/complaining
    of 173-8, 182
  holiness/unholiness of 206, 207, 246, 330, 335, 357
  as inheritance of God 369
  meeting with God 208-10, 223-5
  obedience to God 205, 212, 214-15, 216, 218, 224, 254, 255, 269, 395, 400
  and promised land 69-70, 74, 97-8, 140, 148-9, 163-4, 253-7, 352, 355, 360, 372-3, 375

pursued by Pharaoh...... 153-5, 156-7
rebellion against God.....86, 253, 264,
  335, 341, 343-4,
  346-7, 351-2, 355-6,
  357, 359, 363-4, 369
and renewed covenant............. 363-5,
  371-6, 377-8, 383
revelry of.......... 339, 345-6, 347-8, 349
'Sons of' 47-9, 70, 72, 142, 303, 315
status of................ 82, 203-6, 330, 360
as 'stiff-necked' 341, 355, 356,
  364, 369
submission to God 27
tested by God 170, 182, 264
as 'treasured possession'
  of God................27, 68, 205-6, 369
Ithamar 259, 302, 394

Jacob 47-9, 54, 63-4, 67-8, 71, 77,
  97, 98, 152, 186, 355
Jebel Musa..204
Jehoshaphat, King.................................52
Jephthah 37
Jeremiah............................78, 99, 279, 304
Jeroboam, King....................................339
Jerusalem................ 163-4, 171, 225, 253,
  273, 276, 279-80, 283, 285,
  289, 327, 374-5, 383, 401
Jesus Christ
  blood of..310
  and Book of the Law of Moses 31
  crucifixion of 82, 103, 109
  death of 82, 103, 109, 208
  and descriptive laws 238
  fasting of...264
  genealogy of 101
  mission/message of 32
  and name of God 361
  and power of God 68
  priesthood of.................................307
  rebuke of 151
  redemption through............33-4, 105
  and revelation of God 361
  sacrifice of.............. 33-4, 36, 135, 137,
  140, 145, 293
  and Tent of Meeting 273
Jethro/Reuel 62-3, 65, 80-1, 85,
  189, 190-5
Joab...293-4
Jochebed 57-8, 72, 100, 101
John 145, 273

Joseph........................ 48-9, 50-1, 152, 219
Josephus 62, 186, 213, 271, 295
Joshua 29, 67, 154, 185-6, 255,
  263, 345-6, 358
Josiah, King 134
'jubilee'..208
judicial assistants 195

Keturah...62
kidnapping..................220, 232, 235, 236

Lamech...159
lampstands (in Tent
  of Meeting) 285-6, 290, 299,
  392, 400
Leah..48
leprosy 77
Levi... 100, 101
Levites................31, 57, 79, 261, 289, 305,
  312, 313, 348-9, 364, 394
linen curtains
  (in Tent of Meeting)...........287-8, 295
locusts 125-8
Lord's Supper 137
lying 220-1, 248

Maccabeus, Judas........................283
'malicious witnesses' 247
'manna' 176-8, 252, 279, 385
Marah...169-71
marriage 68, 215, 219-20, 233,
  234-5, 242
Mary..160
Massah..183
Mecca..250
Merarites 394
'mercy-seat' 279, 281
Meribah 182, 183
Midian/Midianites 29, 61-3, 190, 192
midwives...53-5
Migdol 153
milk 252-3
Miriam 58, 59, 165, 186
Moab 163
Moriah 65
Moses
  adopted by Pharaoh's
  daughter............................. 59-60
  altar of 186-7

Subject Index

and Amalekites 185-7
birth of 57-8
Book of the Law of 29, 30-1
and burning bush 65, 66-7, 66n,
    69, 73, 94, 95,
    204, 209
call of 65-80
chosen by God of 65-70, 359-60
and circumcision 83, 84-5
completion of Tent
    of Meeting 403-4
and crossing the
    Red Sea 155, 156, 157
and Decalogue 199-200, 211-12,
    213-14, 224, 227,
    280, 331
and descriptive laws 232, 253
education of 60
fear of God 225
genealogy of 99-102
God attempts to kill 84-5
and God's covenant
    with Israel 199-200, 203,
    204-7, 211-12, 213
and God's judgment
    on Egypt 106-7, 109-11,
    112-13, 115,
    117-32, 136-7
and God's revelation
    of His name 93-8
and golden bull 337-8, 339, 341,
    346-7, 352, 359, 369
and grumbling
    of the Israelites 173, 174-5,
    177-8, 182
inspection of Tent
    of Meeting 397-8
intercession of 343-4, 347
and Israelites freedom
    from slavery 142-3, 154
and Israelites' exit from
    Egypt 147, 149, 153
judicial role 192-5
leads Israelites through
    the desert 169-70, 181
mediator role 31, 73, 79, 98, 203,
    206, 208, 213, 224, 259, 282,
    348, 358, 363, 375, 399
in Midian 61-3, 80-1
mission to Pharaoh 71-2, 74-5, 79,
    80-3, 85-6, 87-90, 91-2,
    99, 100-101, 102-4

on Mount Sinai 204-7, 208, 209-10,
    224-5, 259-60, 263-4,
    335, 337-8, 341, 345, 351,
    363-4, 365, 376, 377
murder of Egyptian overseer .. 61, 80
oratory skills of 78, 99, 102
and Passover 136-7, 139, 141, 146
prayers of 94, 112, 117, 123, 124,
    128, 187, 344, 361, 369, 376
and priestly anointing 308-9, 324
radiant face of 377-8
and ratification of
    covenant 259-60, 261-2
and rebellion of Israel 341, 343-4,
    346-7, 351-2, 356,
    359, 363-4, 369
as refugee 60-4
and renewed covenant 363-5, 372,
    375-6, 377-8
response/objection's to
    God's call 71-80
and revelation of God's
    glory 359, 361-2, 364-5,
    367-9, 378
and revelry of the Israelites 345-6,
    348
saving of 58-9
and scroll of the covenant 29,
    199-201, 259, 261
and signs/miracles/
    wonders of God 71-2, 77-8, 79,
    81, 85-6, 103, 105,
    107-11, 112-15,
    116-30, 133, 136
Song of 155, 158-64, 165
and staff of God 77, 81, 105,
    107-8, 122, 155, 185-6
and temporary meeting
    place 357-8, 364
Tent of Meeting plans/
    construction 273, 274, 275,
    277, 281-2, 285-6, 289,
    294, 383, 385-6, 390,
    393, 395, 399-401
visited by Jethro 190-5
and water from the rock 183
writing of 28-9, 30-1, 35, 199-200
Mount Sinai 30, 34, 65, 71-2, 183,
    203-10, 223-4, 259-60, 263-4,
    335, 337-8, 341, 345, 351, 355,
    363-4, 365, 376, 377, 403
murder 219, 235-6, 239

Subject Index

Naboth..................................220, 248
Nadab 259, 302
Nahshon..101
Nehemiah.....................................30-1
Ninth Word................................220-1
Noah 58, 64, 279, 360
non-resident foreigners,
  treatment of........................ 243-4, 248

Oholiab.............................28, 302, 328,
  386, 389-90
oil for lampstands (in Tent
  of Meeting).......................................299
orphans...244
outline of Book of Exodus..............38-44
oxen..238-9

Parents, respecting..................218, 236,
  245
Passover.................. 115, 121, 131, 133-41,
  140n, 144-6, 145n, 148-9,
  150, 252, 314, 375
Paul 78, 81, 144, 176-7, 203, 218,
  221, 264, 352, 378
pegs (Tent of Meeting)................297, 386
Pentecost...82, 251
Perazim..65
personal relationships................... 246-8
Peter 81-2, 203
Pharaoh
  agrees to free Israelites 142
  defeat of 157-8, 161-2
  first attack on Israelites................50-1
  and God's judgment
    on Egypt.................. 105-7, 109-33,
    142, 150, 157, 191
  hardening of heart...... 81-2, 103, 108,
    110, 113, 114, 117, 118,
    120, 125, 128, 130, 133,
    142, 153, 155
  and Israelites' exit
    from Egypt.......148, 150, 151, 153
  Moses' mission to........ 71-2, 74-5, 79,
    80-3, 85-6, 87-90,
    91-2, 99, 100-101,
    102-4, 107-8
  pursues Israelites........... 153-5, 156-7
  second attack on
    Israelites..........................53, 54, 55
  and signs/miracles/
    wonders of God .107-30, 133, 142
  third attack on Israelites................55
Pharaoh's daughter 59-60, 61
Philistines.........................151-2, 163, 256
Philo...271, 295
Phinehas..349
Pi Hahiroth..................................153, 154
place and significance of
  Exodus in Old Testament.......... 27-8
plagues........................ 105-7, 111-17, 121,
  170, 213, 319
plates, ornamental...........................305-6
pomegranates 305
posts (in Tent of Meeting)..............295-6
priestly garments (for Tent
  of Meeting) 301-7, 313, 321, 394-5
property..................214, 219, 220, 239-42
Puah 53-5
Putiel...100

Rachel..48
ram's horn...208
Rameses..143
ratification of
  covenant.....................259-64, 269, 313
Red Sea 58, 105, 128, 150, 151-9,
  161-2, 164-5, 169, 255
reed basket 58
Rephidim......................181, 185, 203, 204
Reuben....................................99, 100, 101
Reuel/Jethro 62-3, 65, 80-1, 85,
  189, 190-5
revelry...................339, 345-6, 347-8, 349
'ritual decalogue'.................................371
robes...302, 305
ropes (Tent of Meeting).....................386
Ruth..97

Sabbath
  and Decalogue 212, 216-18,
    248-50, 374
  and Passover 138
  provision of food for 174, 177-8
  sabbatical year............218, 233, 248-9
  and Tent of Meeting 34-5,
    329-30, 385
sacrificial system
  and altars 186-7, 227-9, 259,
    260-2, 293-4, 295

Subject Index

burnt offerings 129-30, 192, 228, 260, 309, 310-11, 314-15, 318, 339, 393, 400
  and demands on Pharaoh 116-17, 129-30
  and descriptive laws 243
  and Moses' mission to Pharaoh 74-5, 87-8
  and Passover 134-6, 139-41, 140n, 150
  and ratification of covenant 259, 260-1
  and Tent of Meeting 35-6, 293-4, 295, 297, 301, 306, 307-8, 309-12, 314-15
Samuel 248
Satan 33
Saul, King 185, 308
scroll of the covenant 29, 199-201, 259, 261
second ram, offering of 311-12
Second Word 215-16, 227, 338, 368, 373
servitude 27, 215, 233
Seventh Word 219-20
sexual relations 208, 219-20, 243, 348, 348n, 349
Sheba 325
Shechem 186
Shem 53
Shiphrah 53-5
Shur 169
signs/miracles/ wonders 71-2, 77-8, 79, 81, 85-6, 103, 105-34, 106n, 136-7, 142, 156-7, 170
Simeon 100, 101
sin
  and Decalogue 219, 221, 242, 243
  forgiveness of 368-9
  of Pharaoh 124-5, 128
  and rebellion of Israel 86, 346-7, 351-2, 355-6, 357, 359, 369
  redemption from 33-4, 97
  sin-offering 309-10, 314, 318
  and Tent of Meeting 270, 271, 301, 383
Sinai Peninsula 29, 204
Sixth Word 218-19, 235-6
slander 246

slavery 27, 68-9
  and descriptive laws 232-5, 237, 238-9, 249
  and forced labour 51-3, 61
  Israelites freedom from 33-4, 74-5, 142-4, 149, 154, 234
  and Moses' mission to Pharaoh 89-91
social responsibilities 242-6
Sodom 116
Solomon, King 37-8, 51-2, 134, 139, 163, 228, 255, 290, 308, 401
Song of Moses/Song of the Sea 155, 158-64, 165, 255
'Sons of Israel' 47-9, 70, 72, 142, 303, 315
sorcery 242-3
staff of God 77, 81, 105, 107-8, 109-10, 112, 114, 122, 155, 185-6
Stephen 48, 57, 58, 60, 83
stone tablets 223, 263, 271, 279, 331, 345, 346, 363, 365, 376, 377, 394
'stones' 53
'store cities' 52
straw 89-90
Succoth 143, 152

tabernacle *see* Tent of Meeting
table (in Tent of Meeting) 283-4, 290, 392
Tel Aviv 245
temporary meeting place 357-8, 364, 403
Ten Words *see* Decalogue
Tent of Meeting
  Altar of Burnt Offering 293-4, 393, 400
  Altar of Incense 317-18, 392
  anointing/anointing oil 306, 308-9, 311, 313, 323-4, 325, 387, 399
  and ark of the covenant 279-82, 318, 392, 394
  bronze basin 321-2, 393
  and census tax 275, 319-20
  cloud over 27, 34, 403
  completion of 403-4

consecration of priests
    and Tent... 306, 307-9, 311, 314-15
contributions for 275-7, 386-7, 390
courtyard of 287, 293, 295-7, 313, 393-4, 400
curtains 287-8, 290, 295-6, 317
dimensions of 273-4
as dwelling place
    of God 269, 270-2, 273, 274, 277, 307, 364, 397, 403
dwelling place within 287-90, 391-2, 394
establishment of 27
frames and cross-bars 288-9
future priests 312-15
and God's name 253
importance/significance of 270-2, 274
installation of priests .. 307-9, 313-14
lampstands 285-6, 290, 299, 392, 400
Moses' inspection of 397-8
name of 269, 270-1
offering of the first ram 310-11
offering of the second ram 311-12
pegs 297, 386
plans/construction of 272-3, 274, 257, 276-7, 289, 327-8, 382, 383-4, 385-7, 389-90, 391-5, 399-401
posts 295-6
priestly garments 301-7, 313, 321, 394-5
progress of work on 391-5
and ratification of
    covenant 261, 262
ropes 386
and Sabbath 34-5, 329-30, 385
and sacrificial system 35-6, 293-4, 295, 297, 301, 306, 307-8, 309-12, 314-15
as sanctuary 34-5, 271, 275, 279
serving women 393, 393n
sin-offering 309-10, 314, 318
table 283-4, 290, 392

and Temple of Jerusalem 273-4
veil 289-90
Tenth Word 221
'testimony' 28, 178, 213, 263, 270-1, 280-1, 289, 317, 331, 345, 377, 394
theft 220, 236, 240, 241-2
theology of Book of Exodus 32-6
theophany 122, 206, 208-10, 223-5, 260, 262
Third Word 216
Thummim 303, 304-5
trumpets 207-8, 209, 223-4
tunics 302, 306, 308, 309
turbans 302, 305, 306
Tyre 116

Unbelief 76-8, 189-90, 191
'unblemished' offerings 135
undressed stone 228, 293
unleavened bread 134, 137-9, 148, 169, 250-1, 284, 308, 373-4
Urim 303, 304-5

Veil (in Tent of Meeting) 289-90
vicarious atonement 351-2
victory songs 155, 159
virgins, seduction of 242
visual theology 35-6
Vos, Geerhardus 33

Water from the rock 183
wave offerings 312, 386, 394
'whisper' 348
wicked men 247
widows 244

Zechariah 160
Zilpah 48
Zipporah 63, 84-5, 190

Scripture Index

Genesis
1–3 ... 397
1–11 ... 32, 107
1:20 ... 49
1:26-27 ... 219
1:27 ... 219
1:28 ... 49, 107
1:31 ... 397
2:1-2 ... 397
2:2-3 ... 174
2:3 ... 212, 217, 397
2:18, 23-24 ... 219
3:8-13 ... 397
3:24 ... 209, 281
4:23-24 ... 159
6–8 ... 58
6:8 ... 360
8:1 ... 64
8:13 ... 400
9:4-6 ... 238
9:6 ... 219
9:8-17 ... 375
10:15-17 ... 69
10:21 ... 53
11:14, 16 ... 53
12:1-3 ... 375
12:7 ... 186
13:10 ... 116
14:18-20 ... 62
15:1 ... 154
15:9 ... 338
15:12-16 ... 47
15:12-21 ... 375
15:13 ... 144
15:13-15 ... 191
15:14 ... 131
15:17 ... 209
15:17-19 ... 32
15:18-19 ... 74
15:18-21 ... 69, 97, 140, 355, 372
16:7-13 ... 66
16:13 ... 72
17:1 ... 72, 73
17:7 ... 32
17:8 ... 97, 140
17:10-14 ... 83
17:12-14 ... 189
17:13 ... 146
17:19 ... 32
17:22 ... 175
18:19 ... 138
19:13, 29 ... 116
19:28 ... 119
20:1 ... 169
21:8 ... 60
22:2 ... 65
22:15-18 ... 66
22:16 ... 344
25:2 ... 62
25:22 ... 193
26:3 ... 71
26:24 ... 32, 77, 154
26:31 ... 192
27:34 ... 113
28:13 ... 97
28:13-14 ... 69
28:13-15 ... 355
28:14 ... 52
29:27 ... 212
31:54 ... 192
32:9-10 ... 54
32:22-28 ... 185
32:22-32 ... 83
33:4 ... 85
34:12 ... 242
35:11-12 ... 32
35:13 ... 175
36:15-16 ... 185
37:28 ... 62
38:7-10 ... 49
39:9 ... 219
45:3 ... 80
46:8 ... 47
46:8-17 ... 48
46:8-27 ... 32
46:26-27 ... 27
46:27 ... 48
46:28 ... 389
49:29-30 ... 152
50:25 ... 152

Leviticus
1:5 ... 119
2:2-3 ... 314
3:16-17 ... 252
4:7, 18 ... 318
8:1-36 ... 31
8:7-8 ... 305
8:13 ... 309
8:33 ... 306
9:5 ... 175
9:24 ... 66
14:8 ... 207
16:1 ... 175
16:16 ... 281
16:19 ... 318
16:22 ... 309

16:28...................207	11:31-32...................175	6:4...................215
17:11...................310	12:1...................144, 190	6:4-9...................149, 218
17:15...................207	12:7-8...................194	6:9...................151
18:12...................101	12:8...................358	6:20-25...................125
18:23...................243	13:8, 16...................185	7:1...................69
19:2...................206	14:13-14...................152	7:6...................205
19:11...................220	14:18...................368	7:6-8...................50
19:13...................220	14:30...................98	7:7-8...................28, 68, 122
19:30...................35	15:1-10...................283	7:8...................27, 212
19:33-34...................244	15:8...................192	7:9...................216
19:34...................146	15:29...................146	7:12-15...................170
19:35...................220	15:32-36...................330	7:12-26...................255
20:10...................219	17:1-2...................28	7:18-19...................27
20:15-16...................243	17:7-8...................280	7:24...................341
22:21-22...................135	18:15-16...................150	8:1-20...................372
23:15-22...................251	18:27...................245	8:14...................27
23:34...................251, 374	25:1-18...................349	9:6, 13...................364
23:37...................90	25:1, 6-8...................349	9:7-12...................223
23:43...................250	25:10-13...................349	9:7-21...................27
24:2...................387	27:7...................130	9:9-12...................376
24:5-6...................283	27:21...................193	9:9-21...................335, 343
24:5-9...................284	33:2-49...................28	9:9, 11, 15...................213, 377
24:7...................283	33:3...................153	9:10...................213, 223
24:9...................284	33:6-7...................169	9:15...................377
24:19-20...................237	33:10-11...................128, 152	9:18...................78
24:22...................146	33:11-12...................173	9:19...................376
25:16...................220	35:25, 28...................302	9:20...................344
25:23-34...................220	35:31...................239	9:26...................75
25:35-38...................245	36:5...................130	10:4...................212
25:43, 46, 53...................52		10:5...................263
25:44-46...................232	**Deuteronomy**	10:12-22...................372
26:2...................35	1:37...................78	10:17...................248
26:31-33...................352	2:1-23...................163	10:22...................48
	4:11...................225	11:13-32...................372
Numbers	4:13...................212	12:5, 11...................253
1:51-53...................364	4:15-31...................215, 255	13:10...................182
2:17...................394	4:21...................78	14:2...................205
3:5-9...................31	4:34...................75	14:21...................252
3:7...................394	4:39...................243	15:1-6...................217
3:36-37...................289	4:41-43...................235	15:1-11...................220
4:5...................280	5:1-3...................32	15:12-18...................217, 232
4:7...................284	5:6...................53	15:13-14...................233
4:28, 33...................394	5:12...................330	15:15...................234
4:29-32...................289	5:12-15...................174	16:1-8...................131
5:12-31...................347	5:15...................217	16:3...................136
8:5-22...................31	5:21...................221	16:9-12...................251
8:11...................312	5:22...................223	16:12...................250
9:1...................145	5:22-27...................208	16:13, 16...................251, 374
9:12...................145	5:22-31...................223	16:16-17...................374
9:15...................280	5:23-25...................122	16:19...................247
9:15-23...................404	5:31...................213	16:19-20...................248
11:18...................207	6:1...................213	16:22...................255

Scripture Index

17:5 182
17:15 302
18:10 .... 108, 242
18:15 302
19:1-13 235
19:5 219
19:16-19 247
19:21 237
20:10-15 243
21:1-9 235
21:15-17 .... 82, 147
22:1-4 247
22:9 245
22:22-24 219
22:25-27 242
22:28-29 242
23:18 252
23:19-20 245
24:7 235
24:12-13 245
24:17 247
24:18 234
26:1-11 97
26:5-8 27
26:18 205
27:5 228
27:15-26 206
27:19 247
27:24-25 235
28:1-6 255
28:27 119
28:29 129
28:60-61 170
28:65-68 352
29–30 211
31:1-8 185
31:9-13 301
31:19-22 28
31:24 29
31:26 280
32:1-43 159
32:6 82
32:11-12 205
32:20 82
33:8 305
33:9 348
33:16 66
33:29 158
34:10 64

Joshua
1:2-5 69
3:5 207
3:10 69
4:4-7 260
4:16 280
5:2-3 84
5:10-11 134
5:15 67
6:8 208
7:13 207
7:16-18 195
8:1 154
8:30-31 228
8:30-35 206
8:31 29
9:1-26 255
11:3 69
22:27 192
24 211
24:11 69
24:32 152

Judges
1:16 192
1:27-36 256
5:1-31 159
8:27 303
11:26 37
13:6, 9 66
17:1-5 303

Ruth
4:1-12 97
4:18-22 101

1 Samuel
1:1-8 252
1:3 149
1:9-18 36
2:1-10 159
2:18 303
2:19 149
2:22 393
2:27-28 28
3:10 67
4:4 279
8:3 248
8:8 28
9:9 193
12:18 122
15:1-35 185
18:25 242
27:8 169
27:8-11 185
30:1-20 185

2 Samuel
5:20 65
5:6-10 253
5:6-12 164
6:1-23 164
7:6, 23 28
14:26 319
16:14 249
18:31 348
24:1-17 319

1 Kings
1:50-53 .... 236, 293
2:28-34 .... 236, 294
6:1 37-8
6:13 163
6:38 289
7:18 305
8:8 280
8:9 .... 28, 279
8:11 383
8:12 290
8:21 .... 28, 213
8:22, 38-39 123
8:29 253
8:37 170
8:41-43 139
8:51 28
8:59 90
9:19 52
9:20-21 255
9:25 134
9:26 .... 128, 152, 256
11:28 51
12:28-29 339
18:20-39 65
18:31 260
19:8 .... 208, 264
19:10, 14 228
19:11-12 208
21:1-29 220
21:8-13 248
22:8 193

2 Kings
15:19, 29 63
16:15 314
17:7 28
17:15 213

22-23	30	
23:34-36	63	
25:30	90	

1 Chronicles
1:32	62
2:10	101
2:10-11	101
2:20	327
6:33-37	38
21:15	344
29:3	205

2 Chronicles
1:5	327
6:28	170
7:14	171
8:13	134
17:12	52
19:10	194
19:11	302
25:4	31
29:7	299
32:28	52
34	30
36:23	126

Ezra
1:2	126
6:18	31
6:19-22	135
9:5	123
10:1-5	206

Nehemiah
8:1-9, 14-17	30
8:2-3	301
9:9-15	28
9:12	152
10:28-29	206
10:28-39	30
13:1	31
13:1-3	30

Job
4:12	348
5:14	129
12:25	129
26:14	348
38:2	176

Psalms
10:16	164
19:9-11	54
23:2	163
24	123
24:1	220
25:10	194
32:1-2	368
32:5	368
34:8-14	54
35:11	247
41:13	191
42:4	250
44:20	123
45:14	303
48:2	395
49:7	351
69:28	352
72:18	191
77:7-20	28
78:1-8	125, 218
78:5	377
78:12-16	28
78:12-17	108
78:13	156
78:17, 40, 56	253
78:18	182
78:19-20	173
78:21-22	173
78:22, 32	76
78:24	176
78:25	176
78:32	173
78:42-53	28
78:45	115
80:8-11	164
81:9	373
85:2	368
86:5, 15	368
89:1	160
90:13	344
94:14	369
98:1	162
99:1	279
103:7	65, 360
103:8-10	368
105:23-37	28
105:31	115
105:40	175
105:41	183
105:42-43	173
106:8-9	156-7, 158
106:14, 25, 29	182
106:19-20	338
106:20	264
106:23	344
106:46	131
106:48	191
111:9	116
111:10	122
115:1-8	214
122:4	250
130:7	116
132:12	194
132:13-14	164, 273
135:4	205
138:1	160
139:2	64
139:16	352
141:2	318
147:16	176

Proverbs
1:7	122
4:4, 11	389
6:25	221

Isaiah
1:21-23	220
3:13	182
6:2-7	281
6:4	224
6:5-7	78
6:8	67
7:14	59
7:18	256
19:18	149
28:25	124
40:11	163
40:15	176
44:16	136
44:23	112
49:10	163
50:6	68
52:12	136
57:3-13	220
60:21	112
63:7-9	68
63:9	64

Jeremiah
1:4-8	78
2:3	82
2:6	28
2:9	182
3:4	82

Scripture Index

3:6-9 220
3:16 279
5:7 220
6:10 99
16:14 28
18:3 53
18:8 344
26:3, 19 344
31:9 82
31:11 150
31:33 304
51:11 116

Lamentations
3:56 113

Ezekiel
4:9 124
16:10 288
16:32 219
20:5 98
22:7 218
23:36-49 220
26:4 116
28:13 277
48:35 383

Daniel
9:15 28

Hosea
4:13 219
13:14 150
14:2 368

Joel
2:26-27 307
2:31 110

Amos
2:10 28
3:1 28
5:12-17 220
7:3, 6 344
7:4 182

Jonah
3:10 344

Micah
6:2 182
6:4 28

Zechariah
4:1-7 286

Malachi
1:6-14 135
2:4-7 206
2:6 36
3:17 205

Matthew
1:4 101
2:16-18 56
4:2 264
5:38-42 238
22:23-33 68
23:5 .... 149, 151
27:45-54 208

Mark
12:18-27 68
12:26 31

Luke
1:10 318
1:46-55 160
2:36-38, 41-51 374
3:32-33 101
24:44 32
68-79 160

John
1:14 .... 273, 279
1:18 .... 262, 361
1:19 293
6:33 176
6:46 361
10:25 108
17:6 361
19:32-36 145

Acts
2:22 105
2:22-23 82
5:29 54
7:8 83
7:14 48
7:16 152
7:20 58
7:20-44 57
7:22 .... 29, 60
7:23 .... 60, 61
7:25 .... 57, 61

7:29 62
7:44 .... 273, 289

Romans
1:23 264
9:3 352
9:14-15 361
9:14-18 81
9:18 120

1 Corinthians
2:1 78
2:4 78
5:7 .... 137, 293

2 Corinthians
3:7-18 378
8:15 177
9:6-12 275
10:10 78

Galatians
3:15-21 203
3:17 144

Ephesians
6:1-4 218
6:2 218
6:4 236

Colossians
3:5 221
3:20 218

1 Timothy
6:16 262

2 Timothy
3:16 31

Hebrews
3:5 169
5:1-2 301
6:13-18 344
7:22 121
8–10 272
8:2 36
8:5 .... 273, 277, 289
8:8 113
8:18 115
8:27 118
9:1-7 290

9:5 272	12:22 225	4:12 361
9:6 290	13:12 310	
9:10 400		**Revelation**
9:11 36	**James**	3:5 352
9:22 311	3:9 236	4:8, 9 281
9:23 273	**1 Peter**	5:8 318
9:26-28 293	1:11 36	5:9-10, 12-13 ... 160
11:22 152	1:19 135	8:3-4 318
11:23 58	2:9-10 203	8:6 208
11:23-29 57	**2 Peter**	13:8 352
11:24 61	1:21 31-2	19:11-21 161
11:25-26 60		20:12 352
12:18 225	**1 John**	21:3 383
12:21 225	3:2 206	21:3-4, 22-27 ... 401